D1084133

From the Library of Yvonne Keil-Lauder

The MacArthur New Testament Commentary

REVELATION 12-22

John MacArthur

Moody Publishers/Chicago

ISBN: 978-0-8024-0774-0

Library of Congress Cataloging-in-Publication Data

MacArthur, John, 1939-
Revelation 12-22 / John MacArthur,
p. cm. – (The MacArthur New Testament commentary)
Includes bibliographical references and indexes.
ISBN 0-8024-0774-9
1. Bible. N.T. Revelation XII-XXII–Commentaries. I. Title: Revelation twelve-twenty two. II. Title.

BS2825.3 M29 2000
228'.077–dc21

00-055426

We hope you enjoy this book from Moody Publishers. Our goal is to provide high-quality, thought-provoking books and products that connect truth to your real needs and challenges. For more information on other books and products written and produced from a biblical perspective, go to www.moodypublishers.com or write to:

Moody Publishers
820 N. LaSalle Boulevard
Chicago, IL 60610

10

Printed in the United States of America

With deep gratitude to David Douglass, who for nearly nineteen years served as my editor in the preparation of these commentaries. Dave's obvious love for the Word of God, his skill in theology, and his professionalism as an editor are all indeliby imprinted on these books. His partnership and encouragement over the years have helped keep my own enthusiasm running high. He is finally taking a well-earned rest from the work, and his contribution will be sorely missed.

Contents

Preface

It continues to be a rewarding, divine communion for me to preach expositionally through the New Testament. My goal is always to have deep fellowship with the Lord in the understanding of His Word and out of that experience to explain to His people what a passage means. In the words of Nehemiah 8:8, I strive "to give the sense" of it so they may truly hear God speak and, in so doing, may respond to Him.

Obviously, God's people need to understand Him, which demands knowing His Word of truth (2 Tim. 2:15) and allowing that Word to dwell in them richly (Col. 3:16). The dominant thrust of my ministry, therefore, is to help make God's living Word alive to His people. It is a refreshing adventure.

This New Testament commentary series reflects this objective of explaining and applying Scripture. Some commentaries are primarily linguistic, others are mostly theological, and some are mainly homiletical. This one is basically explanatory, or expository. It is not linguistically technical but deals with linguistics when that seems helpful to proper interpretation. It is not theologically expansive but focuses on the major doctrines in each text and how they relate to the whole of Scripture. It is not primarily homiletical, although each unit of thought is generally treated as one chapter, with a clear outline and logical flow of thought.

Most truths are illustrated and applied with other Scripture. After establishing the context of a passage, I have tried to follow closely the writer's development and reasoning.

My prayer is that each reader will fully understand what the Holy Spirit is saying through this part of His Word, so that His revelation may lodge in the mind of believers and bring greater obedience and faithfulness—to the glory of our great God.

The War of the Ages—Part 1: The Prelude (Revelation 12:1–6) 1

A great sign appeared in heaven: a woman clothed with the sun, and the moon under her feet, and on her head a crown of twelve stars; and she was with child; and she cried out, being in labor and in pain to give birth. Then another sign appeared in heaven: and behold, a great red dragon having seven heads and ten horns, and on his heads were seven diadems. And his tail swept away a third of the stars of heaven and threw them to the earth. And the dragon stood before the woman who was about to give birth, so that when she gave birth he might devour her child. And she gave birth to a son, a male child, who is to rule all the nations with a rod of iron; and her child was caught up to God and to His throne. Then the woman fled into the wilderness where she had a place prepared by God, so that there she would be nourished for one thousand two hundred and sixty days. (12:1–6)

The Bible warns that "pride goes before destruction, and a haughty spirit before stumbling" (Prov. 16:18). The most notorious and tragic illustration of that principle, the one with the most far-reaching consequences, was Satan's prideful rebellion against God. By it Lucifer, having fallen from heaven like lightning (Luke 10:18), was cast down from his exalted position as the "anointed cherub who covers" (Ezek. 28:14). He forfeited his place as the highest created being and became the supreme enemy of God. Satan's rebellion touched off a cosmic war throughout the universe—a war dwarfing any other war in human experience. Satan's war against God is a two-front war. By leading a mutiny against God among the angels, Satan attempted unsuccessfully to destroy the paradise of heaven. By leading a mutiny against God among men, Satan destroyed the earthly paradise of the Garden of Eden, plunged the whole human race into decay and corruption, and usurped (temporarily) the role of the "ruler of this world" (John 12:31; 16:11).

The opening campaign of Satan's war of the ages took place in heaven. When he rebelled (Isa. 14:12–15; Ezek. 28:12–17), one-third of the angels foolishly and wickedly cast their lots with him (see the discussion of v. 4 below). None of them could have known what the eternal consequences of their choice would be. Wanting to be like God, they became as much unlike Him as possible. These fallen angels (or demons) became Satan's storm troopers, doing the bidding of their evil commander. They fight against divine purpose, making war with both the holy angels and the human race.

When Adam and Eve plummeted into corruption by choosing to listen to Satan's lies and disobey God, the human race became embroiled in the cosmic war of the ages. In fact, since the Fall the earth has been the primary theater in which that war has been fought. Though already fallen, every member of the human race faces the same choice as the angels did in eternity past: to fight on God's side or on Satan's. Remaining neutral is not an option, for in Matthew 12:30 Jesus declared, "He who is not with Me is against Me; and he who does not gather with Me scatters."

The final battles of Satan's long war against God are yet to be fought. They will take place in the future, during the last half of the seven-year tribulation period, the time Jesus called the Great Tribulation (Matt. 24:21). At that time Satan, aided by the absence of the raptured church and the presence of increased demon hordes (9:1–11), will mount his most desperate assaults against God's purposes and His people. But despite the savage fury with which those assaults will be carried out, they will not succeed. The Lord Jesus Christ will effortlessly crush Satan and his forces (19:11–21) and send him to the abyss for the duration of the millennial kingdom (20:1–2). After leading a final rebellion at the close of the Millennium, Satan will be consigned to eternal punishment in the lake of fire (20:3, 7–10).

The sounding of the seventh trumpet will proclaim the triumphant victory of the Lord Jesus Christ over the usurper, Satan: "Then the seventh angel sounded; and there were loud voices in heaven, saying, 'The kingdom of the world has become the kingdom of our Lord and of His Christ; and He will reign forever and ever'" (11:15). There will be joy in heaven because Christ has defeated Satan and established His eternal kingdom. Thus, the outcome of the war between Satan and God is not in doubt. Christ's ultimate triumph is certain.

Though chapter 11 records the sounding of the seventh trumpet, the effects it produces are not described until chapters 15–18. The seventh trumpet will sound near the end of the Tribulation, launching the brief, but final and devastating bowl judgments just before Christ's return in power and glory. Chapters 6–11 describe the events of the Tribulation up to the sounding of the seventh trumpet; chapters 12–14 recapitulate that same period, describing events from Satan's vantage point. In addition, the latter section takes the reader all the way back to the original rebellion of Satan (12:3–4). The chronological narrative of the Tribulation events then resumes in chapter 15.

The Tribulation will feature both the unprecedented judgments of God's eschatological wrath and the desperate fury of Satan's efforts to thwart God's purposes. That deadly combination will make the Tribulation the most devastating period in human history (Matt. 24:21–22). During that time, horrifying events will take place, caused both by God's judgments and by Satan's fury.

Before describing that final war, the inspired apostle John first introduces the main characters involved in it: the woman (Israel), the dragon (Satan), and the male child (Jesus Christ).

The Woman

A great sign appeared in heaven: a woman clothed with the sun, and the moon under her feet, and on her head a crown of twelve stars; and she was with child; and she cried out, being in labor and in pain to give birth. (12:1–2)

The first thing John saw in this vision was a **great sign**—the first of seven signs in the last half of Revelation (cf. v. 3; 13:13, 14; 15:1; 16:14; 19:20). *Mega* (**great**) appears repeatedly in this vision (cf. vv. 3, 9, 12, 14); everything John saw seemed to be huge either in size or in significance. *Sēmeion* (**sign**) describes a symbol that points to a reality. The literal approach to interpreting Scripture allows for normal use of symbolic language, but understands that it points to a literal reality. In this case, the description plainly shows that the woman John saw was not an actual woman. Also, the reference to "the rest of her children," those "who keep the commandments of God and hold to the testimony of Jesus" (v. 17), shows that this **woman** is a symbolic mother.

The **woman** is the second of four symbolic women identified in Revelation. The first, though an actual woman, had the symbolic name Jezebel (2:20). She was a false teacher and symbolizes paganism. Another symbolic woman, depicted as a harlot, appears in 17:1–7. She represents the apostate church. The fourth woman, described in 19:7–8 as the bride of the Lamb (cf. 2 Cor. 11:2), represents the true church. Some argue that the **woman** in this present vision represents the church, but as the context makes clear (cf. v. 5), she represents Israel. The Old Testament also pictures Israel as a woman, the adulterous wife of the Lord (Jer. 3:1, 20; Ezek. 16:32–35; Hos. 2:2) whom God will ultimately restore to Himself (Isa. 50:1). A reference to the ark of the covenant (11:19) adds further support for identifying the **woman** as Israel.

That Israel will play a key role in the end-time drama is not surprising. The seventieth week of Daniel's prophecy (the Tribulation) will primarily concern Israel, just as the first sixty-nine did (cf. Dan. 9:24–27). Israel's presence in the end times is consistent with God's emphatic promises of her continued existence as a nation:

> Thus says the Lord,
> Who gives the sun for light by day
> And the fixed order of the moon and the stars for light by night,
> Who stirs up the sea so that its waves roar;
> The Lord of hosts is His name:
> "If this fixed order departs
> From before Me," declares the Lord,
> "Then the offspring of Israel also shall cease
> From being a nation before Me forever."
> Thus says the Lord,
> "If the heavens above can be measured
> And the foundations of the earth searched out below,
> Then I will also cast off all the offspring of Israel
> For all that they have done," declares the Lord.
> (Jer. 31:35–37; cf. 33:20–26; 46:28; Amos 9:8)

Further, Israel's presence during the seventieth week of Daniel's prophecy is in keeping with God's promises to her of a kingdom (Isa. 65:17–25; Ezek. 37:21–28; Dan. 2:44; Zech. 8:1–13) and national salvation (Zech. 12:10–13:1; 13:8–9; Rom. 11:26).

Often as an instrument of God's judgment, Satan has persecuted the Jewish people throughout their history. He knows that to destroy Israel would make it impossible for God to fulfill His promises to the Jewish people. God will not allow him to do that, but will use Satan to chasten Israel. It comes as no surprise that the devil will intensify his persecution of Israel as the establishment of the millennial kingdom draws near. As previously noted, the seventh trumpet will sound near the end of the Tribulation. Only weeks, or perhaps a few months at most, will remain after it sounds until the return of the Lord Jesus Christ. With his time running out (cf. v. 12), Jewish people will become the special target of Satan's hatred and destructive attacks.

John saw that the **woman** was **clothed with the sun, and** had **the moon under her feet, and on her head a crown of twelve stars.** That fascinating description reflects Joseph's dream, recorded in Genesis 37:9–11:

> Now he had still another dream, and related it to his brothers, and said, "Lo, I have had still another dream; and behold, the sun and the moon and eleven stars were bowing down to me." He related it to his father and to his brothers; and his father rebuked him and said to him, "What is this dream that you have had? Shall I and your mother and your brothers actually come to bow ourselves down before you to the ground?" His brothers were jealous of him, but his father kept the saying in mind.

In the imagery of Joseph's dream, the sun represents Jacob, the moon Rachel, and the eleven stars Joseph's brothers. The allusion to Joseph's dream is fitting, since his life parallels Israel's history. Both endured the indignity of captivity in Gentile nations, yet were in the end delivered and exalted to a place of prominence in a kingdom.

That the **woman** was **clothed with the sun** reflects redeemed Israel's unique glory, brilliance, and dignity because of her exalted status as God's chosen nation (cf. Deut. 7:6; 14:2; 1 Kings 3:8; Pss. 33:12; 106:5; Isa. 43:20). It also links her with Jacob (the sun in Joseph's dream), an heir in the Abrahamic covenant; Israel's continued existence as a nation reflects the ongoing fulfillment of that covenant (cf. Gen. 12:1–2). The reference to **the moon under her feet** may be a further description of Israel's exalted status. It could also include the concept of God's covenantal relationship with Israel, since the **moon** was part of the cycle of Israel's required times of worship (cf. Num. 29:5–6; Neh. 10:33; Ps. 81:3; Isa. 1:13–14; Col. 2:16). The **crown** (*stephanos;* the crown associated with triumph in the midst of suffering and struggle) **of twelve stars** (Joseph being the twelfth) on the woman's **head** refers to the twelve tribes of Israel.

Having described the woman's attire, John noted her condition: **she was with child.** That also is familiar Old Testament imagery describing Israel (cf. Isa. 26:17–18; 66:7–9; Jer. 4:31; 13:21; Mic. 4:10; 5:3). That the woman is pregnant further confirms her identity as Israel; the church cannot be a mother since she is not yet married (19:7–9; 2 Cor. 11:2). Being pregnant, the woman **cried out, being in labor and in pain to give birth.** Just like a pregnant woman in labor feels pain, so the nation of Israel was in pain, waiting for Messiah to come forth. The cause of some of the pain is the persecution by Satan, who attempts to destroy the mother. The nation was in pain when the Messiah came the first time. So will it be at His second coming. Ever since the first promise of a Redeemer who would come to destroy him (Gen. 3:15), Satan has attacked Israel. For centuries, Israel agonized and suffered, longing for the Child who would come to destroy Satan, sin, and death, and establish the promised kingdom. No nation in history has suffered as long or as severely as Israel has—both from God's chastening, and also from Satan's furious efforts to destroy the nation through whom the Messiah would come.

Having described the woman's agonizing labor pains, John introduces the cause of her suffering.

The Dragon

Then another sign appeared in heaven: and behold, a great red dragon having seven heads and ten horns, and on his heads were seven diadems. And his tail swept away a third of the stars of heaven and threw them to the earth. And the dragon stood before the woman who was about to give birth, so that when she gave birth he might devour her child. (12:3–4)

With the second sign, a new character emerges on the scene: the woman's mortal enemy, dramatically portrayed by **another sign** that **appeared in heaven.** Verse 9 clearly identifies the **great red dragon** as Satan (cf. 20:2). Satan, of course, is not an actual **dragon** (any more than Israel is an actual woman) but a malevolent spirit being, a fallen angel. The symbolic language used to describe him pictures the reality of his person and character. Only in Revelation is Satan referred to as a **dragon;** before that he is called (among other names) a serpent (Gen. 3:1ff.; 2 Cor. 11:3). A dragon is a far more terrifying symbol. In the Old Testament the same Hebrew word translated *dragon* (Isa. 27:1; 51:9) is also translated *monster* or *sea monster* (Gen. 1:21; Job 7:12; Pss. 74:13; 148:7; Jer. 51:34; Ezek. 29:3; 32:2). It pictures a large, ferocious, and terrifying animal. **Red,** the color of fiery destruction and bloodshed, further stresses Satan's vicious, deadly, destructive nature. In the words of Jesus, "He was a murderer from the beginning" (John 8:44). The Hebrew word for "serpent" (*nachash*) used in Genesis 3:1 is used interchangeably in some texts with the Hebrew word for dragon (*tannin*) (cf. Ex. 7:9, 15). So the animal Satan used in the Garden of Eden was a reptile, but one not yet cast down to its belly (Gen. 3:14). Likely, it was more upright—a dragon standing upon two legs, cursed to walk on four legs close to the ground, or slither like a snake. **Red** is a fitting color for the **dragon,** since he attacks both the woman and her child.

Ezekiel 29:1–5, which describes Pharaoh as the enemy of God, captures the essence of this frightening imagery used to describe Satan:

> In the tenth year, in the tenth month, on the twelfth of the month, the word of the Lord came to me saying, "Son of man, set your face against Pharaoh king of Egypt and prophesy against him and against all Egypt. Speak and say, 'Thus says the Lord God,
> "Behold, I am against you, Pharaoh king of Egypt,
> The great monster that lies in the midst of his rivers,
> That has said, 'My Nile is mine, and I myself have made it.'
> I shall put hooks in your jaws
> And make the fish of your rivers cling to your scales.
> And I shall bring you up out of the midst of your rivers,
> And all the fish of your rivers will cling to your scales.
> I shall abandon you to the wilderness, you and all the fish of your rivers;
> You will fall on the open field; you will not be brought together or gathered.
> I have given you for food to the beasts of the earth and to the birds of the sky."'"

The **dragon** is further described as **having seven heads and ten horns, and on his heads were seven diadems.** He is depicted as a seven-headed monster that rules the world. Satan has been allowed by God to rule the world since the Fall and will continue to do so until the seventh trumpet sounds (11:15). The **seven heads** with their **seven diadems** (*diadema;* royal crowns symbolizing power and authority) represent seven consecutive world empires running their course under Satan's dominion: Egypt, Assyria, Babylon, Medo-Persia, Greece, Rome, and Antichrist's future empire (17:9–10). The final kingdom, ruled by Antichrist, will be a ten-nation confederacy; the **ten horns** represent the kings who will rule under Antichrist (17:12; cf. 13:1; Dan. 7:23–25). The shifting of the **diadems** from the dragon's **heads** to the beast's horns (13:1) reveals the shift in power from the seven consecutive world empires to the ten kings under the final Antichrist.

Satan's pervasive, evil influence is not limited to the human realm, but extended first into the angelic realm. In the picturesque language of

John's vision, the dragon's **tail swept away a third of the stars of heaven and threw them to the earth.** The references to the dragon's angels in verses 7 and 9 indicate that the **stars of heaven** are angels. The genitive case offers further support for that interpretation: these are **stars** belonging to **heaven;** that is their proper abode. Angels are depicted symbolically as **stars** elsewhere in Scripture (9:1; Job 38:7).

When Satan fell (Isa. 14:12–15; Ezek. 28:12–17), he **swept away a third of the** angelic host with him. Along with their defeated leader, those evil angels were cast from heaven **to the earth.** (It should be noted that although he was cast from his dwelling in heaven, Satan, in this present age, has access to God's presence; see 12:10; Job 1, 2. As noted in the discussion of 12:7–9 in chapter 2 of this volume, he will be permanently barred from heaven after his defeat by Michael and the holy angels during the Tribulation.)

The number of angels who joined Satan in his rebellion is not revealed, but is vast. Revelation 5:11 says that the number of the angels around God's throne numbered "myriads of myriads, and thousands of thousands." *Myriad* does not represent an exact number; it was the highest number the Greeks expressed in a word. Since one-third of the angels fell, and 9:16 reveals that two hundred million demons will be released from captivity near the Euphrates River, there must be at least four hundred million holy angels. Uncounted thousands of other demons will have already been released from the abyss earlier in the Tribulation (9:1–3). In addition to those two groups of bound demons, there are millions of others who are currently free to roam the earth and the heavenly realm (cf. Eph. 6:12; Col. 2:15). They, along with evil men under his control, assist Satan in his unholy war against God. Adding the (unrevealed) number of these unbound demons to the calculations given above increases the numbers of both the holy angels and the demons.

As the next event in his dramatic vision unfolded, John noted that **the dragon stood before the woman who was about to give birth, so that when she gave birth he might devour her child.** Throughout history, Satan has bent all of his efforts toward persecuting the people of God. Abel was a righteous, obedient man; Satan prompted Cain to kill him. In his first epistle, John wrote, "Cain . . . was of the evil one and slew his brother. And for what reason did he slay him? Because his deeds were evil, and his brother's were righteous" (1 John 3:12). Seeking to produce a mongrel, half-human half-demon and thus unredeemable race of men, Satan sent demons ("sons of God"; the same Hebrew phrase refers to angels in Job 1:6; 2:1; 38:7; Pss. 29:1; 89:6) to cohabit with human women (Gen. 6:1–4).

Because they were the chosen people through whom the Messiah was to come, and by whom the good news of forgiveness was to be proclaimed, Satan reserved his special hatred for Israel. After Joseph's death, the Israelites became slaves in Egypt. In that place, the fates both of the nation and of its human deliverer hung by a slender thread.

> Now a new king arose over Egypt, who did not know Joseph. He said to his people, "Behold, the people of the sons of Israel are more and mightier than we." . . .
>
> Then the king of Egypt spoke to the Hebrew midwives, one of whom was named Shiphrah and the other was named Puah; and he said, "When you are helping the Hebrew women to give birth and see them upon the birthstool, if it is a son, then you shall put him to death; but if it is a daughter, then she shall live." But the midwives feared God, and did not do as the king of Egypt had commanded them, but let the boys live. So the king of Egypt called for the midwives and said to them, "Why have you done this thing, and let the boys live?" The midwives said to Pharaoh, "Because the Hebrew women are not as the Egyptian women; for they are vigorous and give birth before the midwife can get to them." So God was good to the midwives, and the people multiplied, and became very mighty. It came about because the midwives feared God, that He established households for them. Then Pharaoh commanded all his people, saying, "Every son who is born you are to cast into the Nile, and every daughter you are to keep alive."
>
> Now a man from the house of Levi went and married a daughter of Levi. The woman conceived and bore a son; and when she saw that he was beautiful, she hid him for three months. But when she could hide him no longer, she got him a wicker basket and covered it over with tar and pitch. Then she put the child into it and set it among the reeds by the bank of the Nile. His sister stood at a distance to find out what would happen to him.
>
> The daughter of Pharaoh came down to bathe at the Nile, with her maidens walking alongside the Nile; and she saw the basket among the reeds and sent her maid, and she brought it to her. When she opened it, she saw the child, and behold, the boy was crying. And she had pity on him and said, "This is one of the Hebrews' children." Then his sister said to Pharaoh's daughter, "Shall I go and call a nurse for you from the Hebrew women that she may nurse the child for you?" Pharaoh's daughter said to her, "Go ahead." So the girl went and called the child's mother. Then Pharaoh's daughter said to her, "Take this child away and nurse him for me and I shall give you your wages." So the woman took the child and nursed him. The child grew, and she brought him to Pharaoh's daughter and he became her son. And she named him Moses, and said, "Because I drew him out of the water." (Ex. 1:8–9; 1:15–2:10)

From a human perspective, Pharaoh attempted to destroy the Israelites because he believed them to be a threat to his power. But in reality, Pharaoh was an operative of Satan, who sought to wipe out the people from whom the Messiah would come. It is also true to say that Satan was acting within the purposes of God for Israel. The courage of the Hebrew midwives and God's sovereign protection of Moses, whom He would later use to deliver Israel from Egyptian bondage, thwarted Satan's schemes.

During the period of the judges, Satan used Israel's pagan neighbors in an attempt to destroy them. Yet God preserved His people through all of those assaults, raising up judges to rescue them from their oppressors. Later, Satan tried to use Saul to murder David and thus eliminate the messianic line (cf. 1 Sam. 18:10–11). During the days of the divided kingdom, the messianic line twice dwindled to one fragile child (2 Chron. 21:17; 22:10–12). Still later, Satan inspired Haman to undertake his genocidal mission against the Jewish people (Est. 3–9). But God used Esther to save her people from disaster. Throughout their history, the devil incited the Israelites to murder their own children as sacrifices to idols (cf. Lev. 18:21; 2 Kings 16:3; 2 Chron. 28:3; Ps. 106:37–38; Ezek. 16:20).

Having failed to wipe out the people of God and the messianic line, Satan desperately attempted to murder the Messiah Himself before He could do His saving work. John saw that **the dragon stood before the woman who was about to give birth, so that when she gave birth he might devour her child** (Christ). Satan attacked Jesus first through Herod, who attempted to kill the baby Jesus:

> An angel of the Lord appeared to Joseph in a dream and said, "Get up! Take the Child and His mother and flee to Egypt, and remain there until I tell you; for Herod is going to search for the Child to destroy Him." . . .
>
> Then when Herod saw that he had been tricked by the magi, he became very enraged, and sent and slew all the male children who were in Bethlehem and all its vicinity, from two years old and under, according to the time which he had determined from the magi. (Matt. 2:13, 16)

At the outset of our Lord's earthly ministry, Satan tempted Him to mistrust God (Matt. 4:1–11). But the devil's efforts to get Jesus to abandon His mission did not succeed. Satan tried to use the people of Nazareth to kill Jesus (Luke 4:28–30), but their enraged attempt to "throw Him down the cliff" (v. 29) ended in failure when He calmly "pass[ed] through their midst, [and] went His way" (v. 30). Satan's other attempts to cut short Jesus' earthly ministry also ended in failure, "because His hour had not yet come" (John 7:30; 8:20). Even the devil's seeming victory at the Cross was in reality his ultimate defeat (Col. 2:15; Heb. 2:14; 1 Pet. 3:18–20; 1 John 3:8).

The Male Child

And she gave birth to a son, a male child, who is to rule all the nations with a rod of iron; and her child was caught up to God and to His throne. Then the woman fled into the wilderness where she had a place prepared by God, so that there she would be nourished for one thousand two hundred and sixty days. (12:5–6)

In spite of all of Satan's relentless efforts to prevent it, the woman (Israel) **gave birth to a son.** The incarnation of the **male child,** the Lord Jesus Christ, "who was born of a descendant of David according to the flesh" (Rom. 1:3; cf. Rom. 9:5), was the fulfillment of prophecy (cf. Gen. 3:15; Isa. 7:14; 9:6; Mic. 5:2). Israel brought forth the Messiah. The Bible emphasizes that Jesus was of Jewish lineage. He was a son of Abraham (Matt. 1:1), a member of the tribe of Judah (Gen. 49:10; Mic. 5:2; Rev. 5:5), and a descendant of David (Matt. 1:1; cf. 2 Sam. 7:12–16).

Nor will Satan be able to hinder Christ's coronation; He will **rule all the nations with a rod of iron** during His earthly, millennial kingdom (v. 10; 2:26–27; 11:15; 19:15). Psalm 2:7–9 indicates that this rule is a breaking, shattering work of judgment. In fact, the verb *poimainō* (**rule**) carries the connotation of "destroy," as it does in 2:27. The Messiah will come and destroy **all the nations** (19:11–21) and in His kingdom have dominion over the nations that enter to populate that kingdom. An iron rod is also one that cannot be broken. Just as all of Satan's past efforts to hinder Christ have failed, so also will his future efforts fail (cf. 11:15). The phrase **rod of iron** speaks of the resoluteness of Christ's rule; He will swiftly and immediately judge all sin and put down any rebellion.

Between Christ's incarnation and His coronation came His exaltation, when He **was caught up to God and to His throne** at His ascension. Christ's exaltation signifies the Father's acceptance of His work of redemption (Heb. 1:3). Satan could not stop Christ from accomplishing redemption and therefore being exalted to the right hand of the Father as a perfect Savior. In his sermon on the Day of Pentecost, Peter declared, "God raised [Christ] up again, putting an end to the agony of death, since it was impossible for Him to be held in its power" (Acts 2:24).

But though he is a defeated foe, Satan will not give up. Unable to stop Christ's birth, ascension, or rule, Satan still assaults His people. He has already instigated the genocidal massacre of Jews in Europe, as well as the death of countless thousands throughout history. During the Tribulation, Satan will increase his efforts to destroy the Jewish people, so that the nation cannot be saved as the Bible promises (Zech. 12:10–13:1;

Rom. 11:25–27). And so that there will be none left alive to enter the millennial kingdom, he will seek to kill believing Jews. As always, Israel will be his prime target. In a brief glimpse of what will be described more fully in verses 13–17, John noted that **the woman fled into the wilderness where she had a place prepared by God, so that there she would be nourished for one thousand two hundred and sixty days** (cf. v. 14). God will frustrate Satan's attempt to destroy Israel during the Tribulation by hiding His people, just as the Lord Jesus Christ predicted:

> "Therefore when you see the abomination of desolation which was spoken of through Daniel the prophet, standing in the holy place (let the reader understand), then those who are in Judea must flee to the mountains. Whoever is on the housetop must not go down to get the things out that are in his house. Whoever is in the field must not turn back to get his cloak. But woe to those who are pregnant and to those who are nursing babies in those days! But pray that your flight will not be in the winter, or on a Sabbath. For then there will be a great tribulation, such as has not occurred since the beginning of the world until now, nor ever will." (Matt. 24:15–21)

Antichrist's desecration of the temple will send the Jewish people fleeing **into the wilderness.** The exact location where God will hide them is not revealed, but it is probably somewhere east of the Jordan River and south of the Dead Sea, in the territory formerly occupied by Moab, Ammon, and Edom (cf. Dan. 11:40–41). Wherever their hiding place will be, they will be **nourished** and defended by God (cf. vv. 14–16), just as their ancestors were during the forty years of wandering in the wilderness. The length of Israel's stay in hiding, **one thousand two hundred and sixty days** (three and a half years; cf. 11:2–3; 12:14; 13:5) corresponds to the last half of the Tribulation, the period Jesus called the Great Tribulation (Matt. 24:21). Those Jews who remain behind in Jerusalem will come under the influence of the two witnesses, and many in that city will be redeemed (11:13). Eventually, in spite of Satan's efforts, "all Israel will be saved" (Rom. 11:26).

The great cosmic war of the ages between God and Satan that began with Satan's rebellion is set to reach its climax. In this passage John provided important background information on that war and introduced its key figures. Then his vision turned to a description of the war, both in its heavenly and earthly phases, and its inevitable outcome.

The War of the Ages—Part 2: War in Heaven (Revelation 12:7–12)

2

And there was war in heaven, Michael and his angels waging war with the dragon. The dragon and his angels waged war, and they were not strong enough, and there was no longer a place found for them in heaven. And the great dragon was thrown down, the serpent of old who is called the devil and Satan, who deceives the whole world; he was thrown down to the earth, and his angels were thrown down with him. Then I heard a loud voice in heaven, saying, "Now the salvation, and the power, and the kingdom of our God and the authority of His Christ have come, for the accuser of our brethren has been thrown down, he who accuses them before our God day and night. And they overcame him because of the blood of the Lamb and because of the word of their testimony, and they did not love their life even when faced with death. For this reason, rejoice, O heavens and you who dwell in them. Woe to the earth and the sea, because the devil has come down to you, having great wrath, knowing that he has only a short time." (12:7–12)

In his classic book *The Screwtape Letters*, C. S. Lewis wrote, "There are two equal and opposite errors into which our race can fall about the devils. One is to disbelieve in their existence. The other is to believe, and to feel an excessive and unhealthy interest in them. They themselves are equally pleased by both errors and hail a materialist or a magician with the same delight" ([New York: Macmillan, 1961], 9). The same is true of the leader of the demons, Satan. He is pleased when people hold any unbiblical view of him, whether they deny his existence or worship him. The devil always seeks to create confusion about his true nature and purposes.

The Bible exposes Satan's devious and deceitful nature as the "father of lies" (John 8:44), cautioning that he "disguises himself as an angel of light" (2 Cor. 11:14; cf. 2 Cor. 11:3) so that he can more easily deceive people. The apostle Paul expressed his concern "that no advantage would be taken of us by Satan, for we are not ignorant of his schemes" (2 Cor. 2:11). "Put on the full armor of God," the apostle urged the Ephesians, "so that you will be able to stand firm against the schemes of the devil" (Eph. 6:11).

One of the most pervasive and persistent popular myths about Satan pictures him (complete with pitchfork, horns, and pointed tail) as being in charge of hell. In reality, Satan is not in hell; in fact, he has never been there. He will not be sentenced to the lake of fire until after his final rebellion is crushed at the end of the Millennium (20:7–10). And when he does enter hell, Satan will not be in charge; he will be the lowest inmate there, the one undergoing the most horrible punishment ever inflicted on any created being.

Far from being in hell, Satan currently divides his time between roaming the earth "seeking someone to devour" (1 Pet. 5:8) and being in heaven, where he also engages in his doomed attempt to overthrow God's Person, purposes, plans, and people. One way he seeks to do that is by constantly accusing believers before God's throne (cf. 12:10). Satan ceaselessly harangues God about the unworthiness of believers, hypocritically appealing to God's righteousness to further his own unrighteous aims. The unachievable goal of his accusations is to shatter the unbreakable bonds that inseparably link believers to the Lord Jesus Christ (Rom. 8:29–39). There is no possibility of that happening, however, since no one can snatch a believer out of the hands of Jesus or the Father (John 10:28–29). Still, Satan works on earth to turn God's children against Him and in heaven to turn God against His children. But, as John proves, saving faith and eternal life are unbreakable realities.

As part of their war against God, Satan and his demon hosts also battle the holy angels. That is not surprising, since Scripture describes the devil as "the prince of the power of the air" (Eph. 2:2), as well as "the ruler of this world" (John 12:31; 14:30; 16:11). His theater of operations thus includes both the heavens and the earth, and the war of the ages is being fought at every conceivable level—moral, ideological, philosophical, theological, and supernatural.

Satan's battle plan for the earthly phase of the war of the ages is brutally simple: to eliminate all those who serve God. If he could, he would kill them all. If not that, he would destroy their faith, if that were possible. Were he able to rid the earth of all those who serve God, the devil would achieve his goal of unifying the entire world under his rule. It may be noted at this point that such a reality will occur when the believers on earth are raptured to heaven (John 14:1–6; 1 Cor. 15:51–54; 1 Thess. 4:13–18). The Rapture will be followed by the Tribulation, in which Satan does gain the fullest rule of the planet he will ever have (13:4–10). Satan longs to be permanently what he is only temporarily, the god of an unrighteous world (cf. 2 Cor. 4:4), and to be worshiped by everyone (cf. Matt. 4:9). To achieve those goals, Satan desperately wants to prevent the Lord Jesus Christ from establishing His kingdom—both now spiritually in the hearts of men and in its future millennial and eternal forms.

Satan's evil plans will not succeed, however, for Scripture reveals that he is already a defeated foe. Anticipating His victory over Satan at the Cross, Jesus said in John 12:31, "Now judgment is upon this world; now the ruler of this world will be cast out." To the Romans Paul wrote, "The God of peace will soon crush Satan under your feet" (Rom. 16:20; cf. Gen. 3:15), while the writer of Hebrews declared that through His death Jesus "render[ed] powerless him who had the power of death, that is, the devil" (Heb. 2:14). In 1 John 4:4 the apostle John declared, "Greater is He who is in you than he who is in the world."

Though Satan was defeated at the Cross, his sentence has not yet been fully carried out. And though he understands his destiny as revealed in Scripture, Satan nevertheless relentlessly continues to fight his losing battle against God. Thus, the war of the ages will continue until Satan is incarcerated temporarily in the abyss (20:1–3) and then permanently in hell (20:10).

The epochal, long, supernatural war of Satan against God reaches its climax in this profound passage. The sounding of the seventh trumpet in 11:15–17 will anticipate Christ's triumph over Satan, although the final battle will not yet have been fought (cf. 19:11–21). The effects of the seventh trumpet's sounding will be described beginning in chapter 15. The intervening chapters, 12–14, recapitulate the events of chapters 6–11, viewing them from Satan's perspective. They recount the beginning of the war of the ages with Satan's initial rebellion against God and describe its climactic battle during the Tribulation. They also chronicle Antichrist's rise to power and the ultimate failure of Satan's efforts.

Having introduced the combatants in 12:1–6, John describes the first phase of Satan's final assault on God before Christ's return. Verses 7–12, which describe the war in heaven, may be divided into three sections: the battle, the victory, and the celebration.

The Battle

And there was war in heaven, Michael and his angels waging war with the dragon. The dragon and his angels waged war, and they were not strong enough, and there was no longer a place found for them in heaven. (12:7–8)

There has been **war in heaven** since the fall of Satan (Isa. 14:12–14; Ezek. 28:11–19). Though at present he still has access to God's presence in heaven (v. 10; cf. Job 1,2), Satan's domain is the earth and the air around the earth. That is why the Bible describes him as the "god of this world" (2 Cor. 4:4) and the "prince of the power of the air" (Eph. 2:2) and his demon hosts as "spiritual forces of wickedness in the heavenly places" (Eph. 6:12).

Satan (along with the evil angels) has actively opposed both the holy angels and God's people since his fall. In the Old Testament, demons sought to hinder the ministry of the holy angels to Israel (cf. Dan. 10:12–13). In the present age, Satan "prowls around like a roaring lion, seeking someone to devour" (1 Pet. 5:8), opposes the spread of the gospel (Matt. 13:19, 37–39; Acts 13:10), oppresses individuals (Luke 13:10–16; Acts 10:38), and uses sin to disrupt and pollute the church (Acts 5:1–11). Believers are to be wary of his schemes (2 Cor. 2:11), give him no opportunity (Eph. 4:27), and resist him (James 4:7).

The war raging between supernatural beings in the heavenly sphere will reach its peak during the Tribulation. That future conflict will find **Michael and his angels waging war with the dragon.** The grammatical construction of that phrase in the Greek text indicates that Satan (**the dragon**) will start this battle. It could be translated "Michael and his angels had to fight the dragon." The Bible does not reveal how angels fight, nor does our limited knowledge of the heavenly realm permit us to speculate. Henry Morris wrote:

> With what weapons and by what tactics this heavenly warfare will be waged is beyond our understanding. Angels cannot be injured or slain with earthly weapons, and such physical forces as we know about are not able to move spiritual beings. But these beings do operate in a physical universe, so there must exist powerful physico-spiritual energies of which we yet can have only vague intimations, energies which can propel angelic bodies at superluminary velocities through space and which can move mountains and change planetary orbits. It is with such energies and powers that this heavenly battle will be waged and the spectators in heaven (including John) will watch in awe. When Michael finally prevails, and Satan is forced forever out of the heavens, a tremendous cry of thanksgiving will resound through the heavens. (*The Revelation Record* [Wheaton, Ill: Tyndale, 1983], 224)

The key interpretive question is not how the battle will be fought, but what will cause it. While it is impossible to be dogmatic, this ultimate battle may be triggered by the Rapture of the church. Describing that event the apostle Paul wrote, "For the Lord Himself will descend from heaven with a shout, with the voice of the archangel and with the trumpet of God, and the dead in Christ will rise first. Then we who are alive and remain will be caught up together with them in the clouds to meet the Lord in the air, and so we shall always be with the Lord" (1 Thess. 4:16–17). Possibly, as the raptured believers pass through their realm, the prince of the power of the air and his demon hosts will try to hinder their passage. That may trigger the battle with Michael and the holy angels.

Michael and **the dragon** (Satan) have known each other since they were created, and the battle during the Tribulation will not be the first time they have opposed each other. **Michael** is always seen in Scripture as the defender of God's people against satanic destruction. In Daniel chapter 10 the inspired prophet gives an Old Testament example of him in action. A holy angel, dispatched with an answer to Daniel's prayer (Dan. 10:12), was delayed for three weeks by a powerful demon who was in control of the Persian Empire (Dan. 10:13; cf. v. 20). It was not until "Michael, one of the chief princes, came to help" him (v. 13) that he was able to prevail. Daniel 12:1 also speaks of Michael's defense of God's people: "Now at that time [the Tribulation; cf. v. 7] Michael, the great prince who stands guard over the sons of your people, will arise. And there will be a time of distress such as never occurred since there was a nation until that time; and at that time your people, everyone who is found written in the book, will be rescued."

The New Testament also reveals Michael to be the defender of God's people. Jude 9 describes his conflict with Satan over the body of Moses: "Michael the archangel, when he disputed with the devil and argued about the body of Moses, did not dare pronounce against him a railing judgment, but said, 'The Lord rebuke you!'" After Moses' death (Deut. 34:5–6), Michael contested Satan for possession of Moses' body, which Satan apparently wanted to use for some pernicious purpose. In the Lord's power, Michael won the battle and subsequently "[the Lord] buried [Moses] in the valley in the land of Moab, opposite Beth-peor; but no man knows his burial place to this day" (Deut. 34:6).

Significantly, Jude 9 describes Michael as an archangel. The only other reference to an archangel in Scripture is in 1 Thessalonians 4:16, which reveals that at the Rapture "the Lord Himself will descend from heaven with a shout, with the voice of the archangel." It is possible that the archangel in that passage is Michael and that he is shouting as he confronts Satan's attempt to interfere with the Rapture.

The reference to **the dragon and his angels** reinforces the truth that the demon hosts are under Satan's command—a principle stated by Jesus in Matthew 25:41: "Then He will also say to those on His left, 'Depart from Me, accursed ones, into the eternal fire which has been prepared for the devil and his angels.'" The repetition of the phrase **waging war . . . waged war** emphasizes the force and fury of the battle; this will be no minor skirmish, but an all-out battle. Satan will fight desperately to prevent Christ from establishing His millennial kingdom (just as he opposed Israel's restoration from captivity and was rebuked for it; Zech. 3:2). Thus, the supernatural war will reach a crescendo as the time for Christ to establish His earthly and eternal kingdom draws near.

All of Satan's attempts to oppose God throughout history have failed, and he will lose this final angelic battle as well. The devil and his angels are **not strong enough** to defeat God, Michael, and the holy angels. Satan will suffer such a complete defeat that **there** will **no longer** be **a place found for** him and his demon hosts **in heaven.** Every inch of heaven, as it were, will be thoroughly scoured and all the rebellious fallen angels permanently cast out. They will no longer have access to God's presence, and Satan will never again accuse believers before God's throne. This defeat will also mark the end of Satan's reign as "the prince of the power of the air" (Eph. 2:2).

But heaven's cleansing is earth's pollution, as Satan's full fury explodes on humanity when he is cast to the earth (cf. 12:12). At exactly what point in the Tribulation Satan and the demons will be evicted from heaven is not revealed, nor is the duration of their battle with Michael and the holy angels. All that can be said with certainty is that Satan and the demons will be cast out of heaven, possibly at the Rapture, but no later than the midpoint of the Tribulation. Verse 12 says that Satan and his forces have only "a short time" after they leave heaven, supporting the view that they will have only the last three and a half years of the Tribulation to operate, rather than the full seven years. They will not arrive on earth later than that, since they clearly are present during the terrible events of the last three and a half years, the Great Tribulation (cf. 9:1ff.). During that last period, Satan's full power will be directed at anyone belonging to God, especially Israel.

The Victory

And the great dragon was thrown down, the serpent of old who is called the devil and Satan, who deceives the whole world; he was thrown down to the earth, and his angels were thrown down with him. (12:9)

As a result of his defeat, **the great dragon was thrown down** from heaven to the earth. This describes Satan's second and permanent expulsion from heaven (for comments on his first expulsion [Isa. 14:12; Luke 10:18], see the discussion of 12:4 in chapter 1 of this volume). The **dragon** is called **great** because of his formidable power to inflict harm and bring disaster. Earlier, he was described as having seven heads, seven crowns, and ten horns. That description pictures Satan as the ruler of the world (see the discussion of 12:3 in chapter 1 of this volume).

The fourfold description of the **dragon** leaves no doubt as to his identity. First, he is called **the serpent of old** (cf. 20:2), identifying him as the serpent in the Garden of Eden (Gen. 3:1ff.; cf. 2 Cor. 11:3) and emphasizing his subtlety and treachery.

The **dragon is** also **called the devil.** *Diabolos* (**devil**) means "slanderer," "defamer," or "false accuser"—a fitting title for Satan, the ultimate false accuser (cf. v. 10). He accuses men to God, God to men, and men to other men. Satan is a malicious prosecutor of God's people, constantly trying to arraign them before the bar of God's holy justice. Part of his "prowl[ing] around like a roaring lion" (1 Pet. 5:8) no doubt includes seeking evidence of believers' sins with which to accuse them before God's throne. But the glorious truth is that "there is now no condemnation for those who are in Christ Jesus" (Rom. 8:1), because "if anyone sins, we have an Advocate with the Father, Jesus Christ the righteous" (1 John 2:1). In Romans 8:31–34 the apostle Paul eloquently and emphatically stated the impossibility of Satan successfully accusing believers:

> What then shall we say to these things? If God is for us, who is against us? He who did not spare His own Son, but delivered Him over for us all, how will He not also with Him freely give us all things? Who will bring a charge against God's elect? God is the one who justifies; who is the one who condemns? Christ Jesus is He who died, yes, rather who was raised, who is at the right hand of God, who also intercedes for us.

Then the text plainly identifies the dragon as **Satan. Satan** is a Hebrew word that means "adversary," and is a fitting proper name for the malevolent enemy of God and God's people. Tragically, the most glorious created being, the "star of the morning" (Isa. 14:12), is now and forever branded "the adversary." He assaulted God in his original rebellion when he demanded to be "like the Most High" (Isa. 14:14), and he deceitfully led Eve into sin by manipulating her to distrust the character and word of God (Gen. 3:2–5).

Finally, the **dragon** is described as the one **who deceives the whole world. Deceives** translates the present participle of the verb *planaō* ("to lead astray," "to mislead," or "to deceive"). The use of the present tense indicates that this is Satan's habitual, continual activity; as he constantly accuses believers, so also he **deceives the whole world.** Beginning with the Fall, Satan has duped the human race throughout its history. He is, warned Jesus, "a liar and the father of lies" (John 8:44). Satan lures people to their destruction by causing them to pay "attention to deceitful spirits and doctrines of demons" (1 Tim. 4:1). He seduces people to believe him and not God—to believe he tells the truth and God lies (cf. Gen. 3:4).

His deception will dominate the world during the Tribulation, as he mounts his last, desperate assault against God. Through his agent the false prophet (the associate of the Antichrist), Satan will deceive "those who dwell on the earth" (13:14). Deceitful demons under Satan's control will gather the world's armies for the Battle of Armageddon (16:14; cf. 19:19). Satan will also use Babylon, the great end-time commercial empire, to deceive the unbelieving world (18:23). In addition to energizing his servants, Satan himself will be actively involved in deception. At the end of the Tribulation, he will be thrown into the abyss for a thousand years, "so that he [will] not deceive the nations any longer" (20:3). Released for a brief time at the end of the Millennium, Satan "will come out to deceive the nations which are in the four corners of the earth" (20:8). But in the end, "the devil who deceived them [will be] thrown into the lake of fire and brimstone," with two other notorious deceivers, "the beast and the false prophet." There the three of them (along with all the demons) "will be tormented day and night forever and ever" (20:10; cf. Matt. 25:41).

As they were cast out of heaven with Satan at his original rebellion (12:4), so also will **his angels** be **thrown down with him** after his final expulsion from heaven. The arrival of the excommunicated demon host (and their evil commander) on earth will add immeasurably to the horror of the Tribulation. They will join the innumerable demons already roaming the earth, the lately arrived demons belched forth from the abyss (9:1–3), and two hundred million other formerly bound demons (9:13–16) to create an unimaginable holocaust of evil.

THE CELEBRATION

Then I heard a loud voice in heaven, saying, "Now the salvation, and the power, and the kingdom of our God and the authority of His Christ have come, for the accuser of our brethren has been thrown down, he who accuses them before our God day and night. And they overcame him because of the blood of the Lamb and because of the word of their testimony, and they did not love

their life even when faced with death. For this reason, rejoice, O heavens and you who dwell in them. Woe to the earth and the sea, because the devil has come down to you, having great wrath, knowing that he has only a short time." (12:10–12)

The defeat of Satan and his demon hosts and the cleansing of their foul presence from heaven forever will trigger an outburst of praise there. Such sudden outbursts frequently punctuate the prophetic narrative of Revelation (e.g., 4:8–11; 5:9–10, 11–14; 7:9–12; 11:15–18; 15:3–4; 19:1–8). The identity of those whom John heard crying out with **a loud voice in heaven** is not stated. This collective voice (as the use of the plural pronoun **our** indicates) cannot be angels, since angels could not refer to humans as their brethren. The Bible describes angels as believers' fellow servants (19:10; 22:8–9), but never as their brethren. These worshipers, then, are most likely the redeemed, glorified saints in heaven.

The saints began by rejoicing that **the salvation, and the power, and the kingdom of our God and the authority of His Christ have come. Salvation** is to be understood in its broadest sense. It encompasses not only the redemption of individual believers, but also the deliverance of all creation from the ravages of sin's curse and the power of Satan (cf. Rom. 8:19–22). **Power** speaks of God's omnipotence, His triumphant, sovereign power that crushes all opposition and will establish His **kingdom** (cf. 11:15). They rejoiced further that **the authority of . . . Christ** has **come** (cf. 11:15). The rule of Christ is by authority from God (Ps. 2:8; Matt. 28:18; John 17:2). So certain is the establishing of the kingdom and the rule of Christ that, though yet future, they are spoken of in the past tense. The heavenly worshipers rejoice that the first step, Satan's defeat and final ejection from heaven, has already taken place. They know that, having been expelled from heaven to earth, he will shortly be cast from the earth into the abyss (20:1–3), and then from the abyss into his ultimate destination—the lake of fire (20:10).

The event that will cause the kingdom and authority of Christ to be established is the expulsion of Satan from heaven. So the saints offer praise that **the accuser of our brethren has been thrown down, he who accuses them before our God day and night.** As redeemed and glorified individuals, there was nothing Satan could legitimately accuse them of. Still, it must have grieved them that their suffering brethren on earth were subject to the devil's slanderous accusations. Satan's defeat will put an end to those relentless accusations (cf. Job 1:11; 2:5; Zech. 3:1; 1 Pet. 5:8).

The heavenly worshipers also offer praise because of events on earth, where their brethren **overcame** Satan. Ejected from heaven, Satan and his hellish hosts will vent their full fury on God's people on earth (cf.

12:6, 13–17). There too, however, they will suffer defeat. Again speaking of a future event in the past tense because of its certainty, the inspired apostle John sees the victory already won and notes that the believers alive on earth **overcame** Satan, though it is yet to happen. How they did so is most instructive. They did not defeat him by means of incantations, exorcisms, ritual formulas, or by "binding" or rebuking him. Satan, being far more powerful than any human, is impervious to such fleshly tricks and gimmicks. Nor was it through their own personal power that the Tribulation believers defeated Satan. To the Corinthians Paul wrote, "For though we walk in the flesh, we do not war according to the flesh, for the weapons of our warfare are not of the flesh, but divinely powerful for the destruction of fortresses. We are destroying speculations and every lofty thing raised up against the knowledge of God, and we are taking every thought captive to the obedience of Christ" (2 Cor. 10:3–5).

The apostle John gave the only basis for victory over Satan when he wrote, "You are from God, little children, and have overcome them; because greater is He who is in you than he who is in the world" (1 John 4:4). It is only through God's power that any believer in any age can defeat Satan. Accordingly, the Tribulation believers **overcame** Satan first of all **because of the blood of the Lamb.** Like their martyred brethren already in heaven, they "washed their robes and made them white in the blood of the Lamb" (Rev. 7:14). "You were not redeemed with perishable things like silver or gold from your futile way of life inherited from your forefathers," wrote Peter, "but with precious blood, as of a lamb unblemished and spotless, the blood of Christ" (1 Pet. 1:18–19). These suffering believers knew the forgiveness that Paul wrote of in Romans 4:7–8: "Blessed are those whose lawless deeds have been forgiven, and whose sins have been covered. Blessed is the man whose sin the Lord will not take into account." The truth that "there is now no condemnation for those who are in Christ Jesus" (Rom. 8:1) applied to them. No accusation against the suffering saints of the Great Tribulation will stand, just as no accusation against any believer in any age will stand, because the Lamb's blood was shed for all their sins. The first and most important key to defeating Satan's assaults is to "take the helmet of salvation" (Eph. 6:17; cf. 1 Thess. 5:8). The unshakable foundation of all spiritual victory is Christ's purchase of redemption at Calvary.

A second way these Tribulation saints overcame Satan's assaults was through **the word of their testimony.** Despite all the persecution (and even martyrdom) they suffered, they will remain faithful witnesses to Jesus Christ; their testimony will never waver.

The suffering Tribulation saints also were able to fend off Satan's onslaught because **they did not love their life even when faced with death.** Their faithfulness extended all the way to death; they willingly paid the ultimate price for their loyalty to Christ. They knew that all martyrdom could do to them was usher them into the eternal bliss of Christ's presence (Phil. 1:21, 23; cf. Matt. 10:38–39; Acts 20:24; Rom. 8:38–39). Because their faith was genuine, it not only justified and sanctified them, but also enabled them to persevere all the way to glorification. A sure mark of true believers is that they continue in the faith even to death (cf. 1 John 2:19). In the words of Jesus, "The one who endures to the end, he will be saved" (Matt. 24:13).

The passage concludes with a final note of praise: **For this reason,** because of the defeat of Satan and the triumph of the saints, the heavenly chorus calls on the **heavens and** all **who dwell in them** to **rejoice.** That joyous note is followed by the sobering warning **"Woe to the earth and the sea, because the devil has come down to you, having great wrath, knowing that he has only a short time."** *Thumos* (**wrath**) refers to a violent outburst of rage. The word depicts a turbulent, emotional fury rather than a rational anger. John Phillips wrote, "Satan is now like a caged lion, enraged beyond words by the limitations now placed upon his freedom. He picks himself up from the dust of the earth, shakes his fist at the sky, and glares around, choking with fury for ways to vent his hatred and his spite upon humankind" (*Exploring Revelation,* rev. ed. [Chicago: Moody, 1987; reprint, Neptune, N.J.: Loizeaux, 1991], 160). Satan's rage is all the more violent because he knows **that he has only a short time**—the remainder of the Tribulation—for his final assault on God's people. His actual time will be the three and a half years of the reign of Antichrist (13:5), whom Satan places in power immediately after being cast down from heaven. It is the same period referred to in 12:6, 14. It is a short time because Jesus Christ will return to establish His earthly millennial kingdom.

No matter how desperate their situation looks, no matter how furiously Satan rages against them, believers can take comfort in knowing that his ultimate defeat is certain. In the words of Martin Luther's magnificent hymn "A Mighty Fortress Is Our God,"

> The Prince of Darkness grim,
> We tremble not for him;
> His rage we can endure,
> For lo, his doom is sure;
> One little word shall fell him.

The War of the Ages—Part 3: War on Earth (Revelation 12:13–17)

3

And when the dragon saw that he was thrown down to the earth, he persecuted the woman who gave birth to the male child. But the two wings of the great eagle were given to the woman, so that she could fly into the wilderness to her place, where she was nourished for a time and times and half a time, from the presence of the serpent. And the serpent poured water like a river out of his mouth after the woman, so that he might cause her to be swept away with the flood. But the earth helped the woman, and the earth opened its mouth and drank up the river which the dragon poured out of his mouth. So the dragon was enraged with the woman, and went off to make war with the rest of her children, who keep the commandments of God and hold to the testimony of Jesus. (12:13–17)

One of the darkest stains on the history of mankind has been the persistent specter of anti-Semitism. Over the centuries the Jews have faced more hatred and persecution than any other people. Much of that suffering was chastisement from God to turn the nation away from their sin and unbelief and back to Him. God repeatedly warned Israel of the consequences of disobedience (cf. Deut. 28:15–68) and punished them when they failed to obey (cf. 2 Kings 17:7–23). Within the paradigm of God's sovereign purpose for His people, Israel also has suffered constantly and severely at the hands of Satan, acting as God's instrument. Unlike God, however, Satan's purpose in causing the Jewish people to suffer is not remedial, but destructive. He seeks to bring them not to repentance and salvation, but to death and destruction.

Israel faced constant threats from her neighbors during the periods of the judges and of the kings. Later, first the northern kingdom of Israel (722 B.C.) and then the southern kingdom of Judah (586 B.C.) were conquered by their enemies. As a result, the Jewish people lost their independence and became subject to foreign powers, including Assyria, Babylon, Medo-Persia, Greece, and Rome.

In postbiblical times the story has, tragically, been much the same. The history of the Jewish people for the last two thousand years is a sad litany of prejudice, persecution, and pogroms. The first widespread persecution of the Jewish people in Europe took place during the First Crusade (1095–99). As they made their way across Europe toward Palestine, mobs of unruly crusaders destroyed Jewish homes and villages and massacred their inhabitants. When they captured Jerusalem in 1099, the crusaders herded Jerusalem's Jewish population into a synagogue and set it on fire. Most of the Jews perished, and the survivors were sold into slavery. King Edward I banished all Jews from England in 1290, thus giving England the dubious honor of being the first country to expel its Jewish population. They would not be permitted to return until the time of Oliver Cromwell, nearly three and a half centuries later. France followed suit in 1306, Spain in 1492—ironically, the year of Columbus's voyage of discovery to the New World. Throughout the Middle Ages, the Jews were blamed for various natural disasters—most notably the Black Death (1348–50)—and savagely persecuted.

The nineteenth century saw an outbreak of anti-Semitism in Russia, where Jews were blamed for the assassination of Tsar Alexander II (1881). In the ensuing pogroms of the next four decades, tens of thousands of Jews were killed, and hundreds of thousands of others driven from their homes. Nearly 3 million more were killed during Stalin's reign, part of the tens of millions of people massacred by that notorious dictator. 1894 saw the scandalous Dreyfus affair in France, in which a Jewish army officer, Captain Alfred Dreyfus, was falsely convicted of treason. Only after twelve years of public turmoil over the case was Dreyfus exonerated.

But the darkest hour in the long history of anti-Semitism was yet to come. In the early 1930s the Nazi party came to power in Germany and their insane racial theories became public policy. Unlike others who had persecuted the Jewish people, the Nazis and their maniacal leader, Adolf Hitler, did not merely seek to persecute the Jews, but to eliminate them. In the Holocaust that ensued when the Nazis sought to implement their "final solution" to the "Jewish problem," 6 million Jews—more than half the Jewish population of Europe—were slaughtered.

But despite millennia of savage persecution, the Jewish people still survive. John Phillips wrote:

> Significantly, the turning point came in Moses' life when he saw, in the desert, that mysterious burning bush, which flamed and blazed away but, for all the crackling of the fire, was not consumed. That bush clearly symbolized Israel, which cannot be consumed despite the ceaseless hatred of her foes, because God is in her midst. Israel cannot be assimilated into the nations, nor can she be exterminated by the nations. She is a burning bush in the wilderness. (*Exploring Revelation*, rev. ed. [Chicago: Moody, 1987; reprint, Neptune, N.J.: Loizeaux, 1991], 156)

It is the fervent hope of the Jewish people that the horrors of the Holocaust will never again be repeated. Tragically, however, they will. The Bible warns that a time of suffering lies ahead for Israel that will be worse than anything the nation has endured in the past. Jeremiah called that time "the time of Jacob's distress" (Jer. 30:7). Jesus described it as "a great tribulation, such as has not occurred since the beginning of the world until now, nor ever will" (Matt. 24:21).

The Tribulation will be the worst of times for Israel for two reasons. During that seven-year period God will pour out His final fury on the unrepentant and unbelieving world (including the unrepentant rebels of Israel). At the same time, Satan will make his last, desperate attempt to prevent the promised reign of the Lord Jesus Christ on Israel's throne and thus negate the salvation and kingdom promised to Israel. He will savagely assault the Jewish people, seeking to destroy both those Jews who have already come to faith in Christ, and those who still might. The devil will also do everything in his power to hinder the ministries of the 144,000 Jewish evangelists (7:4) and the two witnesses (11:3–14).

But Satan's efforts will not succeed. His worst fears will be realized when the Jews "look on [the One] whom they have pierced; and . . . mourn for Him, as one mourns for an only son, and . . . weep bitterly over Him like the bitter weeping over a firstborn" (Zech. 12:10). The believing remnant of Israel will be saved (Rom. 11:25–29), and their promised kingdom will be established (cf. Hos. 2:14–23).

The prophet Daniel foresaw this tragic and triumphant time for Israel:

> "Now at that time Michael, the great prince who stands guard over the sons of your people, will arise. And there will be a time of distress

> such as never occurred since there was a nation until that time; and at that time your people, everyone who is found written in the book, will be rescued. Many of those who sleep in the dust of the ground will awake, these to everlasting life, but the others to disgrace and everlasting contempt. Those who have insight will shine brightly like the brightness of the expanse of heaven, and those who lead the many to righteousness, like the stars forever and ever. But as for you, Daniel, conceal these words and seal up the book until the end of time; many will go back and forth, and knowledge will increase."
>
> Then I, Daniel, looked and behold, two others were standing, one on this bank of the river and the other on that bank of the river. And one said to the man dressed in linen, who was above the waters of the river, "How long will it be until the end of these wonders?" I heard the man dressed in linen, who was above the waters of the river, as he raised his right hand and his left toward heaven, and swore by Him who lives forever that it would be for a time, times, and half a time; and as soon as they finish shattering the power of the holy people, all these events will be completed. As for me, I heard but could not understand; so I said, "My lord, what will be the outcome of these events?" He said, "Go your way, Daniel, for these words are concealed and sealed up until the end time. Many will be purged, purified and refined, but the wicked will act wickedly; and none of the wicked will understand, but those who have insight will understand. From the time that the regular sacrifice is abolished and the abomination of desolation is set up, there will be 1,290 days." (Dan. 12:1–11)

Daniel, like Jeremiah and Jesus, saw essentially the same scenario that John reveals in Revelation 12: a future time of unparalleled distress, persecution, and slaughter for Israel. Two-thirds of the Jews alive at that time will be killed as God uses Satan to purge the rebels from the nation (Zech. 13:8–9; cf. Ezek. 20:38). But the elect, believing remnant will enter the Messiah's kingdom, along with those resurrected Old Testament saints who at that time will "awake . . . to everlasting life" (Dan. 12:2).

Satan's onslaught against the Jews during the Tribulation will begin with the rise to power of Antichrist. During the first three and a half years of the Tribulation, Satan will work to extend Antichrist's power. Once he becomes the ruler of the world, Satan will make use of him for his evil purposes. Thus, Antichrist will pose as the protector of the Jews during the first half of the Tribulation. The covenant mentioned in Daniel 9:27 is a protection pact with the Antichrist that he will break in the middle of that seven-year period. At that point, Antichrist will become Israel's persecutor for the last half of the Tribulation. He will reveal his true nature when he breaks the covenant and sets up the abomination of desolation (Dan. 11:31; 12:11; Matt. 24:15–16; 2 Thess. 2:3–4) three and a half years into the Tribulation. At that time, Antichrist's persecution of God's people, which has been going on throughout the first half of the Tribulation (see the discussion of 6:9–11 in *Revelation 1–11*, The MacArthur New Testament Commentary [Chicago: Moody, 1999], 187–97), will focus on Israel and intensify.

This passage describes three attacks that Satan's forces will mount against Israel during the Tribulation.

Attack One

And when the dragon saw that he was thrown down to the earth, he persecuted the woman who gave birth to the male child. But the two wings of the great eagle were given to the woman, so that she could fly into the wilderness to her place, where she was nourished for a time and times and half a time, from the presence of the serpent. (12:13–14)

The reason is now given for Israel's flight, which was first mentioned in 12:6. Following his defeat by Michael and the holy angels (cf. the discussion the vision of 12:7–9 in chapter 2 of this volume) **the dragon** (Satan) **was thrown down to the earth.** Frustrated and enraged by his ejection from heaven and desperate, "knowing that he has only a short time" (12:12) left to oppose God's plans before he is incarcerated in the abyss (20:1–3), the devil furiously **persecuted the woman** (Israel; cf. 12:1), **who gave birth** (12:2) **to the male child** (Christ; cf. 12:5). The Greek verb translated **persecuted** (*diōkō*) means "to pursue," "to chase," or "to hunt." It is used in the New Testament of pursuit with hostile intent (cf. Matt. 23:34; Acts 26:11) and thus, by implication, can mean "to persecute." Here it describes Satan's hostile pursuit and persecution of the Jews as they flee into the wilderness (12:6; cf. 13:4–7).

The flight of the Jews from Satan's forces should come as no surprise to anyone familiar with our Lord's Olivet discourse. In that sermon on the end times, Jesus warned the Jewish people of the desperate danger they will face:

> "Therefore when you see the abomination of desolation which was spoken of through Daniel the prophet, standing in the holy place (let the reader understand), then those who are in Judea must flee to the mountains. Whoever is on the housetop must not go down to get the things out that are in his house. Whoever is in the field must not turn back to get his cloak. But woe to those who are pregnant and to those who are nursing babies in those days! But pray that your flight will not be in the winter, or on a Sabbath. For then there will be a great tribulation, such as has not occurred since the beginning of the world until

> now, nor ever will. Unless those days had been cut short, no life would have been saved; but for the sake of the elect those days will be cut short." (Matt. 24:15–22)

The only appropriate response to the imminent danger will be immediate flight; there will be no time even to return home to gather belongings. Pregnant women and those nursing infants will be especially vulnerable, since it will be difficult for them to flee quickly. So severe will the peril be that God will intervene and "for the sake of the elect [both Jews and Gentiles] those days will be cut short" (Matt. 24:22). Were it not for that intervention, even the elect would perish.

Israel's situation when the storm of Antichrist's persecution breaks upon them during the Tribulation will be terrifying and tragic. The Jews will be in desperate need of any assistance they can get and, in God's providence, there will be some people who will help them:

> "But when the Son of Man comes in His glory, and all the angels with Him, then He will sit on His glorious throne. All the nations will be gathered before Him; and He will separate them from one another, as the shepherd separates the sheep from the goats; and He will put the sheep on His right, and the goats on the left.
>
> "Then the King will say to those on His right, 'Come, you who are blessed of My Father, inherit the kingdom prepared for you from the foundation of the world. For I was hungry, and you gave Me something to eat; I was thirsty, and you gave Me something to drink; I was a stranger, and you invited Me in; naked, and you clothed Me; I was sick, and you visited Me; I was in prison, and you came to Me.' Then the righteous will answer Him, 'Lord, when did we see You hungry, and feed You, or thirsty, and give You something to drink? And when did we see You a stranger, and invite You in, or naked, and clothe You? When did we see You sick, or in prison, and come to You?' The King will answer and say to them, 'Truly I say to you, to the extent that you did it to one of these brothers of Mine, even the least of them, you did it to Me.'" (Matt. 25:31–40)

In the Jews' time of peril and flight they will receive help from individual Gentiles. Those Gentiles will demonstrate the genuineness of their faith in Christ by their willingness to help the persecuted Jews—even at the risk of their own lives.

Not only will God providentially use believing Gentiles to aid the Jewish people, but He will also intervene directly on their behalf. John saw in his vision that **the two wings of the great eagle were given to the woman, so that she could fly into the wilderness to her place, where she was nourished for a time and times and half a time, from the presence of the serpent.** This is figurative language that symbolically depicts Israel's escape from Satan's assault. The striking imagery of **the two wings of the great eagle** is taken from Exodus 19:4: "You yourselves have seen what I did to the Egyptians, and how I bore you on eagles' wings, and brought you to Myself." God will bring Israel to safety, just as He delivered the nation from bondage in Egypt.

Wings in Scripture symbolize strength (e.g., Isa. 40:31) and speed (e.g., 2 Sam. 22:11; Pss. 18:10; 104:3). Most commonly, however, **wings** speak of protection. In Deuteronomy 32:9–11 Moses exulted:

> "For the Lord's portion is His people;
> Jacob is the allotment of His inheritance.
> He found him in a desert land,
> And in the howling waste of a wilderness;
> He encircled him, He cared for him,
> He guarded him as the pupil of His eye.
> Like an eagle that stirs up its nest,
> That hovers over its young,
> He spread His wings and caught them,
> He carried them on His pinions."

The psalms repeatedly use the imagery of **wings** to describe God's protection of His people:

> Keep me as the apple of the eye;
> Hide me in the shadow of Your wings.
>
> (Ps. 17:8)

> How precious is Your lovingkindness, O God!
> And the children of men take refuge in the shadow of Your wings.
>
> (Ps. 36:7)

> In the shadow of Your wings I will take refuge
> Until destruction passes by.
>
> (Ps. 57:1)

> Let me dwell in Your tent forever;
> Let me take refuge in the shelter of Your wings.
>
> (Ps. 61:4)

> For You have been my help,
> And in the shadow of Your wings I sing for joy.
>
> (Ps. 63:7)

> He will cover you with His pinions,
> And under His wings you may seek refuge.
>
> (Ps. 91:4)

Eagle translates *aetos*, which can also refer to the griffon, or vulture (cf. Matt. 24:28; Luke 17:37). These large birds with enormous wingspans serve as a fitting symbol for God's protection and sheltering of Israel. This is not, of course, a reference to an actual **eagle** with literal **wings;** rather, it is picturesque language depicting God's miraculous assistance of **the woman, so that she could fly** swiftly **into the wilderness to her place** of shelter and safety.

The location of the **place** to which the Jews will flee is not revealed. Some have suggested the fortresslike city of Petra, carved into the rocky cliffs of Edom between the Dead Sea and the Gulf of Aqaba. Approachable only through a narrow gorge, Petra was easy to defend in ancient times. The term **wilderness** does not reveal the exact location of Israel's **place** of refuge, since that term is a general one often used to describe the desolate area east of Jerusalem (cf. Matt. 3:1; Mark 1:4; John 11:54). Jesus' warning to flee to the mountains (Matt. 24:15–16) suggests that the **place** of refuge will not be in the coastal plain to the west of Jerusalem, or the relatively flat Negev (desert region) to the south. More likely, it will be in the mountainous region east of Jerusalem. Daniel 11:41 provides further evidence for that view: "[Antichrist] will also enter the Beautiful Land, and many countries will fall; but these will be rescued out of his hand: Edom, Moab and the foremost of the sons of Ammon." Perhaps God will spare Edom, Moab, and Ammon, ancient countries to the east of Israel, to provide a refuge for His people.

In her place of safety and refuge, Israel will be supernaturally **nourished** (fed) by God. Cut off from the world system, and unable in any case to buy and sell (cf. 13:17), the Jews will need outside help to survive. God will supernaturally supply them with food, just as he did by providing their ancestors with manna and quail in the wilderness (Ex. 16:12ff.), and Elijah with food at the brook Cherith (1 Kings 17:1–6). Certainly it is not incredible that, in a time of devastating miraculous judgments, God will miraculously provide provisions for His people.

The duration of Israel's hiding and God's provision is defined as **a time and times and half a time.** That phrase, drawn from Daniel 7:25 and 12:7, refers to the second half of the Tribulation (the three-and-a-half year period Jesus called the Great Tribulation; Matt. 24:21). It is the same period defined in 12:6 as "one thousand two hundred and sixty days" (cf. 11:3) and in 13:5 as "forty-two months" (cf. 11:2). This period, initiated by the setting up of the abomination of desolation (Dan. 11:31; 12:11; Matt. 24:15; 2 Thess. 2:3–4), will mark the visibly, overtly evil career of Antichrist. During that time God will protect Israel **from the presence of the serpent.** Although Satan may know where the Jews are hiding, he will be unable to get at them because of divine protection. Frustrated by this defeat of his first assault on the Jewish people, the devil will launch a second attack.

Attack Two

And the serpent poured water like a river out of his mouth after the woman, so that he might cause her to be swept away with the flood. But the earth helped the woman, and the earth opened its mouth and drank up the river which the dragon poured out of his mouth. (12:15–16)

Thwarted in his initial attempt to massacre the Jewish people, and unable to directly assault them in their hiding place, Satan will resort to long-range tactics. Since the **serpent** is not an actual snake but a symbolic representation of Satan, the **water** he spews **like a river out of his mouth** is likely symbolic as well. The imagery once again derives from the Old Testament, where floods symbolize trouble in general (cf. 2 Sam. 22:17; Job 27:20; Pss. 18:16; 32:6; 69:1–2, 13–14; 124:2–5; 144:7) and an invading, destroying army (cf. Jer. 46:8; 47:2; Dan. 11:26). Satan's attacking force will sweep toward the Jews' hiding place like a great flood. The devil will seek to **cause** Israel **to be swept away with the flood;** to be drowned by it, to be consumed and destroyed.

But just as He sheltered Israel from Satan's initial onslaught, so also will God defeat this second assault. In dramatic fashion, **the earth helped the woman;** it **opened its mouth and drank up the river which the dragon poured out of his mouth.** The imagery is reminiscent of Moses' description of God's destruction of Pharaoh's army in Exodus 15:12: "You stretched out Your right hand, the earth swallowed them." Another Old Testament parallel is the dramatic story of Korah, Dathan, and Abiram, whose rebellion against Moses was crushed by God in a shocking, dramatic fashion:

> Moses said, "By this you shall know that the Lord has sent me to do all these deeds; for this is not my doing. If these men die the death of all men or if they suffer the fate of all men, then the Lord has not sent me. But if the Lord brings about an entirely new thing and the ground opens its mouth and swallows them up with all that is theirs, and they descend alive into Sheol, then you will understand that these men have spurned the Lord."
>
> Then it came about as he finished speaking all these words, that the ground that was under them split open; and the earth opened its mouth and swallowed them up, and their households, and all the men who belonged to Korah with their possessions. So they and all that belonged to them went down alive to Sheol; and the earth closed over them, and they perished from the midst of the assembly. (Num. 16:28–33)

It may be that one of the frequent earthquakes during the Tribulation (cf. 6:12; 8:5; 11:13, 19; 16:18; Matt. 24:7) will cause the ground to split open and swallow Satan's forces. Whatever this symbolic language pictures, it marks the destruction of the attacking army and the end of Satan's second assault.

Attack Three

So the dragon was enraged with the woman, and went off to make war with the rest of her children, who keep the commandments of God and hold to the testimony of Jesus. (12:17)

By now thoroughly frustrated and **enraged** by his inability to destroy **the woman** (Israel), the **dragon** (Satan) will turn his fury toward new targets. Some have identified **the rest of her children** with whom Satan will **make war** as the 144,000 (cf. 7:2–8; 14:1–5); others see them as believing Gentile Tribulation saints (cf. 7:9–14), who are sons of Abraham by faith (Gal. 3:7). It seems best to take this as an all-inclusive phrase, referring to all those who name the name of Jesus Christ.

They are further described as those **who keep the commandments of God and hold to the testimony of Jesus.** *Entolas* (**commandments**) is a word used frequently in John's writings to refer to New Testament commands (e.g., 14:12; John 14:15, 21; 15:10, 12; 1 John 2:3–4; 3:22–24; 5:2–3). The **testimony of Jesus** is not testimony about Him, but the testimony He gave, the truths He taught that are revealed in the New Testament. These persecuted believers will give further evidence that their salvation is real by their obedience to the truth of Scripture.

Like his first two attacks directed against Israel, Satan's third attack on God's people will also fail. At the sounding of the seventh trumpet, "loud voices in heaven" will proclaim, "The kingdom of the world has become the kingdom of our Lord and of His Christ; and He will reign forever and ever" (11:15). All of Satan's efforts to prevent Christ's kingdom from being established are doomed. The Lord Jesus Christ will triumph; He will reign on earth, and the surviving Tribulation saints, both Jews and Gentiles, will enter His earthly kingdom.

For the long-suffering people of Israel, the darkest hour lies ahead. But it will be followed by a glorious dawn. The elect remnant of Israel, having survived the most savage persecution in the nation's long history, will be saved and enjoy the bliss of the millennial kingdom, "and so all Israel will be saved; just as it is written" (Rom. 11:26).

The Beast out of the Sea (Revelation 13:1–10)

4

And the dragon stood on the sand of the seashore. Then I saw a beast coming up out of the sea, having ten horns and seven heads, and on his horns were ten diadems, and on his heads were blasphemous names. And the beast which I saw was like a leopard, and his feet were like those of a bear, and his mouth like the mouth of a lion. And the dragon gave him his power and his throne and great authority. I saw one of his heads as if it had been slain, and his fatal wound was healed. And the whole earth was amazed and followed after the beast; they worshiped the dragon because he gave his authority to the beast; and they worshiped the beast, saying, "Who is like the beast, and who is able to wage war with him?" There was given to him a mouth speaking arrogant words and blasphemies, and authority to act for forty-two months was given to him. And he opened his mouth in blasphemies against God, to blaspheme His name and His tabernacle, that is, those who dwell in heaven. It was also given to him to make war with the saints and to overcome them, and authority over every tribe and people and tongue and nation was given to him. All who dwell on the earth will worship him, everyone whose name has not been written from the foundation of the

world in the book of life of the Lamb who has been slain. If anyone has an ear, let him hear.

If anyone is destined for captivity, to captivity he goes; if anyone kills with the sword, with the sword he must be killed. Here is the perseverance and the faith of the saints. (13:1–10)

In the chaotic times of confusion, uncertainty, and unrest that will prevail during the Tribulation, the world will long for a leader. People will be desperately hoping for someone powerful and influential to unite the divided and contentious nations of the world; someone to bring hope in the midst of helplessness; someone to provide a sense of security in an unsettled time of apprehension and fear. People will be desperately seeking a strong, charismatic, authoritative leader to pull the world back from the brink of disaster.

Those longings will be fulfilled. The powerful leader people desire will come and unify the world under his rule. He will appear at first to be everything people thought they were looking for. And for a brief time he will bring peace and prosperity. But he will turn out to be far more than the world bargained for. He will be a dictator more cruel and powerful than any other leader the world has ever known. This man, often called the Antichrist, will be the culmination of a long line of would-be world conquerors. What men like Alexander the Great and the Roman emperors in ancient times and Hitler and Stalin in modern times only dreamed of doing, the Antichrist actually will do—he will rule the entire world and receive its worship.

Just as the Antichrist will be the culmination of a long line of political rulers, so also will he be the ultimate false religious leader. In the broadest sense, an "antichrist [is any] one who denies the Father and the Son" (1 John 2:22), because one who does "not acknowledge Jesus Christ as coming in the flesh . . . is the deceiver and the antichrist" (2 John 7). Such charlatans have been around throughout human history; in the first century the apostle John lamented that "even now many antichrists have appeared" (1 John 2:18; cf. 1 John 4:3). But the Bible predicts that the end times will see an unprecedented proliferation of false christs and antichrists. Jesus warned, "Many will come in My name, saying, 'I am He!' and will mislead many. . . . [I]f anyone says to you, 'Behold, here is the Christ'; or, 'Behold, He is there'; do not believe him; for false Christs and false prophets will arise, and will show signs and wonders, in order to lead astray, if possible, the elect" (Mark 13:6, 21–22). Those satanic impostors will culminate in the final Antichrist, who will be more vile, evil, and powerful than all the rest.

The astounding description of the Antichrist presented in the opening verses of this chapter is the most gripping, thorough, and dramatic one in all of Scripture. However, it was not new teaching to John's readers. John wrote in his first epistle that his readers had "heard that antichrist is coming" (1 John 2:18). After describing Antichrist and his activity, the apostle Paul reminded the Thessalonians, "Do you not remember that while I was still with you, I was telling you these things?" (2 Thess. 2:5). Those passages indicate that the truth about Antichrist was common knowledge in New Testament times.

The original source of the biblical teaching about the Antichrist is the book of Daniel. Daniel 7 pictures the Antichrist as a little horn (v. 8), arising from the ten horns of the fourth beast of Daniel's vision. That horn represents a person, since it "possessed eyes like the eyes of a man and a mouth uttering great boasts" (v. 8). Earlier in that verse, Daniel notes that "three of the first horns were pulled out by the roots before [Antichrist]," indicating that he will destroy three of the other rulers (cf. v. 24) and subjugate the rest during his rise to power.

Later in chapter 7, Daniel saw that the "horn [Antichrist] was waging war with the saints and overpowering them" (v. 21). Antichrist is seen leading a savage persecution of God's people "until the Ancient of Days came and judgment was passed in favor of the saints of the Highest One, and the time arrived when the saints took possession of the kingdom" (v. 22). Daniel described Antichrist's kingdom (a revived Roman Empire) as one "which will be different from all the other kingdoms and will devour the whole earth and tread it down and crush it" (v. 23). As previously noted, Antichrist, unlike other tyrants in human history, will rule the entire world. In verse 25 Daniel said that Antichrist "will speak out against the Most High and wear down the saints of the Highest One, and he will intend to make alterations in times and in law; and they will be given into his hand for a time, times, and half a time." This counterfeit Christ will, as previously noted, persecute God's people. He will also institute a new religion (the worship of himself; cf. Dan. 11:36–37; 2 Thess. 2:4), a reign of evil, and will rewrite history to suit his purposes. Helping him do so will be his associate, the false prophet (see the discussion of 13:11–18 in chapter 5 of this volume).

Daniel 8:23*b*–25 gives another glimpse of Antichrist and his reign of terror:

> "A king will arise,
> Insolent and skilled in intrigue.
> His power will be mighty, but not by his own power,
> And he will destroy to an extraordinary degree
> And prosper and perform his will;
> He will destroy mighty men and the holy people.
> And through his shrewdness
> He will cause deceit to succeed by his influence;

> And he will magnify himself in his heart,
> And he will destroy many while they are at ease.
> He will even oppose the Prince of princes,
> But he will be broken without human agency."

He will be an insolent intimidator, devious, possessing a power not his own, a fierce destroyer of his victims, and so arrogant that he will dare even to "oppose the Prince of princes" (cf. v. 11), who is the Lord Christ. That move will prove fatal, however, and God's power will fall on Antichrist, who "will be broken without human agency."

Daniel's prophecy of the seventy weeks describes Antichrist as "the prince who is to come" (Dan. 9:26). He

> "will destroy the city [Jerusalem] and the sanctuary. And its end will come with a flood; even to the end there will be war; desolations are determined. And he will make a firm covenant with the many for one week, but in the middle of the week he will put a stop to sacrifice and grain offering; and on the wing of abominations will come one who makes desolate, even until a complete destruction, one that is decreed, is poured out on the one who makes desolate." (Dan. 9:26–27)

Antichrist will make a pact with Israel for seven years. Halfway through that seven-year period, however, he will break that covenant and attack the Jewish people. His plan will be to wipe them out, so that God's promised kingdom cannot come. Antichrist's assault will also include believing Gentiles, as he seeks to destroy all believers.

Another important passage regarding Antichrist and his career is found in Daniel 11:36–45:

> "Then the king will do as he pleases, and he will exalt and magnify himself above every god and will speak monstrous things against the God of gods; and he will prosper until the indignation is finished, for that which is decreed will be done. He will show no regard for the gods of his fathers or for the desire of women, nor will he show regard for any other god; for he will magnify himself above them all. But instead he will honor a god of fortresses, a god whom his fathers did not know; he will honor him with gold, silver, costly stones and treasures. He will take action against the strongest of fortresses with the help of a foreign god; he will give great honor to those who acknowledge him and will cause them to rule over the many, and will parcel out land for a price.
>
> "At the end time the king of the South will collide with him, and the king of the North will storm against him with chariots, with horsemen and with many ships; and he will enter countries, overflow them and pass through. He will also enter the Beautiful Land, and many countries will fall; but these will be rescued out of his hand: Edom, Moab

> and the foremost of the sons of Ammon. Then he will stretch out his hand against other countries, and the land of Egypt will not escape. But he will gain control over the hidden treasures of gold and silver and over all the precious things of Egypt; and Libyans and Ethiopians will follow at his heels. But rumors from the East and from the North will disturb him, and he will go forth with great wrath to destroy and annihilate many. He will pitch the tents of his royal pavilion between the seas and the beautiful Holy Mountain; yet he will come to his end, and no one will help him."

According to this prophecy, Antichrist will have absolute power; he "will do as he pleases." As the leader of a worldwide false religion, he "will exalt and magnify himself above every god. . . . He will show no regard for the gods of his fathers . . . nor will he show regard for any other god; for he will magnify himself above them all" (vv. 36–37). Worse, his arrogant pride will lead him to blasphemy, and he "will speak monstrous things against the God of gods." Like his evil master, Satan, Antichrist will be blasphemous, profane, and proud. But also like his master, "he will come to his end, and no one will help him."

In addition to Daniel's prophecy, the original readers of Revelation had information about the Antichrist from the teaching of the Lord Jesus Christ. In Matthew 24:15–16, Jesus quoted Daniel's prophecy about Antichrist, warning those alive in that day "Therefore when you see the abomination of desolation which was spoken of through Daniel the prophet, standing in the holy place (let the reader understand), then those who are in Judea must flee to the mountains."

Another source of information about the Antichrist available to John's readers was the book of 2 Thessalonians, written several decades earlier. The apostle Paul describes the Antichrist in words reminiscent of Daniel's prophecy:

> Let no one in any way deceive you, for it will not come unless the apostasy comes first, and the man of lawlessness is revealed, the son of destruction, who opposes and exalts himself above every so-called god or object of worship, so that he takes his seat in the temple of God, displaying himself as being God. Do you not remember that while I was still with you, I was telling you these things? And you know what restrains him now, so that in his time he will be revealed. For the mystery of lawlessness is already at work; only he who now restrains will do so until he is taken out of the way. Then that lawless one will be revealed whom the Lord will slay with the breath of His mouth and bring to an end by the appearance of His coming; that is, the one whose coming is in accord with the activity of Satan, with all power and signs and false wonders, and with all the deception of wickedness for those who perish, because they did not receive the love of the truth so as to be saved. (2 Thess. 2:3–10)

In that passage, Paul clearly delineated Antichrist's character, describing Him as the "man of lawlessness . . . the son of destruction" (v. 3). He also described Antichrist's wicked career. When Antichrist "takes his seat in the temple of God, displaying himself as being God," he will break his covenant with Israel, and commit the abomination of desolation that both Daniel (Dan. 11:31) and Jesus (Matt. 24:15) warned about. After deceiving the world into worshiping him during the last half of the Tribulation "with all power and signs and false wonders," Antichrist will be destroyed. The "Lord will slay [Antichrist] with the breath of His mouth and bring [him] to an end by the appearance of His coming" (cf. 19:11–21).

Though chapter 13 gives the most detailed description of Antichrist in Revelation, this is not his first appearance in the Apocalypse. Antichrist was introduced in 11:7 as the "beast" who will assault and kill God's two witnesses. His wicked career, which began in chapter 11, is fully developed beginning in chapter 13.

Chapter 12 records the beginning of Satan's long war against God and His people; chapter 13 follows logically to record that war's culmination. In chapter 12 Satan is seen being cast from heaven to earth; in chapter 13 he is described beginning his massive effort on earth to defeat God and His purposes. Satan will try to prevent Jesus Christ from setting up His earthly kingdom by setting up his own under Antichrist.

As a spirit being, Satan depends on humans to carry out his evil plans on earth. He controls all unbelievers; since they are "of [their] father the devil, and [want] to do the desires of [their] father" (John 8:44), and walk "according to the course of this world, according to the prince of the power of the air, of the spirit that is now working in the sons of disobedience" (Eph. 2:2).

But some humans have been (and are) under Satan's (or his demons') direct control. For example, Satan used Judas to betray Jesus to His death. In the terrifying words of Luke 22:3, "Satan entered into Judas who was called Iscariot, belonging to the number of the twelve." During His earthly ministry, Jesus showed His mastery over Satan by casting demons out of people. He also delegated power over the demonic realm to the apostles, to aid them as they confronted Satan's kingdom (Mark 3:14–15). By so doing, He and the apostles not only freed people from demonic bondage, but also hindered Satan from carrying out his earthly agenda.

Having been cast permanently from heaven (12:9), Satan will know that the time remaining to him is brief (12:12). To lead his last, desperate onslaught against God, he will empower his final Antichrist. The opening verses of this chapter reveal seven features of this ultimate dictator: his ancestry, authority, acclaim, adoration, arrogance, activity, and admirers.

His Ancestry

And the dragon stood on the sand of the seashore. Then I saw a beast coming up out of the sea, having ten horns and seven heads, and on his horns were ten diadems, and on his heads were blasphemous names. (13:1)

The first sentence of this chapter belongs as the last sentence of chapter 12, since it concludes the account of **the dragon** (Satan; cf. 12:9) and his war against God and His people. While some Greek manuscripts read "I stood," the older and more reliable ones read "he stood." In the 1994 and 1995 texts of the *New American Standard Bible*, the translators inserted the phrase **the dragon** in place of "he," since **the dragon** is the antecedent of the verb translated "he stood." The imagery of the **sand of the seashore** depicts the nations of the world (cf. 20:8). In John's vision, Satan takes his place dominantly in their midst as if they were his rightful possession. But in reality, he is a usurper who seeks the world's worship and adoration.

As John's vision unfolded, **the dragon** summoned the Antichrist, described as **a beast coming up out of the sea.** *Thērion* (**beast**) is also used to describe Antichrist in 11:7. It does not refer to a domesticated animal, but to a wild, savage, vicious monster, thus describing Antichrist as a ferocious and rapacious personality. The **beast** must be understood as representing both a kingdom and a person. The **beast** must represent a kingdom, because of the complex description of him in the latter half of verse 1. Yet the **beast** must also represent a person, since he is always described with personal pronouns (e.g., "his," "him," "he"; cf. vv. 1–8; 14:9, 11; 15:2; 16:2, 10). Daniel (Dan. 7:25; 8:24–25; 11:36–45) and Paul (2 Thess. 2:4) also describe the Antichrist as a person. In this manner, Scripture views the final world empire as inseparable from its ruler, much as Hitler is inseparably linked to the Third Reich.

There has been much discussion about what the **sea** symbolizes. Some argue, based on such passages as Isaiah 17:12, 57:20, and Revelation 17:15, that it refers to the Gentile nations. But since 11:7 and 17:8 state that the **beast** comes up out of the abyss, it is best to equate the **sea** with the abyss. That interpretation is in harmony with the Old Testament, which also uses the metaphor of the sea to picture the realm of satanic activity (cf. Job 26:12; Pss. 74:13–14; 89:9–10; Isa. 27:1). Some of the demons are currently incarcerated in the abyss (cf. 9:1–11; Luke 8:31), and Satan will be imprisoned in that abyss during the millennial kingdom (20:1–3).

The Antichrist will be a man (2 Thess. 2:4), but at some point in his life, he will be indwelt by a powerful demon from the abyss. This demon-possessed man will be a gifted orator, an intellectual genius, possess great charm and charisma, and have immense leadership power. Added to those natural qualities will be the hellish power of Satan. The result will be a person of superhuman power, vast intelligence, and consummate wickedness.

While all unbelievers are children of Satan (John 8:44), no one in human history will be more completely the devil's child than the Antichrist. His "family likeness" to Satan becomes strikingly apparent from John's description of him as **having ten horns and seven heads, and on his horns were ten diadems.** That same grotesque description was applied to Satan in 12:3: "Then another sign appeared in heaven: and behold, a great red dragon having seven heads and ten horns, and on his heads were seven diadems." The description of Antichrist emphasizes the importance of the **ten horns** by mentioning them first and associating the **diadems** with them instead of the heads.

Horns in Scripture symbolize strength and power, both for attack and defense (cf. 1 Sam. 2:1, 10; 2 Sam. 22:3; Job 16:15; Pss. 18:2; 75:4–5; 89:17, 24; 92:10; 112:9; Jer. 48:25; Mic. 4:13). In this passage, they represent the great power of the kings who will rule under Antichrist's absolute authority. **Ten** fits the imagery of the fourth beast in Daniel 7:7, 24, and is a symbolic number representing all the world's political and military might. Antichrist will rise from among these ten (Dan. 7:16–24) and will not rule merely ten nations, but the entire world (cf. Dan. 7:23). Unlike the **seven heads,** which represent successive world empires, all of the rulers symbolized by the **ten horns** will rule at the same time (cf. 17:12).

Daniel described this final coalition, headed by Antichrist, in Daniel 2:41–44:

> "In that you saw the feet and toes, partly of potter's clay and partly of iron, it will be a divided kingdom; but it will have in it the toughness of iron, inasmuch as you saw the iron mixed with common clay. As the toes of the feet were partly of iron and partly of pottery, so some of the kingdom will be strong and part of it will be brittle. And in that you saw the iron mixed with common clay, they will combine with one another in the seed of men; but they will not adhere to one another, even as iron does not combine with pottery. In the days of those kings the God of heaven will set up a kingdom which will never be destroyed, and that kingdom will not be left for another people; it will crush and put an end to all these kingdoms, but it will itself endure forever."

The final world empire will be in some sense a revival of the Roman Empire (the iron legs and ten toes of the statue in Daniel 2), but will far exceed it both in power and extent. It will be much more than a European confederacy; it will cover the entire world. Ultimately, Antichrist's empire will be crushed by Christ (the "stone [that] was cut out without hands"; Dan. 2:34,45) when He comes to establish His earthly kingdom.

In addition to his ten horns, the beast is described by John as having **seven heads.** As will be seen in the discussion of Revelation 17 later in this volume, those seven heads represent seven successive world empires: Egypt, Assyria, Babylon, Medo-Persia, Greece, Rome, and Antichrist's final world kingdom. The **ten diadems** (royal crowns) indicate the horns' regal authority and victorious power. John also noted that on the beast's **heads were blasphemous names.** Like many of the Roman emperors and other monarchs before them, these rulers will blasphemously arrogate divine names and titles to themselves that dishonor the true and living God. They will follow the pattern of their master, Antichrist, "who opposes and exalts himself above every so-called god or object of worship, so that he takes his seat in the temple of God, displaying himself as being God" (2 Thess. 2:4).

His Authority

And the beast which I saw was like a leopard, and his feet were like those of a bear, and his mouth like the mouth of a lion. And the dragon gave him his power and his throne and great authority. (13:2)

As John looked more closely at the **beast,** he **saw** that it incorporated the characteristics of the animals from the vision recorded in Daniel 7:3–7:

> "And four great beasts were coming up from the sea, different from one another. The first was like a lion and had the wings of an eagle. I kept looking until its wings were plucked, and it was lifted up from the ground and made to stand on two feet like a man; a human mind also was given to it. And behold, another beast, a second one, resembling a bear. And it was raised up on one side, and three ribs were in its mouth between its teeth; and thus they said to it, 'Arise, devour much meat!' After this I kept looking, and behold, another one, like a leopard, which had on its back four wings of a bird; the beast also had four heads, and dominion was given to it. After this I kept looking in the night visions, and behold, a fourth beast, dreadful and terrifying and extremely strong; and it had large iron teeth. It devoured and crushed and trampled down the remainder with its feet; and it was different from all the beasts that were before it, and it had ten horns."

The **leopard, bear,** and **lion** were well-known in Palestine. They dramatically emphasize the characteristics of the nations they represent. The **lion** was a fitting symbol for the fierce, consuming power of the Babylonian Empire. The ferocity, strength, and stability of the Medo-Persian Empire led to its depiction as a **bear.** The Greeks' swift conquests, particularly under the mercurial Alexander the Great, reflect the speed and viciousness of the **leopard.** John lists the three animals in reverse order from Daniel, since he was looking backward in time. Daniel, looking forward in time, listed the animals and the kingdoms they represent in chronological order.

Like the indescribable fourth beast of Daniel 7:7, which represents the Roman Empire, Antichrist's final empire will be a composite of the empires that preceded it. It will incorporate all the ferocity, viciousness, swiftness, and strength of the other world empires. This powerful empire, unparalleled in human history, will be Satan's last and greatest attempt to stop the reign of Christ. But, like all Satan's other attempts to thwart God's purposes, it will ultimately fail.

Because the **dragon** (Satan) is the source of Antichrist's **power,** no human force will be able to withstand him. **The dragon** works his **power** through **the beast,** using him to make war against God. Nor will the holy angels intervene, because God's supernatural restraint of Antichrist will be removed (2 Thess. 2:7). That will allow Antichrist to rise to power at God's appointed time, and will temporarily let sin run its course. The Antichrist will share Satan's **throne** (cf. 2:13), just as the true Christ shares His Father's throne (cf. 3:21; 22:1, 3). Antichrist will possess **great authority** over the entire world; he will have complete, unrestrained freedom of action and will answer to no one.

Some find it incredible that anyone could rise to such a position of absolute authority. But there are parallels in human history, albeit on a much smaller scale. Inevitably, turmoil in society aids such a ruler's rise to power. Dictators gain control by offering solutions to society's seemingly unsolvable problems. Adolf Hitler, for example, took advantage of the chaotic economic and political conditions in Germany following World War I. He promised the German people that, under his leadership, their downtrodden nation would again rise to a place of prominence, power, and wealth. Desperate for a way out of their dilemma, many people believed his message. Eventually, the Nazi party grew so strong that Hitler was appointed chancellor of Germany. From that position he went on to seize absolute power. Antichrist, a dictator more powerful and evil than Hitler, will rise to power amid the frightening and unprecedented chaos of the Tribulation.

HIS ACCLAIM

I saw one of his heads as if it had been slain, and his fatal wound was healed. And the whole earth was amazed and followed after the beast; (13:3)

A startling event will help Antichrist solidify his hold on the world. John saw **one of his heads as if it had been slain, and his fatal wound was healed.** The interpretation of that phrase has been much debated. Some commentators argue that the head whose fatal wound was healed was a kingdom that will have been destroyed and restored. They see the death and resurrection miracle as the revival of the Roman Empire. Antichrist, they believe, will unite the countries occupying the territory of the ancient Roman Empire into a new empire. That revival of power will so amaze the rest of the nations that they will also submit to his rule.

There are several difficulties with that view, however. The most obvious problem is that while verse 3 speaks of **one** of the **heads** being **slain,** other passages specify that the beast himself is slain (13:12, 14; 17:8, 11). The personal pronoun in the phrase **his fatal wound** also indicates that one of the kings is in view, not the empire as a whole. Nor does it seem likely that merely reviving the Roman Empire would cause the worldwide astonishment and wonder mentioned in this verse. Finally, the phrase **as if . . . slain** is used in 5:6 of the Lord Jesus Christ, implying that it is also used of a person in this passage.

Granting that it is a person who dies and is restored to life, the question remains as to the identity of that person. The view that it will be the resurrected Judas Iscariot has little to commend it. That idea is based on the fact that Judas (John 17:12) and Antichrist (2 Thess. 2:3) are both called "son of perdition [or destruction]," and that Jesus called Judas a "devil" (John 6:70–71). But there would be little point in a resurrected Judas; how would anyone recognize him, since no one would know what he looked like?

A more popular view links the death and resurrection in this passage with Emperor Nero. It was widely believed at the end of the first century that Nero, who had committed suicide in A.D. 68, would rise from the dead. But it is doubtful that many Christians (especially the divinely inspired apostle John) believed in the Nero resurrection myth. Further, the beast will suffer violent death at the hands of another (13:14) while Nero, as previously noted, took his own life.

The head whose **fatal wound** will be **healed** can only be the future Antichrist. Whether his death is real or fake (cf. v. 14; 2 Thess. 2:9) is not clear. It may be that Antichrist is really killed, and God, for His own purposes, allows him to be resurrected. More likely, Antichrist's alleged death and resurrection will be a counterfeit of Christ's death and resurrection, staged, as one of the "lying wonders" perpetrated by the false prophet (13:12–15; 2 Thess. 2:9 NKJV). Antichrist's resurrection will also be phony, since he never really died. Or perhaps Antichrist will explain his extraordinary powers by claiming to be the reincarnation of the Christ spirit, as some have suggested. Certainly, in a world where New Age pantheism and Eastern mysticism are extremely popular, more people would be inclined to believe in a reincarnation than a resurrection.

Whatever actually happens, the people of the world will believe that Antichrist, already popular because of his great powers, has also transcended death. Since the Tribulation will be a time where the world will experience death on a scale unprecedented in human history, Antichrist's seeming invulnerability to death will win him greater, more widespread acclaim. As a result, the **whole earth** will be **amazed and** follow **after the beast** (cf. v. 14; 2 Thess. 2:8–12).

His Adoration

they worshiped the dragon because he gave his authority to the beast; and they worshiped the beast, saying, "Who is like the beast, and who is able to wage war with him?" (13:4)

The world's fascination with Antichrist will quickly become worship. He will encourage and demand that worship by "exalt[ing] himself above every so-called god or object of worship, so that he takes his seat in the temple of God, displaying himself as being God" (2 Thess. 2:4). Not content with acclaim, Antichrist will seek adoration; not content with respect, he will require reverence; not content with being hailed and heralded, he will demand to be worshiped. And those who "did not receive the love of the truth so as to be saved" (2 Thess. 2:10) will be deceived into worshiping him. That deception will be fostered by the Antichrist's associate, the false prophet, who "makes the earth and those who dwell in it to worship the first beast [Antichrist], whose fatal wound was healed" (13:12).

Not only will the deceived unbelievers worship Antichrist, but they will also (wittingly or unwittingly) worship **the dragon** (Satan) **because he gave his authority to the beast.** By worshiping Antichrist, unbelievers will actually be worshiping Satan, the real power behind him. Some people will fully understand that; most will probably be deceived, like those of whom Paul wrote in 1 Corinthians 10:20: "The things which the Gentiles sacrifice, they sacrifice to demons and not to

God." Thinking that they were worshiping the god to whom they sacrificed, the pagans were in reality worshiping the demon impersonating that god. So it will be for many people, who will think they are worshiping a supernaturally powerful leader, but in reality will be worshiping Satan.

As the people of the world worship Antichrist they will cry out in awe, **"Who is like the beast, and who is able to wage war with him?"** By blasphemously referring to Antichrist in superlative language reserved for the worship of God (cf. Ex. 15:11; Pss. 35:10; 113:5; Isa. 40:18, 25; 46:5; Jer. 49:19; Mic. 7:18), Antichrist's deluded worshipers will attribute deity to him (2 Thess. 2:4). The implied answer to both rhetorical questions is "No one!" In the political, military, and religious realms, Antichrist will reign supreme and unchallenged by earth and hell.

His Arrogance

There was given to him a mouth speaking arrogant words and blasphemies, and authority to act for forty-two months was given to him. And he opened his mouth in blasphemies against God, to blaspheme His name and His tabernacle, that is, those who dwell in heaven. (13:5–6)

Like his master, Satan, Antichrist will be an arrogant blasphemer. Blasphemy will not be incidental but central to his operations. The phrase **there was given to him** refers to God's sovereign control of events (6:4, 8; 7:2; 9:5; cf. Dan. 4:17, 25, 32). God will allow Antichrist to blaspheme to give full expression to the satanic wickedness that will cover the earth at that time. He will exhibit a total disregard for the true God by continually **speaking arrogant words and blasphemies.** Antichrist's blasphemy will not be subtle, but open, outrageous, and monstrous—even to the point that he "takes his seat in the temple of God, displaying himself as being God" (2 Thess. 2:4). This is reminiscent of Satan's original desire when he fell from heaven and holiness. He said in his heart, "I will make myself like the Most High" (Isa. 14:14).

Daniel predicted that Antichrist will be characterized by proud, arrogant, blasphemous words. Daniel 7:8 says that he will have "a mouth uttering great boasts" (cf. v. 20), while verse 11 mentions "the sound of the boastful words which the horn was speaking." Daniel further notes that Antichrist "will speak out against the Most High . . . and will speak monstrous things against the God of gods" (7:25; 11:36).

Antichrist's arrogance will surpass that of anyone else in human history. He will be Satan's mouthpiece, voicing his master's frustrated rage against God. He will also be the supreme blasphemer in a world filled with blasphemers. So hardened will sinners' hearts be at that time that God's judgments will elicit not repentance, but more blasphemy. In 16:9, John records a vision in which "men were scorched with fierce heat; and they blasphemed the name of God who has the power over these plagues, and they did not repent so as to give Him glory."

Antichrist's **blasphemies against God** will include blasphemy of **His name and His tabernacle,** and **those who dwell in heaven.** God's **name** represents all that He is; it is the summation of His attributes. So comprehensively evil will Antichrist's blasphemy be that it will even include God's **tabernacle** (heaven; cf. Heb. 9:23–24), and all **those who dwell in heaven** with Him. Thus, Antichrist will utter blasphemous words aimed directly and specifically at God's Person, His abode, and His people, both the redeemed saints and the holy angels.

But neither Antichrist's blasphemies nor his reign of terror will last indefinitely. God will grant Antichrist **authority to act for** only **forty-two months** (the last three and a half years or 1,260 days of the Tribulation, the seventieth week of Daniel's prophecy; Dan. 9:24). Antichrist and Satan will be allowed to operate only within the time limit set for them by the true Ruler of the universe. But for a few years, they will dominate the world.

His Activity

It was also given to him to make war with the saints and to overcome them, and authority over every tribe and people and tongue and nation was given to him. (13:7)

Antichrist will not be all talk; he will also be capable of decisive, deadly action. Once again the text notes that Antichrist can do only what he is **given** permission by almighty God to do, thus stressing that God never relinquishes His absolute control of events. Because they will refuse to worship him, Antichrist will **make war with the saints and overcome them;** believers in the true God will bear the brunt of his murderous fury. He will perceive them as a threat to his **authority over every tribe and people and tongue and nation,** which again **was** temporarily **given to him** by God's sovereignty. The result will be a worldwide slaughter of God's people (cf. 6:9–11; 7:9–17; 11:7; 17:6; Dan. 7:25).

Daniel long before predicted this widespread martyrdom of God's people. He wrote that Antichrist "will . . . wear down the saints of the Highest One . . . and they will be given into his hand for a time, times, and half a time [three and a half years; the last half of the Tribulation]"

(Dan. 7:25). This persecution will begin in earnest at the midpoint of the Tribulation, when Antichrist breaks his covenant with Israel (Dan. 9:27) and sets up the abomination of desolation (Dan. 9:27; 11:31; 12:11; Matt. 24:15; 2 Thess. 2:3–4).

That Antichrist will successfully **make war with the saints and overcome them** does not mean that he will have the power to destroy their faith. He will overpower them physically, but not spiritually. Genuine saving faith cannot be destroyed, because "neither death, nor life, nor angels, nor principalities, nor things present, nor things to come, nor powers, nor height, nor depth, nor any other created thing, will be able to separate us from the love of God, which is in Christ Jesus our Lord" (Rom. 8:38–39). Nor will the Lord Jesus Christ, who is infinitely more powerful than Antichrist or Satan, permit any true child of His to suffer the loss of eternal life (Rev. 3:5; Job 13:15; John 10:27–29). But Antichrist will slaughter God's people on an unprecedented scale as he expresses his world dominance.

His Admirers

All who dwell on the earth will worship him, everyone whose name has not been written from the foundation of the world in the book of life of the Lamb who has been slain. If anyone has an ear, let him hear. If anyone is destined for captivity, to captivity he goes; if anyone kills with the sword, with the sword he must be killed. Here is the perseverance and the faith of the saints. (13:8–10)

As noted previously in the discussion of verse 4, **all who dwell on the earth will worship** the Antichrist. (John here shifts from past tenses to future tenses.) The phrase **all who dwell on the earth** is used throughout Revelation to describe unbelievers (vv. 12, 14; 3:10; 6:10; 8:13; 11:10; 17:2, 8) and does not include everyone who will be alive at that time. Here the limiting factor is specifically stated; it is **everyone whose name has not been written from the foundation of the world in the book of life of the Lamb who has been slain** that will worship Antichrist. Unbelievers, those whose names are not recorded in the **book of life,** will "perish, because they did not receive the love of the truth so as to be saved" (2 Thess. 2:10). Scripture also teaches that the faithless will be judged because they "did not believe the truth, but took pleasure in wickedness" (2 Thess. 2:12). While the eternally elect are saved through faith in the Lord Jesus Christ (John 3:16; 5:24; Acts 13:39; 16:31; Rom. 3:22–30; 4:5; 10:9–10; Gal. 3:22–26; Eph. 2:8–9), the nonelect are lost because they refuse to believe the gospel (John 3:36; Rom. 1:18–32; 2:8;

2 Thess. 1:8–9; 1 Pet. 2:8; 4:17). Unbelief and rejection always indicate those persons whose names were not **written . . . in the book of life.**

Seven times in the New Testament, believers are identified as those whose names are **written** in the **book of life** (cf. 3:5; 17:8; 20:12, 15; 21:27; Phil. 4:3). The **book of life** belonging to the **Lamb,** the Lord Jesus, is the registry in which God inscribed the names of those chosen for salvation before **the foundation of the world.** (This phrase is used as a synonym for eternity past in 17:8; Matt. 13:35; 25:34; Luke 11:50; Eph. 1:4; Heb. 9:26; 1 Pet. 1:20; cf. 2 Thess. 2:13; and 2 Tim. 1:9.) Unlike unbelievers, the elect will not be deceived by Antichrist (Matt. 24:24), nor will they worship him (20:4). Antichrist will not be able to destroy believers' saving faith, for the Lord Jesus Christ promised, "He who overcomes will thus be clothed in white garments; and I will not erase his name from the book of life, and I will confess his name before My Father and before His angels" (Rev. 3:5; cf. 1 John 5:4). Believers have been in the keeping power of God since before creation, and they will be there after the destruction of this order and the establishment of the new heaven and the new earth (21:1ff.).

Believers are doubly secure, because the **book of life** belongs to **the Lamb who has been slain.** Not only the decree of election, but also the atoning work of Christ seals the redemption of the elect forever. Believers "were not redeemed with perishable things like silver or gold . . . but with precious blood, as of a lamb unblemished and spotless, the blood of Christ" (1 Pet. 1:18–19). The Father will not undo the work of Christ in redemption (cf. Rom. 4:25; Heb. 1:3) by allowing any of the elect to be lost. Jesus Christ is "to all those who obey Him the source of eternal salvation" (Heb. 5:9), and it is not within the power of Antichrist, Satan, or all the forces of hell to alter that glorious reality. The very saints that Antichrist massacres during his persecution of God's people are later seen triumphant and victorious in heaven:

> And I saw something like a sea of glass mixed with fire, and those who had been victorious over the beast and his image and the number of his name, standing on the sea of glass, holding harps of God. And they sang the song of Moses, the bond-servant of God, and the song of the Lamb, saying,
>
> "Great and marvelous are Your works,
> O Lord God, the Almighty;
> Righteous and true are Your ways,
> King of the nations!
> Who will not fear, O Lord, and glorify Your name?
> For You alone are holy;
> For all the nations will come and worship before You,
> For Your righteous acts have been revealed."
>
> (Rev. 15:2–4)

Antichrist may take their lives, but he cannot destroy their faith.

This astounding vision of the beast from the sea concludes with a call for spiritual understanding. The warning **If anyone has an ear, let him hear** is used sixteen times in the New Testament (cf. 2:7, 11, 17, 29; 3:6, 13, 22; 13:9; Matt. 11:15; 13:9, 43; Mark 4:9, 23; 7:16; Luke 8:8; 14:35) to emphasize a particularly important truth. In all its previous uses in Revelation (chaps. 2–3), it is followed by the phrase "what the Spirit says to the churches." The omission of that phrase suggests that the church is not in view in this passage, having been raptured before the start of the Tribulation (cf. 3:10).

Here the phrase introduces a proverb that concludes this passage: **If anyone is destined for captivity, to captivity he goes; if anyone kills with the sword, with the sword he must be killed. Here is the perseverance and the faith of the saints.** This proverb contains important practical truth for those believers alive at the time of Antichrist's persecution. They are to depend on God's providence and not take matters into their own hands. Those believers **destined** by God's sovereign plan **for captivity** (imprisonment) are to accept that incarceration as God's will. They are not to resist or fight against Antichrist. Amazingly, the passage upholds the divine institution of capital punishment even by Antichrist's evil government, warning that **if anyone kills with the sword, with the sword he must be killed** (cf. Gen. 9:5–6; Matt. 26:52). God's people must not retaliate against their persecutors; there is no place now, and there will be no place then, for militant, aggressive, violent believers terrorizing their persecutors. "Those also who suffer according to the will of God," wrote Peter, "shall entrust their souls to a faithful Creator in doing what is right" (1 Pet. 4:19).

Instead of reacting violently, believers must exemplify **the perseverance and the faith of the saints.** They must be like the Lord Jesus Christ, who "while being reviled . . . did not revile in return; while suffering . . . uttered no threats, but kept entrusting Himself to Him who judges righteously" (1 Pet. 2:23). When believers follow Christ's example, noted Peter, "those who revile [their] good behavior in Christ will be put to shame" (1 Pet. 3:16). Those who are "reviled for the name of Christ . . . are blessed, because the Spirit of glory and of God rests on [them]" (1 Pet. 4:14).

The message of this passage is clear. Let the monstrous beast from the abyss do his worst. Let Satan and his demon hosts have their hour. God controls the future and believers belong to Him. "In all these things we overwhelmingly conquer through Him who loved us" (Rom. 8:37), and we will triumph on that glorious day when "The kingdom of the world [becomes] the kingdom of our Lord and of His Christ; and He will reign forever and ever" (Rev. 11:15).

The Final False Prophet (Revelation 13:11–18)

5

Then I saw another beast coming up out of the earth; and he had two horns like a lamb and he spoke as a dragon. He exercises all the authority of the first beast in his presence. And he makes the earth and those who dwell in it to worship the first beast, whose fatal wound was healed. He performs great signs, so that he even makes fire come down out of heaven to the earth in the presence of men. And he deceives those who dwell on the earth because of the signs which it was given him to perform in the presence of the beast, telling those who dwell on the earth to make an image to the beast who had the wound of the sword and has come to life. And it was given to him to give breath to the image of the beast, so that the image of the beast would even speak and cause as many as do not worship the image of the beast to be killed. And he causes all, the small and the great, and the rich and the poor, and the free men and the slaves, to be given a mark on their right hand or on their forehead, and he provides that no one will be able to buy or to sell, except the one who has the mark, either the name of the beast or the number of his name. Here is wisdom. Let him who has understanding calculate the number of the beast, for the number is that of a man; and his number is six hundred and sixty-six. (13:11–18)

The major weapon in Satan's arsenal is deception. Satan, Jesus declared, is "a liar and the father of lies" (John 8:44), who "disguises himself as an angel of light" (2 Cor. 11:14) to deceive people. From his first appearance on earth in the Garden of Eden (Gen. 3:2–6) until his final appearance at the end of the Millennium (Rev. 20:7–8), Satan is a liar and a deceiver. He constantly seeks to confuse people, "blind[ing] the minds of the unbelieving so that they might not see the light of the gospel of the glory of Christ, who is the image of God" (2 Cor. 4:4).

Since Satan is a deceiver, it follows that his agents (both human and demonic) are also deceivers. The apostle Paul warned that "[Satan's] servants also disguise themselves as servants of righteousness" (2 Cor. 11:15), though they are purveyors of wickedness, lies, and deceit. The devil uses them to spread his damning "doctrines of demons" (1 Tim. 4:1).

The Bible repeatedly warns of the danger of false prophets. Moses paused in the midst of giving God's law to Israel to warn of those who would lead people astray from it:

> "If a prophet or a dreamer of dreams arises among you and gives you a sign or a wonder, and the sign or the wonder comes true, concerning which he spoke to you, saying, "Let us go after other gods (whom you have not known) and let us serve them," you shall not listen to the words of that prophet or that dreamer of dreams; for the Lord your God is testing you to find out if you love the Lord your God with all your heart and with all your soul. You shall follow the Lord your God and fear Him; and you shall keep His commandments, listen to His voice, serve Him, and cling to Him. But that prophet or that dreamer of dreams shall be put to death, because he has counseled rebellion against the Lord your God who brought you from the land of Egypt and redeemed you from the house of slavery, to seduce you from the way in which the Lord your God commanded you to walk. So you shall purge the evil from among you." (Deut. 13:1–5)

Jeremiah also warned Israel not to listen to false prophets:

> Thus says the Lord of hosts,
> "Do not listen to the words of the prophets who are prophesying to you.
> They are leading you into futility;
> They speak a vision of their own imagination,
> Not from the mouth of the Lord."
>
> (Jer. 23:16)

> "I did not send these prophets,
> But they ran.
> I did not speak to them,

> But they prophesied.
> But if they had stood in My council,
> Then they would have announced My words to My people,
> And would have turned them back from their evil way
> And from the evil of their deeds."
> (Jer. 23:21–22)

> "I have heard what the prophets have said who prophesy falsely in My name, saying, 'I had a dream, I had a dream!' How long? Is there anything in the hearts of the prophets who prophesy falsehood, even these prophets of the deception of their own heart, who intend to make My people forget My name by their dreams which they relate to one another, just as their fathers forgot My name because of Baal? The prophet who has a dream may relate his dream, but let him who has My word speak My word in truth. What does straw have in common with grain?" declares the Lord. "Is not My word like fire?" declares the Lord, "and like a hammer which shatters a rock? Therefore behold, I am against the prophets," declares the Lord, "who steal My words from each other. Behold, I am against the prophets," declares the Lord, "who use their tongues and declare, 'The Lord declares.' Behold, I am against those who have prophesied false dreams," declares the Lord, "and related them and led My people astray by their falsehoods and reckless boasting; yet I did not send them or command them, nor do they furnish this people the slightest benefit," declares the Lord. (Jer. 23:25–32)

> "So do not listen to the words of the prophets who speak to you, saying, 'You shall not serve the king of Babylon,' for they prophesy a lie to you; for I have not sent them," declares the Lord, "but they prophesy falsely in My name, in order that I may drive you out and that you may perish, you and the prophets who prophesy to you." Then I spoke to the priests and to all this people, saying, "Thus says the Lord: Do not listen to the words of your prophets who prophesy to you, saying, 'Behold, the vessels of the Lord's house will now shortly be brought again from Babylon'; for they are prophesying a lie to you." (Jer. 27:14–16)

> "For thus says the Lord of hosts, the God of Israel, 'Do not let your prophets who are in your midst and your diviners deceive you, and do not listen to the dreams which they dream. For they prophesy falsely to you in My name; I have not sent them,' declares the Lord." (Jer. 29:8–9)

As He concluded the Sermon on the Mount, the Lord Jesus Christ solemnly declared, "Beware of the false prophets, who come to you in sheep's clothing, but inwardly are ravenous wolves" (Matt. 7:15). In his second epistle, Peter wrote, "But false prophets also arose among the people, just as there will also be false teachers among you, who will secretly introduce destructive heresies, even denying the Master who bought them, bringing swift destruction upon themselves" (2 Pet. 2:1). The apostle John cautioned, "Beloved, do not believe every spirit, but test the spirits to see whether they are from God, because many false prophets have gone out into the world" (1 John 4:1).

Scripture also records numerous examples of false prophets; some named, some anonymous. Isaiah mentioned unnamed false prophets who were active in his day (Isa. 9:15), as did Jeremiah (Jer. 14:13–15; Lam. 2:14). Jeremiah 28 records Jeremiah's encounter with the false prophet Hananiah, while the next chapter mentions the false prophets Ahab and Zedekiah (Jer. 29:21–23). The Old Testament also names another Zedekiah as a false prophet (1 Kings 22:10–28), as well as two false prophets named Shemaiah (Neh. 6:10–12; Jer. 29:24–32). Ezekiel 13:17 mentions false prophetesses, and Nehemiah encountered the false prophetess Noadiah (Neh. 6:14). The most notorious false prophet in the Old Testament was Balaam, who led Israel into idolatry and sin (Num. 22–24; Josh. 13:22; 24:9–10; Neh. 13:1–2; 2 Pet. 2:15–16; Jude 11; Rev. 2:14). The New Testament records the apostle Paul's encounter on the island of Cyprus with the false prophet Bar-Jesus (Acts 13:6–12).

Several vices characterize false prophets, apart from the obvious one of teaching lies. Scripture denounces them as wicked (Jer. 23:11), adulterers (Jer. 23:14), greedy (Ezek. 22:25; Mic. 3:11; 2 Pet. 2:15), self-deceived (Ezek. 13:2–3), and idolaters (Jer. 2:8; 23:13). Not surprisingly, God will judge them severely. Deuteronomy 18:20 pronounces the death sentence on them: "The prophet who speaks a word presumptuously in My name which I have not commanded him to speak, or which he speaks in the name of other gods, that prophet shall die" (cf. Num. 31:8; Jer. 23:15; 29:21–22). Peter spoke the judgment of God on all false teachers when he wrote that they "will utterly perish in their own corruption, and will receive the wages of unrighteousness . . . for whom is reserved the blackness of darkness forever" (2 Pet. 2:12–13, 17 NKJV).

False prophets have plagued God's people from the beginning of history. But they will proliferate even more as the return of Christ to establish His kingdom approaches. Speaking of that time Jesus said, "Many false prophets will arise and will mislead many" (Matt. 24:11). So persuasive will their efforts be that they "will show signs and wonders, in order to lead astray, if possible, the elect" (Mark 13:22). Those false prophets will be energized by some of Satan's demon hosts. The devil will intensify his efforts to deceive the world as his own doom approaches.

Just as the false christs who have plagued mankind will culminate in the final Antichrist, so also will the false prophets culminate in a final false prophet (cf. 16:13; 19:20; 20:10). He will be Satan's last and most powerful lying deceiver. Along with Satan, the counterfeit of the Father, and Antichrist, the counterfeit of Jesus Christ, the false prophet will form the satanic false trinity. He will be the counterfeit of the Holy Spirit. The false prophet will be Antichrist's partner in Satan's massive final deception of the world. While Antichrist will be primarily a political and military ruler, he will also claim to be God. The false prophet will be his high priest, the religious leader who will lead people into the satanic religion of worshiping Antichrist. The false prophet will deify Antichrist and convince unbelievers that he is the only hope for the world's salvation.

The false prophet will be able to deceive the unbelieving world because the power of religion over men's minds is so great. People are incurable worshipers; everyone worships someone, whether the true God, false gods, or themselves. There is in the heart of man the longing for someone transcendent, someone beyond himself that can deliver him from his troubling circumstances. The terrifying, unparalleled events of the Tribulation will intensify that longing for a supernatural deliverer. The false prophet will convince the unbelieving world that Antichrist is the solution to the world's pressing problems. He may well be the most eloquent, powerful, convincing speaker in human history, and his lofty oratory will persuade the world to worship Antichrist. John Phillips speculated:

> The dynamic appeal of the false prophet will lie in his skill in combining political expediency with religious passion. . . . His arguments will be subtle, convincing, and appealing. His oratory will be hypnotic, for he will be able to move the masses to tears or whip them into a frenzy. He will control the communication media of the world and will skillfully organize mass publicity to promote his ends. He will manage the truth with guile beyond words, bending it, twisting it, and distorting it. . . . He will mold world thought and shape human opinion like so much potter's clay. (*Exploring Revelation*, rev. ed. [Chicago: Moody, 1987; reprint, Neptune, N.J.: Loizeaux, 1991], 171)

The partnership between political and religious power exhibited by Antichrist and the false prophet will not be new. Jannes and Jambres, two false religious leaders, assisted Pharaoh in his confrontations with Moses and Aaron (2 Tim. 3:8). Balak, king of Moab, sought the false prophet Balaam's help to destroy Israel (Num. 22–24). Ahab and Jezebel used the idolatrous priests of Baal to help them accomplish their evil purposes in Israel (1 Kings 18:17ff.). The Roman Empire united political and religious power by demanding that its subjects worship the state (personified as the goddess Roma) and the emperor. In modern times, communism, though officially scorning religion as the "opium of the people," has in effect been a substitute religion for its adherents.

The worldwide joining of political and religious power in the end times is detailed in Revelation 17. For a time, the two powers will coexist (17:1–9). Eventually, however, Antichrist will destroy the false religious system and institute the worship of himself (17:15–17). That will happen at the midpoint of the Tribulation, when Antichrist sets up the abomination of desolation (Dan. 9:27; 11:31; 12:11; Matt. 24:15; 2 Thess. 2:3–4). Having reached the pinnacle of his power, Antichrist will destroy all other religions. The worship of Antichrist, fomented by the false prophet, will become the only religion tolerated (cf. 14:9, 11; 15:2; 16:2; 19:20; 20:4).

John's vision of the false prophet reveals three key elements: his person, power, and program.

His Person

Then I saw another beast coming up out of the earth; and he had two horns like a lamb and he spoke as a dragon. (13:11)

Having seen the terrifying vision of the first beast (Antichrist) in 13:1–10, John then **saw another beast.** Some view this second **beast** as an institution, a form of government, or an ideology. But the use of *allos* (**another** of the same kind) indicates that he, like the first beast, will be a person. Further proof of that comes from 19:20: "And the beast was seized, and with him the false prophet who performed the signs in his presence, by which he deceived those who had received the mark of the beast and those who worshiped his image; these two were thrown alive into the lake of fire which burns with brimstone." Obviously, it is people, not ideologies, institutions, or governments, that God will cast into hell.

In contrast to the first beast, who will come up out of the sea (13:1), the second **beast** will come **up out of the earth.** Like Antichrist, the false prophet will be indwelt by a demon out of the abyss (see the comments on 13:1 in chapter 4 of this volume), which is pictured here as the flaming depths **of the earth.** In the ancient world, the **earth** was less mysterious and foreboding than the sea. That the false prophet arises from the earth suggests that he will be subtler, gentler, less overpowering and terrifying than the Antichrist. He will be winsome and persuasive, the epitome of the wolves in sheep's clothing Jesus warned of (Matt. 7:15).

The description of the first beast, with its ten horns, seven heads, ten crowns, and seven blasphemous names (13:1), was grotesque and frightening. In contrast, the second **beast** merely **had two horns.** That indicates that he is not characterized by the same massive might as Antichrist. And unlike the savage, ferocious, fierce, and deadly Antichrist, who is likened to a leopard, bear, and lion (13:2), the false prophet seems as harmless as **a lamb.** He does not come as a conquering dictator, but on the surface appears as a subtle deceiver, with meekness and gentleness, though not without great authority.

Despite his deceptively mild appearance, the false prophet is no less a child of hell than the Antichrist. That is evident because **he spoke as a dragon**—a strange voice indeed for a lamb. The false prophet, like Antichrist (13:2, 5), will be the **dragon** Satan's mouthpiece, speaking his words. But he will not echo the blasphemous tirades against God that will pour from the lips of Antichrist (Dan. 11:36). Instead, he will speak winsome, deceiving words of praise about the Antichrist, luring the world to worship that vile, satanic dictator.

False prophets often appear meek, mild, and harmless. They offer hope and solutions to the problems troubling men and women. Yet they are ever the voices of hell, and when they open their mouths, Satan speaks. So it will be amid the unspeakable horrors of the Tribulation. The false prophet will come like a lamb, speaking false, deceptive words of comfort. He will promise the suffering, tormented people of the world that all will be well if only they will worship Antichrist. But those who fall for his subtle lies will face the terrifying judgment of God (cf. 14:9–11; 16:2).

His Power

He exercises all the authority of the first beast in his presence. And he makes the earth and those who dwell in it to worship the first beast, whose fatal wound was healed. He performs great signs, so that he even makes fire come down out of heaven to the earth in the presence of men. And he deceives those who dwell on the earth because of the signs which it was given him to perform in the presence of the beast, telling those who dwell on the earth to make an image to the beast who had the wound of the sword and has come to life. (13:12–14)

Though primarily a subtle deceiver, the false prophet will not be impotent. John notes that **he exercises all the authority of the first beast** (Antichrist). Some believe that the false prophet will replace Antichrist and rule alone during the Great Tribulation. That is impossible, however, since the text explicitly says that the false prophet **exercises** his **authority** in the **presence** of Antichrist (cf. v. 14; 19:20). Further, both the false prophet and Antichrist will be alive when Christ returns (19:20).

What is being said here is that the false prophet will exercise the same kind of demonic power and authority as the Antichrist does, since both are empowered by the same hellish source. That he **exercises** his **authority** in Antichrist's **presence** implies that Antichrist will have delegated that **authority** to him. The false prophet's mission will be to use all the means available to him from the Antichrist to cause **the earth and those who dwell in it to worship the first beast.** He will lead the worldwide cult of Antichrist worship.

The false prophet's efforts to promote the worship of the Antichrist will receive a tremendous boost from a startling, spectacular event: the apparent healing of the first beast's (Antichrist's) **fatal wound** (cf. v. 3; 17:8). As noted in the discussion of 13:3 in the previous chapter of this volume, that phrase refers to Antichrist's supposed resurrection from the dead. That is a satanic imitation not only of Christ's resurrection, but also that of the two witnesses (11:11). It is most likely that Antichrist's death will be staged, and hence his "resurrection" is a ruse. It is less likely that God, for His own sovereign purposes, may permit Antichrist to genuinely rise from the dead. In either case, the world will accept Antichrist's resurrection as genuine, thus greatly enhancing both his prestige and that of the false prophet.

Besides his involvement in Antichrist's "resurrection," the false prophet will **perform great signs** of his own. Those signs mimic not only the miracles performed by Jesus Christ (cf. John 2:11, 23; 6:2), but also those of the two witnesses (11:5–6). These satanic "false wonders . . . with all the deception of wickedness" will be extremely persuasive "for those who perish, because they did not receive the love of the truth so as to be saved" (2 Thess. 2:9–10). Those who reject the saving gospel of the Lord Jesus Christ will eagerly accept the damning false gospel preached by the false prophet—a gospel seemingly verified by spectacular supernatural signs.

That Satan can fabricate supernatural signs is clear from Scripture. Jannes and Jambres, the magicians in Pharaoh's court (2 Tim. 3:8–9), imitated some of the miracles God did through Moses and Aaron (Ex. 7:11–12, 22). Acts 8:9–11 describes "a man named Simon, who formerly was practicing magic in the city and astonishing the people of Samaria, claiming to be someone great; and they all, from smallest to greatest, were giving attention to him, saying, 'This man is what is called the Great Power of God.' And they were giving him attention because he had for a long time astonished them with his magic arts." The signs performed by the false prophet will far exceed those of a small-time magician like Simon.

Amazingly, the false prophet, imitating the two witnesses (11:5), **even makes fire come down out of heaven to the earth.** The present tense of *poieō* (**makes**) suggests that he will repeatedly perform this supernatural act **in the presence of men** to impress them with his power. God has often demonstrated His supernatural power by sending fire from heaven (cf. 11:5; Gen. 19:24; Lev. 10:1–2; 1 Kings 18:38; 2 Kings 1:9–12; 1 Chron. 21:26; 2 Chron. 7:1). Satan's henchman will perform a similar sign, but his will be one of the "false wonders" (2 Thess. 2:9) that will lure unbelievers to their doom.

The false prophet will succeed dramatically in his efforts to **deceive those who dwell on the earth**—exactly as Jesus predicted (cf. Matt. 24:5, 11, 24; Mark 13:6). **Deceives** is from *planaō,* and means "to wander." It forms the root of the English word *planet,* since the planets appear to wander through the heavens. The world will be utterly vulnerable to his deception during the Tribulation. There will be unparalleled disasters and unimaginable horrors, leaving people desperate for answers. Having rejected the true gospel and blasphemed the true God (cf. 16:9, 11), the unbelieving world will be eager to believe the deceiving lies propagated by the false prophet.

John defines the people who will be deceived as **those who dwell on the earth**—a technical phrase used throughout Revelation to refer to unbelievers (vv. 8, 12; 3:10; 6:10; 8:13; 11:10; 17:2, 8). Though sorely tested and persecuted, God's elect cannot be deceived (Mark 13:22). Because believers know the truth and are protected by their God (cf. John 10:3–5, 14, 27–30), they will recognize the false prophet's teaching as lies and will not be swayed **because of the signs which it was given him to perform in the presence of the beast.** That the unbelieving world will be deceived is due not only to the wicked deception of Satan, the demons, Antichrist, and the false prophet, but also comes as God's judgment. The false prophet's preaching will succeed in part because it will arrive "with all the deception of wickedness for those who perish, because they did not receive the love of the truth so as to be saved" (2 Thess. 2:10). But it will also succeed because "God will send upon them a deluding influence so that they will believe what is false, in order that they all may be judged who did not believe the truth, but took pleasure in wickedness" (vv. 11–12).

As the power of Antichrist and the persuasiveness of the false prophet grow, Satan will escalate the false world religion of Antichrist worship. Humanity will eventually come to be so completely under the influence of the false prophet that people will obey his command **to make an image to the beast.** The world will engage in the most shocking, blatant idolatry ever seen. Like Nebuchadnezzar before him (Dan. 3), but on a global scale, Antichrist, aided by the false prophet, will set up a statue of himself as a symbol of his deity and worldwide worship. This blasphemous image will probably be set up on the temple grounds in Jerusalem (cf. 2 Thess. 2:4) and will be connected with the abomination of desolation (Dan. 9:27; 11:31; 12:11; Matt. 24:15). It will be a tribute to the awesome power of Antichrist, **who had the wound of the sword**

and has come to life (cf. vv. 3, 12), to seemingly conquer death.

His Program

And it was given to him to give breath to the image of the beast, so that the image of the beast would even speak and cause as many as do not worship the image of the beast to be killed. And he causes all, the small and the great, and the rich and the poor, and the free men and the slaves, to be given a mark on their right hand or on their forehead, and he provides that no one will be able to buy or to sell, except the one who has the mark, either the name of the beast or the number of his name. Here is wisdom. Let him who has understanding calculate the number of the beast, for the number is that of a man; and his number is six hundred and sixty-six. (13:15–18)

The idolatrous image of the Antichrist will be different from any other idol in human history. The Bible scornfully denounces idols as having mouths, yet being unable to speak (Pss. 115:5; 135:15–17; Isa. 46:7; Jer. 10:5; Hab. 2:18–19). But in another display of his power to deceive, the false prophet will **give breath to the image of the beast, so that the image of the beast would even speak. Breath** translates *pneuma,* not *zōē* or *bios,* the Greek words normally translated *life.* The false prophet will animate the image of Antichrist so that it gives the appearance of being alive. With today's amazing special effects technology and robotics, that is not out of the realm of possibility. Add to that the world's desperate need, amid the carnage of the Tribulation, to believe in a death conqueror, and the ruse becomes very believable.

After his immense worldwide success and after dropping his façade of gentleness, the false prophet will **cause as many as do not worship the image of the beast to be killed.** As in the case of Nebuchadnezzar's image (Dan. 3:6), the death sentence will be decreed for those who refuse to worship the image of Antichrist. Many of the martyrs mentioned earlier in Revelation (cf. 6:9–11; 7:13–14) are those who will be killed during this terrible time of persecution. But though the death sentence may be decreed on all, not all believers will be killed. Some will survive until Christ returns and will enter His millennial kingdom as living people (cf. Isa. 65:20–23; Matt. 25:31–40). Nor will Antichrist and his henchmen kill all the Jews (cf. 12:6–7, 14); two-thirds of them will perish, but the rest will be protected (Zech. 13:8–9).

As part of his plan to enforce the worship of Antichrist, the false prophet will require **all** categories of unbelievers, summarized as **the small and the great, and the rich and the poor, and the free men**

and the slaves, to be given a mark on their right hand or on their forehead. Mark (*charagma;* from *charassō,* "I engrave") was the term for images or names of the emperor on Roman coins. In the ancient world, such marks (tattoos or brands) were commonly given to slaves, soldiers, and devotees of religious cults (cf. Gal. 6:17). God sealed, with a mark on the forehead, the 144,000 to preserve them from His wrath against the unbelieving world (7:2–3); the false prophet marks the unsaved to preserve them from Antichrist's wrath against God's people. The mark will signify that the person bearing it is a worshiper and loyal follower of the Antichrist. In much the same way, the Roman emperors required their subjects to prove their loyalty by offering sacrifices to Caesar. Those who refused, like those who refuse to take the Antichrist's mark, were subject to execution.

Besides the constant threat of death, refusing to take the mark of the beast will have dire practical consequences in daily living: **no one will be able to buy or to sell, except the one who has the mark.** Antichrist's empire will maintain strict economic control over the world. Food, clothing, medical supplies, and the other necessities of life potentially in demand in the devastated earth, which has felt the judgment of God (6:5–6), will be unobtainable for those without the **mark.** Currency will probably vanish, to be replaced by controlled credit. Instead of a credit card, which can be lost, people will have a **mark** (possibly a bar code) in their forehead or hand. Scanning people's foreheads or hands would identify them to a central computer system. Life under totalitarian governments in our time provides a faint glimpse of what is to come. A man who had lived under Bulgaria's communist regime remarked:

> You cannot understand and you cannot know that the most terrible instrument of persecution ever devised is an innocent ration card. You cannot buy and you cannot sell except according to that little, innocent card. If they please, you can be starved to death, and if they please, you can be dispossessed of everything you have; for you cannot trade, and you cannot buy and you cannot sell, without permission. (Cited in W. A. Criswell, *Expository Sermons on Revelation* [Grand Rapids: Zondervan, 1969], 4:120–21)

The pressure to give in to the worship of Antichrist will be far worse than anything ever experienced in human history. Life will be virtually unlivable, so the people are forced to bow to the demonized king, not prompted merely by religious deception, but also by economic necessity.

Further describing the mark, John notes that it will consist of **either the name of the beast or the number of his name.** Antichrist will have a universal designation, his name within a numbering system.

The exact identification of that phrase is unclear. What is clear is that everyone will be required to have the identifying **mark** or suffer the consequences.

The exclamation **here is wisdom** is a warning to those alive at that time to be wise and discerning. They will need to recognize what is happening and understand the significance of the number connected with Antichrist's name. Those with **understanding** will be able to **calculate the number of the beast, for the number is that of a man; and his number is six hundred and sixty-six.** Perhaps no detail in Revelation has intrigued people more than this **number.** There has been no end to the speculation as to its significance and how to calculate it. In Greek, Hebrew, and Latin, letters had numerical equivalents, and a myriad of schemes to associate the names of historical individuals with the number 666 have been put forth. Nero, Caligula, Domitian, Napoleon, Hitler, Mussolini, Stalin, and a host of others have been proposed, based on some sort of convoluted mathematical rendering of the letters in their name. All such speculation is futile; since the Antichrist is still to come, the number 666 cannot be associated with any historical individual. The church father Irenaeus cautioned against speculating about the identity of the person associated with the number 666 until that person arrives on the scene (Alan F. Johnson, *Revelation,* The Expositor's Bible Commentary [Grand Rapids: Zondervan, 1996], 137). Robert L. Thomas gives a very reasonable perspective:

> The better part of wisdom is to be content that the identification is not yet available, but will be when the future false Christ ascends to his throne. The person to whom 666 applies must have been future to John's time, because John clearly meant the number to be recognizable to someone. If it was not discernible to his generation and those immediately following him—and it was not—the generation to whom it will be discernible must have lain (and still lies) in the future. Past generations have provided many illustrations of this future personage, but all past candidates have proven inadequate as fulfillments. Christians from generation to generation may manifest the same curiosity as the prophets of old regarding their own prophecies (cf. 1 Pet. 10–11), but their curiosity will remain unsatisfied until the time of fulfillment arrives. (Robert L. Thomas, *Revelation 8–22: An Exegetical Commentary* [Chicago: Moody, 1995], 185)

The precise significance of the number 666 awaits the future time of the Antichrist, but it is noteworthy that **the number is that of a man.** Seven, the number of perfection, is God's number. Since man falls short of perfection, his number is six. Man was created on the sixth day (Gen. 1:26–31); slaves were freed after six years of service (Ex. 21:2); fields were to be sown for only six consecutive years (Lev. 25:3). Repeating the number three times emphasizes that this is man's number, just as the thrice-repeated statement "holy, holy, holy" stresses God's absolute holiness (4:8; Isa. 6:3).

A false religion on a scale never before seen is coming, led by the most notorious of all false prophets. Most people will follow the seemingly safe and prudent course, worshiping the Antichrist, and receiving his mark. But that is a tragic mistake with disastrous consequences, for those who persist in worshiping the beast will face the wrath of God. In a sobering passage, Revelation warns of their fate:

> Then another angel, a third one, followed them, saying with a loud voice, "If anyone worships the beast and his image, and receives a mark on his forehead or on his hand, he also will drink of the wine of the wrath of God, which is mixed in full strength in the cup of His anger; and he will be tormented with fire and brimstone in the presence of the holy angels and in the presence of the Lamb. And the smoke of their torment goes up forever and ever; they have no rest day and night, those who worship the beast and his image, and whoever receives the mark of his name." (14:9–11)

And what of the false prophet, who will usher uncounted millions on to the broadest and most dangerous of all the roads leading to destruction? He will suffer an equally appalling and terrifying fate: "And the beast was seized, and with him the false prophet who performed the signs in his presence, by which he deceived those who had received the mark of the beast and those who worshiped his image; these two were thrown alive into the lake of fire which burns with brimstone" (Rev. 19:20; cf. 20:10).

This sobering passage is not intended to be the source of fruitless speculation about its details. Rather, it stands as a warning to the unbelieving world. It also challenges believers to lead careful, watchful, godly lives (cf. 1 Pet. 4:7; 2 Pet. 3:11), and to evangelize a hopelessly lost world, headed for destruction. Believers are to faithfully proclaim the saving gospel of the Lord Jesus Christ, and thereby rescue the souls of men and women from the disaster that looms just over the horizon.

Triumphant Saints (Revelation 14:1–5)

6

Then I looked, and behold, the Lamb was standing on Mount Zion, and with Him one hundred and forty-four thousand, having His name and the name of His Father written on their foreheads. And I heard a voice from heaven, like the sound of many waters and like the sound of loud thunder, and the voice which I heard was like the sound of harpists playing on their harps. And they sang a new song before the throne and before the four living creatures and the elders; and no one could learn the song except the one hundred and forty-four thousand who had been purchased from the earth. These are the ones who have not been defiled with women, for they have kept themselves chaste. These are the ones who follow the Lamb wherever He goes. These have been purchased from among men as first fruits to God and to the Lamb. And no lie was found in their mouth; they are blameless. (14:1–5)

Our society loves winners. Whether in politics, business, entertainment, sports, or war, we idolize those who succeed. On the other hand, we do not tolerate losers. Coaches who lose are fired; players who lose are traded; executives who fail are replaced; politicians who fail are voted out of office. Our heroes are those who overcome all obstacles and triumph in the end.

While not at all endorsing the world's superficial definition of success, the Bible nevertheless speaks of the Christian life in triumphant terms. Romans 8:37 declares that "we overwhelmingly conquer through Him who loved us." In his first epistle John wrote, "For whatever is born of God overcomes the world; and this is the victory that has overcome the world—our faith. Who is the one who overcomes the world, but he who believes that Jesus is the Son of God?" (1 John 5:4–5). In 1 Corinthians 15:57, Paul exclaimed, "Thanks be to God, who gives us the victory through our Lord Jesus Christ." In 2 Corinthians 2:14, he added another triumphant note, "Thanks be to God, who always leads us in triumph in Christ." Imprisoned, abandoned, and facing imminent execution, Paul could still pen the following victorious epitaph: "I have fought the good fight, I have finished the course, I have kept the faith; in the future there is laid up for me the crown of righteousness, which the Lord, the righteous Judge, will award to me on that day; and not only to me, but also to all who have loved His appearing" (2 Tim. 4:7–8).

But believers' triumphs and victories in this life are incomplete and marred by setbacks and defeats. The world, the flesh, and the devil take their toll on our best efforts. The same apostle Paul who ended his life in victorious triumph earlier described his Christian experience in the following mournful terms:

> For we know that the Law is spiritual, but I am of flesh, sold into bondage to sin. For what I am doing, I do not understand; for I am not practicing what I would like to do, but I am doing the very thing I hate. But if I do the very thing I do not want to do, I agree with the Law, confessing that the Law is good. So now, no longer am I the one doing it, but sin which dwells in me. For I know that nothing good dwells in me, that is, in my flesh; for the willing is present in me, but the doing of the good is not. For the good that I want, I do not do, but I practice the very evil that I do not want. But if I am doing the very thing I do not want, I am no longer the one doing it, but sin which dwells in me.
>
> I find then the principle that evil is present in me, the one who wants to do good. For I joyfully concur with the law of God in the inner man, but I see a different law in the members of my body, waging war against the law of my mind and making me a prisoner of the law of sin which is in my members. Wretched man that I am! Who will set me free from the body of this death? (Rom. 7:14–24)

Abraham, the "friend of God" (James 2:23; cf. 2 Chron. 20:7; Isa. 41:8), twice lied about Sarah, claiming she was his sister and not his wife (Gen. 12:11–20; 20:1–18). David, the man after God's heart (1 Sam. 13:14; Acts

13:22), was guilty of adultery and murder (2 Sam. 11:1–17; 12:9). Peter, the leader and spokesman of the twelve, cravenly denied three times that he even knew Jesus (Matt. 26:69–75). Believer's greatest triumphs are flawed because "there is no man who does not sin . . . there is not a righteous man on earth who continually does good and who never sins" (1 Kings 8:46; Eccl. 7:20), and thus no one can say, "I have cleansed my heart, I am pure from my sin" (Prov. 20:9).

The opening verses of Revelation 14 introduce the most triumphant group of men the world will ever know. Scripture describes other faithful, godly, uncompromising, committed men, such as Joseph, Daniel, and Paul. But never will there be such a large group at one time. They will emerge from the worst holocaust in history, the Tribulation, battle weary but triumphant; they will be like 144,000 Daniels.

Chapter 7 introduced this remarkable group of men. After the horrific events of the sixth seal (6:12–17), the terror-stricken people of the earth will cry out "to the mountains and to the rocks, 'Fall on us and hide us from the presence of Him who sits on the throne, and from the wrath of the Lamb; for the great day of their wrath has come, and who is able to stand?'" (6:16–17). By that point in the Tribulation, the world will have experienced the unimaginable horrors of the first six seals. There will have been widespread wars, severe famines, deadly plagues, and terrible earthquakes and other natural disasters, all of which will result in millions of deaths. Sin will run rampant and unchecked over the earth, fueled by Satan and his demon hosts—both those cast from heaven with him (12:9) and those formerly bound demons who will be released (9:1–11, 14–19). Antichrist will unleash the most terrible persecution the world has ever known, and countless thousands of Christians and Jews will be slaughtered.

In light of that horrifying, unimaginable situation, and the devastating trumpet and bowl judgments to follow, it will seem impossible for anyone to survive.

It is against that backdrop that the 144,000 are introduced. They will survive both Satan's wrath and persecution and God's judgments on the sinful world. Nothing will be able to harm them, because God will seal them (7:3–4). They will be like the remnant of Malachi's day: "Then those who feared the Lord spoke to one another, and the Lord gave attention and heard it and a book of remembrance was written before Him for those who fear the Lord and who esteem His name. 'They will be Mine,' says the Lord of hosts, 'on the day that I prepare My own possession, and I will spare them as a man spares his own son who serves him'" (Mal. 3:16–17). Throughout history, God has protected those who belong to Him. He preserved Noah during the Flood and kept Rahab safe when Jericho was destroyed. He preserved Lot from the destruction of Sodom and kept the children of Israel safe from the plagues that devastated Egypt. Psalm 37:39–40 declares, "The salvation of the righteous is from the Lord; He is their strength in time of trouble. The Lord helps them and delivers them; He delivers them from the wicked and saves them, because they take refuge in Him."

The 144,000 will not be the only ones redeemed during the Tribulation. A great host of others, both Jews (Zech. 12:10–14; 13:1, 9; Rom. 11:26–27) and Gentiles (6:9–11; 7:9, 13–14; Matt. 25:31–46) will be saved. Many, perhaps most, of them will die as martyrs during the savage persecution unleashed by Antichrist. The rest, however, who will live through the horrors of the Tribulation will enter the millennial kingdom (Isa. 65:20–23; Matt. 25:31–36). But the 144,000 Jewish evangelists are unique because all of them will survive. When Christ returns and stands on Mount Zion, they will stand with Him in triumph.

A brief overview sets the stage for the vision of the 144,000. The reader should recall that chapters 12–14 of Revelation form an interlude in the saga of God's final judgments on the sinful world. The unfolding of those judgments is described in chapters 6–11, as God will begin to take back the earth from the usurper, Satan. Chapter 11, verse 15, records the sounding of the seventh trumpet, though the judgments associated with it will not begin to unfold until chapter 15. Chapters 12 and 13 recapitulate the events of the Tribulation, this time giving them from Satan's perspective. They expose Satan's efforts to destroy Israel (chap. 12) and detail the careers of Antichrist and the final false prophet (chap. 13). Chapter 14 returns to what God is doing. It contains three visions that give a general preview of the judgments yet to come that culminate in Christ's return.

Chapter 14 is a bright contrast to the darkness of chapter 13, which describes Satan (the dragon), Antichrist, the final false prophet, deception, the unredeemed, idolatry, and the mark of the beast. Chapter 14 describes the Lamb, angels, redeemed saints, genuine worship, and those sealed by God. In chapter 13 there is falsehood, wickedness, corruption, and blasphemy; in chapter 14 there is truth, righteousness, purity, and praise.

In addition to its prophetic significance, this passage yields important practical principles for triumphant Christian living. Seven such features will characterize the 144,000: power, praise, purity, partisanship, purpose, precision, and perfection.

Power

Then I looked, and behold, the Lamb was standing on Mount Zion, and with Him one hundred and forty-four thousand, having

His name and the name of His Father written on their foreheads. (14:1)

The phrase **I looked, and behold** or its equivalent appears frequently in Revelation to introduce startling, dramatic events (cf. v. 14; 4:1; 6:2, 5, 8; 7:9; 15:5; 19:11). What arrested John's attention was the awe-inspiring sight of **the Lamb . . . standing on Mount Zion.** Revelation depicts the **Lamb** as slain (5:6; 13:8), glorified (5:8, 12–13), exalted (7:9–10), the Redeemer (7:14) and Shepherd (7:17) of His people, and the Lord of Lords and King of Kings (17:14).

The appearance of the **Lamb** on **Mount Zion** is a monumental moment in redemptive history. The psalmist wrote of this moment in Psalm 2:6–9:

> "But as for Me, I have installed My King
> Upon Zion, My holy mountain.
>
> "I will surely tell of the decree of the Lord:
> He said to Me, 'You are My Son,
> Today I have begotten You.
> Ask of Me, and I will surely give the nations as Your inheritance,
> And the very ends of the earth as Your possession.
> You shall break them with a rod of iron,
> You shall shatter them like earthenware'."

Psalm 48:2 describes **Mount Zion** as "Beautiful in elevation, the joy of the whole earth ... [t]he city of the great King." Isaiah wrote that "the Lord of hosts will reign on Mount Zion and in Jerusalem, and His glory will be before His elders" (Isa. 24:23). The fulfillment of those predictions has now arrived.

Strangely, some equate this passage with Hebrews 12:22–24 and view it as a vision of heaven. But the former passage describes the heavenly Mount Zion, the abode of God. This passage describes the return of Christ to the earthly Mount Zion. The whole point would be lost if **Mount Zion** refers to heaven, because that would mean the **one hundred and forty-four thousand** had died. In that case, their sealing with the mark of God (7:3–4; cf. 9:4) would be rendered meaningless. Isaiah 11:9–12 and 24:23, Joel 2:32, and Zechariah 14:4 also support the identification of the **Mount Zion** in this passage with the earthly Mount Zion. That a voice comes out of heaven (v. 2) also suggests that this scene is on earth.

Some commentators insist that the number **one hundred and forty-four thousand** is not to be taken literally. They argue that it symbolizes the church, or the Tribulation saints, or history's most outstanding Christians gathered together in heaven for this scene. Some cults insist that it refers to them—which poses a problem for the ones with more than 144,000 adherents. But all such speculative personal alteration of Scripture is pointless; their identity is not in doubt. This is a group of 144,000 real, live people—12,000 Jewish believers from each of the twelve tribes of Israel (Rev. 7:4–8). (For further evidence that the **one hundred and forty-four thousand** will be Jewish believers alive during the Tribulation, see *Revelation1–11*, The MacArthur New Testament Commentary [Chicago: Moody, 1999], 219–20.)

The **one hundred and forty-four thousand** will be a group unique in redemptive history. John Phillips wrote:

> No other age has produced a company like this, a veritable army of militant believers marching unscathed through every form of danger. It has been theirs to defy the dragon, to bait the Beast, and to give the lie to the false prophet. Their calling has been to preach the gospel from the housetops when even to name the name of Christ called for the most dreadful penalties. They have been surrounded, these latter-day Jobs, with impenetrable hedges, able to laugh to scorn all the grand inquisitors of hell. They have walked the streets in broad daylight, careless of the teeth-gnashing rage of their would-be torturers and assassins, true witnesses of Jehovah in the most terrible era of the history of mankind. The devil knows about this coming band of conquerors, and writhes already in an agony of anticipation. (*Exploring Revelation,* rev. ed. [Chicago: Moody, 1987; reprint, Neptune, N.J.: Loizeaux, 1991], 179–80)

The text also describes the 144,000 as **having His** [the Lamb's] **name and the name of His Father written on their foreheads.** Unbelievers will receive the mark of the beast (13:16–17); the 144,000 will have the mark of God placed on their foreheads (7:3) for their protection. Satan and the unbelieving world will desperately seek to kill these powerful, fearless preachers of the gospel. But, having marked them as His own possession, God will not permit them to be harmed. Throughout the cataclysmic outpouring of God's final judgments and Satan's final fury, they will preach the gospel. They will confront unbelievers with their sins, call them to repentance and faith in the Savior, and proclaim that the catastrophes taking place are God's righteous judgments. And despite Satan's best efforts, all 144,000 will survive to meet Christ on Mount Zion at His second coming. They will enter the millennial kingdom as living men. Most likely, the 144,000 will continue their evangelistic work throughout that thousand-year period. While only redeemed people will enter the kingdom, the children born to them (cf. Isa. 65:23) will not all believe. In fact, there will be enough unregenerate people by the end of the Millennium for Satan to lead a worldwide rebellion against Christ's rule (20:7–10).

Thus, Scripture speaks of salvation during the Millennium (cf. Isa. 60:3; Zech. 8:23)—a salvation thc 144,000 will no doubt proclaim.

The story of these victorious survivors illustrates the divine side of triumphant Christian living: God will preserve His own. The 144,000 will be living proof of the promises found in Psalm 91:5–16:

> You will not be afraid of the terror by night,
> Or of the arrow that flies by day;
> Of the pestilence that stalks in darkness,
> Or of the destruction that lays waste at noon.
> A thousand may fall at your side
> And ten thousand at your right hand,
> But it shall not approach you.
> You will only look on with your eyes
> And see the recompense of the wicked.
> For you have made the Lord, my refuge,
> Even the Most High, your dwelling place.
> No evil will befall you,
> Nor will any plague come near your tent.
>
> For He will give His angels charge concerning you,
> To guard you in all your ways.
> They will bear you up in their hands,
> That you do not strike your foot against a stone.
> You will tread upon the lion and cobra,
> The young lion and the serpent you will trample down.
>
> "Because he has loved Me, therefore I will deliver him;
> I will set him securely on high, because he has known My name.
> He will call upon Me, and I will answer him;
> I will be with him in trouble;
> I will rescue him and honor him.
> With a long life I will satisfy him
> And let him see My salvation."

God will protect His own and bring them triumphantly through their trials. That is true both of survivors on earth, like the 144,000, and of martyrs in heaven, like those depicted in 6:9–11 and 7:9–17. Jesus promised, "All that the Father gives Me will come to Me, and the one who comes to Me I will certainly not cast out" (John 6:37). Believers are eternally secure, Jesus declared, because "no one will snatch them out of My hand. My Father, who has given them to Me, is greater than all; and no one is able to snatch them out of the Father's hand" (John 10:28–29). To the Philippians Paul wrote, "For I am confident of this very thing, that He who began a good work in you will perfect it until the day of Christ Jesus" (Phil. 1:6);

while Jude offered praise "to Him who is able to keep you from stumbling, and to make you stand in the presence of His glory blameless with great joy" (Jude 24). Knowing that they are "protected by the power of God through faith for a salvation ready to be revealed in the last time" (1 Pet. 1:5), believers may both live confidently and minister boldly. The majestic words of Romans 8:31–39 eloquently summarize the marvelous truth that God protects and delivers His own:

> What then shall we say to these things? If God is for us, who is against us? He who did not spare His own Son, but delivered Him over for us all, how will He not also with Him freely give us all things? Who will bring a charge against God's elect? God is the one who justifies; who is the one who condemns? Christ Jesus is He who died, yes, rather who was raised, who is at the right hand of God, who also intercedes for us. Who will separate us from the love of Christ? Will tribulation, or distress, or persecution, or famine, or nakedness, or peril, or sword? Just as it is written,
> "For Your sake we are being put to death all day long;
> We were considered as sheep to be slaughtered."
> But in all these things we overwhelmingly conquer through Him who loved us. For I am convinced that neither death, nor life, nor angels, nor principalities, nor things present, nor things to come, nor powers, nor height, nor depth, nor any other created thing, will be able to separate us from the love of God, which is in Christ Jesus our Lord.

Praise

And I heard a voice from heaven, like the sound of many waters and like the sound of loud thunder, and the voice which I heard was like the sound of harpists playing on their harps. And they sang a new song before the throne and before the four living creatures and the elders; and no one could learn the song except the one hundred and forty-four thousand who had been purchased from the earth. (14:2–3)

Standing with the Lamb on Mount Zion, the 144,000 will join in the heavenly song of redemption. With all the devastation they have seen, with all the trouble they have faced, with all the rejection, hostility, hatred, and persecution they have endured, one might expect them to be too sorrowful to sing (cf. Ps. 137:1–4). But instead they will joyously praise the Lord for their protection and triumph.

This is not the first time John **heard a voice from heaven** (cf. 4:1; 10:4, 8; 11:12; 12:10), nor will it be the last (cf. v. 13; 18:4; 19:1). The voice he heard was very loud and continuous, **like the sound of many**

waters and like the sound of loud thunder. Ezekiel 43:2 likens the voice of God to **the sound of many waters,** while Revelation 1:15 describes the voice of the Lord Jesus Christ in the same way. But since Revelation 19:6 uses both of those phrases to describe the voice of a heavenly multitude, it is best to understand them in that sense here.

The song began in 5:9–10, when the four living creatures and the twenty-four elders "sang a new song, saying, 'Worthy are You to take the book and to break its seals; for You were slain, and purchased for God with Your blood men from every tribe and tongue and people and nation. You have made them to be a kingdom and priests to our God; and they will reign upon the earth.'" The next to join in were myriads of angels, who began "saying with a loud voice, 'Worthy is the Lamb that was slain to receive power and riches and wisdom and might and honor and glory and blessing'" (5:12). Finally, "every created thing which is in heaven and on the earth and under the earth and on the sea, and all things in them [began] saying, 'To Him who sits on the throne, and to the Lamb, be blessing and honor and glory and dominion forever and ever'" (5:13). In 7:9–10, the Tribulation martyrs joined in the escalating chorus of praise: "After these things I looked, and behold, a great multitude which no one could count, from every nation and all tribes and peoples and tongues, standing before the throne and before the Lamb, clothed in white robes, and palm branches were in their hands; and they cry out with a loud voice, saying, 'Salvation to our God who sits on the throne, and to the Lamb.'"

The mighty voice was not mere noise; it had a musical quality, **like the sound of harpists playing on their harps.** The reference to **harpists** and **harps** suggests that the voice expressed not thunderous judgment but joy. **Harps** are frequently associated in the Old Testament with joyous praise (cf. 2 Sam. 6:5; 1 Chron. 13:8; 15:16, 28; 2 Chron. 5:12–13; Neh. 12:27; Pss. 33:2; 71:22; 144:9; 150:3). Heaven will resound with loud praise when the Lord Jesus Christ returns in triumph to establish His earthly kingdom.

The **new song** sung in heaven **before the throne and before the four living creatures and the elders** is the song of redemption (cf. Pss. 33:1–3; 40:3; 96:1–2; 98:1–2; 144:9–10; 149:1; Isa. 42:10). The angels will join the Old Testament saints, the raptured church, and the redeemed Tribulation martyrs in praising God for salvation. While angels do not experience redemption, they do rejoice because of it (Luke 15:10). All heaven will overflow with praise because God's redemptive work culminating in the return of Christ is accomplished.

Heaven's praise overflows to earth, where the **new song** is taken up. John notes that **no one could learn the song except the one hundred and forty-four thousand who had been purchased from the**

earth. The unregenerate cannot, of course, sing the song of redemption; it is only for the redeemed, those **purchased** by Christ's blood. Why the **song** is restricted to **the one hundred and forty-four thousand** is not stated, but Henry Morris has offered a possible explanation:

> Although the words of the song of the 144,000 are not recorded, it surely dwells in part at least on the great truth that they had been "redeemed from the earth." Although in one sense all saved people have been redeemed from the earth, these could know the meaning of such a theme in a more profound way than others. They had been saved after the rapture, at that time in history when man's greatest persecutions and God's greatest judgments were on the earth. It was at such a time that they, like Noah (Genesis 6:8), had "found grace in the eyes of the Lord" and had been separated from "all that dwell upon the earth" (Revelation 13:8). Not only had they been redeemed spiritually but, precursively as it were, they had been redeemed from the very curse on the earth (Genesis 3:17), being protected from pain and death by the guarding seal. (*The Revelation Record* [Wheaton, Ill.: Tyndale, 1983], 260)

The 144,000 will join with the heavenly chorus in praising God for His marvelous work of redemption. Some of the lyrics of their song may be found in 15:3–4:

> And they sang the song of Moses, the bond-servant of God, and the song of the Lamb, saying,
> "Great and marvelous are Your works,
> O Lord God, the Almighty;
> Righteous and true are Your ways,
> King of the nations!
> Who will not fear, O Lord, and glorify Your name?
> For You alone are holy;
> For all the nations will come and worship before You,
> For Your righteous acts have been revealed."

A mark of triumphant Christian living in any era is constant praise to God. The 144,000 no doubt praised God throughout their time of trial and persecution. Because their ordeal is over and they are victorious, they will burst forth in praise to God for their deliverance. Joy is the proper outflow of a heart that trusts in God's sovereign power (Phil. 3:1; 4:4; 1 Thess. 5:16; James 1:2; 1 Pet. 4:13).

Purity

These are the ones who have not been defiled with women, for they have kept themselves chaste. (14:4*a*)

The worship of Antichrist during the Tribulation will be unspeakably vile and perverse. As it did in the fertility cults of ancient times, sexual sin will apparently run rampant. Even in the current grossly immoral day, we can hardly imagine what the deviant sexual perversion of the Tribulation will be like. With all divine restraint removed (2 Thess. 2:6–7) and the unbelieving world judgmentally abandoned by God (cf. Rom. 1:24, 26, 28), sin will be released like a flood, inundating the world. And fanning the hellish flames of wickedness will be Satan and his demon hosts—both those cast from heaven with him (12:9) and those vile demons newly released from imprisonment (9:1–11, 14–19).

In the midst of the darkness of the Tribulation period, the 144,000 will shine forth like beacons of purity. Despite the rampant sexual sin that surrounds them, they will **not** be **defiled with women,** but will keep **themselves chaste.** That the specific sin that they will avoid involves **women** indicates that sexual purity is in view here, not detachment from the corrupt world system. That the 144,000 will be separate from Antichrist's empire has already been made clear; they bear God's mark, not the beast's (7:3–4). Nor does this passage teach that they will all be unmarried, since sex within marriage does not defile anyone (Heb. 13:4). What it means is that they will stand apart from the sin of their culture; 144,000 morally pure preachers amid the defilement that surrounds them.

Sexual purity is essential to triumphant Christian living. In 1 Thessalonians 4:3 Paul wrote plainly, "For this is the will of God, your sanctification; that is, that you abstain from sexual immorality." The apostle admonished the young pastor Timothy to "flee from youthful lusts and pursue righteousness, faith, love and peace, with those who call on the Lord from a pure heart" (2 Tim. 2:22). To the Corinthians Paul wrote, "The body is not for immorality, but for the Lord. . . . Flee immorality. Every other sin that a man commits is outside the body, but the immoral man sins against his own body" (1 Cor. 6:13, 18). Those who would serve God effectively must lead holy, pure lives. The godly nineteenth-century Scottish preacher Robert Murray McCheyne gave the following words of advice to an aspiring young minister:

> Do not forget the culture of the inner man—I mean of the heart. How diligently the cavalry officer keeps his sabre clean and sharp; every stain he rubs off with the greatest care. Remember you are God's sword, His instrument—I trust a chosen vessel unto Him to bear His name. In great measure, according to the purity and perfections of the instrument, will be the success. It is not great talents God blesses so much as great likeness to Jesus. A holy minister is an awful weapon in the hand of God. (Andrew A. Bonar, *Memoirs of McCheyne* [Chicago: Moody, 1978], 95)

Partisanship

These are the ones who follow the Lamb wherever He goes. (14:4*b*)

The 144,000 are further characterized as **the ones who follow the Lamb wherever He goes.** They will be partisans to the party of the Lamb. The *Oxford English Dictionary* defines a partisan as "one who takes part or sides with another; an adherent or supporter of a party, person, or cause . . . a devoted or zealous supporter. . . . One who supports his party 'through thick and thin'; a blind, prejudiced, unreasoning, or fanatical adherent." The triumphant 144,000 will be completely loyal to the Lamb, no matter what the cost. In the words of John Phillips,

> They allow no rivals, no refusals, and no restraint to mar their dedication to Him. Does He need someone to stand upon the steps of the Vatican and cry out against the marriage of Christendom to the Beast? There are 144,000 ready to go! Does the Lord need someone to beard the Beast at some high function of state and roundly denounce him, his policy, his statecraft, his religion, his economic boycott, his mark, his ministers, his alliance with Satan? There are 144,000 eager to go! Does the Lamb need evangelists to proclaim to the untold millions the gospel of the coming kingdom of God? to climb the highest Himalayas, to cross the desert sands, to blaze evangelistic trails through steaming jungles, or to mush huskies across wide arctic wastes? There are 144,000 ready to go! And though the Beast's gestapo [sic] dog their footsteps and wreak upon their converts his direst vengeance, yet on they go undaunted and undeterred. That was the very spirit of their consecration as they followed the Lamb whithersoever He led them on earth, and their reward is in kind. (*Exploring Revelation*, 180–81)

It is such loyal, devoted followers that Jesus seeks. In Matthew 16:24 He said, "If anyone wishes to come after Me, he must deny himself, and take up his cross and follow Me." He advised the rich young ruler, "If you wish to be complete, go and sell your possessions and give to the poor, and you will have treasure in heaven; and come, follow Me" (Matt. 19:21). Jesus told the unbelieving Jews that they were not His sheep, noting that "My sheep hear My voice, and I know them, and they follow Me" (John 10:27). Paul declared himself to be a follower of Jesus Christ (1 Cor. 11:1), while in his first epistle, John reminded his readers that "the one who says he abides in Him ought himself to walk in the same manner as He walked" (1 John 2:6).

PURPOSE

These have been purchased from among men as first fruits to God and to the Lamb. (14:4*c*)

In redemptive language reminiscent of 5:9, John explains that the 144,000 have been **purchased from among men.** But while all believers have been purchased by God (cf. Acts 20:28; 1 Cor. 6:20; 7:23;1 Pet. 1:18–19), the 144,000 were purchased for a special purpose. They will be redeemed as **first fruits to God and to the Lamb.** In the Old Testament the first fruits, the first part of a crop to be harvested, were offered to God (Deut. 26:1–11) to be used in His service (Deut. 18:3–5). The 144,000, like the first fruits offering, will be set apart for divine service. As previously noted, the number 144,000 does not symbolize all the Tribulation saints, but rather designates a group of Jewish evangelists. The purpose of their lives will be to serve the Lord by proclaiming the gospel to the lost, perishing, Christ-rejecting world.

It is also possible to view the 144,000 as **first fruits** in the sense that they represent the first of many others who will be saved. Paul used the term in that sense when he noted that "the household of Stephanas . . . were the first fruits of Achaia" (1 Cor. 16:15). The 144,000 may legitimately be viewed as the first fruits of redeemed Israel, foreshadowing the nation's salvation when Christ returns. In that day "they will look on Me whom they have pierced; and they will mourn for Him, as one mourns for an only son, and they will weep bitterly over Him like the bitter weeping over a firstborn" (Zech. 12:10). Of that day Paul wrote:

> For I do not want you, brethren, to be uninformed of this mystery—so that you will not be wise in your own estimation—that a partial hardening has happened to Israel until the fullness of the Gentiles has come in; and so all Israel will be saved; just as it is written,
>
> "The Deliverer will come from Zion,
> He will remove ungodliness from Jacob.
> This is My covenant with them,
> When I take away their sins."
>
> (Rom. 11:25–27)

The 144,000 will exemplify the purpose, decisiveness, dedication, and clarity of life goal that marks triumphant Christians (cf. Rom. 12:1–2).

PRECISION

And no lie was found in their mouth; (14:5*a*)

The 144,000 will not propagate Satan's lies, but will speak God's truth. They will be like those of whom Zephaniah wrote: "The remnant of Israel will do no wrong and tell no lies, nor will a deceitful tongue be found in their mouths" (Zeph. 3:13). The unbelieving world will be consumed with "false wonders," "all the deception of wickedness," and "a deluding influence" judgmentally decreed by God so that those who reject the gospel "will believe what is false" (2 Thess. 2:9–11). But the 144,000 will accurately proclaim the Word of God without wavering, equivocating, or altering it. They will be like their Lord, of whom the Bible says, "[He] committed no sin, nor was any deceit found in His mouth" (1 Pet. 2:22).

In all generations, triumphant Christians are characterized by "speaking the truth in love" (Eph. 4:15) and "laying aside falsehood [and] speak[ing] truth" (Eph. 4:25). Knowing the vital importance of "accurately handling the word of truth," they will "be diligent to present [themselves] approved to God as [workmen] who [do] not need to be ashamed" (2 Tim. 2:15). They will never be guilty of "walking in craftiness or adulterating the word of God"; rather, "by the manifestation of truth [they will commend themselves] to every man's conscience in the sight of God" (2 Cor. 4:2).

Perfection

they are blameless. (14:5*b*)

Because they will trust in God's power and lead lives characterized by praise, purity, devoted loyalty, and singleness of purpose, the 144,000 will be **blameless.** That does not, of course, mean that they will be sinless (1 Kings 8:46; Job 15:14–16; Ps. 143:2; Prov. 20:9; Eccl. 7:20; 1 John 1:8–10), but they will be sanctified. They will be above reproach, leading godly lives before all who see them.

Like the 144,000, all Christians are called to holiness. In Ephesians 1:4 Paul wrote, "He chose us in Him before the foundation of the world, that we would be holy and blameless before Him" (cf. Col. 1:22). To the Corinthians the apostle wrote, "I betrothed you to one husband, so that to Christ I might present you as a pure virgin" (2 Cor. 11:2; cf. Eph. 5:27). Peter exhorted believers to "like the Holy One who called you, be holy yourselves also in all your behavior; because it is written, 'You shall be holy, for I am holy'" (1 Pet. 1:15–16). Jude reminded his readers that God "is able to keep you from stumbling, and to make you stand in the presence of His glory blameless with great joy" (Jude 24).

The 144,000 deserve a place in the "Hall of Fame" of the Christian faith (Heb. 11). They will lead holy lives and minister effectively for God during history's darkest hour. Their exemplary efforts will spearhead the greatest spiritual awakening the world will ever see (cf. 6:9–11; 7:9). The inspired account of their lives and ministry provides a pattern of triumphant Christian living for all believers to follow.

Angelic Messengers (Revelation 14:6–11)

7

And I saw another angel flying in midheaven, having an eternal gospel to preach to those who live on the earth, and to every nation and tribe and tongue and people; and he said with a loud voice, "Fear God, and give Him glory, because the hour of His judgment has come; worship Him who made the heaven and the earth and sea and springs of waters."

And another angel, a second one, followed, saying, "Fallen, fallen is Babylon the great, she who has made all the nations drink of the wine of the passion of her immorality."

Then another angel, a third one, followed them, saying with a loud voice, "If anyone worships the beast and his image, and receives a mark on his forehead or on his hand, he also will drink of the wine of the wrath of God, which is mixed in full strength in the cup of His anger; and he will be tormented with fire and brimstone in the presence of the holy angels and in the presence of the Lamb. And the smoke of their torment goes up forever and ever; they have no rest day and night, those who worship the beast and his image, and whoever receives the mark of his name." (14:6–11)

People are constantly hoping for a better day. Politicians promise to bring in better times if they are elected. World leaders strive to find common ground between nations, seeking to bring about peace and harmony. Everyone would like to see the stock market up, the crime rate down, poverty and disease eliminated, the environment preserved, and an end to hatred and strife.

But man's efforts to bring about a better world, however well intended, are ultimately doomed. They amount to little more than rearranging the deck chairs on the Titanic to give everyone a better view as the ship sinks. The truth is that not a better day, but an unimaginably worse day lies ahead for man and his world. In the future, God will pour out His wrath and judgment on a scale never before seen. Only after the earth is utterly devastated and unbelievers judged will a better day come —the blessed earthly kingdom of the Lord Jesus Christ.

Revelation has much to say about the coming judgments; as already noted, they are the primary focus of chapters 6–11 and 15–19, with chapters 12–14 forming a brief interlude in the unfolding revelation of God's judgmental wrath. Chapters 12 and 13 have been seen to recount the events of the Tribulation from Satan's perspective; chapter 14 returns to what God is going to do. In three visions, this text previews the remaining judgments of the Tribulation and the return of Christ. The first vision (vv. 1–5) was of the 144,000 Jewish evangelists who will appear with the Lord Jesus Christ on Mount Zion at His second coming. Before us in verses 6 through 11 is the record of the second vision, in which judgment is proclaimed by three angelic messengers.

Angels serve throughout Scripture as God's messengers; in fact, the Greek word *angelos* ("angel") means "messenger." They were instrumental in the giving of the Mosaic Law (Acts 7:38, 53; Gal. 3:19; Heb. 2:2). They also brought messages to individuals, such as Daniel (Dan. 8:15–17; 9:21–22), Zacharias (Luke 1:11–19), Mary (Luke 1:26–27), Joseph (Matt. 1:20; 2:13, 19), the shepherds (Luke 2:9–13), Phillip (Acts 8:26), and Paul (Acts 27:23–24). Angels also minister to and care for believers (Matt. 18:10; Acts 12:7–11; Heb. 1:14).

Angels will play a major role in the end-time events. They will gather the nonelect for judgment (Matt. 13:41–42, 49–50), the elect for glory (Matt. 24:31), and accompany the Lord Jesus Christ when He returns to earth in triumph (Matt. 25:31; 2 Thess. 1:7). In Revelation, angels are involved in the outpouring of God's wrath (8:6ff.; 11:15ff.; 16:1ff.). Unlike those angels, however, the three angels described in verses 6–11 do not bring judgment. Instead, they bring astounding proclamations from God concerning the consummation of the age.

The three angels do not appear in sequential or chronological order. Instead, they address issues and events that stretch across the

Tribulation period. Their messages anticipate the judgment of the seventh trumpet (11:15; chaps. 15, 16), which includes the final, climactic, rapid-fire bowl judgments at the end of the Tribulation. The messages they bring are designed to produce a remedial fear (cf. Luke 12:5; Heb. 10:31) leading to saving faith. God will graciously offer sinners another opportunity to repent before unleashing the terrifying bowl judgments (16:1ff.). The first angel preaches the gospel, the second pronounces judgment, and the third promises damnation.

The First Angel: Preaching the Gospel

And I saw another angel flying in midheaven, having an eternal gospel to preach to those who live on the earth, and to every nation and tribe and tongue and people; and he said with a loud voice, "Fear God, and give Him glory, because the hour of His judgment has come; worship Him who made the heaven and the earth and sea and springs of waters." (14:6–7)

The specific angel or group of angels that John **saw another angel** distinct from is not specified. While angels appear in every chapter from chapters 4 through 12, the nearest antecedent is the reference to Michael and his angels (12:7). The phrase could also point back to the seventh angel (11:15). In any case, another of the countless myriads of angels (5:11) is selected for a very special purpose.

Dramatically, the angel appears in the sky **flying in midheaven.** *Mesouranēma* (**midheaven**) refers to the point in the sky where the sun reaches its meridian, apex, or high point at noon (cf. 8:13; 19:17). From that point, the angel would be most visible to those on the earth. There he will also be beyond the reach of Antichrist, as well as Satan and his demon hosts, whose activity will by that time be restricted to the earth (12:7–9). The battle that currently rages in the heavenlies between the holy angels and the demons (cf. Dan. 10:12–13) will by then be over. This preaching angel will be unreachable, the world's view of him unobstructed, and his ministry unhindered.

By the time the angel begins his ministry, the world will have suffered the incredible devastation of the seal and trumpet judgments. Relentless holocausts will have rocked the globe, and the familiarly stable heavens will have become a disintegrating source of terror (cf. 6:12–14). During this time, the unbelieving world will have heard the gospel preached by the 144,000 Jewish evangelists and the two witnesses, as well as countless thousands of others saved under their ministries. But despite all that, most of the earth's population will reject the gospel

(9:20–21; cf. 16:9, 11); thus God graciously sends this powerful angel to proclaim the gospel to them yet again.

As he flies through the sky, the angel will have **an eternal gospel to preach.** This is the only occurrence of the noun *euangelion* (**gospel**) in John's writings, though the related verb translated **to preach** also appears in 10:7. Like a multifaceted jewel, Scripture describes the gospel in various terms, each looking at it from a different viewpoint. The gospel is called the gospel of the kingdom (Matt. 4:23), the gospel of Jesus Christ (Mark 1:1), the gospel of God (Mark 1:14), the gospel of the grace of God (Acts 20:24), the gospel of the glory of Christ (2 Cor. 4:4), the gospel of salvation (Eph. 1:13), the gospel of peace (Eph. 6:15), and the glorious gospel (1 Tim. 1:11). Here it is described as **eternal** because it provides the means to eternal life. It is the good news that God will forgive all the sins of those who repent and believe in the Lord Jesus Christ as the only way of salvation, and by that repentance and saving faith take them into His eternal kingdom

The **eternal gospel** preached by the angel is the same one proclaimed throughout all history. It is the good news of forgiveness and eternal life. He will declare that people are sinners, facing eternal judgment in hell, but that God has provided atonement for sins through the sacrificial death of the Lord Jesus Christ. That message of forgiveness was given even in Old Testament times based on new covenant terms (cf. Jer. 31:31–34; Ezek. 36:25–27). Its benefits were applied to all who truly repented and sought forgiveness and grace from God, even though the Savior had not yet died. In the purpose of God, the merits of the Lamb slain at Calvary have been granted to all true repenters in all ages. In the Tribulation, most people will already be familiar with the gospel through the preaching of the 144,000, the two witnesses, and other believers. But Jesus declared that before the end comes the whole world will hear the gospel of the kingdom (Matt. 24:14). The preaching of this angel will reach any who still have not heard the gospel message. As earth's darkest hour approaches, the angel will proclaim the good news that it is not too late. There is still time to repent before God's judgment resumes.

The angel's message is addressed **to those who live on the earth**—a phrase always used in Revelation to refer to unbelievers (cf. 3:10; 6:10; 8:13; 11:10; 13:8, 12, 14; 17:2, 8). The all-inclusive phrase **every nation and tribe and tongue and people** (cf. 5:9; 7:9; 11:9; 13:7) stresses the comprehensive, worldwide nature of the angel's proclamation. The angel will call out **with a loud voice** to all unregenerate people everywhere. His loud voice ensures that he will be heard and emphasizes the urgency of his message. The angel's message to sinners is **"Fear God, and give Him glory."** He will call the people of the world to change their allegiance from the beast to the Lamb. He will urge them to no longer fear, reverence, and worship Satan and Antichrist, but instead to **fear,** reverence, and honor God by turning to His Son. As the sovereign ruler of the universe, God alone—Father, Son, and Holy Spirit—has the right to be worshiped (19:10; 22:9; Isa. 42:8; 48:11; Matt. 4:10).

The Bible repeatedly calls people to fear God. In Psalm 111:10 the psalmist declared that "the fear of the Lord is the beginning of wisdom" (cf. Prov. 1:7; 9:10), while Proverbs 23:17 commands, "Live in the fear of the Lord always." A wise father counsels his son to "fear the Lord and the king" (Prov. 24:21), while Peter exhorted his readers to "Honor all people, love the brotherhood, fear God, honor the king" (1 Pet. 2:17). In Matthew 10:28 Jesus warned, "Do not fear those who kill the body but are unable to kill the soul; but rather fear Him who is able to destroy both soul and body in hell." To fear God is to live in the reality of His holiness, His sovereignty, and His judgment of sin. It is to love God, respect Him, reverence Him, adore Him, hold Him in awe, and worship Him. And that can only be done by loving His Son the Savior (John 5:23).

In addition to fearing God, men are to **give Him glory.** This requirement goes to the very essence of the problem of unregenerate people, who "even though they knew God, they did not honor Him as God or give thanks" (Rom. 1:21). Refusing to give God glory is at the core of man's prideful rebellion.

Unbelievers will be called to fear and glorify God immediately **because the hour of His judgment has come.** Opportunity is fading fast; the bowl judgments are about to be poured out, to be followed shortly by the return of the Lord Jesus Christ to judge the unbelieving world (Matt. 25:31–46). This is the first occurrence of the word *krisis* (**judgment**) in Revelation. It will appear again in 16:7, 18:10, and 19:2. (A Greek synonym for *krisis, krima,* appears in 17:1, 18:20, and 20:4.) Up to this point in Revelation, the word *wrath* has been used to describe God's judgment (cf. 6:16–17; 11:18); the two terms will continue to be used interchangeably (cf. vv. 10, 19; 15:1, 7; 16:1, 19; 19:15). God's righteous judgments are the outpouring of His wrath against the stubborn and unrepentant world.

It would seem that the angel's warnings would be superfluous. After all, by this point people will have experienced the devastating seal and trumpet judgments. The earth will have been devastated by worldwide wars, famines, and earthquakes, resulting in the destruction of the environment, witnessed terrifying signs in the heavens, and been attacked by demon hordes. All of that will result in death on a scale unprecedented in human history. Yet, though they will eventually realize that those disasters are God's judgments (cf. 6:15–17), people will defiantly refuse to repent (9:20–21). But God, in grace and mercy, will again call sinners to repentance through the preaching of this angel.

The angel gives one final reason for sinners to turn from Antichrist to God, proclaiming that people should **worship Him who made the heaven and the earth and sea and springs of waters.** The created universe both offers proof of God's existence and provides grounds for worshiping Him. David affirmed in Psalm 19:1–4 that

> The heavens are telling of the glory of God;
> And their expanse is declaring the work of His hands.
> Day to day pours forth speech,
> And night to night reveals knowledge.
> There is no speech, nor are there words;
> Their voice is not heard.
> Their line has gone out through all the earth,
> And their utterances to the end of the world.

Isaiah 40:21–26 also teaches that the creation reveals God's glory and majesty:

> Do you not know? Have you not heard?
> Has it not been declared to you from the beginning?
> Have you not understood from the foundations of the earth?
> It is He who sits above the circle of the earth,
> And its inhabitants are like grasshoppers,
> Who stretches out the heavens like a curtain
> And spreads them out like a tent to dwell in.
> He it is who reduces rulers to nothing,
> Who makes the judges of the earth meaningless.
> Scarcely have they been planted,
> Scarcely have they been sown,
> Scarcely has their stock taken root in the earth,
> But He merely blows on them, and they wither,
> And the storm carries them away like stubble.
> "To whom then will you liken Me
> That I would be his equal?" says the Holy One.
> Lift up your eyes on high
> And see who has created these stars,
> The One who leads forth their host by number,
> He calls them all by name;
> Because of the greatness of His might and the strength of His power,
> Not one of them is missing.

Because God reveals Himself in His creation, men are without excuse for not acknowledging Him:

> For the wrath of God is revealed from heaven against all ungodliness and unrighteousness of men who suppress the truth in unrighteousness, because that which is known about God is evident within them;

for God made it evident to them. For since the creation of the world His invisible attributes, His eternal power and divine nature, have been clearly seen, being understood through what has been made, so that they are without excuse." (Rom. 1:18–20)

When Paul evangelized Jews, he always started from the Old Testament Scripture. But when he evangelized pagans, whether simple common people (Acts 14:14–17) or sophisticated philosophers (Acts 17:22–31), he proclaimed that the true and living God must be worshiped because He is the Creator of everything. Identifying the First Cause was the most important question in philosophy before Darwin. Paul introduced them to Him. In Rev. 4:11 the twenty-four elders praise God because He is the Creator: "Worthy are You, our Lord and our God, to receive glory and honor and power; for You created all things, and because of Your will they existed, and were created" (cf. Gen. 1,2).

The angel's stern warning is that the Creator is also the Judge; He is the one people should fear and worship, rather than Satan and Antichrist. As the world teeters on the brink of final disaster, God graciously offers people another chance to repent. He will snatch those who heed the warning from the fire of judgment (cf. Jude 23), and transfer them from Satan's kingdom of darkness into the soon to be manifest kingdom of His Son (Col. 1:13).

The Second Angel: Pronouncing Judgment

And another angel, a second one, followed, saying, "Fallen, fallen is Babylon the great, she who has made all the nations drink of the wine of the passion of her immorality." (14:8)

John saw **another angel, a second one,** who **followed** the first angel. Unlike the first one, this angel does not preach the good news of the gospel, but rather pronounces the bad news of judgment. Sadly, that implies that the first angel's message was largely rejected. It is almost as if the second angel interrupts the first angel because no one is responding.

The second angel's equally brief and direct message is **"Fallen, fallen is Babylon the great."** The repetition underscores the finality, certainty, and comprehensive nature of Babylon's judgment. Babylon's yet future fall is so certain that it can be spoken of as though it has already taken place. The angel's pronouncement will come as a shock to the unbelieving world. That Antichrist's mighty empire, the most powerful in human history, could be destroyed will be inconceivable to his followers (cf. 13:4). It may be that a restored city of **Babylon** will be

Antichrist's capital city. But **Babylon** in this passage refers not just to the city, but to Antichrist's worldwide political, economic, and religious empire.

Babylon has from its inception symbolized evil and rebellion against God. It was founded by Nimrod (Gen. 10:9), a proud, powerful, God-rejecting ruler. Babel (Babylon) was the site of the first organized system of idolatrous false religion (Gen. 11:1–4). The Tower of Babel, the expression of that false religion, was a ziggurat; an edifice designed to facilitate idolatrous worship. God judged the people's idolatry and rebellion by confusing their language and scattering them over the globe (Gen. 11:5–9). Thus the seeds of idolatry and false religion spread around the world from Babylon, to take root wherever these proud rebels and their descendants settled.

As humanity was united in idolatrous false religion at Babel, so will it again be united in the end times under the aegis of the final Babylon. History will thus come full circle. The final Babylon, personified as a harlot (cf. 17:1–5), is described as **she who has made all the nations drink of the wine of the passion of her immorality.** The world will be intoxicated, deceived, and seduced by the Babylonian false religion headed by Antichrist. *Thumos* (**passion**) describes strong, consuming lusts and desires. As a result of their passion, sinners will engage in an orgy of rebellion, idolatry, and hatred of God. While sexual sin will be rampant, the **immorality** spoken of here is spiritual prostitution to Antichrist's false religion; it pictures unfaithfulness to God. Having imbibed the **wine** of the seductive harlot, **the nations** of the world will continue on their course of spiritual defection from God and end up drinking the "wine of the wrath of God" (v. 10). As the third angel reveals, this will prove disastrous. This judgment will be detailed in the discussions of 16:17–19 and chapters 17 and 18.

The Third Angel: Promising Damnation

Then another angel, a third one, followed them, saying with a loud voice, "If anyone worships the beast and his image, and receives a mark on his forehead or on his hand, he also will drink of the wine of the wrath of God, which is mixed in full strength in the cup of His anger; and he will be tormented with fire and brimstone in the presence of the holy angels and in the presence of the Lamb. And the smoke of their torment goes up forever and ever; they have no rest day and night, those who worship the beast and his image, and whoever receives the mark of his name." (14:9–11)

The three angels appear in a logical, if not chronological, sequence. The rejection of the gospel preached by the first angel results in the pronouncement of judgment by the second angel, which will be carried out in the damnation described by the third angel. The **third** angel will deliver his warning **with a loud voice,** so that all will hear and understand his message. God, being perfectly holy and righteous, judges people because they reject what they know to be true. That is why everyone sentenced to hell will be without excuse (Rom. 1:20; 2:1).

The third angel's dire warning is addressed to **anyone** who **worships the beast and his image, and receives a mark on his forehead or on his hand.** As noted in chapter 5 of this volume, everyone will be required, under pain of death, to worship **the beast and his image.** As sign of loyalty to Antichrist and in order to function in his world economy, everyone will be required to receive **a mark on his forehead or on his hand.** It will seem to the deceived followers of Antichrist who receive that mark that they are backing the winning side. But the angel warns that a terrible fate awaits those who, despite all of God's judgments and warnings, persist in worshiping Antichrist. Once again, God graciously calls on sinners to repent in the final hour.

Those who drank the wine of the harlot Babylon **also will drink of the wine of the wrath of God, which is mixed in full strength in the cup of His anger.** To **drink of the wine of the wrath of God** is to experience His wrath (cf. Job 21:20; Ps. 75:8; Isa. 51:17, 22; Jer. 25:15). The full fury of God's wrath, so long restrained, will be unleashed. Such wrath is not an impulsive outburst of divine emotion aimed at people whimsically. It is the settled, deliberate, merciless, graceless response of the righteous God against all sinners. John describes that terrifying reality by noting that God's wrath will be **mixed in full strength in the cup of His anger. Mixed in full strength** (lit. "mixed unmixed") refers to the ancient practice of diluting wine with water. The wine filling **the cup of** God's **anger,** however, is strong, undiluted wine. God's eschatological wrath will be undiluted vengeance, unmixed with any trace of compassion.

The horrifying fate awaiting the person who drinks **the wine of the wrath of God** is to **be tormented with fire and brimstone.** The verb translated **be tormented** speaks of the ceaseless infliction of unbearable pain. The noun form of that verb is used in Luke 16:23 to describe the agony of the rich man in Hades. Those whom God will force to drink from **the cup of His anger** will know no lessening or diminishing of their torment; they will enjoy no moments of rest throughout eternity. **Fire and brimstone** are often associated in Scripture with divine judgment. God used them to destroy Sodom and Gomorrah (Gen. 19:24–25; Luke 17:29). In Psalm 11:6 David wrote, "Upon the wicked He will rain snares; fire and brimstone and burning wind will be the portion of their cup." Hell, the final resting place of the unregenerate, is described as the "lake of fire which burns with brimstone" (19:20; cf. 20:10; 21:8).

That the unregenerate will be tormented **in the presence of the holy angels and in the presence of the Lamb** will add shame and embarrassment to their suffering. "To suffer in the presence of the hosts of heaven is not to lessen the fierceness of the judgment but to make it more grievous. Christians had borne the shame of public derision and opposition; soon their antagonists will suffer before a more august gathering" (Robert H. Mounce, *The Book of Revelation*, The New International Commentary on the New Testament [Grand Rapids: Eerdmans, 1977], 276). Unrepentant sinners will be banished from God's presence relationally (cf. 21:27; 22:15; Matt. 7:23; 25:41; 2 Thess. 1:9); they will be forever barred from the loving fellowship with Him that believers will enjoy. They will not, however, be away from His presence in the sense of His sovereignty and omnipresence—even in hell. David wrote, "Where can I go from Your Spirit? Or where can I flee from Your presence? If I ascend into heaven, You are there; if I make my bed in hell, behold, You are there" (Ps. 139:7–8 NKJV). Those in hell will suffer eternal punishment at the hands of God, because He is the One who is "able to destroy both soul and body in hell" (Matt. 10:28).

The third angel concludes his message with a final sobering thought about the punishment of those who worship the beast, declaring that **the smoke of their torment goes up forever and ever; they have no rest day and night.** This angel would strongly disagree with those who deny the eternality of hell. His description of hell as the place where **the smoke of** the **torment** of the wicked **goes up forever and ever** (cf. 20:10) is consistent with the rest of Scripture. Isaiah (Isa. 66:24), Daniel (Dan. 12:2), John the Baptist (Matt. 3:12; Luke 3:17), and the apostle Paul (2 Thess. 1:9) also affirm that hell is eternal. But no one taught that sobering truth more clearly than did the Lord Jesus Christ. He spoke of hell as the place of "eternal fire" (Matt. 18:8; 25:41), of "unquenchable fire" (Mark 9:43), where "the fire is not quenched" (Mark 9:48). And in Matthew 25:46, Jesus clearly taught that the torment of the lost in hell will last as long as the blessedness of the redeemed in heaven. Though human sensitivities may balk at the doctrine of eternal punishment, it is both the explicit teaching of the Bible and demanded by God's justice and holiness.

So these three angels deliver God's last call to repentance before the final judgments fall and the Lord Jesus Christ returns. But God's gracious warnings will go unheeded by most of the sinful world. There is perhaps no clearer illustration in Scripture of the sad truth that "men loved the darkness rather than the Light, for their deeds were evil" (John 3:19).

Blessed Are the Dead (Revelation 14:12–13)

8

Here is the perseverance of the saints who keep the commandments of God and their faith in Jesus.

And I heard a voice from heaven, saying, "Write, 'Blessed are the dead who die in the Lord from now on!'" "Yes," says the Spirit, "so that they may rest from their labors, for their deeds follow with them." (14:12–13)

The Bible has much to say about happiness. The familiar New Testament word *makarios* ("blessed") refers to spiritual joy, bliss, fulfillment, and satisfaction. It describes an inner joy that is the fulfillment of every longing, a serene, untouchable, unassailable contentment and peace. The Old and New Testaments reveal much about such blessedness:

> How blessed is the man who does not walk in the counsel of the wicked,
> Nor stand in the path of sinners,
> Nor sit in the seat of scoffers!
> But his delight is in the law of the Lord,
> And in His law he meditates day and night.
>
> (Ps. 1:1–2)

How blessed are all who take refuge in [God's Son]!
(Ps. 2:12)

How blessed is he whose transgression is forgiven,
Whose sin is covered!
How blessed is the man to whom the Lord does not impute iniquity,
And in whose spirit there is no deceit!
(Ps. 32:1–2; cf. Rom. 4:7–8)

How blessed is the man who has made the Lord his trust,
And has not turned to the proud, nor to those who lapse into falsehood.
(Ps. 40:4)

How blessed is he who considers the helpless;
The Lord will deliver him in a day of trouble.
(Ps. 41:1)

How blessed is the one whom You choose and bring near to You
To dwell in Your courts.
(Ps. 65:4)

How blessed are those who dwell in Your house!
They are ever praising You.
(Ps. 84:4)

How blessed is the man whose strength is in You.
(Ps. 84:5)

How blessed are those who keep justice,
Who practice righteousness at all times!
(Ps. 106:3)

How blessed is the man who fears the Lord,
Who greatly delights in His commandments.
(Ps. 112:1)

How blessed are those who observe His testimonies,
Who seek Him with all their heart.
(Ps. 119:2)

Now therefore, O sons, listen to me [wisdom],
For blessed are they who keep my ways.
(Prov. 8:32)

Blessed is the man who listens to me [wisdom],
Watching daily at my gates,
Waiting at my doorposts.
(Prov. 8:34)

> Blessed are the poor in spirit, for theirs is the kingdom of heaven.
> Blessed are those who mourn, for they shall be comforted.
> Blessed are the gentle, for they shall inherit the earth.
> Blessed are those who hunger and thirst for righteousness, for they shall be satisfied.
> Blessed are the merciful, for they shall receive mercy.
> Blessed are the pure in heart, for they shall see God.
> Blessed are the peacemakers, for they shall be called sons of God.
> Blessed are those who have been persecuted for the sake of righteousness, for theirs is the kingdom of heaven.
> Blessed are you when people insult you and persecute you, and falsely say all kinds of evil against you because of Me. Rejoice and be glad, for your reward in heaven is great; for in the same way they persecuted the prophets who were before you. (Matt. 5:3–12)

> Jesus said to him, "Because you have seen Me, have you believed? Blessed are they who did not see, and yet believed." (John 20:29)

> Blessed is a man who perseveres under trial; for once he has been approved, he will receive the crown of life which the Lord has promised to those who love Him. (James 1:12)

> But even if you should suffer for the sake of righteousness, you are blessed. . . . If you are reviled for the name of Christ, you are blessed, because the Spirit of glory and of God rests on you. (1 Pet. 3:14; 4:14)

But the most startling pronouncement of blessing in all of Scripture is found in verse 13. Amazingly, this second of seven beatitudes in Revelation (cf. 1:3; 16:15; 19:9; 20:6; 22:7, 14) pronounces blessing on the dead. Such a thought is incomprehensible to most people, who view death as something to be avoided. "Blessed are the living" would seem a more appropriate motto for most people.

The obvious question that the text provokes is "Why are these dead blessed?" The answer it presents is twofold: The dead in view here are blessed because of how they lived and because of how they died.

How They Lived

Here is the perseverance of the saints who keep the commandments of God and their faith in Jesus. (14:12)

The phrase **the perseverance of the saints** introduces one of the most important and most comforting doctrines in Scripture. It expresses the truth that all those whom God has elected, called, and justified will never lose their faith, but will persevere in it until death. That reality provides assurance, hope, and joy to every true believer in Jesus Christ and brings an end to fear and doubt. It also reveals that believers' deaths are blessed because death ushers them into the glories of heaven.

Some refer to this as the doctrine of eternal security; others dub it the "once saved, always saved" teaching. While those definitions are accurate, they do not express this truth as clearly as the biblical phrase **the perseverance of the saints.** That statement emphasizes the reality that God keeps His own saints by sustaining their faith to the very end, no matter what occurs. True saving faith in its very nature is eternal and cannot be lost or destroyed.

The persevering character of saving faith is never more clearly and powerfully seen than in this passage. No group of believers ever has faced or ever will face stronger assaults on their faith than the Tribulation saints. This large group of believers (7:9, 13–14) will include both Gentiles (7:9) and Jews (12:17). They will be saved through the ministries of the two witnesses (11:3–13) and the 144,000 (7:1–8; 14:1–5). The Tribulation believers will endure the most intense persecution in human history. In Matthew 24:21 Jesus described this period as a time of "great tribulation, such as has not occurred since the beginning of the world until now, nor ever will." So terrible will the conditions be that "unless those days had been cut short, no life would have been saved; but for the sake of the elect those days will be cut short" (Matt. 24:22). God will set a limit on the Tribulation so that the elect will not suffer more than they can bear (cf. 1 Cor. 10:13). There is no stronger evidence that saving faith perseveres than the reality that the most tested believers in history will maintain their saving faith until the end.

The encouraging message of verses 12 and 13 forms a brief respite in the revelation of God's judgment against unbelievers. Verses 9–11 painted a terrifying picture of the damnation of the unrepentant worshipers of Antichrist. The narrative of God's judgment resumes in verse 14 and continues through the rest of the chapter. In the midst of all that carnage, with unprecedented disasters taking place all around them, the Tribulation saints will remain faithful and loyal to Christ. Even the prospect of martyrdom will not persuade them to abandon their faith. Their persevering loyalty to Jesus Christ forms the bright spot in the darkness of the Tribulation. It also answers the question of the unbelieving world, "The great day of [God the Father's and Christ's] wrath has come, and who is able to stand?" (6:17). The Tribulation believers will stand firm until the end.

The biblical doctrine of the perseverance of the saints rests on five solid, unshakable pillars. The first proof of the truthfulness of that doctrine is that God's promise established it. In Psalm 37:23–34, David expressed the truth that God holds on to His own:

> The steps of a man are established by the Lord,
> And He delights in his way.
> When he falls, he shall not be hurled headlong,
> Because the Lord is the One who holds his hand.
> I have been young and now I am old,
> Yet I have not seen the righteous forsaken
> Or his descendants begging bread.
> All day long he is gracious and lends,
> And his descendants are a blessing.
>
> Depart from evil and do good,
> So you will abide forever.
> For the Lord loves justice
> And does not forsake His godly ones;
> They are preserved forever,
> But the descendants of the wicked will be cut off.
> The righteous will inherit the land
> And dwell in it forever.
> The mouth of the righteous utters wisdom,
> And his tongue speaks justice.
> The law of his God is in his heart;
> His steps do not slip.
> The wicked spies upon the righteous
> And seeks to kill him.
> The Lord will not leave him in his hand
> Or let him be condemned when he is judged.
> Wait for the Lord and keep His way,
> And He will exalt you to inherit the land;
> When the wicked are cut off, you will see it.

Isaiah also celebrated this great truth:

> But now, thus says the Lord, your Creator, O Jacob,
> And He who formed you, O Israel,
> "Do not fear, for I have redeemed you;
> I have called you by name; you are Mine!
> When you pass through the waters, I will be with you;
> And through the rivers, they will not overflow you.
> When you walk through the fire, you will not be scorched,
> Nor will the flame burn you.
> For I am the Lord your God,
> The Holy One of Israel, your Savior;
> I have given Egypt as your ransom,
> Cush and Seba in your place.
> Since you are precious in My sight,
> Since you are honored and I love you,

I will give other men in your place and other peoples in exchange
for your life.
Do not fear, for I am with you;
I will bring your offspring from the east,
And gather you from the west.
I will say to the north, 'Give them up!'
And to the south, 'Do not hold them back.'
Bring My sons from afar
And My daughters from the ends of the earth,
Everyone who is called by My name,
And whom I have created for My glory,
Whom I have formed, even whom I have made."
(Isa. 43:1–7)

Israel has been saved by the Lord
With an everlasting salvation;
You will not be put to shame or humiliated
To all eternity.
(Isa. 45:17)

But Zion said, "The Lord has forsaken me,
And the Lord has forgotten me."
"Can a woman forget her nursing child
And have no compassion on the son of her womb?
Even these may forget, but I will not forget you.
Behold, I have inscribed you on the palms of My hands;
Your walls are continually before Me."
(Isa. 49:14–16)

"Lift up your eyes to the sky,
Then look to the earth beneath;
For the sky will vanish like smoke,
And the earth will wear out like a garment
And its inhabitants will die in like manner;
But My salvation shall be forever,
And My righteousness shall not wane."
(Isa. 51:6)

God also promises in the New Testament that salvation is eternal:

"For God so loved the world, that He gave His only begotten Son, that whoever believes in Him shall not perish, but have eternal life." (John 3:16)

"He who believes in the Son has eternal life." (John 3:36)

> "Truly, truly, I say to you, he who hears My word, and believes Him who sent Me, has eternal life, and does not come into judgment, but has passed out of death into life." (John 5:24)

> This is the promise which He Himself made to us: eternal life. (1 John 2:25)

A second truth upon which the doctrine of the perseverance of the saints rests is that God's purpose assures it. Jesus declared:

> "All that the Father gives Me will come to Me, and the one who comes to Me I will certainly not cast out. For I have come down from heaven, not to do My own will, but the will of Him who sent Me. This is the will of Him who sent Me, that of all that He has given Me I lose nothing, but raise it up on the last day. For this is the will of My Father, that everyone who beholds the Son and believes in Him will have eternal life, and I Myself will raise him up on the last day." (John 6:37–40)

God's promise rests upon His sovereign purpose or plan; here it is plainly stated that His will is that none of those whom He gives to His Son should be lost. In John 6:44 Jesus reinforced that truth, noting that "No one can come to Me unless the Father who sent Me draws him; and I will raise him up on the last day." All who come to saving faith in Jesus will be part of the "resurrection of life" (John 5:29); none will be lost. Romans 8:28–30 also teaches that there are no breaks in the process of salvation:

> And we know that God causes all things to work together for good to those who love God, to those who are called according to His purpose. For those whom He foreknew, He also predestined to become conformed to the image of His Son, so that He would be the firstborn among many brethren; and these whom He predestined, He also called; and these whom He called, He also justified; and these whom He justified, He also glorified.

All those whom God foreknew are predestined, called, justified, and glorified. From its beginning in eternity past to its conclusion in eternity future, the salvation process is an uninterrupted continuity; there is no possibility of anyone dropping out along the way. "For I am confident of this very thing," wrote Paul, "that He who began a good work in you will perfect it until the day of Christ Jesus" (Phil. 1:6; cf. 1 Cor. 1:7–9). In Romans 11:29 he added, "The gifts and the calling of God are irrevocable." What God purposes, He will carry out.

A third proof of the doctrine of the perseverance of the saints is that God's power guarantees it. God's power that transforms believers into new creations (2 Cor. 5:17) will sustain them, so that they can never be lost. In John 10:27–29 Jesus stated emphatically that God's power keeps believers secure: "My sheep hear My voice, and I know them, and they follow Me; and I give eternal life to them, and they will never perish; and no one will snatch them out of My hand. My Father, who has given them to Me, is greater than all; and no one is able to snatch them out of the Father's hand." Neither Satan, nor all the forces of hell can take a believer away from God, "because greater is He who is in you than he who is in the world" (1 John 4:4). To the Thessalonians Paul wrote, "But the Lord is faithful, and He will strengthen and protect you from the evil one" (2 Thess. 3:3). The author of Hebrews wrote, "Therefore He is able also to save forever those who draw near to God through Him, since He always lives to make intercession for them" (Heb. 7:25). Jude's epistle closes with the benediction, "Now to Him who is able to keep you from stumbling, and to make you stand in the presence of His glory blameless with great joy" (Jude 24). Along with His promise and His purpose, God has the power to keep believers secure.

The saints will also persevere because salvation is wholly by God's grace (Eph. 2:8–9). Since we did nothing to earn it, so we can do nothing to keep it. As he concluded his first epistle to the Thessalonians, Paul pronounced the following benediction on them: "Now may the God of peace Himself sanctify you entirely; and may your spirit and soul and body be preserved complete, without blame at the coming of our Lord Jesus Christ" (1 Thess. 5:23). Then the apostle explained how the Thessalonians' safekeeping would be accomplished: "Faithful is He who calls you, and He also will bring it to pass" (v. 24).

To argue that saving faith can die, or be lost, contradicts God's promise, purpose, power, and grace. Believers have been "born again to a living hope through the resurrection of Jesus Christ from the dead, to obtain an inheritance which is imperishable and undefiled and will not fade away, reserved in heaven for [them], who are protected by the power of God through faith for a salvation ready to be revealed in the last time" (1 Pet. 1:3–5). God guarantees that believers will persevere.

The repeated biblical exhortations to perseverance make it clear, however, that believers have a responsibility to persevere. "You will be hated by all because of My name," warned Jesus, "but it is the one who has endured to the end who will be saved" (Matt. 10:22). In Matthew 24:13 He added, "The one who endures to the end, he will be saved." Arriving in Antioch, Barnabas "began to encourage them all with resolute heart to remain true to the Lord" (Acts 11:23). Later, Paul and Barnabas spent time at Lystra, Iconium, and Antioch "strengthening the souls of the disciples, encouraging them to continue in the faith, and saying, 'Through many tribulations we must enter the kingdom of God'" (Acts 14:22). To the

Romans Paul wrote, "[God] will render to each person according to his deeds: to those who by perseverance in doing good seek for glory and honor and immortality, eternal life; but to those who are selfishly ambitious and do not obey the truth, but obey unrighteousness, wrath and indignation" (Rom. 2:6–8). Colossians 1:21–23 clearly reveals God's part in salvation and man's responsibility to persevere. Christians are redeemed, "although [they] were formerly alienated and hostile in mind, engaged in evil deeds" because God "has now reconciled [them] in [Christ's] fleshly body through death, in order to present [them] before Him holy and blameless and beyond reproach." But that does not obviate believers' responsibility to "continue in the faith firmly established and steadfast, and not moved away from the hope of the gospel that [they] have heard." In a similar vein the author of Hebrews wrote, "For we have become partakers of Christ, if we hold fast the beginning of our assurance firm until the end" (Heb. 3:14). The apostle John described Christians as overcomers (2:7, 11, 17, 26–28; 3:5, 12, 21; 1 John 5:4–5).

Believers persevere by faith (1 Pet. 1:5; 1 John 5:4–5), fear (Jer. 32:40), love (Eph. 6:24), obedience (John 8:31), and by turning away from sin (2 Cor. 7:1; cf. Rom. 6:12–14). All those means are granted by God—who then exhorts believers to manifest them in their lives. The doctrine of perseverance must not be misconstrued as teaching that believers will be eternally saved regardless of their belief or behavior. What it does teach is that, as noted above, true believers will continue in the faith. Justification will be followed by sanctification that leads to glorification.

That raises the question about those who once professed faith in Christ, but then fell away. The Bible teaches that such people were never saved in the first place. Explaining the parable of the soils to His disciples, Jesus said of the rocky soil, "These are the ones on whom seed was sown on the rocky places, who, when they hear the word, immediately receive it with joy; and they have no firm root in themselves, but are only temporary; then, when affliction or persecution arises because of the word, immediately they fall away" (Mark 4:16–17). Jesus warned in John 15:6: "If anyone does not abide in Me, he is thrown away as a branch and dries up; and they gather them, and cast them into the fire and they are burned." The author of Hebrews noted that "in the case of those who have once been enlightened and have tasted of the heavenly gift and have been made partakers of the Holy Spirit, and have tasted the good word of God and the powers of the age to come, and then have fallen away, it is impossible to renew them again to repentance, since they again crucify to themselves the Son of God and put Him to open shame" (Heb. 6:4–6). In Hebrews 10:29 he asked rhetorically, "How much severer punishment do you think he will deserve who has trampled under foot the Son of God, and has regarded as unclean the blood of the covenant by which he was sanctified, and has insulted the Spirit of grace?" "They went out from us," declared the apostle John, "but they were not really of us; for if they had been of us, they would have remained with us; but they went out, so that it would be shown that they all are not of us" (1 John 2:19).

A scene from John Bunyan's *Pilgrim's Progress* illustrates the fact that true Christians persevere under trials, while false believers fall away from the faith:

> I saw then in my dream, that when CHRISTIAN was got to the borders of the shadow of death, there met him two men, children of them that brought up an evil report of the good land, making haste to go back (Numb. 13:32), to whom CHRISTIAN spake as follows:
>
> *Chr.* Whither are you going?
> *The Two Men.* They said, "Back, back; and we would have you do so too, if either life or peace is prized by you."
> *Chr.* "Why, what is the matter?" said CHRISTIAN.
> *Men.* "Matter!" said they; "we were going that way as you are going, and went as far as we durst; and indeed we were almost past coming back, for had we gone a little farther, we had not been here to bring the news to thee."
> *Chr.* "But what have you met with?" said CHRISTIAN.
> *Men.* Why, we were almost in the Valley of the Shadow of Death (Psa. 44:19; 107:10); but that by good hap we looked before us and saw the danger before we came to it.
> *Chr.* "But what have you seen?" said CHRISTIAN.
> *Men.* Seen! Why the valley itself, which is as dark as pitch. We also saw there the hobgoblins, satyrs, and dragons of the pit; we heard also in that valley a continual howling and yelling, as of a people under unutterable misery, who there sat bound in affliction and irons; and over that valley hangs the discouraging clouds of confusion; death also doth always spread his wings over it; in a word, it is every whit dreadful, being utterly without order (Job 3:5; 10:22).
> *Chr.* Then said CHRISTIAN, "I perceive not yet, by what you have said, but that this is my way to the desired haven."
> *Men.* "Be it thy way, we will not choose it for ours."
>
> So they parted, and CHRISTIAN went on his way; but still with his sword drawn in his hand, for fear lest he should be assaulted. ([Reprint, Grand Rapids: Zondervan, 1967], 61–62)

The perseverance of the Tribulation **saints** will be evident because they will **keep the commandments of God.** That genuine saving faith will result in such obedience is the clear teaching of Scripture. In John 8:31 Jesus said, "If you abide in My word, then you are truly disciples of Mine." In John 14:21 Jesus defined those who truly love Him as those who obey Him: "He who has My commandments and keeps them is the one who loves Me; and he who loves Me will be loved by My Father, and I will love him and will disclose Myself to him." In John 15:14 He added, "You are My friends if you do what I command you." In Luke 6:46 Jesus asked, "Why do you call Me, 'Lord, Lord,' and do not do what I say?" The apostle John wrote, "This is the love of God, that we keep His commandments" (1 John 5:3).

A second way the Tribulation saints will manifest perseverance will be through **their faith in Jesus.** They will remain loyal, even under the tyrannical reign of Antichrist. Even the threat of execution (13:15) will not cause them to abandon their faith in the Lord Jesus Christ. Like the heroes of faith listed in Hebrews 11, they will maintain their testimony until the end—even if that end is a horrifying martyrdom.

Why are these faithful dead believers blessed? Because they lived pure, noble, purposeful, obedient, rich, joyous, exemplary lives. They lived life to the fullest in faith and obedience to God. Even if there were no heaven, that would still be the best way to live. But there is heaven to follow this life for God's people; therefore the deaths of the Tribulation saints will also be eternally blessed.

How They Died

And I heard a voice from heaven, saying, "Write, 'Blessed are the dead who die in the Lord from now on!'" "Yes," says the Spirit, "so that they may rest from their labors, for their deeds follow with them." (14:13)

Having lived with perseverance, the Tribulation saints will die with promise. This is the sixth time in Revelation that John **heard a voice from heaven** (cf. 10:4, 8; 11:12; 12:10; 14:2); he will hear such a voice three more times (18:4; 19:5; 21:3). The **voice** (probably that of God, not an angel) commanded John to write. Twelve times in Revelation John is told to **write** (cf. 1:11, 19; 2:1, 8, 12, 18; 3:1, 7, 14; 19:9; 21:5); the apostle was under a divine mandate to record the visions he saw.

The heavenly **voice** ordered John to write, **"Blessed are the dead who die in the Lord."** That includes martyrs such as Antipas (2:13), those seen underneath the heavenly altar (6:9–11), and the "great multitude which no one could count, from every nation and all tribes and peoples and tongues, standing before the throne and before the Lamb, clothed in white robes . . . the ones who come out of the great tribulation, and they have washed their robes and made them white in the blood of the Lamb" (Rev. 7:9, 14). These martyrs are blessed not only because they lived life to the fullest in obedience and trust, but also because they **died in the Lord.** They will experience in death the fullest reward, because "Precious in the sight of the Lord is the death of His godly ones" (Ps. 116:15). With Paul, they will be able to cry out triumphantly, "O death, where is your victory? O death, where is your sting?" (1 Cor. 15:55).

The **voice** informed John that not only those already dead, but also those who die **from now on** are blessed. The martyred believers from that point until the end of the Tribulation will have nothing to fear. Their deaths, too, will be blessed.

The Holy **Spirit** is quoted directly in Revelation only here and in 22:17. His emphatic **"Yes"** (the Greek particle *nai* indicates strong affirmation) shows that He agrees with the heavenly voice that the dead are blessed. As their sustainer and comforter, who loves them and is grieved by their pain, the Holy Spirit longs to see that suffering end. He adds two further reasons for the Tribulation martyrs' blessedness.

First, the Spirit declares them blessed because **they may rest from their labors.** *Kopos* describes hard, difficult, exhausting toil. It can also refer to bother, annoyance, or trouble. Certainly the Tribulation saints will experience the whole gamut of the word's meanings. They will be filled with deep sorrow as they watch those they love—children, parents, spouses, and friends—suffer torment and death. Their lives will be a hard, difficult, dangerous struggle for survival. Not having the mark of the beast, they will be excluded from society, be unable to buy or sell, and live lives on the run as hunted fugitives. Death, granting **rest** from all the difficulties and sorrows of their lives, will come as a welcome relief. In stark contrast are the damned, who will know not a moment's rest throughout all eternity (14:11).

The Holy Spirit also pronounces the Tribulation martyrs blessed because **their deeds follow with them.** *Erga* (**deeds**) refers to their service to the Lord. When these believers go to heaven, the record of their diligent labor will **follow** along **with them.** The Bible teaches that God will reward believers in heaven for their earthly service to Him. Hebrews 6:10 reads, "For God is not unjust so as to forget your work and the love which you have shown toward His name, in having ministered and in still ministering to the saints." Facing imminent execution, Paul triumphantly declared, "I have fought the good fight, I have finished the course, I have kept the faith; in the future there is laid up for me the crown of righteousness, which the Lord, the righteous Judge, will award to me on that day; and not only to me, but also to all who have loved His appearing" (2 Tim. 4:7–8). First Corinthians 3:12–14 describes God's testing of believers' works. The "gold, silver, [and] precious stones" (v. 12) will be preserved, while the "wood, hay, [and] straw" (v. 12) will be destroyed. What is left will form the basis for believers' rewards (vv. 13–14).

The dead who have lived in obedience and trust will be blessed with rest and reward after they die. Those who live now for wanton pleasure are dead even while they live (1 Tim. 5:6). Being "dead in [their] trespasses and sins" (Eph. 2:1), they face the horror of eternal damnation in hell. The sobering truth is that the choices people make in this life will irreversibly chart the course of their eternal destinies. A Christless eternity of unrelieved torment or the blissful rest and reward of heaven: that is the choice faced by every person.

The Final Reaping of the Earth (Revelation 14:14–20)

9

Then I looked, and behold, a white cloud, and sitting on the cloud was one like a son of man, having a golden crown on His head and a sharp sickle in His hand. And another angel came out of the temple, crying out with a loud voice to Him who sat on the cloud, "Put in your sickle and reap, for the hour to reap has come, because the harvest of the earth is ripe." Then He who sat on the cloud swung His sickle over the earth, and the earth was reaped.

And another angel came out of the temple which is in heaven, and he also had a sharp sickle. Then another angel, the one who has power over fire, came out from the altar; and he called with a loud voice to him who had the sharp sickle, saying, "Put in your sharp sickle and gather the clusters from the vine of the earth, because her grapes are ripe." So the angel swung his sickle to the earth and gathered the clusters from the vine of the earth, and threw them into the great wine press of the wrath of God. And the wine press was trodden outside the city, and blood came out from the wine press, up to the horses' bridles, for a distance of two hundred miles. (14:14–20)

Jesus' first coming was one of humiliation, a time when He, "although He existed in the form of God, did not regard equality with God a thing to be grasped, but emptied Himself, taking the form of a bond-servant, and being made in the likeness of men. Being found in appearance as a man, He humbled Himself by becoming obedient to the point of death, even death on a cross" (Phil. 2:6–8).

Jesus came the first time as a servant; He will return as the sovereign King. In His first coming, He came in humility; in His second coming, He will come in majesty and splendor. The first time He came to earth, "the Son of Man [came] to seek and to save that which was lost" (Luke 19:10); when He returns, it will be to "judge the living and the dead" (2 Tim. 4:1). Jesus came the first time as the sower; He will come again as the reaper.

God's final judgment on the earth is the theme of 14:6–11. Verses 12 and 13 form a brief respite, presenting the encouraging, comforting truth of the perseverance of the saints. After that brief rest to encourage the faithful, the theme of divine wrath resumes in verses 14–20. The judgment introduced in these verses will take place at the worst time in human history, the Great Tribulation (Matt. 24:21–22). After years of enduring Antichrist's oppressive rule, demonic assaults, and the terrifying, devastating, staccato judgments of God, people will wearily hope that things are about to get better. It will seem as if life couldn't possibly get any worse, but it will. Cataclysmic "Day of the Lord" judgment is about to fall on Satan, his demon hordes, Antichrist, and all the wicked, unrepentant people of the world. That judgment is depicted in this passage as the final reaping of the earth. In an unprecedented holocaust, the full fury of the Lord Jesus Christ will be released in devastating judgment.

The theme of coming judgment is certainly not unique to Revelation. Even before the Messiah preached the good news of the gospel, His forerunner proclaimed the bad news of judgment. In Matthew 3:7 John the Baptist said, "You brood of vipers, who warned you to flee from the wrath to come?" During His earthly ministry, Jesus repeatedly warned of the coming day of judgment (e.g., Matt. 10:15; 11:22, 24; 12:36, 41–42; John 5:28–29). Paul wrote, "For the wrath of God is revealed from heaven against all ungodliness and unrighteousness of men who suppress the truth in unrighteousness.... But because of your stubbornness and unrepentant heart you are storing up wrath for yourself in the day of wrath and revelation of the righteous judgment of God, who will render to each person according to his deeds" (Rom. 1:18; 2:5–6). In 2 Thessalonians 1:6–9 the apostle added, "For after all it is only just for God to repay with affliction those who afflict you, and to give relief to you who are afflicted and to us as well when the Lord Jesus will be revealed from heaven with His mighty angels in flaming fire, dealing out retribution to those who do not know God and to those who do not obey the gospel of our Lord Jesus. These will pay the penalty of eternal destruction, away from the presence of the Lord and from the glory of His power." The writer of Hebrews warned, "For if we go on sinning willfully after receiving the knowledge of the truth, there no longer remains a sacrifice for sins, but a terrifying expectation of judgment and the fury of a fire which will consume the adversaries" (Heb. 10:26–27). Peter also wrote of the coming judgment, warning that "the Lord knows how to rescue the godly from temptation, and to keep the unrighteous under punishment for the day of judgment. . . . by His word the present heavens and earth are being reserved for fire, kept for the day of judgment and destruction of ungodly men" (2 Pet. 2:9; 3:7).

The Old Testament, too, speaks of God's eschatological judgment on the world. In Isaiah it is written:

> Thus I will punish the world for its evil
> And the wicked for their iniquity;
> I will also put an end to the arrogance of the proud
> And abase the haughtiness of the ruthless.
> I will make mortal man scarcer than pure gold
> And mankind than the gold of Ophir.
> Therefore I will make the heavens tremble,
> And the earth will be shaken from its place
> At the fury of the Lord of hosts
> In the day of His burning anger.
>
> (Isa. 13:11–13)

The coming judgment is also referred to in Isaiah 24:21–23:

> So it will happen in that day,
> That the Lord will punish the host of heaven on high,
> And the kings of the earth on earth.
> They will be gathered together
> Like prisoners in the dungeon,
> And will be confined in prison;
> And after many days they will be punished.
> Then the moon will be abashed and the sun ashamed,
> For the Lord of hosts will reign on Mount Zion and in Jerusalem,
> And His glory will be before His elders.

Two Old Testament passages present striking parallels with Revelation 14. Isaiah 63:1–6 records a fascinating soliloquy of the Messiah as He comes to execute the bloody final judgment on the unbelieving world:

> Who is this who comes from Edom,
> With garments of glowing colors from Bozrah,
> This One who is majestic in His apparel,
> Marching in the greatness of His strength?
> "It is I who speak in righteousness, mighty to save."
> Why is Your apparel red,
> And Your garments like the one who treads in the wine press?
> "I have trodden the wine trough alone,
> And from the peoples there was no man with Me.
> I also trod them in My anger
> And trampled them in My wrath;
> And their lifeblood is sprinkled on My garments,
> And I stained all My raiment.
> For the day of vengeance was in My heart,
> And My year of redemption has come.
> I looked, and there was no one to help,
> And I was astonished and there was no one to uphold;
> So My own arm brought salvation to Me,
> And My wrath upheld Me.
> I trod down the peoples in My anger
> And made them drunk in My wrath,
> And I poured out their lifeblood on the earth."

This passage, like Revelation 14:19–20, uses the metaphor of trampling grapes in a winepress to depict the devastation of God's final judgment.

The prophet Joel recorded the devastation caused in Israel by drought, fire, and a massive invasion of locusts (Joel 1:1–2:11). Then the prophet used those temporal judgments to warn of the even more devastating judgment of the Day of the Lord (2:18–3:21). In Joel 3:12–13 that judgment is described using the same imagery found in Revelation 14:

> Let the nations be aroused
> And come up to the valley of Jehoshaphat,
> For there I will sit to judge
> All the surrounding nations.
> Put in the sickle, for the harvest is ripe.
> Come, tread, for the wine press is full;
> The vats overflow, for their wickedness is great.

Joel, like Isaiah, depicted God's future judgment of the wicked, in the imagery of a winepress and of a harvest.

The Lord Jesus Christ also used the harvest analogy for judgment. In the parable of the tares He said, "Allow both to grow together until the harvest; and in the time of the harvest I will say to the reapers, 'First gather up the tares and bind them in bundles to burn them up; but gather the wheat into my barn'" (Matt. 13:30). Asked by His disciples to explain that parable Jesus said,

> "The enemy who sowed them is the devil, and the harvest is the end of the age; and the reapers are angels. So just as the tares are gathered up and burned with fire, so shall it be at the end of the age. The Son of Man will send forth His angels, and they will gather out of His kingdom all stumbling blocks, and those who commit lawlessness, and will throw them into the furnace of fire; in that place there will be weeping and gnashing of teeth." (Matt. 13:39–42)

So Joel, Isaiah, and the Lord Jesus Christ all spoke of a coming harvest of divine wrath when the Messiah will execute final judgment. That final outpouring of the judgmental fury of the Lamb is the theme of this chapter's text.

This passage pictures the final harvest of divine wrath in two agricultural motifs: the grain harvest (vv. 14–16) and the grape harvest (vv. 17–20), raising the question as to why John recorded two visions of the same event. There are many depictions of this event by the prophets, including those mentioned above, so it is not unusual for John to record two visions of it. But there is also a specific situation at this point in the book of Revelation that suggests a purpose behind the repetition. As the Tribulation nears its climax, two main aspects of God's eschatological wrath remain to be poured out on the sinful world. The first aspect involves the seven bowl judgments (16:1–21), a rapid-fire sequence of frightening and deadly worldwide judgments that will destroy the final Babylon—the Antichrist's empire. The second aspect is the Battle of Armageddon, at which point Jesus Christ returns to judge and destroy His enemies (19:11–21).

The Grain Harvest

Then I looked, and behold, a white cloud, and sitting on the cloud was one like a son of man, having a golden crown on His head and a sharp sickle in His hand. And another angel came out of the temple, crying out with a loud voice to Him who sat on the cloud, "Put in your sickle and reap, for the hour to reap has come, because the harvest of the earth is ripe." Then He who sat on the cloud swung His sickle over the earth, and the earth was reaped. (14:14–16)

The grain harvest symbolizes the seven bowl judgments, the grape harvest the judgment of Armageddon. Both harvests involve a sickle and reaping, and both can be described by the same three points: the reaper, the ripeness, and the reaping.

THE REAPER

Then I looked, and behold, a white cloud, and sitting on the cloud was one like a son of man, having a golden crown on His head and a sharp sickle in His hand. (14:14)

The familiar phrase **I looked, and behold** often introduces a new and important subject in Revelation (cf. 4:1; 6:2, 5, 8; 7:9; 14:1). What caught John's attention was a **white cloud,** an image drawn from Daniel 7:13–14:

> "I kept looking in the night visions,
> And behold, with the clouds of heaven
> One like a Son of Man was coming,
> And He came up to the Ancient of Days
> And was presented before Him.
> And to Him was given dominion,
> Glory and a kingdom,
> That all the peoples, nations and men of every language
> Might serve Him.
> His dominion is an everlasting dominion
> Which will not pass away;
> And His kingdom is one
> Which will not be destroyed."

John saw **sitting on the cloud one like a son of man**—the Lord Jesus Christ, coming to establish His kingdom in fulfillment of Daniel's prophecy. The brilliant, white **cloud** symbolizes His glory and majesty (cf. 1:7; Matt. 17:5; 24:30; 26:64; Acts 1:9). He is ready to take the dominion of which Daniel prophesied; the reaper is **sitting** as He waits for the proper time to stand and begin the reaping. That reaping (the seven bowl judgments) will be followed by Christ's return to establish His kingdom.

The description of Christ as **one like a son of man** also derives from Daniel's prophecy (Dan. 7:13). It was the Lord's favorite title for Himself during His incarnation (e.g., Matt. 8:20; 9:6; 24:27, 30; Mark 2:10, 28; 8:31; 9:9; Luke 6:22; 7:34; 9:22; 12:8; John 5:27; 6:27, 62; 8:28), when He "emptied Himself, taking the form of a bond-servant, and [was] made in the likeness of men . . . [and was] found in appearance as a man" (Phil. 2:7–8). Why the text does not use the definite article and read *the* **son of man** is not clear. Yet the phrase also appears without a definite article in its only other appearance in Revelation (1:13). Perhaps the article was omitted to strengthen the allusion to Daniel 7:13. In any case, there is no doubt that the **one like a son of man** is the Lord Jesus Christ. This is the last time Scripture refers to Him by that title, and it presents a marked contrast with the first time the New Testament calls Him the **son of man.** Then He had nothing, not even a place to lay His head (Matt. 8:20); now He is about to take possession of the entire earth.

The reaper is further described as **having a golden crown on His head.** This **crown** is not the *diadēma* worn by a king (cf. 19:12), but the *stephanos* worn by victors in war or athletic events; it is the crown of triumph (cf. 2:10; 1 Cor. 9:25; 1 Thess. 2:19; 2 Tim. 4:8; James 1:12; 1 Pet. 5:4). It pictures the Son of Man not in His identity as the sovereign ruler, but as the triumphant conqueror victorious over all His enemies (cf. Matt. 24:30).

The reaper also had **a sharp sickle in His hand.** A **sickle** was a long, curved, razor-sharp iron blade attached to a long, broomsticklike wooden handle. Sickles were used to harvest grain; as they were held with both hands spread apart and swept back and forth, their sharp blades would cut off the grain stalks at ground level. The picture is of the Lord Jesus Christ mowing down His enemies like a harvester cutting grain.

THE RIPENESS

And another angel came out of the temple, crying out with a loud voice to Him who sat on the cloud, "Put in your sickle and reap, for the hour to reap has come, because the harvest of the earth is ripe." (14:15)

Another angel, the fourth one mentioned in this chapter (cf. vv. 6, 8, 9), appears on the scene. The first three angels proclaimed that judgment was coming; the fourth brings the command to execute it. This angel **came out of the** heavenly (cf. v. 17) **temple,** from before the throne of God. In a **loud voice** conveying urgency, power, and the authority delegated to him from God, the angel cried out **to Him who sat on the cloud, "Put in your sickle and reap, for the hour to reap has come, because the harvest of the earth is ripe."** He delivers the message from God the Father to the Son of Man that it is time for Him to move in judgment. God's anger has reached its limit, and His wrath is poured out. The time for grace is over, and there will be no more delaying the harvest of judgment. The Son can now exercise the right to judge that the Father has delegated to Him (John 5:22, 27; Acts 10:42; 17:31) because the **earth is ripe** for judgment. In fact, the verb translated **is ripe** actually means "dried up," "withered," "overripe," or "rotten." The grain (the earth) pictured here has passed the point of any usefulness and is fit only to be "gathered up and burned with fire" (Matt. 13:40).

THE REAPING

Then He who sat on the cloud swung His sickle over the earth, and the earth was reaped. (14:16)

Here is one of the most tragic and sobering statements in all of Scripture. Simply, and without fanfare, it records the executing of divine judgment. The frightening details of that judgment are unfolded in chapter 16: loathsome and malignant sores on the worshipers of Antichrist (v. 2), the death of all life in the world's oceans (v. 3), the turning of the world's rivers and springs of water into blood (v. 4), the intensifying of the sun's heat until it scorches people (v. 8), painful darkness over all of Antichrist's kingdom (v. 10), the drying up of the Euphrates River in preparation for a massive invasion by the kings of the east (v. 12), and the most powerful and destructive earthquake in history (v. 18). Those seven rapid-fire bowl judgments mark the first phase of the final reaping of the earth.

THE GRAPE HARVEST

And another angel came out of the temple which is in heaven, and he also had a sharp sickle. Then another angel, the one who has power over fire, came out from the altar; and he called with a loud voice to him who had the sharp sickle, saying, "Put in your sharp sickle and gather the clusters from the vine of the earth, because her grapes are ripe." So the angel swung his sickle to the earth and gathered the clusters from the vine of the earth, and threw them into the great wine press of the wrath of God. And the wine press was trodden outside the city, and blood came out from the wine press, up to the horses' bridles, for a distance of two hundred miles. (14:17–20)

The vision of the grain harvest is followed by the vision of the grape harvest, which does not speak of the bowl judgments but of the judgment that takes place at the battle of Armageddon. The vintage judgment is more dramatic because of the imagery of the winepress. Like the vision of the grain harvest, the grape harvest can be described in three points: the reaper, the ripeness, and the reaping.

THE REAPER

And another angel came out of the temple which is in heaven, and he also had a sharp sickle. (14:17)

The reaper in this vision is not the Son of Man, as in the grain harvest, but an **angel,** the fifth one mentioned in chapter 14. Like the fourth angel (v. 15), he **came out of the temple which is in heaven.** Like Christ in the previous vision, **he also had a sharp sickle.** Angels have played a prominent role in Revelation up to this point, summoning the four horsemen, sounding the seven trumpets, and defeating Satan and his demon hosts. Angels will also pour out the seven bowl judgments in chapter 16, announce the Battle of Armageddon (19:17), and bind Satan (20:1–3). That an angel is pictured in this vision as the reaper, then, is not surprising. The Son of Man will be assisted by holy angels in His final judgment (cf. Matt. 13:39, 49; 2 Thess. 1:7).

THE RIPENESS

Then another angel, the one who has power over fire, came out from the altar; and he called with a loud voice to him who had the sharp sickle, saying, "Put in your sharp sickle and gather the clusters from the vine of the earth, because her grapes are ripe." (14:18)

As John watched, **another angel** appeared, the sixth one in the vision. He is given the interesting designation of the **one who has power over fire.** That title is closely connected with the fact that he **came out from the altar.** This heavenly **altar** has already been mentioned in 6:9–11:

> When the Lamb broke the fifth seal, I saw underneath the altar the souls of those who had been slain because of the word of God, and because of the testimony which they had maintained; and they cried out with a loud voice, saying, "How long, O Lord, holy and true, will You refrain from judging and avenging our blood on those who dwell on the earth?" And there was given to each of them a white robe; and they were told that they should rest for a little while longer, until the number of their fellow servants and their brethren who were to be killed even as they had been, would be completed also.

It most likely is emblematic of the Old Testament brass incense altar (Ex. 40:5), where twice daily priests burned incense to be offered in the Holy Place as a picture of the people's prayers, since the martyrs underneath it are viewed praying and prayer is associated with incense (5:8; Ps. 141:2; Luke 1:10). Those martyred saints are praying for God to take vengeance on their tormenters and send His wrath.

This altar is also described in 8:3–5:

> Another angel came and stood at the altar, holding a golden censer; and much incense was given to him, so that he might add it to the prayers of all the saints on the golden altar which was before the throne. And the smoke of the incense, with the prayers of the saints, went up before God out of the angel's hand. Then the angel took the censer and filled it with the fire of the altar, and threw it to the earth; and there followed peals of thunder and sounds and flashes of lightning and an earthquake.

Every morning and evening the Old Testament priests would take hot coals from the brazen altar (upon which sacrifices were offered) and bring them to the incense altar. There they would ignite the incense (Ex. 30:7–8; 2 Chron. 29:11), which would rise toward heaven, symbolizing the prayers of God's people (5:8). At that same time, the people outside would be praying (Luke 1:10).

That the angel had **power over** the altar's **fire** (the definite article is present in the Greek text, which literally reads "the fire") indicates that he had been ministering at the heavenly counterpart to the earthly incense altar. Unlike the angel in verse 17, this angel does not come from the throne of God, but from the **altar** associated with the prayers of the saints. His appearance means that the time had come for those prayers to be answered. The time had come for God to take fire associated with intercession and use it for the destruction of His enemies and the enemies of His people.

Leaving the altar, **he called with a loud,** urgent, commanding **voice to him who had the sharp sickle, saying, "Put in your sharp sickle and gather the clusters from the vine of the earth, because her grapes are ripe."** In answer to the saints' prayers, the time for the reaping of judgment comes. Unrepentant sinners are depicted as **clusters** of **grapes,** to be cut off by the reaper's **sharp sickle** from **the vine of the earth;** that is, from earthly existence. The word **ripe** is not the same Greek word used in verse 15. This word refers to something fully ripe and in its prime. It pictures earth's wicked, unregenerate people as bursting with the juice of wickedness and ready for the harvest of righteousness.

THE REAPING

So the angel swung his sickle to the earth and gathered the clusters from the vine of the earth, and threw them into the great wine press of the wrath of God. And the wine press was trodden outside the city, and blood came out from the wine press, up to the horses' bridles, for a distance of two hundred miles. (14:19–20)

What resulted when **the angel swung his sickle to the earth** was catastrophic. All the enemies of God who survive the seven bowl judgments will be **gathered** like grape **clusters from the vine of the earth** and flung **into the great wine press of the wrath of God.** A **wine press** consisted of two stone basins connected by a trough. Grapes would be trampled in the upper basin, and the juice would collect in the lower one. The splattering of the juice as the grapes are stomped vividly pictures the splattered blood of those who will be destroyed (cf. Isa. 63:3; Lam. 1:15; Joel 3:13).

The **wine press** will be **trodden outside the city,** as the Lord protects Jerusalem from the carnage of the Battle of Armageddon (cf. 11:2; Dan. 11:45; Zech. 14:1–4). That battle will take place in the north of Israel on the Plain of Esdraelon near Mount Megiddo (about sixty miles north of Jerusalem). It will rage the entire length of Israel as far south as Bozrah in Edom (cf. Isa. 63:1). Jerusalem will be spared to become the capital of Christ's kingdom.

The staggering, horrifying bloodbath of the Battle of Armageddon will be so widespread that **blood** will come out **from the wine press, up to the horses' bridles, for a distance of two hundred miles.** There will be millions of people engaged in the Battle of Armageddon, as all the nations gather together to fight against the Lord Jesus Christ. Still, it is difficult to imagine that they could produce a flow of blood **up to the horses' bridles** (about four feet deep) **for a distance of two hundred miles** (lit. "1,600 *stadia*"). A better interpretation, whether there are actual horses involved or not, sees this as hyperbole to suggest the slaughter in which blood will splatter into the air profusely along the whole length of the battle. When the slaughter reaches its peak, blood could flow deeply in troughs and streambeds.

Armageddon, as this passage indicates, will actually be a slaughter rather than a battle. When the Lord Jesus Christ returns, Antichrist, the false prophet, and all their human and demonic forces will be immediately destroyed. Revelation 19:11–21 describes the scene in detail:

> And I saw heaven opened, and behold, a white horse, and He who sat on it is called Faithful and True, and in righteousness He judges and wages war. His eyes are a flame of fire, and on His head are many

diadems; and He has a name written on Him which no one knows except Himself. He is clothed with a robe dipped in blood, and His name is called The Word of God. And the armies which are in heaven, clothed in fine linen, white and clean, were following Him on white horses. From His mouth comes a sharp sword, so that with it He may strike down the nations, and He will rule them with a rod of iron; and He treads the wine press of the fierce wrath of God, the Almighty. And on His robe and on His thigh He has a name written, "KING OF KINGS, AND LORD OF LORDS."

Then I saw an angel standing in the sun, and he cried out with a loud voice, saying to all the birds which fly in midheaven, "Come, assemble for the great supper of God, so that you may eat the flesh of kings and the flesh of commanders and the flesh of mighty men and the flesh of horses and of those who sit on them and the flesh of all men, both free men and slaves, and small and great."

And I saw the beast and the kings of the earth and their armies assembled to make war against Him who sat on the horse and against His army. And the beast was seized, and with him the false prophet who performed the signs in his presence, by which he deceived those who had received the mark of the beast and those who worshiped his image; these two were thrown alive into the lake of fire which burns with brimstone. And the rest were killed with the sword which came from the mouth of Him who sat on the horse, and all the birds were filled with their flesh.

Putting the scene in this chapter together with that of chapter 19, while the angel cuts the grapes, it is the Lord Jesus Christ who crushes out their lives.

Unregenerate humanity faces a frightening future, as this incredible scene indicates. Those who refuse to repent, even after repeated warnings, will learn firsthand the sobering truth that "it is a terrifying thing to fall into the hands of the living God" (Heb. 10:31). They would do well to heed the psalmist's admonition:

> Do homage to the Son, that He not become angry,
> and you perish in the way,
> For His wrath may soon be kindled.
> How blessed are all who take refuge in Him!
> (Ps. 2:12)

The Temple of Doom (Revelation 15:1–8)

10

Then I saw another sign in heaven, great and marvelous, seven angels who had seven plagues, which are the last, because in them the wrath of God is finished.

And I saw something like a sea of glass mixed with fire, and those who had been victorious over the beast and his image and the number of his name, standing on the sea of glass, holding harps of God. And they sang the song of Moses, the bond-servant of God, and the song of the Lamb, saying,

"Great and marvelous are Your works,
O Lord God, the Almighty;
Righteous and true are Your ways,
King of the nations!
Who will not fear, O Lord, and glorify Your name?
For You alone are holy;
For all the nations will come and worship before You,
For Your righteous acts have been revealed."

After these things I looked, and the temple of the tabernacle of testimony in heaven was opened, and the seven angels who had the seven plagues came out of the temple, clothed in linen, clean and bright, and girded around their chests with golden

sashes. Then one of the four living creatures gave to the seven angels seven golden bowls full of the wrath of God, who lives forever and ever. And the temple was filled with smoke from the glory of God and from His power; and no one was able to enter the temple until the seven plagues of the seven angels were finished. (15:1–8)

When they think about the future, people worry about many things. The destruction of the environment, global warming, political unrest and instability, terrorism, crime, economic and financial collapse, and the continual decline in moral values that destroy all relationships are all causes for concern. A further cause for anxiety is the sense of forlorn emptiness fostered by the anti-God philosophy of humanism. For those who believe there is no personal God, there is no one home in the universe, so they have nowhere to turn for ultimate answers, help, or meaning.

But what is truly frightening about the future is not any of those things; what should stop the heart of sinners is what God will do. God's judgmental anger and fury is a terrifying reality that looms just over the horizon of human history (cf. Pss. 96:13; 98:9; 110:6; Joel 3:2, 12; Acts 17:31; 2 Tim. 4:1). Because they willfully ignore that reality, people do not fear what they should fear. Jesus exhorted people to "fear Him who is able to destroy both soul and body in hell" (Matt. 10:28), because "God is a just judge, and God is angry with the wicked every day" (Ps. 7:11 NKJV). The writer of Hebrews adds, "It is a terrifying thing to fall into the hands of the living God" (Heb. 10:31).

Throughout human history God has poured out His wrath in judgment on sinners. Adam's sin in Eden brought the entire human race under judgment (Rom. 5:12). By Noah's day, people had become so wicked that God sent the cataclysmic judgment of the Flood to destroy the world (cf. Gen. 6:5–8). Only Noah and those with him on the ark were spared. Centuries of disobedience by the Jewish people ultimately led to their judgment, as first the northern kingdom of Israel and then the southern kingdom of Judah went into captivity.

God's wrath and judgment were the constant themes of the Old Testament prophets. They frequently warned of the coming Day of the Lord, whether an imminent historical judgment, or the final eschatological Day of the Lord. All the historical Day of the Lord judgments were previews of the last and most terrible Day of the Lord. (For more information about the Day of the Lord, see *Revelation 1–11*, The MacArthur New Testament Commentary [Chicago: Moody, 1999], 199ff.)

Isaiah warned of God's coming judgment:

> Wail, for the day of the Lord is near!
> It will come as destruction from the Almighty.
> Therefore all hands will fall limp,
> And every man's heart will melt.
> They will be terrified,
> Pains and anguish will take hold of them;
> They will writhe like a woman in labor,
> They will look at one another in astonishment,
> Their faces aflame.
> Behold, the day of the Lord is coming,
> Cruel, with fury and burning anger,
> To make the land a desolation;
> And He will exterminate its sinners from it.
> (Isa. 13:6–9)

Ezekiel described the Day of the Lord as "a time of doom for the nations" (Ezek. 30:3). Joel exclaimed, "Alas for the day! For the day of the Lord is near, and it will come as destruction from the Almighty" (Joel 1:15). Amos cried out to sinners in Israel, "Prepare to meet your God" (Amos 4:12). The prophet Zephaniah gave the following frightening description of the Day of the Lord:

> Near is the great day of the Lord,
> Near and coming very quickly;
> Listen, the day of the Lord!
> In it the warrior cries out bitterly.
> A day of wrath is that day,
> A day of trouble and distress,
> A day of destruction and desolation,
> A day of darkness and gloom,
> A day of clouds and thick darkness,
> A day of trumpet and battle cry
> Against the fortified cities
> And the high corner towers.
> I will bring distress on men
> So that they will walk like the blind,
> Because they have sinned against the Lord;
> And their blood will be poured out like dust
> And their flesh like dung.
> Neither their silver nor their gold
> Will be able to deliver them
> On the day of the Lord's wrath;
> And all the earth will be devoured
> In the fire of His jealousy,

> For He will make a complete end,
> Indeed a terrifying one,
> Of all the inhabitants of the earth.
> (Zeph. 1:14–18)

Job warned that "the wicked is reserved for the day of calamity; they will be led forth at the day of fury" (Job 21:30).

The historical outpourings of God's wrath fall into several categories. First is what might be called "sowing and reaping" wrath. People sin and suffer the logical consequences of that sin; "Those who plow iniquity and those who sow trouble harvest it" (Job 4:8; cf. Gal. 6:7–8). A second kind of wrath is cataclysmic wrath, when God sends massive, destructive judgment. That judgment may engulf the entire world, as it did with the Flood (Gen. 6–8), or a smaller region, as when God destroyed Sodom and Gomorrah (Gen. 19:1–29). Romans chapter 1 reveals God's wrath of abandonment when Paul three times used the phrase "God gave them over" to demonstrate God's judicial abandonment of sinners, removing restraint to the deadly consequences of their sinful choices (vv. 24, 26, 28). Hosea 4:17 declares, "Ephraim is joined to idols; let him alone." As previously noted, God's temporal judgment is poured out in historical Day of the Lord judgments. Finally, there is eternal wrath, God's eschatological wrath that will in the future be poured out on the whole world (1 Thess. 1:10; 5:9). The ultimate result of eternal wrath will be the sentencing of all unrepentant sinners to hell forever.

But throughout the entire historical outpouring of God's wrath, from Eden to the final explosion of His eschatological wrath, a strange paradox exists: God is busily working to save sinners from His own wrath. God's nature encompasses not only righteousness and holiness, but also grace and mercy. Even during the devastating judgments of the Tribulation, God will call sinners to salvation. He will do so using the 144,000 Jewish evangelists (7:2–8; 14:1–5), the two witnesses (11:3–13), a host of redeemed Gentiles and Jews (7:9–17), even an angel flying in the sky (14:6–7). As the outpouring of divine wrath escalates, God's evangelistic efforts will escalate as well. The result will be the greatest harvest of souls in human history (cf. 7:9). A redeemed Israel and souls from all the nations will be saved, many to survive the Tribulation and enter the millennial kingdom.

Chapters 15 and 16 present the specific phenomena of the final outpouring of God's wrath before Christ's return. That wrath is expressed by the effects of the seventh trumpet (11:15), which are the seven bowl judgments described in chapter 16. Chapter 15, the shortest in Revelation, forms an introduction to those rapid-fire judgments, but this chapter is not written for the specific purpose of defending God's wrath. Since

"His work is perfect [and] all His ways are just" (Deut. 32:4), God's actions need no defense. Nevertheless, several reasons for the outpouring of God's wrath can be discerned in this text.

A scene in **heaven** anticipates the bowl judgments, as it did in the case of the seal (chaps. 4–5) and trumpet (8:2–6) judgments. This is the third heavenly **sign** that John has seen in Revelation. In 12:1 he saw the sign of "a woman clothed with the sun, and the moon under her feet, and on her head a crown of twelve stars," while in 12:3 he saw the sign of "a great red dragon having seven heads and ten horns, and on his heads were seven diadems." The terms **great** and **marvelous** express the enormous importance of this sign as it contains the final outpouring of God's wrath on the wicked, unrepentant sinners of the earth.

The sign itself consists of **seven angels who had seven plagues.** The same beings who care for and minister to God's people (cf. Heb. 1:14) will bring God's wrath to the sinful world (cf. Matt. 13:37–42). *Plēgē* (**plagues**) literally means "a blow," or "a wound," and is so used in such passages as Luke 12:48; Acts 16:23, 33; 2 Corinthians 6:5, and 11:23. In 13:3 and 12 it describes the beast's fatal wound. Thus, the **seven plagues** are not really diseases or epidemics, but powerful, deadly blows (cf. 9:18–20; 11:6) that will strike the world with killing impact.

These **seven plagues** (the seven bowl judgments) **are the last** (and worst) plagues, **because in them the wrath of God is finished.** It is important to note that the fact that they are called the **last** implies that the preceding trumpet and seal judgments were also plagues expressing **the wrath of God.** God's wrath extends throughout the Tribulation and is not confined to a brief period at the very end, as some argue. That they are the **last** also indicates that the bowls come after the seals and trumpets in chronological sequence.

This tremendous outpouring of God's final judgmental fury was actually anticipated earlier in Revelation. It is the culmination of the "great day of [God the Father's and Jesus Christ's] wrath" (6:17). It is the "third woe" predicted in 11:14; the time of destruction (11:18); the unmixed wine of God's wrath (14:10); the final reaping of the earth (14:14–16); the final trampling of the grapes of God's wrath (14:17–20).

Thumos (**wrath**) is a strong word, describing rage, or a passionate outburst of anger. God's anger must be expressed against all unforgiven sin (cf. 14:8, 10). In 16:19 and 19:15 God's final **wrath** is called His "fierce wrath." The prophet Zephaniah wrote of this final outpouring of God's wrath in Zephaniah 3:8:

> "Therefore wait for Me," declares the Lord,
> "For the day when I rise up as a witness.
> Indeed, My decision is to gather nations,
> To assemble kingdoms,

To pour out on them My indignation,
All My burning anger;
For all the earth will be devoured
By the fire of My zeal."

It is true that, as Peter wrote, "The Lord . . . is patient toward you, not wishing for any to perish but for all to come to repentance" (2 Pet. 3:9). Yet those who refuse God's love, reject His grace, and scorn His mercy will inevitably face His wrath.

As this chapter unfolds, three motives for the final outpouring of God's wrath will become evident: the vengeance of God, the character of God, and the plan of God.

THE VENGEANCE OF GOD

And I saw something like a sea of glass mixed with fire, and those who had been victorious over the beast and his image and the number of his name, standing on the sea of glass, holding harps of God. (15:2)

In this remarkable vision, John **saw something like a sea of glass mixed with fire.** The sea was not an actual ocean, because in 21:1 he "saw a new heaven and a new earth; for the first heaven and the first earth passed away, and there is no longer any sea." What John saw was a transparent crystal platform before God's throne, shimmering and glistening like a tranquil, sunlit sea. John saw this same sealike crystal platform in 4:6: "Before the throne there was something like a sea of glass, like crystal." Moses also had a vision of it when he and the elders of Israel "saw the God of Israel; and under His feet there appeared to be a pavement of sapphire, as clear as the sky itself" (Ex. 24:10). Ezekiel described it as "something like an expanse, like the awesome gleam of crystal" (Ezek. 1:22).

But the tranquil beauty of the **sea** was **mixed with** the **fire** of God's judgment, which was about to be poured out on the earth. Those who reject God's grace and mercy face "a terrifying expectation of judgment and the fury of a fire which will consume the adversaries" (Heb. 10:27), because "our God is a consuming fire" (Heb. 12:29). Fire is frequently associated in Scripture with God's judgment (cf. Num. 11:1; 16:35; Deut. 9:3; Pss. 50:3; 97:3; Isa. 66:15; 2 Thess. 1:7–9; 2 Pet. 3:7).

John saw gathered around the throne of God **those who had been victorious over the beast.** These are the believers redeemed during the Tribulation (6:9–11; 7:9–17; 12:11, 17; 14:1–5, 12–13). They will be **victorious over the beast** because of their undying faith in the Lord Jesus Christ. Revelation 20:4–6 describes their resurrection and reward. In 13:7 it says of the beast (Antichrist), "It was also given to him to make war with the saints and to overcome them." But Antichrist's triumph will be short-lived, and in the end the Tribulation saints will be granted triumph over him, prevailing under the pressure to which the world succumbed (cf. 13:4, 14–17; 14:9, 11; 19:20).

Not only will the Tribulation saints triumph over the beast, but also over **his image and the number of his name.** The beast's crony, the false prophet, will perform many lying wonders to deceive people. One of them will be to set up an **image** of the beast, which he will order everyone to worship on pain of death (see the discussion of 13:14–15 in chapter 5 of this volume). The false prophet will also require everyone to receive a mark representing either the beast's name, or **the number of his name.** Those without that mark will face execution and will be unable to buy or sell (see the discussion of 13:17 in chapter 5 of this volume). But the Tribulation believers will, by God's power, eternally triumph over the whole enterprise of Satan, the beast, and the false prophet. Even those martyred for their triumphant faith will receive their glorious rewards (20:4).

That the Tribulation saints are seen **holding harps of God** indicates that they are rejoicing and singing praise to God. **Harps** were also associated with praise earlier in Revelation (5:8; 14:2), as they are frequently in the Old Testament (cf. 2 Sam. 6:5; 1 Chron. 13:8; 15:16, 28; 2 Chron. 5:12–13; Neh. 12:27; Pss. 33:2; 71:22; 144:9; 150:3). These believers rejoice because their prayers for God to take vengeance on their persecutors (6:9–10) are about to be answered.

The appearance of the Tribulation saints makes the point that God sends His wrath as an act of vengeance on those who mistreat His people. Jesus warned:

> "Whoever causes one of these little ones who believe in Me to stumble, it would be better for him to have a heavy millstone hung around his neck, and to be drowned in the depth of the sea.
>
> "Woe to the world because of its stumbling blocks! For it is inevitable that stumbling blocks come; but woe to that man through whom the stumbling block comes!
>
> "If your hand or your foot causes you to stumble, cut it off and throw it from you; it is better for you to enter life crippled or lame, than to have two hands or two feet and be cast into the eternal fire. If your eye causes you to stumble, pluck it out and throw it from you. It is better for you to enter life with one eye, than to have two eyes and be cast into the fiery hell.

> "See that you do not despise one of these little ones, for I say to you that their angels in heaven continually see the face of My Father who is in heaven." (Matt. 18:6–10)

Unbelievers will be condemned to eternal hell for mistreating God's people, because that mistreatment reveals their evil, impenitent hearts:

> "Then He will also say to those on His left, 'Depart from Me, accursed ones, into the eternal fire which has been prepared for the devil and his angels; for I was hungry, and you gave Me nothing to eat; I was thirsty, and you gave Me nothing to drink; I was a stranger, and you did not invite Me in; naked, and you did not clothe Me; sick, and in prison, and you did not visit Me.' Then they themselves also will answer, 'Lord, when did we see You hungry, or thirsty, or a stranger, or naked, or sick, or in prison, and did not take care of You?' Then He will answer them, 'Truly I say to you, to the extent that you did not do it to one of the least of these, you did not do it to Me.'" (Matt. 25:41–45)

The apostle Paul wrote, "Never take your own revenge, beloved, but leave room for the wrath of God, for it is written, 'Vengeance is Mine, I will repay,' says the Lord" (Rom. 12:19). The Old Testament likens persecuting God's people to poking a finger in His eye (Zech. 2:8). The psalmist also wrote of God's vengeance for His people:

> O Lord, God of vengeance,
> God of vengeance, shine forth!
> Rise up, O Judge of the earth,
> Render recompense to the proud.
> How long shall the wicked, O Lord,
> How long shall the wicked exult?
> They pour forth words, they speak arrogantly;
> All who do wickedness vaunt themselves.
> They crush Your people, O Lord,
> And afflict Your heritage.
> They slay the widow and the stranger
> And murder the orphans.
> They have said, "The Lord does not see,
> Nor does the God of Jacob pay heed."
>
> Pay heed, you senseless among the people;
> And when will you understand, stupid ones?
> He who planted the ear, does He not hear?
> He who formed the eye, does He not see?
> He who chastens the nations, will He not rebuke,
> Even He who teaches man knowledge? . . .

They band themselves together against the life of the righteous
And condemn the innocent to death.
But the Lord has been my stronghold,
And my God the rock of my refuge.
He has brought back their wickedness upon them
And will destroy them in their evil;
The Lord our God will destroy them.
(Ps. 94:1–10, 21–23)

The believers pictured here will have undergone the terrors of the Tribulation and suffered painful, violent deaths as martyrs. Yet despite having endured the most intense persecution the world will ever know, their faith, which is a gift from God, will endure. Eventually, they will stand triumphantly before the throne of God, watching as God takes vengeance on their persecutors.

The Character of God

And they sang the song of Moses, the bond-servant of God, and the song of the Lamb, saying,

"Great and marvelous are Your works,
O Lord God, the Almighty;
Righteous and true are Your ways,
King of the nations!
Who will not fear, O Lord, and glorify Your name?
For You alone are holy;
For all the nations will come and worship before You,
For Your righteous acts have been revealed."
(15:3–4)

The song sung by the glorified saints before the throne is an anthem of praise to God. The ultimate motive of God's wrath is His holy, righteous character, which demands that He judge sinners. It is God's holy nature, soon to be revealed in judgment against their persecutors, that elicits this song from the redeemed.

The **song of Moses** is the first of several songs recorded in the Old Testament. The Israelites sang a song of praise when the Lord gave them water in the wilderness (Num. 21:17–18). Moses taught the children of Israel a song of remembrance shortly before his death (Deut. 31:19–22; 32:1–44). That song of Moses is not in view here, because it deals with Israel's unfaithfulness and God's punishment of the nation before her restoration. The context of Revelation 15 is not one of unfaithfulness, but of faithfulness that triumphs. Deborah and Barak sang a triumphant victory song celebrating Israel's defeat of the Canaanites, whose forces were led by the notorious Sisera (Judg. 5:1–31). There was a song sung to the Lord as part of the restoration of true worship in Hezekiah's day (2 Chron. 29:27). In addition, David and others wrote the Psalms, the hymnbook of ancient Israel, and Solomon wrote the Song of Solomon.

The historical setting for the **song of Moses** comes from the time of the Exodus. As **the bond-servant of God, Moses** was called to lead the people of Israel out of captivity in Egypt. God delivered them from Pharaoh's pursuing army by parting the Red Sea, stacking the water on either side of a path, thus allowing the Israelites to cross safely on dry land. After they were safely across, the collapsing waters drowned the Egyptian army. On the far side of the Red Sea, the Israelites sang a song of praise to God for their deliverance.

> Then Moses and the sons of Israel sang this song to the Lord, and said,
> "I will sing to the Lord, for He is highly exalted;
> The horse and its rider He has hurled into the sea.
> The Lord is my strength and song,
> And He has become my salvation;
> This is my God, and I will praise Him;
> My father's God, and I will extol Him.
> The Lord is a warrior;
> The Lord is His name.
> Pharaoh's chariots and his army He has cast into the sea;
> And the choicest of his officers are drowned in the Red Sea.
> The deeps cover them;
> They went down into the depths like a stone.
> Your right hand, O Lord, is majestic in power,
> Your right hand, O Lord, shatters the enemy.
> And in the greatness of Your excellence You overthrow those who rise up against You;
> You send forth Your burning anger, and it consumes them as chaff.
> At the blast of Your nostrils the waters were piled up,
> The flowing waters stood up like a heap;
> The deeps were congealed in the heart of the sea.
> The enemy said, 'I will pursue, I will overtake, I will divide the spoil;
> My desire shall be gratified against them;
> I will draw out my sword, my hand will destroy them.'
> You blew with Your wind, the sea covered them;
> They sank like lead in the mighty waters.
> Who is like You among the gods, O Lord?
> Who is like You, majestic in holiness,
> Awesome in praises, working wonders?
> You stretched out Your right hand,
> The earth swallowed them.

> In Your lovingkindness You have led the people whom You have
> redeemed;
> In Your strength You have guided them to Your holy habitation.
> The peoples have heard, they tremble;
> Anguish has gripped the inhabitants of Philistia.
> Then the chiefs of Edom were dismayed;
> The leaders of Moab, trembling grips them;
> All the inhabitants of Canaan have melted away.
> Terror and dread fall upon them;
> By the greatness of Your arm they are motionless as stone;
> Until Your people pass over, O Lord,
> Until the people pass over whom You have purchased.
> You will bring them and plant them in the mountain of Your
> inheritance,
> The place, O Lord, which You have made for Your dwelling,
> The sanctuary, O Lord, which Your hands have established.
> The Lord shall reign forever and ever."
>
> (Ex. 15:1–18)

The **song of Moses** was a song of victory and deliverance for the righteous, and at the same time of judgment and wrath on God's enemies. The Tribulation saints, gathered in triumph in a place of safety and security, will echo the same song of deliverance sung long ago by the people of Israel.

In addition to singing again with new meaning the **song of Moses,** who led Israel in the redemption from Egypt, the redeemed saints before God's throne also will sing the **song of the Lamb,** who is their eternal Redeemer. That song was first heard in 5:8–14:

> When He had taken the book, the four living creatures and the twenty-four elders fell down before the Lamb, each one holding a harp and golden bowls full of incense, which are the prayers of the saints. And they sang a new song, saying,
>
> "Worthy are You to take the book and to break its seals; for You were slain, and purchased for God with Your blood men from every tribe and tongue and people and nation. You have made them to be a kingdom and priests to our God; and they will reign upon the earth."
>
> Then I looked, and I heard the voice of many angels around the throne and the living creatures and the elders; and the number of them was myriads of myriads, and thousands of thousands, saying with a loud voice,
>
> "Worthy is the Lamb that was slain to receive power and riches and wisdom and might and honor and glory and blessing."
>
> And every created thing which is in heaven and on the earth and under the earth and on the sea, and all things in them, I heard saying,

> "To Him who sits on the throne, and to the Lamb, be blessing and honor and glory and dominion forever and ever."
>
> And the four living creatures kept saying, "Amen." And the elders fell down and worshiped.

Like the **song of Moses,** the **song of the Lamb** expresses the themes of God's faithfulness, deliverance of His people, and judgment of His enemies. Commentator John Phillips compares and contrasts the two songs:

> The song of Moses was sung at the Red Sea, the song of the Lamb is sung at the crystal sea; the song of Moses was a song of triumph over Egypt, the song of the Lamb is a song of triumph over Babylon; the song of Moses told how God brought His people out, the song of the lamb tells how God brings His people in; the song of Moses was the first song in Scripture, the song of the Lamb is the last. The song of Moses commemorated the execution of the foe, the expectation of the saints, and the exaltation of the Lord; the song of the Lamb deals with the same three themes. (*Exploring Revelation,* rev. ed. [Chicago: Moody, 1987; reprint, Neptune, N.J.: Loizeaux, 1991], 187)

The words of the song recorded here do not match exactly either the **song of Moses** in Exodus 15, or the **song of the Lamb** in Revelation 5. But the themes and many of the key terms are similar. This song adds some new stanzas to the triumph song of God's redeemed people, yet every one of its lines finds an echo in the Old Testament. **Great and marvelous are Your works** is reminiscent of Psalm 139:14, "Wonderful are Your works, and my soul knows it very well." The title **Lord God, the Almighty,** celebrating God's omnipotence, essential to the triumphant power of the last judgments, appears frequently in Revelation (cf. 1:8; 4:8; 11:17; 16:7, 14; 19:6, 15; 21:22), and the title "God Almighty" was the name by which God revealed Himself to Abraham (Gen. 17:1; cf. Gen. 35:11; 48:3; Ex. 6:3). The exclamation **righteous and true are Your ways** reflects the Old Testament truth that "all [God's] works are true and His ways just" (Dan. 4:37; cf. Deut. 32:4; Hos. 14:9). God is called the **King of the nations** in Jeremiah 10:7. The phrase **Who will not fear, O Lord, and glorify Your name?** is also drawn from Jeremiah 10:7 (cf. Ps. 86:9). The truth that God **alone** is **holy** is an oft-repeated Old Testament theme (cf. 1 Sam. 2:2; Pss. 22:3; 99:5, 9; 111:9; Isa. 6:3; 57:15; Hab. 1:12). The phrase **for all the nations will come and worship before You** quotes Psalm 86:9 (cf. Jer. 10:7), while the phrase **Your righteous acts have been revealed** echoes such Old Testament passages as Judges 5:11; 1 Samuel 12:7; Psalm 103:6; Daniel 9:16; and Micah 6:5.

The song of these redeemed saints extols God's character as the omnipotent, immutable, sovereign, perfect, and righteous Creator and

Judge. Because He is all that, God must and will judge sinners; if He ignored their sin, He would not be holy, righteous, and true to His nature. The prophet Habbakuk, speaking to God, put it this way, "Your eyes are too pure to approve evil, and You can not look on wickedness with favor" (Hab. 1:13). "Does God pervert justice? Or does the Almighty pervert what is right?" asks Job 8:3. Psalm 19:9 answers, "The judgments of the Lord are true; they are righteous altogether."

The song closes with joyful anticipation of the millennial reign of Christ, when **all the nations will come and worship before** God. In the words of the psalmist, "All the earth will worship You, and will sing praises to You; they will sing praises to Your name" (Ps. 66:4). In the earthly, millennial kingdom, "it will come about that any who are left of all the nations that went against Jerusalem will go up from year to year to worship the King, the Lord of hosts, and to celebrate the Feast of Booths" (Zech. 14:16). After God's **righteous acts** of judgment **have been revealed** during the Tribulation, the time anticipated by Isaiah will come: "'And it shall be from new moon to new moon and from sabbath to sabbath, all mankind will come to bow down before Me,' says the Lord" (Isa. 66:23). That time will mark the first phase of the fulfillment of Philippians 2:10–11: "At the name of Jesus every knee will bow, of those who are in heaven and on earth and under the earth, and . . . every tongue will confess that Jesus Christ is Lord, to the glory of God the Father."

The Plan of God

After these things I looked, and the temple of the tabernacle of testimony in heaven was opened, and the seven angels who had the seven plagues came out of the temple, clothed in linen, clean and bright, and girded around their chests with golden sashes. Then one of the four living creatures gave to the seven angels seven golden bowls full of the wrath of God, who lives forever and ever. And the temple was filled with smoke from the glory of God and from His power; and no one was able to enter the temple until the seven plagues of the seven angels were finished. (15:5–8)

Each of the angelic players in this unfolding drama will fulfill his assigned duty according to God's plan. It has always been God's purpose to judge sinners and destroy sin. The "eternal fire . . . has [already] been prepared for the devil and his angels" (Matt. 25:41) and awaits those whom God will one day sentence to eternal punishment there. God's holy angels await the time when they will play their role in God's judgment of sinners (cf. Matt. 13:41–42, 49–50). Here, in a new vision, they are given the instruments of execution.

As it does throughout Revelation (cf. 4:1; 6:2, 5, 8; 7:9; 14:1, 14; 19:11), the phrase **after these things I looked** introduces a startling, dramatic new vision. Something is about to draw John's attention away from the redeemed saints singing their praises before God's glorious throne. This new vision revealed to him the bowl judgments (16:1–21), but first John saw the angels who will carry out those judgments. As he watched, **the temple of the tabernacle of testimony in heaven was opened.** The apostle had seen a similar sight in an earlier vision, which anticipated this opening, when "the temple of God which is in heaven was opened; and the ark of His covenant appeared in His temple, and there were flashes of lightning and sounds and peals of thunder and an earthquake and a great hailstorm" (11:19). *Naos* (**temple**) refers to the Holy of Holies, the inner sanctuary where God's presence dwells, emphasizing that God is the source of the plagues. The **tabernacle** was sometimes referred to as the **tabernacle of testimony** (Ex. 38:21; Num. 1:50, 53; 10:11; Acts 7:44) because the most important item in it was the ark of the covenant, sometimes called the ark of the testimony (Ex. 25:22; 26:33–34; 30:6; Lev. 16:13; Num. 4:5; 7:89; Josh. 4:16). It was so named because it contained the testimony, the two stone tablets on which God had written the Ten Commandments (Ex. 25:16, 21; 40:20; cf. Ps. 78:5).

In an earlier vision, God's throne room was opened so the faithful could see in (4:1ff.). In this vision, the heavenly tabernacle, of which the earthly tabernacle was only a copy (Heb. 8:2, 5), was opened to reveal the most severe earthly judgment ever on the unfaithful. As John watched, **the seven angels who had the seven plagues came out of the temple.** The time has come in God's sovereign plan for the seven plagues, which represent the final, deadly judgments, to be poured out on the world (cf. Heb. 10:31). These seven angels will execute that plan. They were **clothed in linen, clean and bright,** the fabric representing their holiness and purity (see the discussion of 19:14 in chapter 15 of this volume; cf. Acts 10:30). As befits such glorious, holy, majestic beings, the angels were **girded around their chests with golden sashes,** running across the torso from the shoulder to the waist.

After solemnly proceeding from the inner sanctuary of God's heavenly temple, the seven angels received the means by which they will dump God's judgment. **One of the four living creatures** (cherubim; an order of high-ranking angels; 4:6, 8–9; 5:6, 8, 11, 14; 6:1, 6; 7:11; 14:3; 19:4; Ezek. 1:4–25; 10:15; cf. 1 Sam. 4:4; 2 Sam. 6:2; 22:11; Pss. 80:1; 99:1; Isa. 37:16) **gave to the seven angels seven golden bowls full of the wrath of God, who lives forever and ever.** *Phialas* (**bowls**) refers to shallow saucers. The imagery is not that of a stream being poured gradually out of a pitcher, but of the whole contents of the shallow saucers being hurled down in an instant flood of judgment. **Bowls** were part of the temple furnishings (1 Kings 7:50; 2 Kings 12:13; 25:15; 1 Chron. 28:17; Zech. 14:20) and were associated with the sacrifices (Ex. 27:3; 38:3). Those who refuse to drink the cup of salvation (Ps. 116:13) will be drowned in the judgments poured from the bowls of wrath. Because God **lives forever and ever,** He has the power to put an end to sin, so that it cannot exist again forever in His holy presence.

Out of the heavenly temple came not only the angels, but also **smoke** symbolizing **the glory of God and His power. Smoke,** an emblem of majesty (Ex. 19:16–18), also symbolized God's glorious presence in the Old Testament tabernacle or temple (Ex. 40:34–35; 1 Kings 8:10–11; Isa. 6:1–4). This **smoke** also symbolizes God's wrath; thus **no one was able to enter the temple until the seven plagues of the seven angels were finished.** The glory cloud will remain in the heavenly temple until the earth is completely purged, cleansed, and prepared for the King and His kingdom.

The scene described in this chapter establishes the background for the final, definitive judgments, poured out in chapter 16. Once the wrath of God was poured out on Jesus Christ because of what He did for sinners; in the future, wrath will be poured out on sinners because of what they did to Jesus Christ. It is true that "The Lord is . . . patient toward you, not wishing for any to perish but for all to come to repentance" (2 Pet. 3:9), and that even in His wrath, He will remember mercy (cf. Hab. 3:2). Yet mercy refused brings judgment. By the time God pours out the seven bowls of His final wrath on earth, sinners will have been warned repeatedly to repent. They will have experienced numerous terrifying judgments, which they will acknowledge came from God (6:16–17). They will have heard the saving message of the gospel preached by the 144,000 Jewish evangelists, the two witnesses, other redeemed Gentiles and Jews, even from an angel flying in midheaven. Yet, tragically, they will harden their hearts and fall into calamity (Prov. 28:14). They will pay a fearful price for failing to heed the Scripture's warning: "Today if you hear His voice, do not harden your hearts" (Heb. 3:15; 4:7).

The Seven Final Plagues (Revelation 16:1–21)

11

Then I heard a loud voice from the temple, saying to the seven angels, "Go and pour out on the earth the seven bowls of the wrath of God."

So the first angel went and poured out his bowl on the earth; and it became a loathsome and malignant sore on the people who had the mark of the beast and who worshiped his image.

The second angel poured out his bowl into the sea, and it became blood like that of a dead man; and every living thing in the sea died.

Then the third angel poured out his bowl into the rivers and the springs of waters; and they became blood. And I heard the angel of the waters saying, "Righteous are You, who are and who were, O Holy One, because You judged these things; for they poured out the blood of saints and prophets, and You have given them blood to drink. They deserve it." And I heard the altar saying, "Yes, O Lord God, the Almighty, true and righteous are Your judgments."

The fourth angel poured out his bowl upon the sun, and it was given to it to scorch men with fire. Men were scorched with fierce heat; and they blasphemed the name of God who has the

power over these plagues, and they did not repent so as to give Him glory.

Then the fifth angel poured out his bowl on the throne of the beast, and his kingdom became darkened; and they gnawed their tongues because of pain, and they blasphemed the God of heaven because of their pains and their sores; and they did not repent of their deeds.

The sixth angel poured out his bowl on the great river, the Euphrates; and its water was dried up, so that the way would be prepared for the kings from the east. And I saw coming out of the mouth of the dragon and out of the mouth of the beast and out of the mouth of the false prophet, three unclean spirits like frogs; for they are spirits of demons, performing signs, which go out to the kings of the whole world, to gather them together for the war of the great day of God, the Almighty. ("Behold, I am coming like a thief. Blessed is the one who stays awake and keeps his clothes, so that he will not walk about naked and men will not see his shame.") And they gathered them together to the place which in Hebrew is called Har-Magedon.

Then the seventh angel poured out his bowl upon the air, and a loud voice came out of the temple from the throne, saying, "It is done." And there were flashes of lightning and sounds and peals of thunder; and there was a great earthquake, such as there had not been since man came to be upon the earth, so great an earthquake was it, and so mighty. The great city was split into three parts, and the cities of the nations fell. Babylon the great was remembered before God, to give her the cup of the wine of His fierce wrath. And every island fled away, and the mountains were not found. And huge hailstones, about one hundred pounds each, came down from heaven upon men; and men blasphemed God because of the plague of the hail, because its plague was extremely severe. (16:1–21)

The Bible provides the only true beacon of light and hope in the darkness and despair of the world. In its pages are comforting, encouraging, and affirming words of the peace, goodness, joy, and love of salvation. Believers are reassured as they read of God's love and promises and of their eternal inheritance in His kingdom.

But while the Bible is a book of hope, it is also a book of judgment. Because God loves righteousness and faith, He must hate sin and unbelief. He cannot love truth unless He hates lies. He cannot love goodness unless He hates wickedness. He cannot reward unless He also punishes. The Old Testament repeatedly warns of coming judgment, particularly in those passages that describe the final Day of the Lord judgments (e.g., Joel 2:28–32; Zech. 14:1; Mal. 4:1,5).

The New Testament also reveals God's judgment of sinners. John the Baptist, the forerunner of the Messiah, preached a confronting, even harsh message of judgment. He called some of those who came to him seeking baptism snakes (Luke 3:7) and threatened them with judgment, saying, "I baptize you with water for repentance, but He who is coming after me is mightier than I, and I am not fit to remove His sandals; He will baptize you with the Holy Spirit and fire. His winnowing fork is in His hand, and He will thoroughly clear His threshing floor; and He will gather His wheat into the barn, but He will burn up the chaff with unquenchable fire" (Matt. 3:11–12). John 3:36 warns, "He who believes in the Son has eternal life; but he who does not obey the Son will not see life, but the wrath of God abides on him." The apostle Paul spoke of "the God who inflicts wrath" (Rom. 3:5), noted that "the wrath of God will come upon the sons of disobedience" (Col. 3:6), and described the terrifying time "when the Lord Jesus will be revealed from heaven with His mighty angels in flaming fire, dealing out retribution to those who do not know God and to those who do not obey the gospel of our Lord Jesus. These will pay the penalty of eternal destruction, away from the presence of the Lord and from the glory of His power" (2 Thess. 1:7–9). The writer of Hebrews added,

> For if we go on sinning willfully after receiving the knowledge of the truth, there no longer remains a sacrifice for sins, but a terrifying expectation of judgment and the fury of a fire which will consume the adversaries. Anyone who has set aside the Law of Moses dies without mercy on the testimony of two or three witnesses. How much severer punishment do you think he will deserve who has trampled under foot the Son of God, and has regarded as unclean the blood of the covenant by which he was sanctified, and has insulted the Spirit of grace? For we know Him who said, "Vengeance is Mine, I will repay." And again, "The Lord will judge His people." It is a terrifying thing to fall into the hands of the living God. (Heb. 10:26–31)

The wrath of God against sin and His final, eschatological judgment of sinners, recurring themes in the Bible, take center stage in Revelation. That wrath, displayed earlier in Revelation in the seal and trumpet judgments, reaches its devastating climax with the bowl judgments described in this chapter. Those rapid-fire judgments will take place in a very short period of time, marking the final hour of the Day of the Lord. They are the final outpouring of God's wrath on the unbelieving world before the return of the Lord Jesus Christ (15:1). They are the last expression of divine wrath against the sin, unrighteousness, and blasphemy that is rampant on the earth.

The return of Jesus Christ described in chapter 19 immediately follows these seven judgments. Chapters 17 and 18 go back in time to describe the destruction of Antichrist's worldwide political and religious empire of Babylon. (A similar recapitulation interrupted the chronological flow of Revelation in chapters 12–14.) Immediately following the seven bowl judgments, the Lord Jesus Christ will return, destroy the world's armies at the Battle of Armageddon, and establish His universal rule on the earth. In fact, the bowl judgments foreshadow the Battle of Armageddon. The drying up of the Euphrates River as a result of the sixth bowl will pave the way for the forces of the east to come to that destruction.

Since they are the final outpouring of God's wrath, the bowl judgments will be more severe than all the earlier judgments. Their severity is strong proof of how God feels about those who persistently, willfully reject Him. This particular epoch in human history will be a fitting time for God's wrath to reach its apex, for mankind's rebellion against God will also then be at its apex. Despite years of horrific judgments (which they will acknowledge as coming from God—6:15–17), sinners will stubbornly cling to their sin and persist in their rebellion (9:21). Nor will the powerful preaching of the gospel by the 144,000, the two witnesses, countless other believers, and an angel from heaven bring them to repentance (vv. 9, 11). Instead, their rebellion, defiance, and rejection of God will increase until the final judgments fall. This worldwide rebellion of sinful mankind will bring the worldwide judgments of holy God.

These "seven plagues, which are the last" (15:1), had precursors in two other sets of plagues in Scripture: the plagues God brought upon Egypt (Ex. 7–12) and the seven trumpet judgments (chaps. 8–11). There are similarities and differences between the three sets of plagues. The first plagues were very localized, affecting only Egypt. The second set of plagues destroyed one third of the world (8:7–12; 9:15, 18). The final plagues will affect the entire world. All three sets of plagues include hail, darkness, water turned to blood, and an invasion from the east, whether by insects, demons, or men. The seven bowl judgments will gather together all the horrors and terrors from all the previous judgments of God. They will completely inundate the world, bringing it to the brink of utter ruin.

As the vision of the bowl judgments began to unfold, John **heard a loud voice from the temple.** The startling impact of loud voices is heard some twenty times in Revelation. This **loud voice** is certainly that of God, since there was no one else in the **temple** (15:8). His loud cry of judgment is reminiscent of Isaiah 66:6: "A voice of uproar from the city, a voice from the temple, the voice of the Lord who is rendering recompense to His enemies." *Megalē* (**loud**) appears half a dozen times in this chapter (usually translated "great"), again emphasizing the magnitude of the judgments recorded here. His loud voice is heard again after the seventh bowl is poured out (v. 17).

The **seven angels** were introduced in 15:1, 6–8. There they were given the seven bowls containing the final judgments. Here God commands all seven of them, **"Go and pour out on the earth the seven bowls of the wrath of God."** As are all the judgments, the seven bowls will be supernatural acts of God. The text does not tolerate the attempts of some commentators to give them a purely natural, scientific explanation. They will hit far too rapidly for any explanation other than that they come from God Himself. In fact, there is only a brief pause, just long enough for one of the angels to affirm that the bowl judgments are just and righteous (vv. 5–7).

Some writers have seen these bowl judgments as recapitulating the seal and trumpet judgments. There are similarities, but many more differences, especially in the degree of devastation. The fourth bowl has no parallel in earlier judgments. No personal suffering accompanies the first four trumpets, but the bowls bring torment from the start. The bowls are universal, more intense than the previous judgments, and are called "the last" judgments (15:1), showing they do not go back in time to repeat earlier plagues.

The First Bowl

So the first angel went and poured out his bowl on the earth; and it became a loathsome and malignant sore on the people who had the mark of the beast and who worshiped his image. (16:2)

Responding immediately to God's command, **the first angel went and poured out his bowl on the earth.** As noted in the discussion of 15:7 in the previous chapter, the bowls were actually shallow saucers. Their contents are not slowly, gradually poured out, but dumped all at once. The sloshing out of the first bowl results in a **loathsome and malignant sore** that afflicts people. **Loathsome** and **malignant** translate two general Greek words for evil (*kakos* and *ponēros*). Used together, they stress that the sores will be festering, painful, and incurable. **Sore** translates *helkos*, the Greek equivalent of the Latin word from which the English word *ulcer* derives. It describes inflamed, oozing, ulcerous sores, such as those that affected the Egyptians (Ex. 9:9–11 LXX; cf. Deut. 28:27, 35), Job (Job 2:7), and the ones that covered Lazarus the beggar (Luke 16:21). They will bring unrelieved physical torment to those who have rejected Jesus Christ.

The sores will not affect believers, whose names have been "written from the foundation of the world in the book of life of the Lamb who has been slain" (13:8). They will come only upon those who chose to follow Antichrist, received his **mark** to show their allegiance (13:16–17), and **worshiped his image** (13:12). In 14:9–11, an angel described their ultimate fate:

> Then another angel, a third one, followed them, saying with a loud voice, "If anyone worships the beast and his image, and receives a mark on his forehead or on his hand, he also will drink of the wine of the wrath of God, which is mixed in full strength in the cup of His anger; and he will be tormented with fire and brimstone in the presence of the holy angels and in the presence of the Lamb. And the smoke of their torment goes up forever and ever; they have no rest day and night, those who worship the beast and his image, and whoever receives the mark of his name."

That passage describes eternal judgment; the present one describes temporal judgment. Antichrist's followers are suffering the consequences of having rejected the preaching of the gospel and the warning of the angel given in 14:7: "Fear God, and give Him glory, because the hour of His judgment has come." These inflamed, incurable sores may be similar to those Zechariah wrote about: "Now this will be the plague with which the Lord will strike all the peoples who have gone to war against Jerusalem; their flesh will rot while they stand on their feet, and their eyes will rot in their sockets, and their tongue will rot in their mouth" (14:12).

The Second Bowl

The second angel poured out his bowl into the sea, and it became blood like that of a dead man; and every living thing in the sea died. (16:3)

One of the reasons the bowl judgments will be so devastating is that their effects are cumulative. Before the sores of the first bowl could heal **the second angel poured out his bowl into the sea, and it became blood like that of a dead man; and every living thing in the sea died.** This judgment is similar to the first plague in Egypt (Ex. 7:20–24) and the second trumpet judgment (8:8–9). But this time the effects will be much more intense and widespread; since the oceans cover approximately 70 percent of the earth's surface, the effects of this judgment will be worldwide. After the angel dumped his bowl, the **sea,** which is vitally important to all life on earth, **became blood like that of a dead man.** To the amazement, horror, and despair of the world, the oceans will no longer be fluid, but will become thick, dark, and coagulated, like the pool of blood from someone who has been stabbed to death.

Exactly what supernatural means God will use to destroy the oceans is not revealed, but the effects will resemble those of the phenomenon known as the red tide. Commentator John Phillips writes:

> From time to time, off the coast of California and elsewhere, a phenomenon known as "the red tide" occurs. These red tides kill millions of fish and poison those who eat contaminated shellfish. In 1949, one of these red tides hit the coast of Florida. First the water turned yellow, but by midsummer it was thick and viscous with countless billions of dinoflagellates, tiny one-celled organisms. Sixty-mile windrows of stinking fish fouled the beaches. Much marine life was wiped out, even bait used by fishermen died upon the hooks. Eventually the red tide subsided, only to appear again the following year. Eating fish contaminated by the tide produced severe symptoms caused by a potent nerve poison, a few grams of which, distributed aright, could easily kill everyone in the world. An unchecked population explosion of toxic dinoflagellates would kill all the fish in the sea. (*Exploring Revelation*, rev. ed. [Chicago: Moody, 1987; reprint, Neptune, N.J.: Loizeaux, 1991], 190–91)

The stench from the dead, decaying bodies of **every living thing in the sea** (only partial death occurred at the second trumpet) will be unimaginable. Henry Morris writes:

> In this toxic ocean nothing can survive, and soon all the billions of fishes and marine mammals and marine reptiles and the innumerable varieties of marine invertebrates will perish, thus still further poisoning the oceans and contaminating the sea shores of the world. The oceans will have effectively completed their age-long function in the earth's physical economy, and will die. As God had created every living soul in the waters (Genesis 1:21), so now every living soul died in the sea. (*The Revelation Record* [Wheaton, Ill.: Tyndale, 1983], 298)

The transforming of the world's seas into putrid pools of stinking death will be graphic testimony to the wickedness of man, and the reverse of the day when God originally gave life to all sea creatures (Gen. 1:21).

The Third Bowl

Then the third angel poured out his bowl into the rivers and the springs of waters; and they became blood. And I heard the angel of the waters saying, "Righteous are You, who are and who were, O

Holy One, because You judged these things; for they poured out the blood of saints and prophets, and You have given them blood to drink. They deserve it." And I heard the altar saying, "Yes, O Lord God, the Almighty, true and righteous are Your judgments." (16:4–7)

When **the third angel poured out his bowl,** the same appalling judgment that affected the oceans was visited on **the rivers and the springs of waters . . . they** too **became blood.** What happened to the Nile River in Egypt (Ex. 7:20–24; Ps. 78:43–44) now happens to the world's entire supply of fresh water. The contamination of the world's oceans will be an environmentalist's worst nightmare. But the destruction of the world's remaining fresh water supply will be a catastrophic, staggering blow to fallen humanity.

By the time the third bowl is poured out, fresh water will be in critically short supply. The third trumpet judgment (8:10–11) will result in the poisoning of one third of the world's fresh water. Additionally, the two witnesses will "have the power to shut up the sky, so that rain will not fall during the days of their prophesying [the last three and a half years of the Tribulation]; and they have power over the waters to turn them into blood" (11:6). The temporary restraining of the earth's winds (7:1) will also cause drought. With no wind to move clouds and weather systems, the hydrological cycle will be disrupted and no rain will fall.

The destruction of what is left of the earth's fresh water will cause unthinkable hardship and suffering. There will be no water to drink; no clean water to wash the oozing sores caused by the first bowl judgment; no water to bring cooling relief from the scorching heat that the fourth bowl judgment will shortly bring. The scene is so unimaginably horrible that people will wonder how a God of compassion, mercy, and grace could send such a judgment. And so there is a brief interlude in the pouring out of the judgments while an angel speaks in God's defense.

Appropriately, it is **the angel of the waters** who defends God's righteous judgment in an echo of the overcomers' song in 15:3–4. In contrast to the curses and blasphemies of men (cf. vv. 9, 11) the angel declares, **"Righteous are You, who are and who were** (cf. 11:17; 1:4, 8; 4:8)**, O Holy One, because You judged these things."** God's judgment of sinners is unquestionably **righteous** because He is the **Holy One.** And although His wrath is terrifying and deadly, it is a just, deserved, and appropriate response to sinners' rejection of Him.

The angel declares that the Christ-hating, God-rejecting people receiving these judgments will bear an overwhelming burden of guilt. They will have rejected the clear, powerful, and persuasive preaching of the gospel throughout the Tribulation. More than that, the angel reminds the reader that **they poured out the blood of saints and prophets.**

They will mercilessly persecute and kill believers throughout the Tribulation, beginning with the martyrs of the fifth seal (6:9–11). Later, John saw "a great multitude which no one could count, from every nation and all tribes and peoples and tongues, standing before the throne and before the Lamb, clothed in white robes, and palm branches were in their hands. . . . 'These are the ones who come out of the great tribulation, and they have washed their robes and made them white in the blood of the Lamb'" (7:9, 14). The two witnesses will be martyred (11:7), and the enraged nations (11:18) will be "drunk with the blood of the saints, and with the blood of the witnesses of Jesus" (17:6).

Fittingly, those who have spilled so much innocent blood will be **given blood to drink.** In the angel's chilling words, **"They deserve it."** God is just and holy and will execute vengeance for His people (Rom. 12:19; Heb. 10:30). Having willfully rejected the knowledge of the truth (Heb. 10:26), there is nothing left for the unbelieving world but to receive what they **deserve,** "a terrifying expectation of judgment and the fury of a fire which will consume the adversaries" (Heb. 10:27).

Then the apostle John **heard the altar saying, "Yes, O Lord God, the Almighty, true and righteous are Your judgments."** The personified altar echoes the sentiments of the angel with words similar to 15:3. It may be that the very altar under which the saints were earlier seen praying for vengeance (6:9–11) now affirms that God's **true and righteous judgments** are the answer to those prayers.

That God's **judgments** are **true** and **righteous** is the constant teaching of Scripture. They are not like the capricious judgments associated with false pagan gods. In Genesis 18:25 Abraham asked rhetorically, "Shall not the Judge of all the earth deal justly?" David wrote in Psalm 19:9, "The judgments of the Lord are true; they are righteous altogether," while in Psalm 119:75 the psalmist added, "I know, O Lord, that Your judgments are righteous." Paul wrote of "the day of wrath and revelation of the righteous judgment of God" (Rom. 2:5). In 19:1–2 John "heard something like a loud voice of a great multitude in heaven, saying, 'Hallelujah! Salvation and glory and power belong to our God; because His judgments are true and righteous; for He has judged the great harlot who was corrupting the earth with her immorality, and He has avenged the blood of His bond-servants on her.'"

The Fourth Bowl

The fourth angel poured out his bowl upon the sun, and it was given to it to scorch men with fire. Men were scorched with fierce heat; and they blasphemed the name of God who has the power over these plagues, and they did not repent so as to give Him glory. (16:8–9)

In contrast to the first three angels, who poured out their bowls on the earth, the **fourth angel poured out his bowl upon the sun.** As a result the sun, which has since the fourth day of creation (Gen. 1:14–19) given the world light, warmth, and energy, becomes a deadly killer. Searing heat exceeding anything in human experience will **scorch men** so severely that it will seem that the atmosphere is on **fire.** Those who will be **scorched with** the sun's **fierce heat** are the same "people who had the mark of the beast and who worshiped his image" (v. 2).

This fiery judgment is reminiscent of Isaiah 24:4–6: "The earth mourns and withers, the world fades and withers, the exalted of the people of the earth fade away. The earth is also polluted by its inhabitants, for they transgressed laws, violated statutes, broke the everlasting covenant. Therefore, a curse devours the earth, and those who live in it are held guilty. Therefore, the inhabitants of the earth are burned, and few men are left."

Another serious consequence of the sun's intense heat will be the melting of the polar ice caps. The resulting rise in the oceans' water level will inundate coastal regions, flooding areas miles inland with the noxious waters of the dead oceans. Widespread damage and loss of life will accompany that flooding, adding further to the unspeakable misery of the devastated planet. Transportation by sea will become impossible.

One would think that the unparalleled disasters of the first four bowl judgments would cause people to repent. God's judgment is designed to call sinners to repentance (Rom. 2:4), or, like Pharaoh, to harden their hearts. Instead of blaming their sin, in the most shocking example of hardness of heart in history, **they blasphemed the name of God,** whom they know to be directly responsible for all their misery. Amazingly, they know that it is **God who has the power over** the **plagues** that were afflicting them. Yet, they will love their sin so much, and be so deceived by Antichrist, that **they** will **not repent so as to give** God **glory.** Until this point, only the Antichrist has been described as blaspheming (13:1, 5–6); here the world adopts his evil character. Neither grace nor wrath will move their wicked hearts to repentance (cf. 9:20–21; 16:11). In 11:13 the earthquake brought some to repentance, but not in this judgment series. Such blind, blasphemous hardness of heart is incredible in the face of the devastating judgments they will be undergoing. But like their evil leader, Antichrist, they will continue to hate God and refuse to **repent,** which would give **glory** to God as a just and righteous Judge of sin (cf. Josh. 7:19–25).

The Fifth Bowl

Then the fifth angel poured out his bowl on the throne of the beast, and his kingdom became darkened; and they gnawed their

tongues because of pain, and they blasphemed the God of heaven because of their pains and their sores; and they did not repent of their deeds. (16:10–11)

As He did long ago in Egypt (Ex. 10:21–29), God will turn up the intense suffering of the sinful world by turning out the lights. After **the fifth angel poured out his bowl on the throne of the beast, his kingdom became darkened** (cf. 9:2; Ex. 10:21–23). Commentators disagree over where specifically this **bowl** will be dumped. Some think it will be on the actual **throne** that **the beast** sits on; others on his capital city of Babylon; still others on his entire kingdom. It is best to see the **throne** as a reference to his kingdom, since the bowl poured out on the **throne** darkens the whole kingdom. Regardless of the exact location of where the bowl is dumped, the result is that darkness engulfs the whole earth, which is Antichrist's worldwide **kingdom.** The **beast** will be as helpless before the power of God as anyone else.

Joel described this time of judgment as "a day of darkness and gloom, a day of clouds and thick darkness. . . . Multitudes, multitudes in the valley of decision! For the day of the Lord is near in the valley of decision. The sun and moon grow dark and the stars lose their brightness" (Joel 2:2; 3:14–15). Zephaniah described the Day of the Lord as "a day of darkness and gloom, a day of clouds and thick darkness" (Zeph. 1:15). Jesus declared in His Olivet discourse that "in those days, after that tribulation, the sun will be darkened and the moon will not give its light" (Mark 13:24; cf. Isa. 13:10; 24:23; Luke 21:25; Acts 2:20).

The cumulative effect of the painful sores, fouled oceans, lack of drinking water, intense heat, all engulfed in thick blackness, will bring unbearable misery. Yet, incredibly, the wicked, unbelieving people of the world will still refuse to repent. John notes that they **gnawed their tongues** (lit. "kept on chewing") **because of** the most intense and excruciating **pain,** yet with those same tongues **they blasphemed the God of heaven** (a frequent Old Testament title for God; cf. 11:13; Gen. 24:3; Ezra 5:11–12; Neh. 1:4–5; Ps. 136:26; Dan. 2:18, 19, 37, 44; Jonah 1:9) **because of their pains and their sores** (perhaps related to the lack of sunlight, as well as the effect of previous plagues) **and they did not repent of their deeds**—the ultimate act of defiance by those hopelessly engulfed in Antichrist's satanic system. This is the last reference to their unwillingness to repent. The first five plagues were God's final call to repentance. Sinners ignored that call, and are now confirmed in their unbelief. The final two bowls, containing the severest of all the judgments, will be poured out on hardened, implacable impenitents.

The Sixth Bowl

The sixth angel poured out his bowl on the great river, the Euphrates; and its water was dried up, so that the way would be prepared for the kings from the east. And I saw coming out of the mouth of the dragon and out of the mouth of the beast and out of the mouth of the false prophet, three unclean spirits like frogs; for they are spirits of demons, performing signs, which go out to the kings of the whole world, to gather them together for the war of the great day of God, the Almighty. ("Behold, I am coming like a thief. Blessed is the one who stays awake and keeps his clothes, so that he will not walk about naked and men will not see his shame.") And they gathered them together to the place which in Hebrew is called Har-Magedon. (16:12–16)

Unlike the previous five bowls, the sixth, like the fifth seal (6:9–11), has no specific assault on humanity but prepares for what is to come. When his turn came, **the sixth angel poured out his bowl on the great river, the Euphrates.** The **Euphrates** appeared earlier in Revelation in connection with the sixth trumpet judgment (9:14), when 200 million demons who were bound near it were released. As the longest and most significant river in the Middle East, the **Euphrates** deserves to be called the **great river** (cf. 9:14; Gen. 15:18; Deut. 1:7; Josh. 1:4). Its source is in the snowfields and ice cap high on the slopes of Mount Ararat (located in modern Turkey), from which it flows some eighteen hundred miles before emptying into the Persian Gulf. In ancient times the Garden of Eden was located in the vicinity of the **Euphrates** (Gen. 2:10–14). The **Euphrates** also formed the eastern boundary of the land God gave to Israel (Gen. 15:18; Deut. 1:7; 11:24; Josh. 1:4). Along with the nearby Tigris, the **Euphrates** is still the lifeblood of the Fertile Crescent.

By the time the sixth bowl is poured out, the **Euphrates** will be very different than it is today or has ever been. The blazing heat from the sun associated with the fourth bowl will melt the snow and the ice cap on Mount Ararat. That will vastly increase the volume of water in the **Euphrates,** causing massive damage and flooding along its course. The bridges spanning the river will surely be destroyed. Thus, the reason for the sixth bowl becomes apparent. As the angel dumped his bowl, the Euphrates's **water was dried up, so that the way would be prepared for the kings from the east.** The eastern armies will need to cross the Euphrates to reach their ultimate destination—Armageddon in the land of Palestine.

God's drying up of the Euphrates is not an act of kindness toward the **kings from the east,** but one of judgment. They and their armies will be entering a deadly trap. The evaporation of the Euphrates will lead them to their doom, just as the parting of the Red Sea led to the destruction of the Egyptian army. Why they will make the daunting journey that will take them to their doom, through the drought, scorching heat, darkness, and their painful sores, is stated in vv. 13–14.

Whatever the human motives of this invasion force, whether political rebellion or rabid anti-Semitism, the real reason behind their advance toward Palestine soon becomes evident. In a grotesque vision, like something out of a horror movie, John **saw coming out of the mouth of the dragon and out of the mouth of the beast and out of the mouth of the false prophet, three unclean spirits** (cf. Matt. 10:1; Mark 1:23; Acts 5:16) **like frogs.** From the **mouth** (symbolizing the source of influence) of each member of the unholy trinity (the **dragon** [Satan], the **beast** [Antichrist], and the **false prophet**) came foul, **unclean spirits** resembling **frogs.** Frogs were unclean animals (Lev. 11:10, 41), but these are not literal frogs as in the plague in Egypt (Ex. 8:5; Ps. 78:45). John identified the froglike apparitions as **spirits of demons.** This graphic, revolting, and disgusting illustration pictures the slimy, cold-blooded vileness of these demons, who seduce the kings from the east into making the difficult journey to their doom at Armageddon under their deluding influence (cf. 1 Kings 22:19–22).

As part of their deception, the **demons** will no doubt perform supernatural signs. Earlier in the Tribulation, the false prophet performed "great signs," even making "fire come down out of heaven to the earth in the presence of men" (13:13). As a result, he was able to deceive "those who dwell on the earth because of the signs which it was given him to perform in the presence of the beast" (13:14). He was even able to persuade "those who dwell on the earth to make an image to the beast who had the wound of the sword and has come to life" (13:14). These unclean **spirits of demons** will work lying wonders to deceive the eastern **kings.**

That these demons will have such powers of deception is not surprising. Jesus predicted that "false Christs and false prophets . . . will show signs and wonders, in order to lead astray, if possible, the elect" (Mark 13:22; cf. 2 Thess. 2:9–10). Certainly these demons will have even greater powers of deception. Thus, they will have little difficulty in deceiving **the kings of the whole world, to gather them together.** The mission of the demons is to gather not just the eastern powers, but all of the world's rulers and armies to join the forces from the east **for the war of the great day of God, the Almighty.** In their pride, arrogance, and folly, the demonically deceived nations of the world will converge on Palestine to do battle with God Himself at Armageddon. According to 17:12–14, ten kings will be involved.

Joel prophesied of this time in Joel 3:2,9–13:

"I will gather all the nations
And bring them down to the valley of Jehoshaphat.
Then I will enter into judgment with them there
On behalf of My people and My inheritance, Israel,
Whom they have scattered among the nations;
And they have divided up My land." . . .

Proclaim this among the nations:
Prepare a war; rouse the mighty men!
Let all the soldiers draw near, let them come up!
Beat your plowshares into swords
And your pruning hooks into spears;
Let the weak say, "I am a mighty man."
Hasten and come, all you surrounding nations,
And gather yourselves there.
Bring down, O Lord, Your mighty ones.
Let the nations be aroused
And come up to the valley of Jehoshaphat,
For there I will sit to judge
All the surrounding nations.
Put in the sickle, for the harvest is ripe.
Come, tread, for the wine press is full;
The vats overflow, for their wickedness is great.

Zechariah also wrote of that time:

> For I will gather all the nations against Jerusalem to battle, and the city will be captured, the houses plundered, the women ravished and half of the city exiled, but the rest of the people will not be cut off from the city. Then the LORD will go forth and fight against those nations, as when He fights on a day of battle. (Zech. 14:2–3)

In a similar vein the psalmist wrote,

Why are the nations in an uproar
And the peoples devising a vain thing?
The kings of the earth take their stand
And the rulers take counsel together
Against the Lord and against His Anointed, saying,
"Let us tear their fetters apart
And cast away their cords from us!"
(Ps. 2:1–3)

The **war** will be over quickly: "These will wage war against the Lamb, and the Lamb will overcome them, because He is Lord of lords and King of kings" (17:14). In fact, it will not be a war; it will be a slaughter, as 19:11–21 graphically portrays.

Amid all the horrors of judgment, deception, and war comes a parenthetical word of encouragement to believers: **"Behold, I am coming like a thief. Blessed is the one who stays awake and keeps his clothes, so that he will not walk about naked and men will not see his shame."** This gracious word from heaven will come before the pouring out of the seventh bowl and assure believers that they will not be forgotten.

It is parallel to the beautiful passage in Malachi where the prophet addresses words of comfort from God to the righteous, who were frightened by the approach of the horrible Day of the Lord: "Then those who feared the Lord spoke to one another, and the Lord gave attention and heard it, and a book of remembrance was written before Him for those who fear the Lord and who esteem His name. 'They will be Mine,' says the Lord of hosts, 'on the day that I prepare My own possession, and I will spare them as a man spares his own son who serves him'" (Mal. 3:16–17). God told them not to be afraid because they are His. He never forgets His own. There were similar respites to encourage God's people between the sixth and seventh seals (7:1–17) and between the sixth and seventh trumpets (10:1–11:14). Because the bowl judgments take place in a short period of time, the respite between the sixth and seventh bowls is very brief.

The word of comfort from the Lord Jesus Christ (cf. 22:7, 12, 20) begins **"Behold, I am coming like a thief."** Like a thief comes, Jesus will come quickly and unexpectedly. But unlike a thief, He will come not to steal but to take what is rightfully His. The imagery of Jesus coming like a thief appears elsewhere in the New Testament. Earlier in Revelation Jesus warned the church in Sardis, "If you do not wake up, I will come like a thief, and you will not know at what hour I will come to you" (3:3). In the Olivet discourse He added, "Therefore be on the alert, for you do not know which day your Lord is coming. But be sure of this, that if the head of the house had known at what time of the night the thief was coming, he would have been on the alert and would not have allowed his house to be broken into" (Matt. 24:42–43). The apostle Paul reminded the Thessalonians that "the day of the Lord will come just like a thief in the night" (1 Thess. 5:2), a truth that Peter also affirmed (2 Pet. 3:10). Jesus' sudden, unexpected return will bring fear and dismay to His enemies, but hope and comfort to His people.

Then the exalted Lord pronounced the third of seven beatitudes (blessings, benedictions) in Revelation (cf. 1:3; 14:13; 19:9; 20:6; 22:7, 14): **"Blessed is the one who stays awake and keeps his clothes, so that**

he will not walk about naked and men will not see his shame." This describes those who, like the five prudent virgins (Matt. 25:1–13), will be prepared for His arrival. The imagery here, however, is not that of bridesmaids preparing for a wedding, but of soldiers alert and on duty. Only a soldier **who stays awake and keeps his clothes** on is ready for combat. Those caught unprepared when the battle breaks out will **walk about naked and men will see** their **shame**—the shame of a soldier derelict in his duty. Those whom God has "clothed . . . with garments of salvation" and "wrapped . . . with a robe of righteousness" (Isa. 61:10), who have "put on the Lord Jesus Christ" (Rom. 13:14), will be ready when the judgment comes. "Now, little children, abide in Him," urged John in his first epistle, "so that when He appears, we may have confidence and not shrink away from Him in shame at His coming" (1 John 2:28). Those whom Jesus finds prepared when He returns will be blessed.

After the brief interlude of encouragement for the redeemed, the prophetic narrative returns to the events of the sixth bowl. The deceiving demon spirits will have gathered the nations **together to the place which in Hebrew is called Har-Magedon. Har-Magedon** is a Hebrew word meaning "Mount Megiddo." Since there is no specific mountain by that name, and **Har** can refer to hill country, it is probably a reference to the hill country surrounding the Plain of Megiddo, some sixty miles north of Jerusalem. More than two hundred battles have been fought in that region, including Barak's defeat of the Canaanites (Judg. 4–5; cf. Judg. 5:19), Gideon's victory over the Midianites (Judg. 7; cf. Judg. 6:33; the "valley of Jezreel" is another name for the Plain of Esdraelon), and Josiah's defeat at the hands of Pharaoh Neco (2 Chron. 35:22). The Plain of Megiddo and the nearby Plain of Esdraelon will be the focal point for the Battle of Armageddon, which will rage the entire length of Israel as far south as the Edomite city of Bozrah (Isa. 63:1). Other battles will also occur in the vicinity of Jerusalem (Zech. 14:1–3).

The "battle" will be over almost as soon as it begins, as the Lord Jesus Christ returns to rescue His people (cf. Zech 14:1–3; Joel 3:16) and defeat His enemies. The resulting slaughter of the world's armies will be almost unimaginable, with blood splattered several feet high and perhaps running in streams throughout a distance of two hundred miles (14:20). The sixth bowl sets the final stage, but before the brief "battle," the seventh and final plague will hit.

The Seventh Bowl

Then the seventh angel poured out his bowl upon the air, and a loud voice came out of the temple from the throne, saying, "It is

done." And there were flashes of lightning and sounds and peals of thunder; and there was a great earthquake, such as there had not been since man came to be upon the earth, so great an earthquake was it, and so mighty. The great city was split into three parts, and the cities of the nations fell. Babylon the great was remembered before God, to give her the cup of the wine of His fierce wrath. And every island fled away, and the mountains were not found. And huge hailstones, about one hundred pounds each, came down from heaven upon men; and men blasphemed God because of the plague of the hail, because its plague was extremely severe. (16:17–21)

The **seventh bowl** is the final outpouring of God's wrath on sinners in this present earth. After it Jesus will come and set up His millennial kingdom. At the end of that thousand-year period, there will be one final act of rebellion, which will be quickly crushed (20:7–10). But that judgment will not take place in the world as we know it, for the earth will be changed dramatically before the kingdom arrives.

This final judgment of the present era will take place during the time when "the mystery of God is finished" (10:7). It is the last of the "seven plagues, which are the last, because in them the wrath of God is finished" (15:1). The seventh bowl will be the worst calamity in the world's history, the most complete and devastating catastrophe the earth will ever experience. Its effects carry all the way to the establishment of the earthly kingdom of Christ. Like the fourth angel, **the seventh angel** did not dump his bowl on the earth, but **poured** it **out** . . . **upon the air.** Its first effects were on the earth's atmosphere, as if God were cleansing the former domain of Satan and his demon hosts (12:9). The earth (v. 2), the sea (v. 3), the waters (v. 4), the sun (v. 8), and finally the **air** are the targets of judgment.

As the angel dumped his bowl, **a loud voice came out of the temple from the throne.** The voice is that of God Most High, possessor of heaven and earth. His solemn declaration **"It is done"** announces the climax of the final Day of the Lord that will spread doom over the entire globe. The perfect tense verb *gegonen* (**it is done**) describes a completed action with ongoing results. It is similar to Jesus' final words from the cross, "It is finished" (John 19:30). God's judgment of Christ on Calvary provided salvation for repentant sinners; the judgment of the seventh bowl brings doom to unrepentant sinners.

The pouring out of the seventh bowl dramatically affected the atmosphere; **there were flashes of lightning and sounds and peals of thunder.** Like the seventh seal (8:5) and the seventh trumpet (11:19), the seventh bowl is introduced with the imagery of a violent thunderstorm. But those earlier storms were mere previews of the mighty storm of wrath that now bursts upon the earth.

Though the seventh bowl was dumped on the earth's atmosphere, it will also have a devastating effect on the earth itself. God will punctuate this final judgment against sinners with an earthquake (cf. Isa. 24:19–20; Hag. 2:6), just as He did His judgment of sin at Calvary (Matt. 27:51–54). This earthquake will be the most powerful one ever to strike the earth; John described it as **a great earthquake, such as there had not been since man came to be upon the earth, so great an earthquake was it, and so mighty.** While there have always been and will continue to be local earthquakes (Matt. 24:7), this **great earthquake** will be unique in that God will shake the globe, as prophesied in Haggai 2:6 and Hebrews 12:26–27. The shaking will be so severe that it will renovate and reconfigure the earth in preparation for the millennial kingdom, restoring it to something like its pre-Flood condition (v. 20).

The first effect of this **great** and **mighty** earthquake was that **the great city was split into three parts.** The great city cannot be Babylon, as some think, because it is distinguished from "Babylon the great" mentioned later in verse 19. A comparison with 11:8 clearly identifies the **great city** as Jerusalem, "the great city . . . where also [the] Lord was crucified." That the **great city** is distinct from **the cities of the nations** offers further evidence that Jerusalem is in view. The massive earthquake will **split** Jerusalem **into three parts,** beginning a series of geophysical alterations to the city and its surrounding region that will conclude when the Lord Jesus Christ returns. Zechariah 14:4–10 describes these changes in detail. The Mount of Olives will split in two, and a new valley running east and west will be created (Zech. 14:4). A spring of water will flow year-round from Jerusalem to the Mediterranean and Dead Seas (Zech. 14:8), causing the desert to blossom like a rose (cf. Isa. 35:1). Jerusalem will be elevated, and the surrounding region flattened into a plain (Zech. 14:10). Thus, the purpose of the earthquake as it relates to Jerusalem is not to judge the city, but to enhance it. Jerusalem was judged earlier in the Tribulation by an earthquake, which led to the salvation of those who were not killed (11:13). Thus, there is no need for further judgment on that city. The physical changes will prepare Jerusalem for the central role it will play during the millennial kingdom, when Christ will reign there as King (Ps. 110:2; Isa. 2:3; 24:23; Mic. 4:7).

Unlike Jerusalem, which was enhanced by the earthquake, **the cities of the nations fell,** perhaps simultaneously with the defeat of Antichrist by the Lamb (17:12–14). Naturally, such a powerful earthquake will cause massive, widespread destruction. Specifically singled out is **Babylon the great,** which **was remembered before God, to give her the cup of the wine of His fierce wrath.** As the capital city of

Antichrist's empire, **Babylon** especially will be made to drink **the cup of the wine of His fierce wrath.** The downfall of **Babylon,** mentioned here in passing, will be described at length in chapters 17 and 18.

The final effect of the earthquake, as noted above, is to prepare the earth for the millennial rule of the Lord Jesus Christ. To that end, the earth's topography will be drastically altered; **every island fled away, and the mountains were not found. Islands,** which are undersea mountains, will disappear and the **mountains** on land will be flattened (cf. Isa. 40:4), completing the process that began during the sixth seal (6:12–14). "The gentle rolling topography of the world as originally created will be restored. No more will there be great inaccessible, uninhabitable mountain ranges or deserts or ice caps. The physical environment of the millennium will be, in large measure, a restoration of the antediluvian [pre-Flood] environment" (Henry M. Morris, *The Revelation Record,* 321). That may leave Jerusalem as the highest point on earth, making it a fitting throne for the Great King who will rule there during the Millennium (Jer. 3:17).

Those who somehow escape the devastation caused by the earthquake will face another catastrophe, one unprecedented in earth's history. They will be pelted with **huge hailstones, about one hundred pounds each,** that will hurtle **down from heaven upon men.** Unlike the seventh Egyptian plague (Ex. 9:23–24) and the first trumpet judgment (8:7), the force of these hailstones is unimaginable. The Greek term translated **about one hundred pounds** described the most weight a normal man could carry, anywhere from 90 to 135 pounds. The heaviest hailstones ever recorded weighed about 2 pounds; these gigantic chunks of ice will be fifty times heavier. They will add to the devastation caused by the earthquake and crush humanity, who, because of the earthquake's power, have no adequate shelter.

Fixed in their impenitence, the survivors of the hailstorm **blasphemed God because of the plague of the hail, because its plague was extremely severe.** Incredibly, tortured humanity defiantly remains hardened against God—a truth that should give pause to those who think that signs and wonders will convince people to believe the gospel. Those who reject the wonder, glory, and majesty of the Son of God, who spurn the gracious, free gift of salvation, will not be convinced by any sign (cf. Luke 16:31). It is too late for these hardened sinners; they have sold their souls to Satan; they are totally committed to Antichrist's blasphemous, idolatrous, anti-God system. Children of wrath they are, catapulting into hell.

God's eschatological and eternal wrath is inevitable; no one can prevent or hinder it from coming (Isa. 43:13). But there is a way to escape it, because "there is now no condemnation for those who are in Christ

Jesus" (Rom. 8:1). Those who by faith trust in Christ alone for salvation will escape both God's eschatological wrath (3:10) and His eternal wrath (1 Thess. 1:10). They will not face judgment, because their sins were judged when Jesus died in their place on the cross (2 Cor. 5:21; 1 Pet. 2:24). In light of the inevitable judgment to come, the warning to all unrepentant sinners is "Today if you hear His voice, do not harden your hearts" (Heb. 4:7).

The Destruction of the Final World Religion (Revelation 17:1–18)

12

Then one of the seven angels who had the seven bowls came and spoke with me, saying, "Come here, I will show you the judgment of the great harlot who sits on many waters, with whom the kings of the earth committed acts of immorality, and those who dwell on the earth were made drunk with the wine of her immorality." And he carried me away in the Spirit into a wilderness; and I saw a woman sitting on a scarlet beast, full of blasphemous names, having seven heads and ten horns. The woman was clothed in purple and scarlet, and adorned with gold and precious stones and pearls, having in her hand a gold cup full of abominations and of the unclean things of her immorality, and on her forehead a name was written, a mystery, "BABYLON THE GREAT, THE MOTHER OF HARLOTS AND OF THE ABOMINATIONS OF THE EARTH." And I saw the woman drunk with the blood of the saints, and with the blood of the witnesses of Jesus. When I saw her, I wondered greatly. And the angel said to me, "Why do you wonder? I will tell you the mystery of the woman and of the beast that carries her, which has the seven heads and the ten horns.

"The beast that you saw was, and is not, and is about to come up out of the abyss and go to destruction. And those who

dwell on the earth, whose name has not been written in the book of life from the foundation of the world, will wonder when they see the beast, that he was and is not and will come. Here is the mind which has wisdom. The seven heads are seven mountains on which the woman sits, and they are seven kings; five have fallen, one is, the other has not yet come; and when he comes, he must remain a little while. The beast which was and is not, is himself also an eighth and is one of the seven, and he goes to destruction. The ten horns which you saw are ten kings who have not yet received a kingdom, but they receive authority as kings with the beast for one hour. These have one purpose, and they give their power and authority to the beast. These will wage war against the Lamb, and the Lamb will overcome them, because He is Lord of lords and King of kings, and those who are with Him are the called and chosen and faithful."

And he said to me, "The waters which you saw where the harlot sits, are peoples and multitudes and nations and tongues. And the ten horns which you saw, and the beast, these will hate the harlot and will make her desolate and naked, and will eat her flesh and will burn her up with fire. For God has put it in their hearts to execute His purpose by having a common purpose, and by giving their kingdom to the beast, until the words of God will be fulfilled. The woman whom you saw is the great city, which reigns over the kings of the earth." (17:1–18)

There is a certain element of truth in Karl Marx's oft-quoted statement that religion is "the opium of the people." People are incurably religious, because God created them to be worshipers. They will inevitably worship someone or something, if not the true God, then false gods of their own making. People are made with a God-shaped vacuum that they are constantly seeking to fill.

Since the Fall, man's innate longing to know God has been twisted and perverted. People still seek something to worship but no longer seek the true God. In fact, "there is none who seeks for God" (Rom. 3:11), because, as Jesus declared, "No one can come to Me unless the Father who sent Me draws him" (John 6:44). Sadly, man's need for a relationship with God has been corrupted by his love of sin. Paul wrote in Romans 1:21 that "even though [people] knew God, they did not honor Him as God or give thanks, but they became futile in their speculations, and their foolish heart was darkened."

Into mankind's spiritual vacuum step Satan, "the father of lies" (John 8:44) and his demon hosts, disguised as angels of light (2 Cor. 11:14–15) and purveying "doctrines of demons" (1 Tim. 4:1). Playing on people's religious bent, they energize religious deception. False religion's powerful appeal comes from its promise to satisfy man's longing for the spiritual realm without bringing him under God's authority. In their rebellion against the true God, and because of their love of sin, fallen men willingly turn to these damning satanic religions. But wonderfully, graciously, mercifully, though man no longer seeks God, God still seeks man. Indeed, it was to "seek and to save that which was lost" (Luke 19:10) that Jesus came into the world.

Because false religion is so much a part of this fallen world, it is no surprise that it will play a major role in the end times. During the Tribulation, all the world's diverse false religions will be reunited into one great world religion. That ultimate expression of false religion will be an essential element of Antichrist's final world empire, in holding together his military, economic, and political structure. Only religion can unite the world in the most compelling way. Politics, economics, even military force are unable to overcome the world's cultural diversity. Only religion, with its appeal to the supernatural, can transcend the physical, geographical, historical, economic, and cultural barriers to world unity. Chapter 17 reveals the spiritual nature of Antichrist's kingdom; chapter 18 follows with its material aspects. God will destroy both aspects of Antichrist's kingdom.

Chapters 17 and 18 are inserted into the chronological flow of Revelation, which continues in chapter 19. The pouring out of the seventh bowl (16:17) is actually followed immediately in time by the return of the Lord Jesus Christ to end the great world battle (19:11). Chapters 17 and 18 digress to look not at God's specific judgments, but at what is being judged. Those two chapters go back to describe the world system led by Satan, Antichrist, and the false prophet, before recording its destruction. John had already heard harbingers of Babylon's destruction (14:8; 16:19); now the details of that destruction will be given in these remarkable visions.

During the Tribulation, people will desperately seek religion because of what will be happening in the world. As the hammer blows of God's judgment (the seal, trumpet, and bowl judgments) devastate the earth and terrorize its inhabitants, people will turn in desperation to Antichrist as their savior. Aided by the false prophet and hordes of deceiving demons, Antichrist will establish a worldwide religion, **"BABYLON THE GREAT, THE MOTHER OF HARLOTS AND OF THE ABOMINATIONS OF THE EARTH."** How can the future religious Babylon be the mother of all false religion? To comprehend the Babylonian false religion of the future requires an understanding of Babylon's role in the false religion of the past.

The story of Babylon begins with the Tower of Babel, recorded in Genesis 11:1–9:

> Now the whole earth used the same language and the same words. It came about as they journeyed east, that they found a plain in the land of Shinar and settled there. They said to one another, "Come, let us make bricks and burn them thoroughly." And they used brick for stone, and they used tar for mortar. They said, "Come, let us build for ourselves a city, and a tower whose top will reach into heaven, and let us make for ourselves a name, otherwise we will be scattered abroad over the face of the whole earth." The Lord came down to see the city and the tower which the sons of men had built. The Lord said, "Behold, they are one people, and they all have the same language. And this is what they began to do, and now nothing which they purpose to do will be impossible for them. Come, let Us go down and there confuse their language, that they may not understand one another's speech." So the Lord scattered them abroad from there over the face of the whole earth; and they stopped building the city. Therefore its name was called Babel, because there the Lord confused the language of the whole earth; and from there the Lord scattered them abroad over the face of the whole earth.

Journeying east after the Flood, Noah's descendants arrived at the site of Babylon (the "land of Shinar"). In history's first great humanistic effort, they decided to build a monument to themselves, to "make for [themselves] a name." But this act of rebellion against God also had religious implications. Brick towers, like the one they built (known as ziggurats), were later used in false religions. Ziggurats had on their tops the sign of the zodiac, which was used by pagan priests to chart the stars. Through their observations of the stars, the priests supposedly gained spiritual insights and knowledge of the future.

Such blatant, defiant rebellion against God is incredible on the part of those to whom the Flood was a recent event. In fact Nimrod, the apparent leader of the plot, was Noah's great-grandson. Genesis describes him as "a mighty hunter before the Lord" (10:9), and notes that "the beginning of his kingdom was Babel and Erech and Accad and Calneh, in the land of Shinar. From that land he went forth into Assyria, and built Nineveh and Rehoboth-Ir and Calah, and Resen between Nineveh and Calah; that is the great city" (Gen. 10:10–12). This proud, arrogant leader (his name may derive from a Hebrew verb meaning "to rebel") foreshadowed the final Antichrist.

God judgmentally scattered those proud rebels from Babel (Gen. 11:8), and they took their false religion around the world with them. In spite of the scattering, Babylon remained an idolatrous center of false worship. At one point in the city's sordid history, it contained no less than 180 shrines dedicated to the goddess Ishtar (Charles L. Feinberg, "Jeremiah," in *The Expositor's Bible Commentary,* Frank E. Gaebelein, ed., [Grand Rapids: Zondervan, 1986], 6:643).

Even some of the Israelites were caught up in the idolatrous worship of Ishtar, one of whose titles was "Queen of Heaven." Jeremiah rebuked the Jewish remnant that had fled to Egypt for the idolatry that had led to their downfall. Instead of repenting, however, they remained defiant:

> Then all the men who were aware that their wives were burning sacrifices to other gods, along with all the women who were standing by, as a large assembly, including all the people who were living in Pathros in the land of Egypt, responded to Jeremiah, saying, "As for the message that you have spoken to us in the name of the Lord, we are not going to listen to you! But rather we will certainly carry out every word that has proceeded from our mouths, by burning sacrifices to the queen of heaven and pouring out drink offerings to her, just as we ourselves, our forefathers, our kings and our princes did in the cities of Judah and in the streets of Jerusalem; for then we had plenty of food and were well off and saw no misfortune. But since we stopped burning sacrifices to the queen of heaven and pouring out drink offerings to her, we have lacked everything and have met our end by the sword and by famine." "And," said the women, "when we were burning sacrifices to the queen of heaven and were pouring out drink offerings to her, was it without our husbands that we made for her sacrificial cakes in her image and poured out drink offerings to her?" (Jer. 44:15–19)

God, through Jeremiah, pronounced judgment on those Jews for their stubborn, defiant adherence to the Ishtar cult:

> Then Jeremiah said to all the people, to the men and women—even to all the people who were giving him such an answer—saying, "As for the smoking sacrifices that you burned in the cities of Judah and in the streets of Jerusalem, you and your forefathers, your kings and your princes, and the people of the land, did not the Lord remember them and did not all this come into His mind? So the Lord was no longer able to endure it, because of the evil of your deeds, because of the abominations which you have committed; thus your land has become a ruin, an object of horror and a curse, without an inhabitant, as it is this day. Because you have burned sacrifices and have sinned against the Lord and not obeyed the voice of the Lord or walked in His law, His statutes or His testimonies, therefore this calamity has befallen you, as it has this day."
>
> Then Jeremiah said to all the people, including all the women, "Hear the word of the Lord, all Judah who are in the land of Egypt, thus says the Lord of hosts, the God of Israel, as follows: 'As for you and your wives, you have spoken with your mouths and fulfilled it with your hands, saying, "We will certainly perform our vows that we have vowed, to burn sacrifices to the queen of heaven and pour out drink offerings to her." Go ahead and confirm your vows, and certainly perform your

> vows!' Nevertheless hear the word of the Lord, all Judah who are living in the land of Egypt, 'Behold, I have sworn by My great name,' says the Lord, 'never shall My name be invoked again by the mouth of any man of Judah in all the land of Egypt, saying, "As the Lord God lives." Behold, I am watching over them for harm and not for good, and all the men of Judah who are in the land of Egypt will meet their end by the sword and by famine until they are completely gone.'" (Jer. 44:20–27)

Ezekiel also refers to the worship of Ishtar and Tammuz: "Then He brought me to the entrance of the gate of the Lord's house which was toward the north; and behold, women were sitting there weeping for Tammuz" (Ezek. 8:14).

Throughout history, then, Babylon has been an important center of false religion. In the end times, false religion will come back to where it started. The devil who deceived the people at Babel, and from there launched false religion over the earth, will deceive the world once again.

The final world religion, depicted as a harlot, is the theme of this vision, which records the exposure of the harlot, the explanation of the harlot, and the extermination of the harlot.

The Exposure of the Harlot

Then one of the seven angels who had the seven bowls came and spoke with me, saying, "Come here, I will show you the judgment of the great harlot who sits on many waters, with whom the kings of the earth committed acts of immorality, and those who dwell on the earth were made drunk with the wine of her immorality." And he carried me away in the Spirit into a wilderness; and I saw a woman sitting on a scarlet beast, full of blasphemous names, having seven heads and ten horns. The woman was clothed in purple and scarlet, and adorned with gold and precious stones and pearls, having in her hand a gold cup full of abominations and of the unclean things of her immorality, and on her forehead a name was written, a mystery, "BABYLON THE GREAT, THE MOTHER OF HARLOTS AND OF THE ABOMINATIONS OF THE EARTH." And I saw the woman drunk with the blood of the saints, and with the blood of the witnesses of Jesus. When I saw her, I wondered greatly. . . .

And he said to me, "The waters which you saw where the harlot sits, are peoples and multitudes and nations and tongues. (17:1–6, 15)

That it was **one of the seven angels who had the seven bowls** who **came and spoke with** John connects the judgment of the harlot with the seven last plagues (16:1–21). As previously noted, chronology halts in chapters 17 and 18 as the scene shifts from God's judgments to Antichrist's world empire, the target of those judgments. The **great harlot** that will be judged is not an actual prostitute. The term **harlot** is a metaphor for false religion, spiritual defection, idolatry, and religious apostasy. Besides Babylon, several cities in Scripture are designated harlot cities because of their idolatry and pursuit of false religion. Nineveh (Nah. 3:1, 4), Tyre (Isa. 23:15–17), and, sadly, Jerusalem (Isa. 1:21) are examples of cities that committed spiritual fornication.

John's vision exposes several aspects of the harlot city of Babylon: her authority, alliances, apparel, abominations, and accusation.

THE AUTHORITY OF THE HARLOT

who sits on many waters. . . . And he said to me, "The waters which you saw where the harlot sits, are peoples and multitudes and nations and tongues. (17:1*b*, 15)

The harlot in John's vision **sits** in a position of authority and sovereignty like a king on his throne **on** or beside **many waters.** Cities in ancient times were usually located near a source of water, either the ocean, a river, lake, or spring. That was true of Babylon, which was located on the Euphrates River. Jeremiah 51:13 addresses ancient Babylon as "you who dwell by many waters," the same phrase applied in this passage to her future counterpart. Just as the proud capital of the Babylonian empire took her seat beside "many waters," so also will the Babylonian harlot city of the future.

The phrase **many waters** does not, however, refer to the harlot's geographical location. Instead, as the angel explains to John in verse 15, **"The waters which you saw where the harlot sits, are peoples and multitudes and nations and tongues."** The metaphor is an apt one, since a city situated in a commanding position on a great waterway would be highly influential. The **harlot** will not merely influence, but will dominate all the unredeemed **peoples and multitudes and nations and tongues** of the earth (cf. the similar phrases in 5:9; 7:9; 11:9; 13:7; 14:6). The harlot's authority will be universal; the entire world will be committed to the false worship of the Babylonian system, rather than the true God.

THE ALLIANCES OF THE HARLOT

with whom the kings of the earth committed acts of immorality, and those who dwell on the earth were made drunk with the wine of her immorality." And he carried me away in the Spirit into a wilderness; and I saw a woman sitting on a scarlet beast, full of blasphemous names, having seven heads and ten horns. (17:2–3)

Her association with the **kings of the earth** reveals that the scope of the harlot's influence will be immense. Those at the highest levels of power and influence will commit spiritual fornication with her. The phrase **committed acts of immorality** translates a form of the Greek verb *porneuō* ("to commit sexual immorality"). It aptly describes the harlot's interaction with the **kings of the earth.** The symbolism of spiritual adultery, used in the Old Testament to describe Israel's apostasy from Jehovah (cf. Ezek. 16, 23) is inappropriate here. The unredeemed rulers and the nations they represent do not know God and are never pictured as His wife.

Rulers from around the world will become obsessed with the Babylonian harlot. Deceived by the false prophet, Antichrist, and Satan and his demon hosts, they will become enamored with the false world religion. "All who dwell on the earth will worship [Antichrist], everyone whose name has not been written from the foundation of the world in the book of life of the Lamb who has been slain" (13:8). But having joined themselves to the harlot, economically, socially, militarily, politically, and religiously, they will share her disastrous fate.

The harlot will not be allied just with the rulers and influential people of the world. All **those who dwell on the earth** (a technical term for unbelievers; cf. v. 8; 3:10; 6:10; 8:13; 11:10; 13:8, 12, 14; 14:6) **were made drunk with the wine of her immorality.** All the unredeemed will be caught up in the final false religion; they will give their hearts and souls to the abominable Babylonian harlot. The angel is not describing people who are physically **drunk** with literal **wine** committing sexual **immorality** with an actual prostitute, though that may be happening. Instead, he is talking about those who are passionately intoxicated with Antichrist's illicit false world religion. The imagery derives from Jeremiah 51:7, which says of ancient Babylon, "Babylon has been a golden cup in the hand of the Lord, intoxicating all the earth. The nations have drunk of her wine; therefore the nations are going mad."

Before the next alliance of the harlot is revealed, the scene of John's vision changes. The angel with whom John had been speaking **carried** him **away in the Spirit into a wilderness** (cf. 1:10; 4:2; 21:10).

Wilderness translates *erēmos,* which describes a deserted, desolate wasteland like the region where modern Babylon is located. In that place John **saw a woman**—the Babylonian harlot whom the angel had just described (vv. 1–2). She was **sitting on a scarlet beast,** whose description identifies him as Antichrist (cf. 13:1, 4; 14:9; 16:10). That the **woman** was sitting on the **scarlet beast** signifies that he was supporting her. The initial unifying and controlling factor of Antichrist's kingdom will be religion. With the heavens and the earth being ravaged by God's judgments, and the world's political, economic, and military might crumbling, people will turn in desperation to the supernatural. The **beast** and the **woman** will coexist for a while; that is, the religion will be separate from the kingdom of Antichrist at first. But eventually "the beast . . . will hate the harlot and will make her desolate and naked, and will eat her flesh and will burn her up with fire" (v. 16). It will be at that point that the false prophet will make the whole world worship Antichrist (13:11–14), and everything will be one in the beast's universal and comprehensive rule.

Scarlet is the color associated with luxury (2 Sam. 1:24), splendor, and royalty. It is also the color associated with sin (Isa. 1:18) and the hue of blood. Antichrist will be a splendorous, royal, sinful, bloody beast, **full of blasphemous names** (cf. 13:1). In his arrogant self-deification, Antichrist will take for himself the names and titles that belong to God. He will not only blaspheme God by what he claims, but also by what he says. Antichrist "will speak out against the Most High. . . . and will speak monstrous things against the God of gods" (Dan. 7:25; 11:36).

This demonic **scarlet beast** is further described as **having seven heads and ten horns,** showing the extent of his alliances. As will be seen in the discussion of verses 9 and 10 below, the **seven heads** "are seven mountains on which the woman sits, and they are seven kings; five have fallen, one is, the other has not yet come; and when he comes, he must remain a little while" (vv. 9–10). They represent seven mountains, seven past, present, and future governments. The **ten horns** represent ten kings (v. 12), who will rule as subordinates to Antichrist (v. 13).

The harlot's alliances will be comprehensive. Her deadly embrace will encompass all the unredeemed, from kings and rulers to common people; all will worship and submit to her religion. Far from being separated, church and state will be united as never before in human history.

THE APPAREL OF THE HARLOT

The woman was clothed in purple and scarlet, and adorned with gold and precious stones and pearls, (17:4*a*)

Prostitutes usually dress so as to attract attention to themselves, and metaphorically the harlot Babylon will be no different. John saw her **clothed in purple and scarlet,** the colors of royalty, prosperity, nobility, and wealth (cf. Judg. 8:26; Est. 8:15; Lam. 4:5; Ezek. 23:6; Dan. 5:7, 16, 29). That she is **adorned with gold and precious stones and pearls** portrays her as a prostitute who is both attractive (cf. Prov. 7:10) and has plied her trade successfully and become extremely wealthy.

THE ABOMINATIONS OF THE HARLOT

having in her hand a gold cup full of abominations and of the unclean things of her immorality, and on her forehead a name was written, a mystery, "BABYLON THE GREAT, THE MOTHER OF HARLOTS AND OF THE ABOMINATIONS OF THE EARTH." (17:4*b*–5)

As a further indication of her wealth, the harlot had **in her hand a gold cup.** Like prostitutes who want to take everything their victims have, she will make her victims drunk, as did ancient Babylon: "Babylon has been a golden cup in the hand of the Lord, intoxicating all the earth. The nations have drunk of her wine; therefore the nations are going mad" (Jer. 51:7). The harlot's **gold cup** was **full of abominations and of the unclean things of her immorality.** Commenting on that graphic description Donald Grey Barnhouse wrote:

> It is also highly significant that the abominations and filthiness should be spoken of as coming from a golden cup. "Babylon hath been a golden cup in the Lord's hand, that made all the earth drunken: the nations have drunken of her wine; therefore the nations are mad" (Jer. 51:7). To those who are acquainted with the history of ancient religions this significance is heightened by comparisons with the rites of the pagan religious mysteries. A French scholar, Salverte, writing on *The Occult Sciences,* tells of the drinking in connection with these demon ceremonies. "To drink of mysterious beverages," he says, "was indispensable on the part of all who sought initiation in these mysteries. These mysterious beverages were composed of wine, honey, water, and flour, with various other ingredients used locally. From the nature of the ingredients avowedly used, and from the nature of others not avowed, but certainly used, there can be no doubt that they were of an intoxicating nature; and till the aspirants had come under their power, till their understandings had been dimmed, and their passions excited by the medicated draught, they were not duly prepared for what they were either to hear or see." (*Revelation: An Expository Commentary* [Grand Rapids: Zondervan, 1971], 324)

All idolatry is abominable to God (cf. 1 Kings 14:22–24; 2 Kings 21:1–9; Ezek. 20:30–33), and the gross idolatry of Antichrist's false religion will be the worst ever. No wonder Babylon's sins will be "piled up as high as heaven" (18:5), bringing her destruction.

As was customary for prostitutes to identify themselves in the Roman world, the harlot Babylon also had **a name written on her forehead** (cf. Jer. 3:3). The name John saw was **"mystery BABYLON THE GREAT, THE MOTHER OF HARLOTS AND OF THE ABOMINATIONS OF THE EARTH."** (The word **mystery** should be rendered as part of the title.) The harlot is called **mystery BABYLON** to indicate that BABYLON in this context does not refer to a geographical location. This is not ancient Babylon, the Babylon of John's day, or the rebuilt city of Babylon in the end times. The details of this vision can't be applied to any actual city. Here is a previously undisclosed Babylon, a secret reality to be revealed in the end times. This **BABYLON** is the symbol of all worldly resistance to God; it is described as **THE GREAT** because of its far-reaching influence. In fact, so great will be its influence that it is called **THE MOTHER OF HARLOTS AND OF THE ABOMINATIONS OF THE EARTH.** Babylon will be the source of all the false, idolatrous, blasphemous worship in the end times. Her designation as the **MOTHER OF HARLOTS** is appropriate, since harlotry in Scripture often symbolizes idolatry (cf. Judg. 2:17; 8:27, 33; 1 Chron. 5:25; 2 Chron. 21:11; Jer. 3:6, 8–9; Ezek. 16:30–31, 36). So Babylon, the city that spawned the system that corrupted the world with false religion, will do so again.

THE ACCUSATION OF THE HARLOT

And I saw the woman drunk with the blood of the saints, and with the blood of the witnesses of Jesus. When I saw her, I wondered greatly. (17:6)

Like many harlots, this **woman** was **drunk,** but not from drinking alcoholic beverages. In a graphic indictment of her for her murderous persecution of God's people, the Babylonian harlot is pictured as **drunk with the blood of the saints, and with the blood of the witnesses of Jesus.** That vivid expression was commonly used in the ancient world to depict a murderous lust for violence. Some commentators see the **saints** and the **witnesses of Jesus** as two distinct groups, the former being the Old Testament saints and the latter the New Testament saints. More likely, however, the two descriptions refer to the same group and describe God's people throughout history. The important point is that false religion, represented here by the harlot, is a murderer. It has killed millions of believers over the centuries. The history of the church has demonstrated that apostate Christianity is relentless in its persecution of those who hold to true faith in Jesus Christ. While the world becomes drunk with lust for her, the harlot becomes drunk with the blood of God's people. The vision was so appalling that **when** John **saw her,** he **wondered greatly;** expressing that he was confused, shocked, astonished, and frightened by the ghastly vision of such a contrastingly magnificent figure of the woman and such a deadly intent.

The Explanation of the Harlot

And the angel said to me, "Why do you wonder? I will tell you the mystery of the woman and of the beast that carries her, which has the seven heads and the ten horns.

"The beast that you saw was, and is not, and is about to come up out of the abyss and go to destruction. And those who dwell on the earth, whose name has not been written in the book of life from the foundation of the world, will wonder when they see the beast, that he was and is not and will come. Here is the mind which has wisdom. The seven heads are seven mountains on which the woman sits, and they are seven kings; five have fallen, one is, the other has not yet come; and when he comes, he must remain a little while. The beast which was and is not, is himself also an eighth and is one of the seven, and he goes to destruction. The ten horns which you saw are ten kings who have not yet received a kingdom, but they receive authority as kings with the beast for one hour. These have one purpose, and they give their power and authority to the beast. These will wage war against the Lamb, and the Lamb will overcome them, because He is Lord of lords and King of kings, and those who are with Him are the called and chosen and faithful." . . .

"The woman whom you saw is the great city, which reigns over the kings of the earth." (17:7–14, 18)

In response to John's confusion and amazement, **the angel said to** him rhetorically, **"Why do you wonder?"** There was no need for John to remain puzzled by the relation of the beast to this beautiful yet bloody woman in the vision; the angel was about to explain to him **the mystery of the woman** (v. 18) **and of the beast that carries her** (vv. 8–17). The apostle understood that **the woman** represented a false religious system, and that **the beast** was the Antichrist, as the reference to his **seven heads and . . . ten horns** indicates (cf. v. 3; 13:1). What he did not understand was the connection between the two figures. It had been revealed to John in a previous vision that the whole world would worship Antichrist (13:4, 8, 12). That may have been what raised the question in John's mind as to how **the woman** fits into the picture, particularly how it is that **the beast . . . carries her.**

Skipping for the moment the angel's digression in verses 8–14 describing the beast, verse 18 identifies **the woman whom** John **saw** as **the great city, which reigns over the kings of the earth.** Some commentators deny that **the great city** is a literal city, preferring to see it as a symbol of the religious aspect of Antichrist's empire. Some of those who view **the great city** as an actual city identify it as Rome, others as Jerusalem. But the angel quite clearly and repeatedly refers to Babylon on the Euphrates throughout chapters 17–18. Those allusions can be seen by comparing 17:1 with Jeremiah 51:13; 17:2, 4 with Jeremiah 51:7; 18:7 with Isaiah 47:5; 18:2 with Isaiah 13:21 and Jeremiah 51:8; 18:4 with Jeremiah 50:8 and 51:6, 45; 18:5 with Jeremiah 51:9; 18:6 with Jeremiah 50:15 and 51:24; 18:21 with Jeremiah 51:63–64. The description of Babylon's destruction (cf. 18:10, 18, 21) also suggests that an actual city is in view. Thus, a rebuilt city of Babylon will be closely identified with Antichrist's world empire, perhaps as its capital city. That city will be the center of his kingdom, the extent of which will be the whole earth.

The Old Testament predictions of Babylon's total destruction (e.g., Isa. 13:1–14:27; Jer. 50–51) also favor identifying **the great city** with Babylon on the Euphrates. The detailed description those passages give of Babylon's destruction was only partially fulfilled when the Medes and Persians sacked the ancient city of Babylon. As is the case with many Old Testament prophecies, those predictions had both a near and a far fulfillment. Henry Morris noted that

> Babylon, indeed, will be permanently destroyed, as recorded in the very next chapter (18:21), but this has not happened yet. The prophecies of Isaiah and Jeremiah also refer to this future destruction, not merely to Babylon's present-day condition, as is evident from the following considerations, among others: (1) The destruction will take place in the time that the stars and sun are darkened (Isaiah 13:1, 9, 10). (2) The city will become as desolate as Sodom and Gomorrah, burned completely, with no remains whatever (Isaiah 13:19; Jeremiah 50:40). (3) It shall become desolate forever, with neither man nor beast entering it any more (Isaiah 13:20; Jeremiah 51:62). (4) It will be a time of judgment not only for Babylon, but for all nations (Isaiah 13:11–13; Jeremiah 51:49). (5) Its destruction will be followed by universal rest and peace (Isaiah 14:7, 8). (6) Its destruction is directly associated also with the casting of Lucifer into Sheol (Isaiah 14:12–15). (7) Babylon's stones will never be used in future construction elsewhere, whereas the present-day ruins of Babylon have been frequently plundered and

reused in later constructions (Jeremiah 51:26). (*The Revelation Record* [Wheaton, Ill.: Tyndale, 1983], 348)

The site of modern Babylon is strategically located at the crossroads of Asia, Europe, and Africa and is not far from the Persian Gulf. It is also near the world's richest oil fields and has a virtually unlimited water supply from the Euphrates. Those considerations led the famed historian Arnold Toynbee to proclaim that Babylon would be an ideal site for an important political and cultural center (Morris, *Revelation Record,* 349).

In verses 8–14 the angel gives John a lengthy description of the beast. He is explaining to John the relationship between the harlot and the beast, which had mystified the apostle (vv. 6–7). But for John to grasp that connection, the angel needed first to give him further details about the beast. This further describes the nature of the beast and his kingdom, enhancing the description of him in chapter 13.

As previously noted, the **beast that** John **saw** is Antichrist, the satanic ruler of the last and most powerful empire in human history, who will serve as Satan's instrument to attack Israel, persecute believers, conquer the world for Satan, and oppose Christ. Scripture portrays him as an intellectual genius (Dan. 7:8); an outstanding orator (Dan. 7:20); a military leader without parallel in human history (Dan. 7:23); a shrewd, calculating, manipulating politician (Dan. 8:25; 11:21); and the ultimate religious charlatan (2 Thess. 2:4). The angel briefly reviews the detailed description of him given in 13:1–10.

The **beast** is described as one who **was, and is not, and is about to come** again. As noted in the discussion of 13:3 and 12 in chapters four and five of this volume, that phrase refers to Antichrist's faked death and resurrection. The false prophet will use that alleged miracle to deceive the entire world into worshiping Antichrist (13:14). Up till that point, Antichrist's political and economic empire will coexist with the false religious system headed by the false prophet. But after his staged "resurrection," Antichrist, then indwelt by a powerful demon **out of the abyss** (the place where certain demons are incarcerated; cf. 9:11; 11:7; 20:1, 3; Luke 8:31; and the discussion in *Revelation 1–11,* The MacArthur New Testament Commentary [Chicago: Moody, 1999], 257–58), will turn on the false religious system and destroy it. He will tolerate only one religion—the worship of himself.

Antichrist's faked resurrection and his destruction of the false religious system will take place approximately halfway through the Tribulation period. At that point, he will be the undisputed ruler of the world, with unilateral power. He will appear to have reached the apex of his sovereignty, and be ready to thwart the coming of Christ and His kingdom. Yet in reality, Antichrist will be about to be crushed and sent **to**

destruction—eternal damnation in the lake of fire (19:20; 20:10). That will be the appropriate punishment for the "son of destruction" (2 Thess. 2:3), who dared in his insolent pride to copy the sin of Lucifer (cf. Isa. 14:12–14) and challenge the King of Kings and Lord of Lords.

Antichrist's phony resurrection and swift destruction of the false religious system will shock the world. As it does throughout Revelation, the phrase **those who dwell on the earth** describes unbelievers (cf. v. 2; 3:10; 6:10; 8:13; 11:10; 13:8, 12, 14; 14:6). They are the ones **whose name has not been written in the book of life from the foundation of the world** (see the discussion of 13:8 in chapter 4 of this volume), since the names of the elect are recorded in the book of life (3:5; 20:15; 21:27; Phil. 4:3). Amazed and deceived by Antichrist (cf. 2 Thess. 2:9–10), his followers **will wonder when they see the beast, that he was and is not and will come.** The specific cause for their amazement will be Antichrist's seemingly miraculous return to life after receiving an apparently fatal wound (cf. 13:3–4). Only the elect will not fall for Antichrist's deception (Matt. 24:24).

The angel's statement **here is the mind which has wisdom** invites John and his readers to pay close attention to what follows. This unusual expression introduces a difficult and complex aspect of this vision. It will take much wisdom and spiritual insight to understand it, and perhaps only those alive at the time will fully comprehend it.

The first aspect of the vision that needs to be understood is that **the seven heads** of the beast (v. 3) **are seven mountains** or hills **on which the woman sits.** Some commentators associate the **seven mountains** with Rome, famous for being built on seven hills, and identify the **woman** as the Roman Catholic Church. But such an interpretation is too narrow; something more than just Rome must be in view, because Antichrist's empire is worldwide. Nor can the **woman** be the Roman Catholic Church, since, as noted above, verse 18 identifies her as the city of Babylon. Also "when the woman sits on the 'many waters' (v. 1) this must be taken as metaphorical since it is interpreted in v. 15; when the woman sits upon 'a scarlet coloured beast' this again is symbolic; thus when she sits upon the 'seven mountains' this too must be figurative" (James Allen, *What the Bible Teaches: Revelation* [Kilmarnock, Scotland: John Ritchie Ltd., 1997], 424). Finally, the angel's call for spiritual discernment would have been pointless if the seven mountains were an obvious geographical reference to Rome.

All such speculation is unnecessary, because the text plainly identifies the mountains as **seven kings.** Mountains are sometimes used metaphorically in the Old Testament to represent rule, or power (e.g., Ps. 30:7; Isa. 2:2; Jer. 51:25; Dan. 2:35). Here they represent seven world empires embodied in their rulers. The angel tells John that **five have fallen, one is, the other has not yet come.** The five Gentile world empires that had fallen by the time of John's vision are Egypt, Assyria, Babylon, Medo-Persia, and Greece. The **one** that existed at that time was obviously Rome. The **other** one that **has not yet come** is Antichrist's final world empire. Commenting on the significance of the first six empires, Henry Morris writes,

> Though none of these empires ever actually ruled the whole world, each was the greatest kingdom of its own time, particularly in reference to the land and people of Israel and these kingdoms' opposition to the proclamation of God's Word and the accomplishment of His purposes in the world. . . .
>
> These, of course, have not been the *only* kingdoms that have been at enmity with God and His purposes. In this category could also be placed such kingdoms as Syria, Edom, Moab, Midian, and many others, but none of these were empires of great size and influence. On the other hand, there were other great and powerful empires in the ancient world—China, India, and the Incas, for example—but these had only peripheral contact with the Word of God and the chosen people. There were only six kingdoms that met both criteria up to the time of Christ and the apostles. Furthermore, all six of these were not only legitimate heirs of political Babel but also of religious Babel as well. Babylonia, Egypt, Assyria, Persia, Greece, and Rome were all strongholds of the world religion of evolutionary pantheism and idolatrous polytheism. Thus, they appropriately are represented as six heads on the great beast that supports the harlot. (Morris, *Revelation Record,* 337. Italics in the original.)

The angel further explains that **when** Antichrist **comes, he must remain a little while** (cf. 12:12). His empire will be short-lived; he will be given "authority to act for forty-two months" (13:5; the second half of the Tribulation). Then the angel offered the enigmatic comment that **the beast which was and is not, is himself also an eighth and is one of the seven, and he goes to destruction.** How can the **beast** (Antichrist) be **an eighth** king and also **one of the seven?** The answer lies in the phrase **the beast . . . was and is not.** Antichrist will be one of the seven kings before his supposed demise and resurrection and **an eighth** king afterwards during the second phase of his rule. As noted earlier in verse 8, Antichrist will go to **destruction**—eternal damnation in the lake of fire (19:20; 20:10). Unlike the first six empires, his empire will be destroyed by a direct act of God.

The angel further explained that **the ten horns which** John **saw are ten kings.** They cannot be known to any earlier generation because they **have not yet received a kingdom,** since they are part of Antichrist's future empire. **They** will **receive authority as kings with the beast for one hour.** Perhaps Antichrist's empire will be divided into ten administrative regions, which these **ten kings** will rule under him. The reference to **one hour** is a figure of speech that emphasizes the brevity of their rule; their reign will be short-lived because their master's empire itself will be short-lived. During their brief reign, they will be unanimously devoted to Antichrist; they will **have one purpose, and** will **give their power and authority to the beast.** They will do his will, and his will alone.

The agenda of the **ten kings,** like that of Satan and Antichrist, will be to **wage war against the Lamb** at the Battle of Armageddon. Three exceptionally deceitful and powerful demons will be the agents to gather them for that battle:

> And I saw coming out of the mouth of the dragon and out of the mouth of the beast and out of the mouth of the false prophet, three unclean spirits like frogs; for they are spirits of demons, performing signs, which go out to the kings of the whole world, to gather them together for the war of the great day of God, the Almighty. . . . And they gathered them together to the place which in Hebrew is called Har-Magedon. (16:13–14, 16)

John will describe this ill-fated battle in detail in chapter 19, so here he merely notes that **the Lamb will overcome them.** The battle will in reality be a slaughter; the Lord Jesus Christ will utterly destroy the forces gathered against Him at His second coming. The reason all the forces of hell cannot defeat the Lamb is **because He is Lord of lords and King of kings** (cf. 19:14; Deut. 10:17; 1 Tim. 6:15). With Christ when He returns will be **the called and chosen and faithful**—a reference that can only apply to believers (cf. 19:14; Matt. 22:14). The terms are rich in their definition of believers as the eternally elect, **chosen** in the Son before the foundation of the world (Eph. 1:4); the **called,** summoned in time by the Father to repentance and faith that saves (John 6:44); and **faithful,** demonstrating the true saving faith, the genuine eternal life that endures by the power of the Spirit (Rom. 8:9). The Lord Jesus Christ will effortlessly crush the greatest armed force ever assembled when He returns with His elect and the holy angels (Matt. 24:30–31; 2 Thess. 1:7).

Verse 15 was discussed earlier in connection with verse 1, since that is what it explains.

The Extermination of the Harlot

And the ten horns which you saw, and the beast, these will hate the harlot and will make her desolate and naked, and will eat her flesh and will burn her up with fire. For God has put it in their

hearts to execute His purpose by having a common purpose, and by giving their kingdom to the beast, until the words of God will be fulfilled. (17:16–17)

Antichrist's alliance with the false religious system will not last. Eventually **the ten horns** (the ten kings who rule under Antichrist) and **the beast** (Antichrist himself) will come to **hate the harlot.** Having used the false religious system to help him gain control of the world, Antichrist will discard it. In his rampant megalomania, he will want the world to worship only him. He will also no doubt covet the vast wealth of the false religious system. Thus, he will turn on the harlot **and will make her desolate and naked, and will eat her flesh and will burn her up with fire.** That graphic language of extreme violence is used to make clear that Antichrist and his henchmen will utterly and completely obliterate all vestiges of the false religious system.

Antichrist's self-serving, satanically inspired actions are, however, precisely in the scope of God's sovereign plan. In fact, it is **God** who will **put it in** the **hearts** of Antichrist's followers **to execute His purpose by having a common purpose, and by giving their kingdom to the beast.** God's power is behind the destruction and consolidation of the evil empire; as always, Satan is the instrument of God's purposes. The one-world unification government so long sought by the humanists will have finally arrived, only to be destroyed in one great act of divine judgment. All **the words of God**—every prophecy of Christ's return and the setting up of His kingdom—**will be fulfilled** completely.

God hates every form of false religion and will not tolerate those who seek to rob Him of His glory (Isa. 42:8). Antichrist's religious empire will be judged and destroyed. So also, as chapter 18 of Revelation reveals, will be the political and economic aspects of that evil world empire.

Babylon Is Fallen (Revelation 18:1–24)

13

After these things I saw another angel coming down from heaven, having great authority, and the earth was illumined with his glory. And he cried out with a mighty voice, saying, "Fallen, fallen is Babylon the great! She has become a dwelling place of demons and a prison of every unclean spirit, and a prison of every unclean and hateful bird. For all the nations have drunk of the wine of the passion of her immorality, and the kings of the earth have committed acts of immorality with her, and the merchants of the earth have become rich by the wealth of her sensuality."

I heard another voice from heaven, saying, "Come out of her, my people, so that you will not participate in her sins and receive of her plagues; for her sins have piled up as high as heaven, and God has remembered her iniquities. Pay her back even as she has paid, and give back to her double according to her deeds; in the cup which she has mixed, mix twice as much for her. To the degree that she glorified herself and lived sensuously, to the same degree give her torment and mourning; for she says in her heart, 'I sit as a queen and I am not a widow, and will never see mourning.' For this reason in one day her plagues will come,

pestilence and mourning and famine, and she will be burned up with fire; for the Lord God who judges her is strong.

"And the kings of the earth, who committed acts of immorality and lived sensuously with her, will weep and lament over her when they see the smoke of her burning, standing at a distance because of the fear of her torment, saying, 'Woe, woe, the great city, Babylon, the strong city! For in one hour your judgment has come.'

"And the merchants of the earth weep and mourn over her, because no one buys their cargoes any more—cargoes of gold and silver and precious stones and pearls and fine linen and purple and silk and scarlet, and every kind of citron wood and every article of ivory and every article made from very costly wood and bronze and iron and marble, and cinnamon and spice and incense and perfume and frankincense and wine and olive oil and fine flour and wheat and cattle and sheep, and cargoes of horses and chariots and slaves and human lives. The fruit you long for has gone from you, and all things that were luxurious and splendid have passed away from you and men will no longer find them. The merchants of these things, who became rich from her, will stand at a distance because of the fear of her torment, weeping and mourning, saying, 'Woe, woe, the great city, she who was clothed in fine linen and purple and scarlet, and adorned with gold and precious stones and pearls; for in one hour such great wealth has been laid waste!' And every shipmaster and every passenger and sailor, and as many as make their living by the sea, stood at a distance, and were crying out as they saw the smoke of her burning, saying, 'What city is like the great city?' And they threw dust on their heads and were crying out, weeping and mourning, saying, 'Woe, woe, the great city, in which all who had ships at sea became rich by her wealth, for in one hour she has been laid waste!' Rejoice over her, O heaven, and you saints and apostles and prophets, because God has pronounced judgment for you against her."

Then a strong angel took up a stone like a great millstone and threw it into the sea, saying, "So will Babylon, the great city, be thrown down with violence, and will not be found any longer. And the sound of harpists and musicians and flute-players and trumpeters will not be heard in you any longer; and no craftsman of any craft will be found in you any longer; and the sound of a mill will not be heard in you any longer; and the light of a lamp will not shine in you any longer; and the voice of the bridegroom and bride will not be heard in you any longer; for your mer-

chants were the great men of the earth, because all the nations were deceived by your sorcery. And in her was found the blood of prophets and of saints and of all who have been slain on the earth." (18:1–24)

Throughout history the petty kingdoms and empires built by proud, arrogant, God-rejecting rebels have come and gone. The spirit of humanism first expressed at Babel has permeated human history ever since. Unshakably optimistic despite centuries of war, slaughter, injustice, and cruelty, people still seek a utopia, to be brought about by humanity's upward scientific progress. Having taken control (so they think) of their own destiny through science, sinners have no use for God and haughtily replace Him as self-styled gods devoted to their own sovereignty.

But God cannot be so easily replaced, nor His plans thwarted by the whims of sinful men (Isa. 43:13; 46:10). In fact, in a profound, if brief, statement in Acts 14:16, Scripture says that God "permitted all the nations to go their own ways." In Psalm 2:2–4 the psalmist recorded God's reaction to man's impotent fury against Him:

> The kings of the earth take their stand
> And the rulers take counsel together
> Against the Lord and against His Anointed, saying,
> "Let us tear their fetters apart
> And cast away their cords from us!"
>
> He who sits in the heavens laughs,
> The Lord scoffs at them.

Compared to the glorious, indescribable majesty of the omnipotent God, all of man's vaunted empires are a mere "drop from a bucket" (Isa. 40:15). In His sight, they are but "a speck of dust on the scales" (Isa. 40:15), so insignificant that they "are as nothing before Him, they are regarded by Him as less than nothing and meaningless" (Isa. 40:17). The inescapable reality is that God, not man, will have the last word in human history, and that word will be a word of judgment.

From beginning to end, the Bible warns of coming judgment on sinners who reject God and blaspheme His holy name. Job declared that "the wicked is reserved for the day of calamity; they will be led forth at the day of fury" (Job 21:30). David noted that "the Lord . . . has established His throne for judgment, and He will judge the world in righteousness" (Ps. 9:7–8). Psalm 96:13 warns that God "is coming to judge the earth. He will judge the world in righteousness and the peoples in His faithfulness." Isaiah wrote, "According to their deeds, so He will repay, wrath to His adversaries, recompense to His enemies; to the coastlands He will make recompense" (Isa. 59:18). In His kingdom parables, Jesus also described the coming time of judgment:

> "So just as the tares are gathered up and burned with fire, so shall it be at the end of the age. The Son of Man will send forth His angels, and they will gather out of His kingdom all stumbling blocks, and those who commit lawlessness, and will throw them into the furnace of fire; in that place there will be weeping and gnashing of teeth. Then the righteous will shine forth as the sun in the kingdom of their Father. He who has ears, let him hear.
>
> "The kingdom of heaven is like a treasure hidden in the field, which a man found and hid again; and from joy over it he goes and sells all that he has and buys that field.
>
> "Again, the kingdom of heaven is like a merchant seeking fine pearls, and upon finding one pearl of great value, he went and sold all that he had and bought it.
>
> "Again, the kingdom of heaven is like a dragnet cast into the sea, and gathering fish of every kind; and when it was filled, they drew it up on the beach; and they sat down and gathered the good fish into containers, but the bad they threw away. So it will be at the end of the age; the angels will come forth and take out the wicked from among the righteous, and will throw them into the furnace of fire; in that place there will be weeping and gnashing of teeth." (Matt. 13:40–50)

The apostle Paul declared to the Greek philosophers gathered on Mars Hill in Athens that God "has fixed a day in which He will judge the world in righteousness through a Man whom He has appointed, having furnished proof to all men by raising Him from the dead" (Acts 17:31). To the Thessalonians he wrote:

> The Lord Jesus will be revealed from heaven with His mighty angels in flaming fire, dealing out retribution to those who do not know God and to those who do not obey the gospel of our Lord Jesus. These will pay the penalty of eternal destruction, away from the presence of the Lord and from the glory of His power, when He comes to be glorified in His saints on that day, and to be marveled at among all who have believed—for our testimony to you was believed. (2 Thess. 1:7–10)

In 2 Peter 2:9 Peter added, "The Lord knows how to rescue the godly from temptation, and to keep the unrighteous under punishment for the day of judgment."

But nowhere in Scripture is there a more detailed description of the coming judgment than in Revelation 6–18. Those chapters describe the future seven-year period known as the Tribulation. Summing up what they reveal about that period, God's judgment will rain down on the earth in the form of the seal, trumpet, and bowl judgments. Although those judgments will be worldwide in scope, they will focus particularly on Antichrist's world empire of Babylon. That empire will involve both a religious and a commercial aspect. At the midpoint of the Tribulation, Antichrist will destroy the false Babylonian religious system, which will be absorbed into commercial Babylon (cf. the discussion in chap. 12 of this volume). Religion will not cease to exist, but will be restricted to the worship of Antichrist. The Babylon in view in chapter 18 is Antichrist's worldwide commercial empire, which will rule the world during the last three and a half years of the Tribulation. That Antichrist will be able to build the greatest commercial empire the world has ever known in the midst of the devastating judgments of the Tribulation reveals his incredible power.

God's destruction of commercial Babylon is the theme of chapter 18. It is thus a very somber chapter; it is a requiem, a dirge for the funeral of humanity. With the destruction of the satanic last and greatest human empire, the stage is set for the triumphant return of the Lord Jesus Christ.

Though some commentators view it as a symbol for Antichrist's whole godless system, the Babylon described in chapter 18 is most likely an actual city. It is called a city five times in the chapter (vv. 10, 16, 18, 19, 21), and other features in the text imply that a literal city is in view. Since the text plainly describes Babylon as a city, and there is nothing in the context to indicate otherwise, it is safest to view it as a real city. The specific Old Testament prophecies of Babylon's destruction and perpetual desolation (Isa. 13:19–22; 14:22–23; Jer. 50:13, 39; 51:37), as yet unfulfilled, also argue that chapter 18 describes an actual city (cf. the discussion in chap. 12 of this volume). But while Babylon will be an actual city, its influence will be worldwide. As Antichrist's capital city, it will be the hub of and represent his commercial empire. Thus, the judgment and destruction of Babylon will kill the head, and the rest of the body of Antichrist's whole world empire will follow in death.

Babylon will have received plenty of warnings of its impending doom by the occurrence of the events of chapter 18. The 144,000 Jewish evangelists, the two witnesses, the rest of the redeemed, and an angel flying in the heavens will have proclaimed the gospel message. That message includes the truth that God will judge those who refuse to repent. In addition, earlier in the Tribulation an angel specifically warned of Babylon's impending doom, crying out "Fallen, fallen is Babylon the great, she who has made all the nations drink of the wine of the passion of her immorality" (14:8). The angel spoke of Babylon's yet future fall as if it had already happened, emphasizing the certainty of its doom.

But despite the repeated warnings, the people of the world will refuse to repent (cf. 9:20–21; 16:9, 11), and God's judgment will fall on Babylon. Chapter 18 records seven aspects of that judgment on Antichrist's commercial empire: judgment pronounced, judgment avoided, judgment defined, judgment lamented, judgment enjoyed, judgment completed, and judgment justified.

Judgment Pronounced

After these things I saw another angel coming down from heaven, having great authority, and the earth was illumined with his glory. And he cried out with a mighty voice, saying, "Fallen, fallen is Babylon the great! She has become a dwelling place of demons and a prison of every unclean spirit, and a prison of every unclean and hateful bird. For all the nations have drunk of the wine of the passion of her immorality, and the kings of the earth have committed acts of immorality with her, and the merchants of the earth have become rich by the wealth of her sensuality." (18:1–3)

This solemn opening pronouncement of judgment gives two reasons for Babylon's impending destruction: pervasive demonic activity and wretched sensuality. As it often does in Revelation (cf. 4:1; 7:9; 15:5; 19:1), the phrase **after these things** marks the beginning of a new vision. While still discussing the general theme of Antichrist's world empire, destroyed finally by the seven bowl judgments (chap. 16), chapter 18 moves from its religious aspects to its commercial aspects. As this new vision opened, John **saw another angel,** distinct from the one in 17:1. Some view this angel as Christ, but the use of *allos* (another of the same kind) instead of *heteros* (another of a different kind) indicates that this is an angel of the same type as the one in 17:1. He may be the angel who had earlier predicted Babylon's downfall (14:8). Three features in the text reveal his unusual power and importance.

First, he came **down from heaven** with **great authority.** He left the presence of God with delegated authority to act on God's behalf.

Second, when he arrived, **the earth was illumined with his glory.** He will make his dramatic appearance onto a darkened stage, for the fifth bowl will have plunged the world into darkness (16:10). Manifesting the flashing brilliance of a glorious heavenly being against the blackness, the angel will be an awe-inspiring sight to the shocked and terrified earth dwellers.

Third, the angel **cried out with a mighty voice.** No one will be able to ignore him; everyone will hear him as well as see him. His message will add to the consternation and terror caused by his appearance. It will be a word of woe, ill tidings for Antichrist and his followers: **"Fallen, fallen is Babylon the great!"** The judgment predicted in 14:8 will now be carried out. This will be a greater and more far-reaching judgment than the one pronounced in identical words on ancient Babylon (Isa. 21:9). A comparison of this passage with 16:17–19 suggests that this judgment takes place when the seventh bowl is poured out:

> Then the seventh angel poured out his bowl upon the air, and a loud voice came out of the temple from the throne, saying, "It is done." And there were flashes of lightning and sounds and peals of thunder; and there was a great earthquake, such as there had not been since man came to be upon the earth, so great an earthquake was it, and so mighty. The great city was split into three parts, and the cities of the nations fell. Babylon the great was remembered before God, to give her the cup of the wine of His fierce wrath.

The first cause given for Babylon's destruction is that **she has become a dwelling place of demons and a prison of every unclean spirit** (a synonym for **demons,** cf. 16:13–14). It was in the vicinity of Babylon that 200 million formerly bound demons were released at the sounding of the sixth trumpet (9:13–16). They, along with the demons released from the abyss at the sounding of the fifth trumpet (9:1–11), those cast from heaven with Satan (12:4, 9), and those previously on earth, will be confined in Babylon. God will, so to speak, gather all the rotten eggs into one basket before disposing of them.

Babylon will also be **a prison of every unclean and hateful bird.** That phrase symbolizes the city's total destruction (cf. Isa. 34:11). Like grotesque carrion birds, the demons will hover over the doomed city, waiting for its fall. The depiction of the demons as **unclean and hateful** reflects heaven's view of them.

Babylon's destruction will also come because **all the nations have drunk of the wine of the passion of her immorality, and the kings of the earth have committed acts of immorality with her, and the merchants of the earth have become rich by the wealth of her sensuality.** Antichrist's evil religious and commercial empire will spread its hellish influence to **all the nations** of the world. Having **drunk of the wine of the passion of her immorality** (cf. 14:8; 17:2), the people of the world will fall into a religious and materialistic stupor. The all-encompassing terms **all the nations, the kings of the earth,** and **the merchants of the earth** reveal that Babylon will seduce the entire world. The unregenerate people of the world will lust for Babylon, passionately desiring to commit **acts of** spiritual **immorality** with her. Likewise, **the merchants of the earth** will **have become rich by the wealth of her sensuality.** In the beginning, the world will cash in on Babylon's financial prosperity.

Having thrown off any semblance of self-control or self-restraint, sinners will indulge in a wild materialistic orgy. Like those in ancient Babylon, they will be partying when their city is destroyed (cf. Dan. 5:1–30). James's condemnation of the ruthless wealthy could also apply to them:

> Come now, you rich, weep and howl for your miseries which are coming upon you. Your riches have rotted and your garments have become moth-eaten. Your gold and your silver have rusted; and their rust will be a witness against you and will consume your flesh like fire. It is in the last days that you have stored up your treasure! Behold, the pay of the laborers who mowed your fields, and which has been withheld by you, cries out against you; and the outcry of those who did the harvesting has reached the ears of the Lord of Sabaoth. You have lived luxuriously on the earth and led a life of wanton pleasure; you have fattened your hearts in a day of slaughter. (James 5:1–5)

Judgment Avoided

I heard another voice from heaven, saying, "Come out of her, my people, so that you will not participate in her sins and receive of her plagues; for her sins have piled up as high as heaven, and God has remembered her iniquities." (18:4–5)

God's judgment on this commercially prosperous but morally bankrupt society can be avoided, as **another voice from heaven** makes clear. The use of *allos* (**another** of the same kind) suggests that the speaker is an angel like the one in verse 1. The message he proclaims, **"Come out of her, my people,"** is a call for God's people to disentangle themselves from the world system. It may also be an evangelistic call to God's elect to come to faith in Christ and come out of Satan's kingdom (cf. Col. 1:13). In both cases, the message is to abandon the system.

Throughout the terrifying judgments of the Tribulation, God will save people. The result of the gospel preaching by the 144,000 Jewish evangelists, the two witnesses, and an angel flying in midheaven will be the greatest harvest of souls the world has ever known (cf. 7:9). Many of these believers will be martyred for their faith in Christ when they refuse to take the mark of the beast (13:15–16). The survivors will face powerful temptations to participate in the system. Family and friends will no doubt pressure them to save themselves by accepting the mark of the beast. The need to obtain the basic necessities of life will also pressure them to conform to the system (cf. 13:17).

The exhortation to flee Babylon finds an Old Testament parallel in the prophets' warnings to flee ancient Babylon. "Go forth from Babylon!" cried Isaiah. "Flee from the Chaldeans!" (Isa. 48:20). Jeremiah echoed Isaiah's warning: "Wander away from the midst of Babylon and go forth from the land of the Chaldeans. . . . Flee from the midst of Babylon, and each of you save his life! Do not be destroyed in her punishment, for this is the Lord's time of vengeance; He is going to render recompense to her. . . . Come forth from her midst, My people, and each of you save yourselves from the fierce anger of the Lord" (Jer. 50:8; 51:6, 45).

Believers in the present day must also avoid the temptation to get caught up in the world system. "Do not be conformed to this world," Paul commanded the believers at Rome, "but be transformed by the renewing of your mind, so that you may prove what the will of God is, that which is good and acceptable and perfect" (Rom. 12:2). To the Corinthians he wrote,

> Do not be bound together with unbelievers; for what partnership have righteousness and lawlessness, or what fellowship has light with darkness? Or what harmony has Christ with Belial, or what has a believer in common with an unbeliever? Or what agreement has the temple of God with idols? For we are the temple of the living God; just as God said,
> "I will dwell in them and walk among them;
> And I will be their God, and they shall be My people.
> Therefore, come out from their midst and be separate," says the Lord.
> "And do not touch what is unclean;
> And I will welcome you." (2 Cor. 6:14–17)

James wrote that "pure and undefiled religion in the sight of our God and Father is . . . to keep oneself unstained by the world" (James 1:27), and sharply rebuked those caught up in the world system: "You adulteresses, do you not know that friendship with the world is hostility toward God? Therefore whoever wishes to be a friend of the world makes himself an enemy of God" (James 4:4). In his first epistle, the apostle John exhorted believers, "Do not love the world nor the things in the world. If anyone loves the world, the love of the Father is not in him" (1 John 2:15).

The biblical truth that believers are not to be involved in the world system will take on new urgency as Babylon faces imminent destruction. The angel's message to the believers still in that city is the same one that the angels brought to Lot (Gen. 19:12–13): Get out before you are caught up in God's judgment of that wicked place.

Believers are to flee Babylon so that they **will not participate in her sins.** The materialistic, pleasure-mad, demon-infested city of Babylon will exert an almost irresistible influence on believers to **participate in her sins.** Like Joseph (Gen. 39:7–12; cf. 1 Cor. 10:14; 1 Tim. 6:11;

2 Tim. 2:22) they must flee to avoid succumbing to "the lust of the flesh and the lust of the eyes and the boastful pride of life" (1 John 2:16).

God's people must also flee Babylon so they do not **receive of her plagues.** Some view the **plagues** as a reference to the bowl judgments, which are also called plagues (15:1, 6, 8; 16:9). The bowl judgments, however, are worldwide in scope; hence, there would be no place to escape to (cf. 18:9–10). Therefore it is best to see these **plagues** as specific judgments on Babylon, perhaps, as noted above, in conjunction with the outpouring of the seventh bowl (cf. 16:17–19).

Finally, believers must flee Babylon because **her sins have piled up as high as heaven** (cf. Jer. 51:9). **Piled** is from *kollaō,* which literally means "to glue together," or "to join." Babylon's sins will pile up like a new Tower of Babel (Gen. 11:3–4), but unlike the ancient tower, her sins will reach **as high as heaven.** Then the angel adds that **God has remembered her iniquities** (cf. 16:19). He will take note of them as He did that earlier monument to man's sinful, arrogant, prideful rebellion at Babel. The blessed truth is that God says of believers, "I will not remember your sins. . . . I will forgive their iniquity, and their sin I will remember no more" (Isa. 43:25; Jer. 31:34). But for defiant, unrepentant Babylon there will be no forgiveness, only judgment.

Judgment Defined

"Pay her back even as she has paid, and give back to her double according to her deeds; in the cup which she has mixed, mix twice as much for her. To the degree that she glorified herself and lived sensuously, to the same degree give her torment and mourning; for she says in her heart, 'I sit as a queen and I am not a widow, and will never see mourning.' For this reason in one day her plagues will come, pestilence and mourning and famine, and she will be burned up with fire; for the Lord God who judges her is strong." (18:6–8)

Babylon's judgment is defined as the angel now speaks not to John, but to God. His call for vengeance on Babylon, **pay her back even as she has paid,** parallels the prayers of the martyred saints recorded in 6:9–10: "When the Lamb broke the fifth seal, I saw underneath the altar the souls of those who had been slain because of the word of God, and because of the testimony which they had maintained; and they cried out with a loud voice, saying, 'How long, O Lord, holy and true, will You refrain from judging and avenging our blood on those who dwell on the earth?'" The angel's prayer for justice is based on the Old Testament principle of *lex talionis,* the law of retaliation, the principle of "an eye for an eye, and a tooth for a tooth" (Matt. 5:38; cf. Ex. 21:23–24; Lev. 24:19–20; Deut. 19:21). Babylon has been extended enough grace and heard enough warnings. It is time for vengeance. It is time for her destruction.

The angel's plea is reminiscent of the Old Testament saints' pleas for vengeance on ancient Babylon. In Psalm 137:8 the psalmist wrote, "O daughter of Babylon, you devastated one, how blessed will be the one who repays you with the recompense with which you have repaid us." Jeremiah also pleaded for vengeance on Babylon:

> "Draw up your battle lines against Babylon on every side,
> All you who bend the bow;
> Shoot at her, do not be sparing with your arrows,
> For she has sinned against the Lord.
> Raise your battle cry against her on every side!
> She has given herself up, her pillars have fallen,
> Her walls have been torn down.
> For this is the vengeance of the Lord:
> Take vengeance on her;
> As she has done to others, so do to her."
> (Jer. 50:14–15)

> "Summon many against Babylon,
> All those who bend the bow:
> Encamp against her on every side,
> Let there be no escape.
> Repay her according to her work;
> According to all that she has done, so do to her;
> For she has become arrogant against the Lord,
> Against the Holy One of Israel."
> (Jer. 50:29)

> "But I will repay Babylon and all the inhabitants of Chaldea for all their evil that they have done in Zion before your eyes," declares the Lord. (Jer. 51:24)

> For the destroyer is coming against her, against Babylon,
> And her mighty men will be captured,
> Their bows are shattered;
> For the Lord is a God of recompense,
> He will fully repay.
> (Jer. 51:56)

It is important to note that retaliation belongs to God alone. The Bible explicitly forbids Christians to take their own vengeance. Believers must "not say, 'I will repay evil'"; instead they are to "wait for the Lord, and He will save [them]" (Prov. 20:22). They are to "bless those who persecute [them]" (Rom. 12:14), "never pay[ing] back evil for evil to anyone" (Rom. 12:17). They must "never take [their] own revenge . . . but leave room for the wrath of God, for it is written, 'Vengeance is Mine, I will repay,' says the Lord." If their "enemy is hungry, [they must] feed him, and if he is thirsty, give him a drink; for in so doing [they] will heap burning coals on his head." Instead of being "overcome by evil, [they must] overcome evil with good" (Rom. 12:19–21). Christians are to "see that no one repays another with evil for evil, but always seek after that which is good for one another and for all people" (1 Thess. 5:15), "not returning evil for evil or insult for insult, but giving a blessing instead" (1 Pet. 3:9). But those commands do not preclude holy God's righteous judgment of sinners.

The angel's request that God **give back to** Babylon **double according to her deeds** (literally in the Greek "double the double things") is a request that Babylon's punishment fit her crimes. Double has been her iniquity; double must be her punishment. Babylon's sins have overflowed, piling up as high as the heavens, and the angel calls for God's judgment to overflow on her in equal measure.

Double has the sense of fullness or completeness. In the Mosaic Law, wrongdoers were often required to pay double restitution for their crimes:

> "If what he stole is actually found alive in his possession, whether an ox or a donkey or a sheep, he shall pay double. . . .
>
> "If a man gives his neighbor money or goods to keep for him and it is stolen from the man's house, if the thief is caught, he shall pay double. . . . For every breach of trust, whether it is for ox, for donkey, for sheep, for clothing, or for any lost thing about which one says, 'This is it,' the case of both parties shall come before the judges; he whom the judges condemn shall pay double to his neighbor." (Ex. 22:4, 7, 9).

The prophets note that Israel received double for her sins (Isa. 40:1–2; Jer. 16:18). Jeremiah prayed that God would "crush [his persecutors] with twofold destruction!" (Jer. 17:18).

Further stating his request that God fully punish Babylon, the angel asks that **in the cup which she has mixed,** God would **mix twice as much for her.** Fittingly, in the very cup that Babylon used to deceive the nations (v. 3; 14:8; 17:2, 4; Jer. 51:7) she is to receive a double portion of God's wrath. The imagery of the cup of God's wrath also appears in 14:10 and 16:19.

Then the angel calls on God a third time to exact complete vengeance on Babylon: **"To the degree that she glorified herself and lived sensuously, to the same degree give her torment and**

mourning; for she says in her heart, 'I sit as a queen and I am not a widow, and will never see mourning.'" To the degree is a call to match the punishment to the crime, a biblical principle (Isa. 3:16ff.; Prov. 29:23; Luke 1:51; 14:11). Three sins call for Babylon's judgment. First, she was proud; **she glorified herself.** God, who said, "I will not give My glory to another" (Isa. 42:8), hates pride (Prov. 6:16–17; James 4:6). Second, she pursued self-gratification; she **lived sensuously.** The Bible pronounces those who do so to be dead even while they live (1 Tim. 5:6). Third, she was guilty of self-sufficiency, of presumptuously overestimating her power; **she** said **in her heart, "I sit as a queen and I am not a widow, and will never see mourning."** That proud boast echoes that of ancient Babylon, who said "I will be a queen forever. . . . I will not sit as a widow, nor know loss of children" (Isa. 47:7, 8; cf. Ezek. 27:3; 28:2; Zeph. 2:15). Yet God's devastating reply was that "these two things shall come on you suddenly in one day: Loss of children and widowhood. They shall come on you in full measure in spite of your many sorceries, in spite of the great power of your spells" (Isa. 47:9).

For those three sins Babylon will receive **torment and mourning.** *Basanismos* (**torment**) literally means torture (cf. vv. 10, 15; 9:5; 14:11). **Mourning** refers to the grief that the torture produces. Hell will be a place of both unimaginable torment (20:10; Luke 16:23–24, 28) and crushing grief (Matt. 8:12; 13:42, 50; 22:13; 24:51; 25:30).

Then the angel notes that **for this reason,** the sins catalogued above, **in one day her plagues will come.** Babylon's destruction will not be progressive. The wicked city will be instantly destroyed (cf. vv. 10, 17, 19). Daniel 5 records the similar fate that befell ancient Babylon; the city fell the very night that God wrote its doom on the wall of the king's palace (cf. Dan. 5:30). As noted above, the **plagues** that will destroy Babylon are specific judgments on that city, possibly in connection with the seventh bowl. Three **plagues** will result in Babylon's complete devastation: **pestilence and mourning and famine**—heaven's fitting answer to her proud boast in verse 7. After those three plagues have run their course, Babylon **will be burned up with fire.**

Babylon's doom is certain and cannot be avoided **for the Lord God who judges her is strong.** No one can frustrate God's plans, or keep Him from accomplishing what He purposes to do. Job said to God, "I know that You can do all things, and that no purpose of Yours can be thwarted" (Job 42:2). Despite the "plans [that] are in a man's heart . . . the counsel of the Lord, it will stand" (Prov. 19:21). "For the Lord of hosts has planned," declared Isaiah, "and who can frustrate it? And as for His stretched-out hand, who can turn it back?" (Isa. 14:27). A chastened and humbled Nebuchadnezzar affirmed that God "does according to His will in the host of heaven and among the inhabitants of earth; and no one can ward off His hand or say to Him, 'What have You done?'" (Dan. 4:35). God Himself declares that "there is none who can deliver out of My hand; I act and who can reverse it? . . . My purpose will be established, and I will accomplish all My good pleasure" (Isa. 43:13; 46:10). All the power of wicked men and demons will not be enough to deliver Babylon from God's judgment.

Judgment Lamented

"And the kings of the earth, who committed acts of immorality and lived sensuously with her, will weep and lament over her when they see the smoke of her burning, standing at a distance because of the fear of her torment, saying, 'Woe, woe, the great city, Babylon, the strong city! For in one hour your judgment has come.'

"And the merchants of the earth weep and mourn over her, because no one buys their cargoes any more—cargoes of gold and silver and precious stones and pearls and fine linen and purple and silk and scarlet, and every kind of citron wood and every article of ivory and every article made from very costly wood and bronze and iron and marble, and cinnamon and spice and incense and perfume and frankincense and wine and olive oil and fine flour and wheat and cattle and sheep, and cargoes of horses and chariots and slaves and human lives. The fruit you long for has gone from you, and all things that were luxurious and splendid have passed away from you and men will no longer find them. The merchants of these things, who became rich from her, will stand at a distance because of the fear of her torment, weeping and mourning, saying, 'Woe, woe, the great city, she who was clothed in fine linen and purple and scarlet, and adorned with gold and precious stones and pearls; for in one hour such great wealth has been laid waste!' And every shipmaster and every passenger and sailor, and as many as make their living by the sea, stood at a distance, and were crying out as they saw the smoke of her burning, saying, 'What city is like the great city?' And they threw dust on their heads and were crying out, weeping and mourning, saying, 'Woe, woe, the great city, in which all who had ships at sea became rich by her wealth, for in one hour she has been laid waste!'" (18:9–19)

Nothing so clearly reveals the hardness of sinners' hearts as their lack of sorrow over their sin. Through the years of devastating judgments, the Tribulation sinners will relentlessly refuse to mourn over their sin. But though they will not lament over their sin, they will cry over the destruction of Babylon. When the glorious centerpiece, the head of Antichrist's empire, is judged and destroyed, there will be worldwide dismay and mourning.

The first mourners introduced are the leaders, **the kings of the earth.** This group includes the ten kings who rule Antichrist's kingdom under his authority (17:12), as well as the rest of the world's leaders under them. They will greet the news of Babylon's destruction with shock and dismay. The destruction of the seat of Antichrist's political and economic power will strike a fatal blow to his empire. The fall of Babylon will be a symbol of the fall of that entire evil world system.

These leaders are the same ones **who committed acts of immorality and lived sensuously with her** (v. 3). Once again, Babylon is pictured as a harlot (cf. 17:1, 15, 16), whose death causes her lovers to **weep and lament over her.** Some of those crossing the Euphrates on their way to Armageddon (16:12) may actually **see the smoke** rising from the **burning** city (cf. Gen. 19:28; Josh. 8:20–21; Isa. 34:10). The rest will watch Babylon's destruction through the world's media. All will be careful to keep their **distance** from the stricken city. They will be powerless to help and will **fear** that they may share **her torment.** This fearful scene supports the idea that Babylon is an actual city, not a symbol for the entire world system. Obviously, the entire world is not destroyed at this point, since those watching Babylon burn are safe for the moment. Babylon's destruction is, however, a precursor to the doom that will soon fall on the entire world.

As they watch her burn, the leaders will cry out in anguish, **"Woe, woe, the great city, Babylon, the strong city! For in one hour your judgment has come."** As the crown jewel of Antichrist's empire, Babylon will be a **great city.** And since it will have survived the devastating judgments of the Tribulation up to that point, the leaders will believe it to be a **strong city.** Thus, Babylon's swift destruction will shock and amaze them, and they will cry out to her in dismay, **"For in one hour your judgment has come."** The judgment on Babylon will happen rapidly, just as verse 8 predicted.

The next mourners to appear on the scene are **the merchants of the earth.** These businessmen will **weep and mourn over** Babylon **because no one buys their cargoes any more.** The destruction of Antichrist's capital will end any semblance of normalcy on the devastated planet. Whatever economic activity will have been taking place on an earth reeling under the escalating difficulty brought on by the catastrophic divine judgments will then come to a halt.

Then follows a list of twenty-eight items or categories of merchandise that comprised the merchants' cargoes: **gold and silver and precious stones and pearls and fine linen and purple and silk and scarlet, and every kind of citron wood and every article of ivory and every article made from very costly wood and bronze and iron and marble, and cinnamon and spice and incense and perfume and frankincense and wine and olive oil and fine flour and wheat and cattle and sheep, and cargoes of horses and chariots and slaves and human lives** (lit. "bodies and souls of men"). These items were common commodities in the ancient world (many of them are included on the list in Ezek. 27:12–24) and were the source of immense financial gain. They are only representative of the great wealth of Antichrist's future commercial empire. John Phillips writes:

> What a catalog of opulence! What a vivid picture of a great, commercial city, trafficking in every luxury the heart could desire. This is the world's great Vanity Fair. It offers articles of adornment and display, beautiful things to grace the mansions of the world's millionaires. It deals in exotic spices and perfumes, in delicacies for the table, in provisions for banquets, in slaves, and in the souls of men. And Babylon imported all these things. . . . Babylon's demand for this world's goods was insatiable; ever it clamored for more and more! (*Exploring Revelation,* rev. ed. [Chicago: Moody, 1987; reprint, Neptune, N.J.: Loizeaux, 1991], 225)

Continuing their lament, the merchants now address Babylon directly: **The fruit you long for has gone from you, and all things that were luxurious and splendid have passed away from you and men will no longer find them.** All of the city's **luxurious and splendid** (Gk., *lampros,* a word that may refer to clothing) possessions **have passed away from** her and **men will no longer find them.** They will be gone forever as God bankrupts the system. The words **no longer** translate a double double negative in the Greek text, which is the strongest form of negation in the Greek language. That indicates these items will never be found again.

Joining the leaders, **the merchants of these things, who became rich from her, will stand at a distance because of the fear of her torment, weeping and mourning, saying, "Woe, woe, the great city, she who was clothed in fine linen and purple and scarlet, and adorned with gold and precious stones and pearls; for in one hour such great wealth has been laid waste!"** They weep and mourn, not out of some emotional sympathy for the decimated city, but because with its collapse they have been stripped of the key source of their financial resources. The merchants lament because their materialistic passions can no longer be fulfilled. The weeping that begins then will last for eternity in hell (Matt. 8:12; 13:42, 50; 22:13; 24:51; 25:30). These greedy merchants are the classic illustration of all those in all times who gain the whole world, but forfeit their souls (Mark 8:36).

Then a third and final group in the vision joins the funeral dirge for Babylon: **every shipmaster and every passenger and sailor, and as many as make their living by the sea.** In addition to her political and economic importance, Babylon will also be an important distribution center. With its destruction, there will be no more goods to be transported by those who **make their living by the sea.** Like the rulers and merchants, the sailors were careful to stand **at a** safe **distance** from the city. As they gazed on the ruined city they **were crying out as they saw the smoke of her burning, saying, "What city is like the great city?"** Their lament is reminiscent of the proud boast of Antichrist's deluded followers in 13:4, "Who is like the beast, and who is able to wage war with him?" But the seemingly indestructible city is already destroyed before their eyes, and its seemingly invincible ruler will shortly meet his end (19:20).

Then, in a typical ancient expression of grief, the sailors **threw dust on their heads** (cf. Josh. 7:6; 1 Sam. 4:12; 2 Sam. 1:2; 15:32; Job 2:12; Lam. 2:10; Ezek. 27:30). Like the rulers (vv. 9–10) and the merchants (vv. 15–16), they too will cry out, **"Woe, woe, the great city."** That is an expression of pain, suffering, and grief, but not of repentance. The sailors do not mourn over their sins, or those of Babylon, but because of their lost business, since **all who had ships at sea became rich by** Babylon's **wealth.** Like the rulers (v. 10) and the merchants (v. 17), the sailors also express amazement at the swiftness of Babylon's downfall, exclaiming, **"In one hour she has been laid waste!"** In an astonishingly short period of time, the city that was the source of their wealth was destroyed.

Judgment Enjoyed

"Rejoice over her, O heaven, and you saints and apostles and prophets, because God has pronounced judgment for you against her." (18:20)

Heaven will have quite a different perspective on Babylon's judgment than that of Antichrist's earthly followers. The angel who began speaking in verse 4 then addressed the redeemed in heaven: the **saints** (a general term for all believers) **and apostles and prophets** (the special class of saints given to the church, as indicated in Eph. 2:20; 4:11). He calls on them to **rejoice over** Babylon's fall, **because God has pronounced judgment for** them **against her.** The long-awaited moment of vindication, retribution, and vengeance, for which the martyred Tribulation believers prayed (6:9–10) and for which all the redeemed hoped, will have arrived. Heaven rejoices, not over the damnation of sinners, but because of the triumph of righteousness, the exaltation of Jesus Christ, the elimination of His enemies, and the arrival of His kingdom on the earth.

Judgment Completed

Then a strong angel took up a stone like a great millstone and threw it into the sea, saying, "So will Babylon, the great city, be thrown down with violence, and will not be found any longer. And the sound of harpists and musicians and flute-players and trumpeters will not be heard in you any longer; and no craftsman of any craft will be found in you any longer; and the sound of a mill will not be heard in you any longer; and the light of a lamp will not shine in you any longer; and the voice of the bridegroom and bride will not be heard in you any longer; (18:21–23*a*)

Another **strong angel** (cf. 5:2; 10:1) now appeared in the vision. In a dramatic act picturing Babylon's destruction, he **took up a stone like a great millstone** (like those used to grind grain; they were four to five feet in diameter, a foot thick, and very heavy) **and threw it into the sea. "So,"** explained the angel, "**will Babylon, the great city, be thrown down with violence, and will not be found any longer."** In one moment, as that stone disappeared into the sea, Babylon will disappear. A similar demonstration predicted the doom of ancient Babylon:

> Then Jeremiah said to Seraiah, "As soon as you come to Babylon, then see that you read all these words aloud, and say, 'You, O Lord, have promised concerning this place to cut it off, so that there will be nothing dwelling in it, whether man or beast, but it will be a perpetual desolation.' And it will come about as soon as you finish reading this scroll, you will tie a stone to it and throw it into the middle of the Euphrates, and say, 'Just so shall Babylon sink down and not rise again because of the calamity that I am going to bring upon her; and they will become exhausted.'" (Jer. 51:61–64)

So complete will be Babylon's destruction that none of the normal activities of human life will take place. There will be no one making music at all; **the sound of harpists and musicians and flute-players and trumpeters will not be heard.** There will be no one working; **no craftsman of any craft will be found.** There will be no one preparing food; **the sound of a mill will not be heard.** The city will be so completely abandoned that even **the light of a lamp will not shine in** her **any longer.** There will be no more falling in love; **the voice of the bridegroom and bride will not be heard in** her **any longer.** Babylon will be so thoroughly destroyed that it will never rise again, as predicted by the Old Testament prophets (Isa. 13:19–22; 14:22–23; Jer. 50:13, 39; 51:37).

Judgment Justified

"for your merchants were the great men of the earth, because all the nations were deceived by your sorcery. And in her was found the blood of prophets and of saints and of all who have been slain on the earth." (18:23*b*–24)

Three final reasons are given for Babylon's judgment. First, her **merchants were the great men of the earth,** using their wealth to ascend to positions of power, prominence, and influence. The abuses of the proud, arrogant rich are well documented in Scripture. "Is it not the rich who oppress you and personally drag you into court?" asked James (James 2:6). Later in his epistle James further indicted the rich for their abuse of the poor:

> Behold, the pay of the laborers who mowed your fields, and which has been withheld by you, cries out against you; and the outcry of those who did the harvesting has reached the ears of the Lord of Sabaoth. You have lived luxuriously on the earth and led a life of wanton pleasure; you have fattened your hearts in a day of slaughter. You have condemned and put to death the righteous man; he does not resist you. (James 5:4–6)

Isaiah (Isa. 3:14–15; 5:8) and Amos (Amos 4:1; 5:11; 8:4–6) also condemned the rich for their self-aggrandizement and maltreatment of the poor.

A second reason for Babylon's being judged is that **all the nations were deceived by** her **sorcery. Sorcery** is from *pharmakeia,* the root word of the English words "pharmacy" and "pharmaceuticals." The word is used in the New Testament to refer to magic and occult practices (9:21; Gal. 5:20). Babylon's hold on the world will not be entirely due to her military and economic power, but also to her occult influence.

A final reason given for Babylon's judgment is her murderous slaughter of God's people; **in her was found the blood of prophets**

and of saints and of all who have been slain on the earth (cf. 6:10; 11:7; 13:7, 15; 16:6; 17:6). The heavenly rejoicing over Babylon's downfall also mentions this: "After these things I heard something like a loud voice of a great multitude in heaven, saying, 'Hallelujah! Salvation and glory and power belong to our God; because His judgments are true and righteous; for He has judged the great harlot who was corrupting the earth with her immorality, and He has avenged the blood of His bond-servants on her'" (19:1–2).

The words of Jesus in Luke 12:16–21 form a fitting conclusion to the message of judgment on commercial Babylon:

> And He told them a parable, saying, "The land of a rich man was very productive. And he began reasoning to himself, saying, 'What shall I do, since I have no place to store my crops?' Then he said, 'This is what I will do: I will tear down my barns and build larger ones, and there I will store all my grain and my goods. And I will say to my soul, "Soul, you have many goods laid up for many years to come; take your ease, eat, drink and be merry."' But God said to him, 'You fool! This very night your soul is required of you; and now who will own what you have prepared?' So is the man who stores up treasure for himself, and is not rich toward God."

Heavenly Hallelujahs (Revelation 19:1–10) 14

After these things I heard something like a loud voice of a great multitude in heaven, saying, "Hallelujah! Salvation and glory and power belong to our God; because His judgments are true and righteous; for He has judged the great harlot who was corrupting the earth with her immorality, and He has avenged the blood of His bond-servants on her." And a second time they said, "Hallelujah! Her smoke rises up forever and ever." And the twenty-four elders and the four living creatures fell down and worshiped God who sits on the throne saying, "Amen. Hallelujah!" And a voice came from the throne, saying, "Give praise to our God, all you His bond-servants, you who fear Him, the small and the great." Then I heard something like the voice of a great multitude and like the sound of many waters and like the sound of mighty peals of thunder, saying, "Hallelujah! For the Lord our God, the Almighty, reigns. Let us rejoice and be glad and give the glory to Him, for the marriage of the Lamb has come and His bride has made herself ready." It was given to her to clothe herself in fine linen, bright and clean; for the fine linen is the righteous acts of the saints.

Then he said to me, "Write, 'Blessed are those who are

invited to the marriage supper of the Lamb.'" And he said to me, "These are true words of God." Then I fell at his feet to worship him. But he said to me, "Do not do that; I am a fellow servant of yours and your brethren who hold the testimony of Jesus; worship God. For the testimony of Jesus is the spirit of prophecy." (19:1–10)

The Bible lists many reasons for giving thanks to God. He is to be praised first of all for all the perfections of His glorious being. "Through Him then," urged the writer of Hebrews, "let us continually offer up a sacrifice of praise to God, that is, the fruit of lips that give thanks to His name" (Heb. 13:15; cf. 2 Sam. 22:50; Pss. 7:17; 44:8; 122:4; 140:13). One of the perfections God is to be praised for is His holiness. In Psalm 30:4 David declared, "Sing praise to the Lord, you His godly ones, and give thanks to His holy name" (cf. 1 Chron. 16:35; Pss. 97:12; 106:47). God is also to be praised for His mercy. Concluding a psalm in which God's lovingkindness is praised in every verse, Psalm 136:26 commands, "Give thanks to the God of heaven, for His lovingkindness is everlasting" (cf. 1 Chron. 16:41; 2 Chron. 20:21; Pss. 107:8, 15, 21, 31; 118:1, 29; Jer. 33:11). Scripture also extols God's goodness: "Praise the Lord!" cried the psalmist, "Oh give thanks to the Lord, for He is good" (Ps. 106:1; cf. 1 Chron. 16:34; Ezra 3:11; Pss. 54:6; 107:1). The comforting knowledge of God's nearness caused the psalmist to exclaim, "We give thanks to You, O God, we give thanks, for Your name is near" (Ps. 75:1).

God is to be praised not only for His attributes, but also for His mighty works. Isaiah wrote, "O Lord, You are my God; I will exalt You, I will give thanks to Your name; for You have worked wonders" (Isa. 25:1; cf. 1 Chron. 16:9; Pss. 9:1; 26:7; 89:5; 105:2; 107:8, 15, 21, 31). Chief among those works are creation (Ps. 139:14; Rev. 4:11) and salvation (1 Sam. 2:1; Pss. 9:14; 13:5; 35:9; Acts 11:21–23; 16:34; Rom. 6:17; 2 Thess. 2:13).

The many rich blessings God bestows on His people also call forth praise, chief of which is the gift of His Son. That matchless gift caused Paul to exclaim, "Thanks be to God for His indescribable gift!" (2 Cor. 9:15; cf. Isa. 9:6; Luke 2:38; John 3:16). Paul also praised God for his deliverance from indwelling sin (Rom. 7:23–25), believers' triumph over death and the grave (1 Cor. 15:57), and the triumph of the gospel (2 Cor. 2:14; 4:15). His call to the ministry (1 Tim. 1:12), the faith exhibited by others (Rom. 1:8; 2 Thess. 1:3), and the grace God poured out on believers (1 Cor. 1:4) also caused Paul to be thankful. The apostle also modeled and taught the truth that Christians are to give thanks for all the basic necessities of life (Acts 27:35; Rom. 14:6; 1 Tim. 4:3–4), which are tangible expressions of God's love and care for them. In summary, giving thanks to God is to be done always (Eph. 5:20) and for everything (1 Thess. 5:18).

But of all the things God is to be praised for, perhaps the least expected is for His destruction of the wicked. Yet that, too, is an important theme in Scripture. Deuteronomy 32:43 reads, "Rejoice, O nations, with His people; for He will avenge the blood of His servants, and will render vengeance on His adversaries." Psalm 48:11 adds, "Let Mount Zion be glad, let the daughters of Judah rejoice because of Your judgments," while Psalm 58:10–11 notes that "The righteous will rejoice when he sees the vengeance; he will wash his feet in the blood of the wicked. And men will say, 'Surely there is a reward for the righteous; surely there is a God who judges on earth!'" In Psalm 96:11–13 the psalmist declared, "Let the heavens be glad, and let the earth rejoice; let the sea roar, and all it contains; let the field exult, and all that is in it. Then all the trees of the forest will sing for joy before the Lord, for He is coming, for He is coming to judge the earth. He will judge the world in righteousness and the peoples in His faithfulness." As man's day draws to a close and the true King prepares to return to earth, heaven will rejoice. Heavenly hallelujahs ring out in chapter 19 over the final destruction of the evil world system and the glorious victory of the returning Messiah (cf. 5:9–14).

As that long-awaited time approaches, the scene in Revelation shifts from earth, where it has been since chapter 6, to heaven. The intervening chapters have detailed God's cataclysmic explosion of judgmental fury on the sinful world. That fury began to be poured out when the Lord Jesus Christ, the rightful heir to the universe, received the title deed to the earth from His Father (5:1–14). As He unrolled that scroll and broke its seven seals, terrifying judgments struck the earth. The seal judgments were followed by the equally devastating trumpet and bowl judgments.

The particular target of God's wrath was Antichrist's worldwide religious, political, and economic empire, symbolized by its capital city of Babylon. Babylon's destruction was described in detail in chapters 17 and 18. That destruction, which caused dismay and mourning on earth (18:9–11, 15–19), now brings joy to heaven. With the devastation of its capital city, Antichrist's empire was dealt a fatal blow. The final destruction of the world's forces will take place shortly at Armageddon (19:11–21).

Some might think heaven's rejoicing over Babylon's destruction to be insensitive and uncaring. But that shortsighted view ignores the reality that those sinners will have had the greatest opportunity to repent of any people who have ever lived. They will have experienced the unprecedented disasters of the Tribulation, which they will acknowledge to be God's judgments (6:17). They will also have heard the most powerful preaching of the gospel in history, from the 144,000 Jewish evangelists, the two witnesses, the host of the redeemed saved during the Tribulation, and even a powerful angel (14:6–7). Yet despite all that, they will remain unrepentant to the very end (9:20–21; 16:9, 11), hardened into irreversible unbelief and defiant hatred of God.

The praise seen in heaven throughout Revelation (4:8–11; 5:9–14; 7:10–12; 11:15–18; 15:3–4; 16:5–6) reaches a crescendo in this text. The heavenly rejoicing is not over the damnation of those who reject God (cf. Ezek. 18:23, 32; 33:11), but because Jesus Christ will soon remove those obstinate sinners from the world. God will then be properly honored, the Lord Jesus Christ enthroned, and the earth restored to its lost glory. Heaven rejoices because history is finally going to reach its culmination as the true King establishes His kingdom on earth.

As the text unfolds, five reasons for heaven's joy become evident. Heaven rejoices because full salvation has come, because justice is meted out, because rebellion is ended, because God is in control, and because the marriage of the Lamb is completed.

Because Full Salvation Has Come

After these things I heard something like a loud voice of a great multitude in heaven, saying, "Hallelujah! Salvation and glory and power belong to our God; (19:1)

As it does throughout Revelation (cf. 4:1; 7:9; 15:5; 18:1), the phrase **after these things** marks the beginning of a new vision. This new vision takes place after the destruction of Babylon (chaps. 17–18) and before the triumphant return of Jesus Christ (19:11–21) to establish the Millennial Kingdom (20:1–10). As the loud laments over Babylon's destruction fade into silence, loud hallelujahs ring out in heaven.

In his vision John **heard something like a loud voice of a great multitude in heaven.** The text does not identify those whose composite voices make up the **loud voice** John heard, but they are likely angels. This **great multitude** does not appear to include the redeemed saints, since they are encouraged to join in the praise later (vv. 5–8). The uncounted millions of holy angels make up a majestic, awe-inspiring choir.

The angelic chorus opens with the important word **Hallelujah,** an exclamation of praise to God. The Greek word *Allēlouia* is a transliteration of a Hebrew phrase comprised of the verb *halal* ("to praise") and the noun *Yah* ("God"). It appears only in this chapter in the New Testament (cf. vv. 3–4, 6). The Hebrew phrase first appears in Psalm 104:35, "Let sinners be consumed from the earth and let the wicked be no more. Bless the Lord, O my soul. Praise the Lord!" In its first Old Testament appearance, as in its first New Testament appearance, **Hallelujah** expresses praise for God's judgment on the wicked oppressors of His people. The Hebrew phrase is associated with God's deliverance of His people from Egypt in Psalms 113–18, which are known collectively as the Egyptian Hallel. It is a word often associated with both the judgment of the ungodly and the salvation of God's people.

Heaven rejoices specifically because **salvation** has come for God's people, and with it the **glory and power** that **belong to God** (cf. 1 Chron. 29:11) have been put on display. The word **salvation** does not focus on justification or sanctification, but celebrates the final aspect of salvation history, the glorification of the saints in the kingdom of Christ. The imminent coming of Jesus Christ prompts this praise as the angels anticipate the glory of His kingdom.

Because Justice Is Meted Out

"because His judgments are true and righteous; for He has judged the great harlot who was corrupting the earth with her immorality, and He has avenged the blood of His bond-servants on her." (19:2)

Heaven also rejoices **because** God's **judgments are true and righteous** (cf. 16:7), as evidenced by the destruction of wicked, deserving Babylon. That joy over the imminent triumph of God's justice is something that all who pray and work for righteousness can relate to. Throughout history God's people have been disturbed by the inequity, injustice, and unrighteousness in the world, and have longed for God's justice to come. Anticipating the coming of the Messiah, Isaiah wrote:

> For a child will be born to us, a son will be given to us;
> And the government will rest on His shoulders;
> And His name will be called Wonderful Counselor, Mighty God,
> Eternal Father, Prince of Peace.
> There will be no end to the increase of His government or of peace,
> On the throne of David and over his kingdom,
> To establish it and to uphold it with justice and righteousness
> From then on and forevermore.
> The zeal of the Lord of hosts will accomplish this.
> (Isa. 9:6–7)

Jeremiah also anticipated the time when the Messiah would bring justice and righteousness to the earth: "'Behold, the days are coming,' declares the Lord, 'When I shall raise up for David a righteous Branch; and He will reign as king and act wisely and do justice and righteousness in the land'" (Jer. 23:5). Earlier in Revelation the martyred Tribulation believers "cried out with a loud voice, saying, 'How long, O Lord, holy and true, will You refrain from judging and avenging our blood on those who dwell on the earth?'" (Rev. 6:10). Like Isaiah and Jeremiah, they eagerly anticipated the day when God's justice would triumph. God's people hate sin because it mocks God and love righteousness because it exalts Him. They long for a world characterized by holiness and justice. But that will only happen when Christ establishes His righteous kingdom and rules with a rod of iron (v. 15; 2:27; 12:5; Ps. 2:9).

The stage was set for establishing that kingdom when God **judged the great harlot who was corrupting the earth with her immorality.** Babylon is identified as **the great harlot** (cf. 17:1, 15–16), Satan and Antichrist's system that seduced the unbelieving world to believe the lies of Satan. Because that system rules the whole world, it is thus guilty of **corrupting the earth with** its **immorality** (cf. 14:8; 17:2; 18:3, 9). The evil of the commercial and religious Babylon will be pervasive and dominant, leading to equitable retribution from God.

A further reason for Babylon's judgment was her maltreatment of God's people (cf. 18:24). As a result, **He has avenged the blood of His bond-servants on her.** That God will exact vengeance for His people is clearly taught in Scripture. Deuteronomy 32:42–43 reads:

> "'I will make My arrows drunk with blood,
> And My sword shall devour flesh,
> With the blood of the slain and the captives,
> From the long-haired leaders of the enemy.'
> Rejoice, O nations, with His people;
> For He will avenge the blood of His servants,
> And will render vengeance on His adversaries,
> And will atone for His land and His people."

"It is only just," wrote Paul to the Thessalonians, "for God to repay with affliction those who afflict you, and to give relief to you who are afflicted and to us as well when the Lord Jesus will be revealed from heaven with His mighty angels in flaming fire, dealing out retribution to those who do not know God and to those who do not obey the gospel of our Lord Jesus" (2 Thess. 1:6–8). Revelation 18:20 commands, "Rejoice over [Babylon], O heaven, and you saints and apostles and prophets, because God has pronounced judgment for you against her" (cf. 16:5–6; 2 Sam. 22:48; Pss. 58:10–11; 79:10; 94:1–2; Jer. 15:15; 20:12; 51:36; Joel 3:20–21). It is both fitting and just that those who caused the moral ruin of the world and persecuted God's people should face His vengeance.

Because Rebellion Is Ended

And a second time they said, "Hallelujah! Her smoke rises up forever and ever." (19:3)

Babylon's judgment provoked the first outburst of heavenly rejoicing; the aftermath of her destruction prompts the heavenly chorus for **a second time** to say, **"Hallelujah!"** At the climax of her judgment, Babylon was "burned up with fire" (18:8; cf. 17:16), and sinners mourned as they watched the pall of smoke rise into the sky (18:9, 18). That the **smoke rises up forever and ever** indicates that this judgment is final, permanent, and irreversible. The language is similar to that used of God's destruction of Sodom and Gomorrah (Gen. 19:28), and Edom (Isa. 34:10). The flames and smoke will eventually die out, but the judgment is eternal on the souls of the sinners destroyed. And hell is a place "where their worm does not die, and the fire is not quenched" (Mark 9:48), where the damned "will be tormented with fire and brimstone in the presence of the holy angels and in the presence of the Lamb. And the smoke of their torment goes up forever and ever" (14:10–11).

The destruction of the last and most powerful empire in human history marks the end of man's day. The rebellion that began long ago in the Garden of Eden is finally ended (apart from a futile, short-lived revolt at the end of the Millennium; 20:7–10). There will be no more false religion, worldly philosophy, injustice, unrighteousness; all the sorry results of human depravity will be vanquished.

Because God Is in Control

And the twenty-four elders and the four living creatures fell down and worshiped God who sits on the throne saying, "Amen. Hallelujah!" And a voice came from the throne, saying, "Give praise to our God, all you His bond-servants, you who fear Him, the small and the great." Then I heard something like the voice of a great multitude and like the sound of many waters and like the sound of mighty peals of thunder, saying, "Hallelujah! For the Lord our God, the Almighty, reigns." (19:4–6)

In agreement with the angelic chorus, hallelujahs ring out from other heavenly residents. The **twenty-four elders** are best seen as representatives of the church (for a discussion of the identity of the twenty-four elders, see *Revelation 1–11,* The MacArthur New Testament Commentary [Chicago: Moody, 1999], 148–50). The **four living creatures** are cherubim, a high-ranking order of angels (for more information on the four living creatures, see *Revelation 1–11*, 152–54). These two groups have **worshiped** God throughout Revelation (cf. 4:8–11; 5:8–12, 14; 7:11; 11:16–18). Prostrate before God's **throne** the two new additions to the heavenly chorus cried out, **"Amen. Hallelujah!"** That phrase comes from Psalm 106:48 and indicates their solemn agreement (cf. the use of **Amen,** "so let it be," in 5:14; 7:12) with the heavenly rejoicing over Babylon's downfall.

The text does not identify the owner of the **voice** that **came from the throne,** but it is likely an angel, since he refers to God as **our God.** The voice authoritatively calls another group to join in the anthem of praise, **saying, "Give praise to our God, all you His bond-servants, you who fear Him, the small and the great."** The redeemed believers in heaven are described as God's **bond-servants** (cf. v. 2; 1:1; 2:20; 7:3; 11:18; 15:3; 22:3, 6; Luke 2:29; Acts 4:29; 16:17; Rom. 1:1; Gal. 1:10; Phil. 1:1; Col. 1:7; 4:7; 2 Tim. 2:24; Titus 1:1; James 1:1; 2 Pet. 1:1; Jude 1), and those **who fear Him** (cf. Deut. 6:13; 8:6; 10:12, 20; 13:4; Josh. 24:14; 1 Sam. 12:14, 24; 2 Kings 17:39; Pss. 22:23, 25; 25:14; 33:18; 34:7, 9; 85:9; 103:11, 13, 17; Luke 1:50). The all-inclusive phrase **the small and the great** (cf. 11:18) transcends all human categories and distinctions to embrace everyone. All the redeemed are called to praise God.

When the redeemed obeyed the command from the heavenly voice and added their voices to the heavenly chorus, the dramatic sound John heard was **something like the voice of a great multitude.** The loud chorus of praise rose to a deafening crescendo, which the apostle likened to **the sound of many waters** (cf. 1:15; 14:2) **and . . . the sound of mighty peals of thunder** (cf. 6:1; 14:2). The fitting finale to the heavenly oratorio of praise is a fourth **"Hallelujah!"** followed by the motive for it—**"For the Lord our God, the Almighty, reigns."** The evil world system has been completely destroyed, and God's kingdom has come in its fullness. This usage of **Hallelujah** is reminiscent of Psalms 146–50, which repeatedly offer praise for God's sovereign rule and eternal fellowship with the redeemed. The title **Almighty** is used nine times in Revelation (v. 15; 1:8; 4:8; 11:17; 15:3; 16:7, 14; 21:22).

Because the Marriage of the Lamb Is Completed

"Let us rejoice and be glad and give the glory to Him, for the marriage of the Lamb has come and His bride has made herself ready." It was given to her to clothe herself in fine linen, bright and clean; for the fine linen is the righteous acts of the saints.

Then he said to me, "Write, 'Blessed are those who are

invited to the marriage supper of the Lamb.'" And he said to me, "These are true words of God." Then I fell at his feet to worship him. But he said to me, "Do not do that; I am a fellow servant of yours and your brethren who hold the testimony of Jesus; worship God. For the testimony of Jesus is the spirit of prophecy." (19:7–10)

The heavenly praise continues with a call for gladness, rejoicing, and giving God **glory** for yet a fifth reason—**the marriage of the Lamb.** The imagery of marriage is used frequently in Scripture. A marriage was the single greatest celebration and social event of the biblical world. Wedding preparations and celebrations in ancient times were even more elaborate and involved than those of today and also lasted longer. They consisted of three distinct stages. First was the betrothal, or engagement. This was an arrangement by both sets of parents contracting the marriage of their children. It was legally binding and could only be broken by a divorce (cf. Matt. 1:18–19). A betrothal contract was often signed long before the children reached the marriageable age of thirteen or fourteen. Since a marriage represented the union of two families, it was natural for the parents to be involved. And there were years of preparation for the time of marriage, as the boy prepared for his bride. The second stage of a wedding was the presentation, a time of festivities just before the actual ceremony. Those festivities could last up to a week or more, depending on the economic and social status of the bride and groom. The third and most significant stage of a wedding was the actual ceremony, during which the vows were exchanged. At the end of the presentation festivities, the groom and his attendants would go to the bride's house and take her and her bridesmaids to the ceremony. After the ceremony would come a final meal, followed by the consummation of the marriage.

Scripture uses the familiar imagery of a wedding to picture the Lord's relationship with His church. Second Corinthians 11:2 mentions the betrothal of the church to Christ. Paul wrote, "For I am jealous for you with a godly jealousy; for I betrothed you to one husband, so that to Christ I might present you as a pure virgin." The church's betrothal contract was signed in eternity past when the Father promised the Son a redeemed people and wrote their names in the Book of Life. The apostle Paul described the church's presentation in Ephesians 5:25–27: "Husbands, love your wives, just as Christ also loved the church and gave Himself up for her, so that He might sanctify her, having cleansed her by the washing of water with the word, that He might present to Himself the church in all her glory, having no spot or wrinkle or any such thing; but that she would be holy and blameless." That presentation will take place at the Rapture. Speaking of both the present time of preparation, as He makes a home for His bride, and the moment of presentation, when He comes for her, Jesus said, "In My Father's house are many dwelling places; if it were not so, I would have told you; for I go to prepare a place for you. If I go and prepare a place for you, I will come again and receive you to Myself, that where I am, there you may be also" (John 14:2–3). In the imagery of an ancient wedding, the Rapture marks the time when the Bridegroom, the Lord Jesus Christ (cf. Matt. 9:15; Mark 2:19–20; Luke 5:34–35; John 3:28–29), takes His bride to His Father's house. During the Tribulation, the raptured church will be presented in heaven. But at the end of those seven years of joyous fellowship and wonderful celebration, the time will come for the wedding ceremony, the marriage of the Lamb. That final union of the Bridegroom and the bride is marked by a great supper.

Some have attempted to combine the marriage parables in Matthew 22:1–14 and Matthew 25:1–13 with Revelation 19:7–10 to form a sort of "marriage theology." But that violates the hermeneutical principle that doctrine cannot be formulated by combining elements from various illustrations or parables. Marriage is incidental in the two Matthew parables; in fact, neither one even mentions a bride. The theme of the parable of the marriage feast (Matt. 22:1–14) is Israel's apostasy and rejection of God. The invited guests who rejected the King's invitation to the great celebration symbolize Israel; the uninvited guests brought in from the streets symbolize the Gentile church (cf. Matt. 8:11–12). Thus, in this parable the church does not represent the bride, but the guests. The parable of the ten virgins (Matt. 25:1–13) emphasizes the importance of spiritual preparedness. Again, believers in that parable are not represented by the bride, but the virgins (the bride's attendants). The five foolish virgins were like professing believers, unprepared for Christ's return (i.e., unsaved); the five wise ones were true believers, genuinely prepared. The point of the parable is that professed believers must be ready (i.e., truly saved) when Christ returns to set up His kingdom. There will be no second opportunity for the unprepared (unsaved) because the Day of the Lord judgment is total and final. Only believers will survive to enter the kingdom.

Because the New Testament uses marriage to illustrate such a variety of spiritual principles, those illustrations cannot be used to interpret Revelation 19. Each parable or illustration must be interpreted in its own context. To blend together details from such unconnected illustrations with a common theme is not the way to interpret this text (or any text).

The entire heavenly chorus, including angels (v. 1), the twenty-four elders (v. 4), the four living creatures (v. 4), and all the host of the redeemed (v. 5), is exhorted to **rejoice and be glad and give the glory to Him** because all the preparation is complete and **the marriage of the Lamb has come.** Betrothed in eternity past, presented in the Father's house since the Rapture, the church is now ready for the wedding ceremony to begin. That ceremony will coincide with the establishment of the millennial kingdom, and stretch throughout that thousand-year period to be finally consummated in the new heavens and the new earth (cf. 21:1–2). The idea of a thousand-year-long ceremony may seem far-fetched; yet it is no more difficult than several thousand years of betrothal. And it must be remembered that "a thousand years in [God's] sight are like yesterday when it passes by" (Ps. 90:4), and that "with the Lord one day is like a thousand years, and a thousand years like one day" (2 Pet. 3:8). In the new heavens and the new earth, the bride concept will be expanded to include not only the church, but also all the redeemed of all ages as the New Jerusalem becomes the bridal city (21:1–2). It should be noted that in the Old Testament, God is the Bridegroom of Israel (Isa. 54:5–6; 62:5; Jer. 31:32; Ezek. 16:7–14; Hos. 2:16, 19).

In preparation for her marriage to the Lamb, **His bride has made herself ready.** That was not, of course, by her own works, but rather by God's gracious working. Paul taught that believers, by God's grace, participate in His work in their lives: "So then, my beloved, just as you have always obeyed, not as in my presence only, but now much more in my absence, work out your salvation with fear and trembling; for it is God who is at work in you, both to will and to work for His good pleasure" (Phil. 2:12–13). To the Colossians he wrote, "I labor, striving according to His power, which mightily works within me" (Col. 1:29). The bride has made herself ready in the power of God, by the grace of God, through the work of the Spirit of God. Purged from all sin and impurity (cf. 1 Cor. 3:12–15), she is a flawless, blameless, unblemished virgin.

Having been presented glorified, purified, and spotless before God's throne, **it was given to** the church **to clothe herself in fine linen, bright and clean. Fine linen** was expensive and beautiful cloth (cf. 18:12, 16), like that worn by Joseph (Gen. 41:42), David (1 Chron. 15:27), and Mordecai (Est. 8:15); *lampros* (**bright**) means glistening, shining, or radiant (cf. its use in Acts 10:30); *katharos* (**clean**) is translated "pure" in 21:18, 21. Such dazzling garments were worn earlier in Revelation by angels (15:6), and will be the clothing of the armies of heaven (made up of both angels and the redeemed saints) that accompany Christ when He returns to earth (v. 14).

The **fine linen** with which the bride is clothed in the vision represents **the righteous acts of the saints.** At salvation, believers were clothed with Christ's righteousness, imputed to them (Rom. 3:21–24; 4:5; 5:19; 1 Cor. 1:30; 2 Cor. 5:21; Phil. 3:8–9). But now the church is clothed with a righteousness of its own; the glorified believers are intrinsically righteous, like the holy angels. No longer will the church have only an imputed righteousness, but also then an imparted holy perfection. The promise of 1 John 3:2, "Beloved, now we are children of God, and it has not appeared as yet what we will be. We know that when He appears, we will be like Him, because we will see Him just as He is" (cf. Rom. 8:19–21) is then fulfilled.

Then the angel who had been speaking with John (cf. 17:1, 15) **said to** the apostle, **"Write, 'Blessed are those who are invited to the marriage supper of the Lamb.'"** This is the fourth of seven beatitudes in Revelation (cf. 1:3; 14:13; 16:15; 20:6; 22:7, 14), all introduced by the word **blessed,** which means "happy," "joyous," "satisfied," and "fulfilled." The recipients of this blessing are **those who are invited to the marriage supper of the Lamb.** That they are **invited** guests marks them as a distinct group from the church, since a bride would hardly be invited to her own wedding.

These guests represent Old Testament believers. Matthew 8:11 and Luke 13:28 both refer to Abraham, Isaac, and Jacob as being in the kingdom, and Luke 13:28 also mentions the prophets. All the heroes of the faith mentioned in Hebrews 11 will be among the invited guests. So will John the Baptist, the greatest of all Old Testament believers (Matt. 11:11), who described himself as the friend of the bridegroom (John 3:29) and hence one of the invited guests. All the Tribulation saints, glorified and still alive on earth and entering the millennial kingdom, will be guests.

Some may question why the church age believers should be granted the honor of being the bride, while believers from other ages are merely guests. But one may equally ask why God singled out Israel to be the covenant people. The only answer to both questions is that God sovereignly purposed that it be so (cf. Deut. 7:7–8). It must be remembered that the wedding imagery is just that; imagery that is not reality, but pictures God's intimate union with His people. There will be no "second-class citizens" in God's kingdom, just as all the participants in a wedding enjoy the celebration. And in the new heavens and the new earth, as noted above, the imagery of the bride will be expanded to encompass all the redeemed from all ages (21:1–2).

Israel looked forward to this great wedding banquet:

> The Lord of hosts will prepare a lavish banquet for all peoples on this mountain;
> A banquet of aged wine, choice pieces with marrow,
> And refined, aged wine.
> And on this mountain He will swallow up the covering which is over all peoples,

> Even the veil which is stretched over all nations.
> He will swallow up death for all time,
> And the Lord God will wipe tears away from all faces,
> And He will remove the reproach of His people from all the earth;
> For the Lord has spoken.
> And it will be said in that day,
> "Behold, this is our God for whom we have waited that He might save us.
> This is the Lord for whom we have waited;
> Let us rejoice and be glad in His salvation."
> For the hand of the Lord will rest on this mountain,
> And Moab will be trodden down in his place.
> (Isa. 25:6–10)

Isaiah 26:1–4 records one of the joyous songs the redeemed of Israel will sing:

> In that day this song will be sung in the land of Judah:
> "We have a strong city;
> He sets up walls and ramparts for security.
> Open the gates, that the righteous nation may enter,
> The one that remains faithful.
> The steadfast of mind You will keep in perfect peace,
> Because he trusts in You.
> Trust in the Lord forever,
> For in God the Lord, we have an everlasting Rock."

Verse 19 of that chapter describes the resurrection that will bring the Old Testament saints to the banquet: "Your dead will live; their corpses will rise. You who lie in the dust, awake and shout for joy, for your dew is as the dew of the dawn, and the earth will give birth to the departed spirits."

Daniel 12:2 promises the resurrection of Old Testament believers, whose bodies have long been in decay: "Many of those who sleep in the dust of the ground will awake, these to everlasting life, but the others to disgrace and everlasting contempt." The souls of those believers are already with the Lord. Their bodies will be raised for the kingdom. Daniel 12:1 connects the resurrection with the Tribulation: "Now at that time Michael, the great prince who stands guard over the sons of your people, will arise. And there will be a time of distress such as never occurred since there was a nation until that time; and at that time your people, everyone who is found written in the book, will be rescued." It is best to place that resurrection at the end of the Tribulation. They are raised to be guests at the wedding and enjoy all the festivities of the glory of the kingdom.

Israel's inclusion in the festivities is a testimony to God's gracious promise to restore her. Israel was pictured as God's wife in the Old Testament (Isa. 54:5–6)—tragically, God's unfaithful, apostate wife, as the book of Hosea illustrates. Yet Israel's estrangement will not be permanent. In Hosea 14:4 God promises, "I will heal their apostasy, I will love them freely, for My anger has turned away from them." In the kingdom, God will restore His relationship with His unfaithful wife. And Israel will have a prominent place in the New Jerusalem, as the description given of it in Revelation 21:10–14 reveals:

> And he carried me away in the Spirit to a great and high mountain, and showed me the holy city, Jerusalem, coming down out of heaven from God, having the glory of God. Her brilliance was like a very costly stone, as a stone of crystal-clear jasper. It had a great and high wall, with twelve gates, and at the gates twelve angels; and names were written on them, which are the names of the twelve tribes of the sons of Israel. There were three gates on the east and three gates on the north and three gates on the south and three gates on the west. And the wall of the city had twelve foundation stones, and on them were the twelve names of the twelve apostles of the Lamb.

Whatever distinctions are made in Scripture, all believers of all ages will enjoy the full glories of eternity. Henry Morris writes:

> Whatever distinctions may exist between the saints of the pre-Abrahamic period, the saints in Israel before Christ, the saints among the Gentiles from Abraham to Christ, the saints of the tribulation, and the saints in the churches from Christ to the rapture . . . such distinctions are secondary to the great primary truth that all will be there by virtue of the saving work of Christ and their personal trust in the true Creator God and His provision of salvation. (*The Revelation Record* [Wheaton, Ill.: Tyndale, 1983], 389)

The blessed truth that God will be in personal fellowship forever with all the redeemed saints of all the ages is so significant that the angel solemnly affirmed to John, **"These are true words of God."** To the beleaguered and aged apostle, in exile on the harsh, barren island of Patmos, it must have seemed amazing, almost impossible that God's kingdom would eventually triumph. In John's day, the church was being persecuted from without and attacked by heresies from within, and it was crumbling (see the discussion of the seven churches in *Revelation 1–11*, The MacArthur New Testament Commentary [Chicago: Moody, 1999], chaps. 4–10). The revelation that God's redemptive plan cannot and will not be thwarted brought great relief, comfort, and joy to the apostle.

So great was John's astonishment at the angel's message that he involuntarily and thoughtlessly **fell at his feet to worship him** (cf.

22:8)—a practice strictly prohibited in Scripture (Col. 2:18; cf. Matt. 4:10). Calling him back to his senses with a sharp rebuke, the angel said, **"Do not do that; I am a fellow servant of yours and your brethren who hold the testimony of Jesus; worship God."** Like John, the angel was a **servant** of God, sent to minister to John and his **brethren who hold the testimony of Jesus.** Angels serve all believers (cf. Heb. 1:14), particularly those who, like John, are involved in preaching the gospel (cf. 22:9). The angel reminds John that he is to **worship God** only. Worship is the theme of redemptive history, and the purpose for which believers were redeemed (John 4:23). It will also be their occupation throughout eternity.

The angel's final word to John is a reminder that **"the testimony of Jesus is the spirit of prophecy."** The central theme of Old Testament prophecy and New Testament preaching is the Lord Jesus Christ. Until the coming of His kingdom, all who proclaim the gospel must be faithful to **the testimony of Jesus,** the saving gospel message, which was His message. Those who are not will forfeit heavenly affirmation of their ministry.

The glorious reality that God will judge the wicked and usher believers into His kingdom should cause all believers to rejoice. "For after all," wrote Paul, "it is only just for God to repay with affliction those who afflict you, and to give relief to you who are afflicted and to us as well when the Lord Jesus will be revealed from heaven with His mighty angels in flaming fire, dealing out retribution to those who do not know God and to those who do not obey the gospel of our Lord Jesus" (2 Thess. 1:6–8). Because believers are defined as those who "have loved His appearing" (2 Tim. 4:8), they are to eagerly wait for His return from heaven (Phil. 3:20).

The Glorious Return of Jesus Christ (Revelation 19:11–21) 15

And I saw heaven opened, and behold, a white horse, and He who sat on it is called Faithful and True, and in righteousness He judges and wages war. His eyes are a flame of fire, and on His head are many diadems; and He has a name written on Him which no one knows except Himself. He is clothed with a robe dipped in blood, and His name is called The Word of God. And the armies which are in heaven, clothed in fine linen, white and clean, were following Him on white horses. From His mouth comes a sharp sword, so that with it He may strike down the nations, and He will rule them with a rod of iron; and He treads the wine press of the fierce wrath of God, the Almighty. And on His robe and on His thigh He has a name written, "KING OF KINGS, AND LORD OF LORDS."

Then I saw an angel standing in the sun, and he cried out with a loud voice, saying to all the birds which fly in midheaven, "Come, assemble for the great supper of God, so that you may eat the flesh of kings and the flesh of commanders and the flesh of mighty men and the flesh of horses and of those who sit on them and the flesh of all men, both free men and slaves, and small and great."

And I saw the beast and the kings of the earth and their armies assembled to make war against Him who sat on the horse and against His army. And the beast was seized, and with him the false prophet who performed the signs in his presence, by which he deceived those who had received the mark of the beast and those who worshiped his image; these two were thrown alive into the lake of fire which burns with brimstone. And the rest were killed with the sword which came from the mouth of Him who sat on the horse, and all the birds were filled with their flesh. (19:11–21)

A century ago most people believed that history was progressing inexorably toward a man-made utopia. The Industrial Revolution, the march of scientific discovery, and the increasing pace of social reform seemed to augur nothing but brighter days ahead. Today, however, two world wars; innumerable regional, civil, and national wars; countless acts of terrorism and senseless violence; and the nearly complete collapse of moral values make such rosy optimism seem quaintly naive.

The Bible teaches that things will be wonderfully better, but only after they become unimaginably worse. There is only one solution for the world's problems: the return of its true King, the Lord Jesus Christ, to establish absolute monarchy and unilateral authority in His earthly kingdom. Only under His rule will there be peace instead of war, justice instead of inequity, and righteousness instead of wickedness. But that glorious event will not occur without fierce opposition from Satan, his demon hordes, and the world of wicked sinners. The Tribulation, the seven-year period immediately before Christ's return, will see the greatest of all human world empires, headed by the evil genius known as Antichrist. The earth will be infested with demons, those who have been here all along, those cast from heaven with Satan (12:9), and those released from imprisonment during the Tribulation (9:1–10, 14–20). The Tribulation will also be a time of escalating human wickedness, despite the unprecedented outpouring of God's wrath in the seal, trumpet, and bowl judgments. Stubbornly hardening their hearts against the truth of the gospel, people even then will obstinately refuse to repent (9:20–21; 16:9, 11). Even the destruction of Antichrist's magnificent capital city of Babylon (chaps. 17–18) will provoke loud laments, but no repentance.

But while chaos and turmoil reigns on earth during the Tribulation, the raptured church will be presented in heaven. The church, the bride of the Lamb, will be eagerly awaiting the marriage supper of the Lamb in the millennial earth (19:7). But before that wonderful celebration can take place, the warrior King must win the final battle. The forces of heaven and hell will meet in the climactic slaughter of human history, the Battle of Armageddon. At that final holocaust, man's day will end, all of Christ's foes will be vanquished, and His kingdom will be established.

God's people throughout redemptive history have eagerly anticipated the return of the Lord Jesus Christ to defeat His foes and set up His kingdom. That will be the time when the destruction of Satan is completed (Gen. 3:15; Rom. 16:20), when the true King receives the ruling scepter (Gen. 49:10), when God will establish the throne of David's greater Son (2 Sam. 7:13; Isa. 9:7), when the Son will rule the earth with a rod of iron (Ps. 2:6–9), when the armies of Gog and Magog will be shattered (Ezek. 38–39), when the nations will be judged (Joel 3:1–2, 12–14) after their defeat in battle by the returning King (Zech. 14:3–4), when Jerusalem will be the center of Messiah's kingdom (Zech. 12:3–9), when the angels will gather the wicked for judgment (Matt. 13:41–42; 25:41), when the wicked will face God's wrath and indignation (Rom. 2:5–9), and when the Lord Jesus Christ will descend visibly (Rev. 1:7) from heaven in flaming fire, bringing retribution on the persecutors of His people (2 Thess. 1:6–9; cf. Rev. 6:9–11).

The second coming of Jesus Christ is thus the culmination of redemptive history. Believers of all ages have eagerly anticipated that glorious event (cf. Isa. 64:1–2). In fact, the apostle Paul defined Christians as those "who have loved His appearing" (2 Tim. 4:8). Many believers, however, are enamored by the things of the world and do not love Christ's appearing as they should. Certainly the Tribulation believers will have no such problem. They will be persecuted, hunted outcasts (cf. 13:17), living constantly under the sentence of death (13:15) in an unspeakably vile, demon-infested world. Christ's coming will be what they long for and pray for.

So important is the second coming of Christ that the Bible lists several compelling reasons why Jesus must return to earth. First, the numerous promises of God in Scripture, such as those noted above, demand Christ's return. Likewise, the promises of Jesus Himself also demand His return (e.g., 3:11; 22:7, 12, 20; Matt. 24:27, 30, 37–44; 25:31; 26:64). The guarantee of the Holy Spirit, the Spirit of truth (John 14:17; 15:26; 16:13), is another reason that Jesus must return, since He inspired the New Testament writers to write of Christ's return (cf. 1 Cor. 1:7; Phil. 3:20; Col. 3:4; 1 Thess. 4:16–17; Heb. 9:28; James 5:7–8; 1 Pet. 1:13; 5:4; 1 John 3:2). If Christ does not return, the Father, Son, and Holy Spirit would be guilty of making false promises—which, of course, is impossible, since God is incapable of lying (Num. 23:19; Titus 1:2; Heb. 6:18). God's plan for the church also necessitates Christ's return. He must take her to heaven to present her in preparation for the marriage supper of the Lamb (19:7–10). Jesus must also return because of God's plan for the nations—their judgment (14:14–20; Joel 3:1–2, 12–14; Matt. 25:31–46), and for Israel—the salvation of the remnant of believing Jews (Ezek. 36:25–35; 37:1ff.; Rom. 11:25–27). Christ's humiliation at His first coming, when He was scorned, hated, and despised (Isa. 53:3; Matt. 26:67; 27:27–31), demands His return to display His glory (Matt. 25:31). Satan's exaltation is another reason Jesus must return to earth. The "god of this world" (2 Cor. 4:4; cf. John 12:31; 14:30; 16:11; 1 John 5:19) will not be permitted to keep his usurped throne (cf. Luke 4:5–6) forever. The rightful Heir to earth's throne must return, defeat the usurper, and take what is rightfully His (cf. 20:1–3, 10). Finally, the hope and expectation of God's people demands that Christ return (6:9–10; Titus 2:13; 1 John 3:2–3).

The Second Coming must be distinguished from the Rapture of the church prior to the seven-year Tribulation; the differing biblical descriptions of the two events indicate that they are distinct from each other. At the Rapture, Christ comes for His saints (John 14:3; 1 Thess. 4:16–17); at the Second Coming, He comes with them (see the discussion of v. 14 below). Furthermore, at the Rapture, Christ meets His saints in the air (1 Thess. 4:17) to take them to heaven (John 14:2–3); at the Second Coming, He descends with them from heaven to the earth (Zech. 14:4).

Some attempt to harmonize those two distinctions by arguing that believers meet Christ in the air, then descend to earth with Him. By so doing, they essentially make the Rapture and the Second Coming the same event. But that view, championed by posttribulationists, trivializes or marginalizes the Rapture and renders it pointless, as Thomas R. Edgar notes:

> What can be the purpose for keeping a remnant alive through the tribulation so that some of the church survive and then take them out of their situation and make them the same as those who did not survive? Why keep them for this? [The] explanation that they provide an escort for Jesus does not hold up. Raptured living saints will be exactly the same as resurrected dead saints. Why cannot the dead believers fulfill this purpose? Why keep a remnant alive [through the Tribulation], then rapture them and accomplish no more than by letting them die? There is no purpose or accomplishment in [such] a rapture.
>
> With all the saints of all the ages past and the armies [of angels] in heaven available as escorts and the fact that [raptured] saints provide no different escort than if they had been killed, why permit the church to suffer immensely, most believers [to] be killed, and spare a few for a rapture which has no apparent purpose, immediately before the [Tribulation] period ends? . . . Is this the promise? You will suffer, be killed, but I will keep a few alive, and take them out just before the good times come. Such reasoning, of course, calls for some explanation of the apparent lack of purpose for a posttribulational rapture of any sort.
>
> We can note the following:

(1) An unusual, portentous, one-time event such as the rapture must have a specific purpose. God has purposes for his actions. This purpose must be one that can be accomplished only by such an unusual event as a rapture of living saints.
(2) This purpose must agree with God's general principles of operation.
(3) There is little or no apparent reason to rapture believers when the Lord returns and just prior to setting up the long-awaited kingdom with all of its joyful prospects.
(4) There is good reason to deliver all who are already believers from the tribulation, where they would be special targets of persecution.
(5) To deliver from a period of universal trial and physical destruction such as the tribulation requires a removal from the earth by death or rapture. Death is not appropriate as a promise in Rev. 3:10.
(6) Deliverance from the tribulation before it starts agrees with God's previous dealings with Noah and Lot and is directly stated as a principle of God's action toward believers in 2 Pet. 2:9. ("Robert H. Gundry and Revelation 3:10," *Grace Theological Journal* 3 [Spring 1982]: 43–44)

Richard L. Mayhue gives another reason that a posttribulational rapture (one that happens at the Second Coming) is pointless: "If the rapture took place in connection with our Lord's posttribulational [second] coming, the subsequent separation of the sheep from the goats (see Matt. 25:31 and following) would be redundant. Separation would have taken place in the very act of [the rapture]" (*Snatched Before the Storm! A Case for Pretribulationism* [Winona Lake, Ind.: BMH, 1980], 9).

There is not even a hint of judgment in passages describing the Rapture (John 14:1–3; 1 Thess. 4:13–18), but judgment plays a prominent role in the Second Coming (cf. 19:11, 15, 17–21).

The dramatic signs accompanying the Second Coming, the darkening of the sun and moon and the disruption of the "powers of the heavens" (Matt. 24:29–30), are not mentioned in the passages describing the Rapture.

In its description of the Second Coming, Revelation 19 does not mention either a translation (rapture) of living believers (1 Cor. 15:51–52), or a resurrection of dead believers (cf. 1 Thess. 4:16).

This monumental, climactic passage may be divided into four sections: the return of the Conqueror, the regiments of the Conqueror, the rule of the Conqueror, and the victory of the Conqueror.

THE RETURN OF THE CONQUEROR

And I saw heaven opened, and behold, a white horse, and He who sat on it is called Faithful and True, and in righteousness He judges and wages war. His eyes are a flame of fire, and on His head are many diadems; and He has a name written on Him which no one knows except Himself. He is clothed with a robe dipped in blood, and His name is called The Word of God. (19:11–13)

As it did in 4:1, **heaven opened** before John's wondering eyes. But unlike 4:1, heaven opens this time not to let John in, but to let Jesus out. The time has come at last for the full, glorious revelation of the sovereign Lord. This is the time to which all of Revelation (as well as all of redemptive history) has been pointing, the time of which Jesus Himself spoke in Matthew 24:27–31:

> "For just as the lightning comes from the east and flashes even to the west, so will the coming of the Son of Man be. Wherever the corpse is, there the vultures will gather.
>
> "But immediately after the tribulation of those days the sun will be darkened, and the moon will not give its light, and the stars will fall from the sky, and the powers of the heavens will be shaken. And then the sign of the Son of Man will appear in the sky, and then all the tribes of the earth will mourn, and they will see the Son of Man coming on the clouds of the sky with power and great glory. And He will send forth His angels with a great trumpet and they will gather together His elect from the four winds, from one end of the sky to the other."

As the dramatic scene unfolds, John stands transfixed, his attention riveted on the majestic, regal, mighty Rider. Jesus, the One who ascended to heaven (Acts 1:9–11) where He has been seated at the Father's right hand (Acts 5:31; 7:55–56; Rom. 8:34; Eph. 1:20; Col. 3:1; Heb. 1:3, 13; 8:1; 10:12; 12:2; 1 Pet. 3:22), is about to receive the kingdom that the Father promised Him. In an earlier vision, John saw Jesus receive the title deed to the earth:

> I saw in the right hand of Him who sat on the throne a book written inside and on the back, sealed up with seven seals. And I saw a strong angel proclaiming with a loud voice, "Who is worthy to open the book and to break its seals?" And no one in heaven or on the earth or under the earth was able to open the book or to look into it. Then I began to weep greatly because no one was found worthy to open the book or to look into it; and one of the elders said to me, "Stop weeping; behold, the Lion that is from the tribe of Judah, the Root of David, has overcome so as to open the book and its seven seals."

> And I saw between the throne (with the four living creatures) and the elders a Lamb standing, as if slain, having seven horns and seven eyes, which are the seven Spirits of God, sent out into all the earth. And He came and took the book out of the right hand of Him who sat on the throne. (5:1–7)

The Lamb of that vision has become the conquering King.

No longer is Jesus portrayed as He was in His humiliation, "humble, and mounted on a donkey, even on a colt, the foal of a donkey" (Zech. 9:9). Instead, He rides the traditional **white horse** ridden by victorious Roman generals in their triumphal processions through the streets of Rome. **White** also symbolizes the spotless, unblemished, absolutely holy character of the Rider. The **horse,** like the crowns (v. 12), the sharp sword (v. 15), the rod of iron (v. 15), and the wine press (v. 15) is symbolic; Christ's coming is reality. The symbolic language represents various aspects of that reality—Christ's victory over His enemies, His sovereign rule, and His judgment of sinners.

Continuing his description of the astonishing scene before him, John notes that **He who sat on** the white horse **is called Faithful and True.** There is no more appropriate name for the Lord Jesus Christ, who earlier in Revelation was called "the faithful and true Witness" (3:14). He is **faithful** to His promises (cf. 2 Cor. 1:20) and what He speaks is always true (John 8:45–46; Titus 1:2). Though some would like to pick and choose which teachings of Jesus they wish to accept, He is just as faithful to His promises of wrath and judgment as He is to His promises of grace and salvation. The description of Jesus as **Faithful and True** is in marked contrast with the unfaithfulness and lies of Satan (12:9), Antichrist's evil empire (18:23), and wicked people (2 Tim. 3:13). The very fact that He is coming again as He promised confirms that Jesus is **Faithful and True.**

Because Jesus is faithful to His word and righteous character, it follows that **in righteousness He judges.** His holy nature demands a holy, righteous reaction to sin. And because He always does what He says, He must judge the wicked (Matt. 16:27; 25:31–46; John 5:22, 27; cf. Acts 10:42; 17:31; Rom. 2:16; 2 Thess. 1:7–9; 2 Tim. 4:1). Jesus came the first time as Savior; He will return as Judge. When He came the first time, wicked people, including Pilate, Herod, Annas, and Caiaphas judged Him; when He returns, He will judge all wicked people (Acts 17:31). And He will not only be their judge, but also their executioner (vv. 15, 21). Angels may gather the wicked for judgment (Matt. 13:41), but the Lord Jesus will pass sentence on them.

No longer the Suffering Servant of His incarnation, the Lord Jesus Christ is seen in this vision as the warrior King who **wages war** against

His foes. He is the executioner of all ungodly, unbelieving sinners. The only other reference in Scripture to Jesus waging war is in 2:16, when He warned the worldly church at Pergamum, "Repent; or else I am coming to you quickly, and I will make war against them with the sword of My mouth." This is not out of keeping with God's character, however. After their deliverance from the Egyptian forces at the Red Sea, Israel sang, "The Lord is a warrior" (Ex. 15:3; cf. Pss. 24:8; 45:3–5). John Phillips writes:

> The Lord is a man of war! It is an amazing title for the Son of God. Says Alexander White, comenting on Bunyan's *Holy War*,
>
> > Holy Scripture is full of wars and rumours of wars; the wars of the Lord; the wars of Joshua and the Judges; the wars of David, with his and many other magnificient battle-songs; till the best known name of the God of Israel in the Old Testament is the Lord of Hosts; and then in the New Testament we have Jesus Christ described as the Captain of our salvation. . . . And then the whole Bible is crowned with a book all sounding with battle-cries. . . . till it ends with that city of peace where they hang the trumpet in the hall and study war no more.
>
> The Lord is a man of war! In righteousness He judges and makes war. The judging has been going on throughout the breaking of the seals, the blowing of the trumpets, and the pouring out of the bowls. Now He makes war. He, who for long centuries has endured patiently the scoffings, the insults, the bad manners of men; who for ages has contemplated Calvary and all that it displayed of human hatred and contempt; and who, through the millennia has made peace through the blood of that cross, now makes war over that blood. (*Exploring Revelation*, rev. ed. [Chicago: Moody, 1987; reprint, Neptune, N.J.: Loizeaux, 1991], 232)

Jesus' adversaries this time will be the hardened sinners who have defied His judgments and scorned the gospel message during the Tribulation. Despite all the devastating judgments they will have experienced, and the powerful gospel preaching they will have heard, they will stubbornly refuse to repent (9:20–21; 16:9, 11). Since neither judgment nor preaching moves them to repent, Jesus will return to destroy them and send them to hell.

Unlike other conquerors the world has seen, covetousness, ambition, pride, or power will not motivate this Conqueror. He will come in utter righteousness, in perfect holiness, and in strict accord with every holy interest. Heaven cannot be at peace with sin, for God's "eyes are too pure to approve evil, and [He] can not look on wickedness with favor" (Hab. 1:13). There is a limit to God's patience. Justice cannot always tolerate injustice; truth cannot forever tolerate lies; rebellion cannot be permitted to go on forever. Incorrigible, incurable, hardened sinners will face destruction; mercy abused and grace rejected will ultimately bring judgment.

Describing the personal appearance of the majestic, awe-inspiring Rider, John writes that **His eyes are a flame of fire** (see the discussion of 1:14 in *Revelation 1–11,* The MacArthur New Testament Commentary [Chicago: Moody, 1999], 46). Nothing escapes the notice of His penetrating, piercing vision. He can see into the deepest recesses of the human heart, because "all things are open and laid bare to the eyes of Him with whom we have to do" (Heb. 4:13). Those **eyes** had reflected tenderness and joy as He gathered little children to Himself. They had reflected compassion when He observed distressed and dispirited people, wandering aimlessly through life like sheep without a shepherd. And they had reflected forgiveness when He restored Peter, who had been crushed by guilt over his shocking denial of his Master. The eyes that wept over the fate of unrepentant Jerusalem and over the sorrow, suffering, and death in this sin-cursed world, John sees flashing with the fire of judgment.

On His head John noted that Christ wore **many diadems,** a transliteration of the Greek word *diadēma,* which refers to a ruler's crown (cf. 12:3; 13:1). In this case, they are worn by Jesus to signify His royal rank and regal authority. **Many** indicates His collecting of all the rulers' crowns, signifying that He alone is the sovereign ruler of the earth. Collecting the crown of a vanquished king was customary in the ancient world. After defeating the Ammonites, David "took the crown of their king from his head . . . and it was placed on David's head" (2 Sam. 12:30). Christ alone will be sovereign, since He alone is "King of kings, and Lord of lords" (v. 16), and "the kingdom of the world has become the kingdom of our Lord and of His Christ; and He will reign forever and ever" (11:15). The many crowns Christ will wear are indeed a fair exchange for a crown of thorns (cf. Phil. 2:8–11).

Further, John notes that Jesus had **a name written on Him which no one knows except Himself.** All speculation as to the meaning of that **name** is obviously pointless, since the text plainly states that **no one knows** it **except** Jesus **Himself.** Even the inspired apostle John could not comprehend it. Maybe it will be made known after His return.

Describing the final element of Christ's appearance, John writes that **He is clothed with a robe dipped in blood.** The **blood** is not representative of that which He shed on the cross; this is a picture of judgment, not redemption. The **blood** is the blood of His slaughtered enemies. The imagery of this passage is similar to that of Isaiah 63:1–6:

> Who is this who comes from Edom,
> With garments of glowing colors from Bozrah,
> This One who is majestic in His apparel,

Marching in the greatness of His strength?
"It is I who speak in righteousness, mighty to save."
Why is Your apparel red,
And Your garments like the one who treads in the wine press?
"I have trodden the wine trough alone,
And from the peoples there was no man with Me.
I also trod them in My anger
And trampled them in My wrath;
And their lifeblood is sprinkled on My garments,
And I stained all My raiment.
For the day of vengeance was in My heart,
And My year of redemption has come.
I looked, and there was no one to help,
And I was astonished and there was no one to uphold;
So My own arm brought salvation to Me,
And My wrath upheld Me.
I trod down the peoples in My anger
And made them drunk in My wrath,
And I poured out their lifeblood on the earth."

The question arises as to why His garments are blood spattered before the battle has begun. But this is not His first battle; it is His last battle. He has fought for His people throughout redemptive history, and His war clothes bear the stains of many previous slaughters. At that day, they will be stained as never before when He "treads the wine press of the fierce wrath of God, the Almighty" (v. 15).

That the Rider's **name is called The Word of God** identifies Him unmistakably as the Lord Jesus Christ (John 1:1, 14; 1 John 1:1). The second Person of the Trinity, the incarnate Son of God is called **The Word of God** because He is the revelation of God. He is the full expression of the mind, will, and purpose of God, "the radiance of His glory and the exact representation of His nature" (Heb. 1:3).

The Regiments of the Conqueror

And the armies which are in heaven, clothed in fine linen, white and clean, were following Him on white horses. (19:14)

The Lord Jesus Christ will not return alone, but will be accompanied by **the armies which are in heaven** (cf. 17:14). Four divisions make up these glorified troops. Earlier in chapter 19 the bride of the Lamb (the church) was pictured wearing **fine linen, white and clean** (vv. 7–8). Those glorified believers will accompany Christ. So will the

Tribulation believers, who are also pictured in heaven wearing white robes (7:9). The third group is the Old Testament saints, who are resurrected at the end of the Tribulation (Dan. 12:1–2). Finally, the holy angels will also accompany Christ (Matt. 25:31). The **white horses** ridden by the heavenly cavalry are not literal horses, anymore than those ridden by hell's cavalry in 9:7 and 16. Unlike the Lord Jesus Christ, the heavenly army is unarmed; He alone will destroy His enemies. The saints will come not to fight with Jesus, but to reign with Him (20:4–6; 1 Cor. 6:2).

The Rule of the Conqueror

From His mouth comes a sharp sword, so that with it He may strike down the nations, and He will rule them with a rod of iron; and He treads the wine press of the fierce wrath of God, the Almighty. And on His robe and on His thigh He has a name written, "KING OF KINGS, AND LORD OF LORDS." (19:15–16)

The rule of the King is described in graphic, powerful imagery. John notes first that **from His mouth comes a sharp sword.** The apostle had seen that **sword** in an earlier vision (1:16), where it was used to defend the church against the onslaught of Satan's forces. Here it is the **sword** of judgment, the flaming **sword** dealing death to the King's foes. That the **sword comes** out of **His mouth** symbolizes the deadly power of Christ's words. Once He spoke words of comfort, but now He speaks words of death. As previously noted, the armies that accompany Christ when He returns carry no weapons. He alone wields the **sword** with which He will slay the wicked.

And Christ will wield that **sword** with deadly effect as He **strikes down the nations.** His elect, both from the Gentile nations and from Israel, will be preserved; the wicked He will slaughter instantly. The dead will include all those gathered for battle at Armageddon; none will escape. The rest of the world's unredeemed people will be judged and executed at the sheep and goat judgment (Matt. 25:31–46) that follows Christ's return. This is the final stroke of death in the Day of the Lord (cf. Isa. 66:15–16; Ezek. 39:1–4, 17–20; Joel 3:12–21; Matt. 25:31–46; 2 Thess. 1:6–9; 2:8).

The stern, swift judgment that marks the onset of Christ's kingdom will be the pattern of His rule throughout the Millennium. During His thousand-year reign, **He will rule** the nations **with a rod of iron** (cf. 12:5; Ps. 2:8–9); He will swiftly judge all sin and instantly put down any rebellion. All people will be required to conform to His law or face immediate judgment. Using the same imagery of ruling **with a rod of**

iron, Jesus promised that believers would rule under Him in the kingdom: "He who overcomes, and he who keeps My deeds until the end, to him I will give authority over the nations; and he shall rule them with a rod of iron, as the vessels of the potter are broken to pieces, as I also have received authority from My Father" (2:26–27).

Returning to the judgment at the outset of Christ's rule, John writes that **He treads the wine press of the fierce wrath of God, the Almighty.** That vivid symbol of God's wrath comes from the ancient practice of stomping on grapes as part of the wine-making process. The splattering of the grape juice pictures the pouring out of the blood of Christ's enemies (cf. 14:18–20). The imagery of a **wine press** also portrays judgment in the Old Testament. Isaiah 63:1–3 describes Messiah's destruction of Israel's implacable foe, Edom, which represents the God-hating world:

> Who is this who comes from Edom,
> With garments of glowing colors from Bozrah,
> This One who is majestic in His apparel,
> Marching in the greatness of His strength?
> "It is I who speak in righteousness, mighty to save."
> Why is Your apparel red,
> And Your garments like the one who treads in the wine press?
> "I have trodden the wine trough alone,
> And from the peoples there was no man with Me.
> I also trod them in My anger
> And trampled them in My wrath;
> And their lifeblood is sprinkled on My garments,
> And I stained all My raiment."

Joel 3:12–14 also uses the wine press imagery to depict Messiah's judgment of His enemies:

> Let the nations be aroused
> And come up to the valley of Jehoshaphat,
> For there I will sit to judge
> All the surrounding nations.
> Put in the sickle, for the harvest is ripe.
> Come, tread, for the wine press is full;
> The vats overflow, for their wickedness is great.
> Multitudes, multitudes in the valley of decision!
> For the day of the Lord is near in the valley of decision.

In a final look at the returning King, John saw in his vision that Christ wore a banner around **His robe and on His thigh** (across His chest and hanging down on His upper leg as He rides), on which **He has**

a name written, "KING OF KINGS, AND LORD OF LORDS" (cf. 17:14; Deut. 10:17; 1 Tim. 6:15). This is the third name given to the Lord Jesus Christ in this passage. The incomprehensible name of verse 12 may express the mystery of His essential deity. Verse 13 calls Him the Word of God, expressing His incarnation as the Son of God. The name **"KING OF KINGS, AND LORD OF LORDS"** expresses His sovereign triumph over all foes and His absolute rule in His soon to be established kingdom.

The Victory of the Conqueror

Then I saw an angel standing in the sun, and he cried out with a loud voice, saying to all the birds which fly in midheaven, "Come, assemble for the great supper of God, so that you may eat the flesh of kings and the flesh of commanders and the flesh of mighty men and the flesh of horses and of those who sit on them and the flesh of all men, both free men and slaves, and small and great."

And I saw the beast and the kings of the earth and their armies assembled to make war against Him who sat on the horse and against His army. And the beast was seized, and with him the false prophet who performed the signs in his presence, by which he deceived those who had received the mark of the beast and those who worshiped his image; these two were thrown alive into the lake of fire which burns with brimstone. And the rest were killed with the sword which came from the mouth of Him who sat on the horse, and all the birds were filled with their flesh. (19:17–21)

Once again **an angel** plays a key role in one of the end-time scenarios described in the Apocalypse. John saw this **angel standing in the sun;** that is, in the proximity of the sun, possibly in front of it, partially eclipsing it. He stands in a conspicuous, prominent place to make this important announcement. Evidently the worldwide darkness associated with the fifth bowl (16:10) has been lifted, since the **sun** is again visible. The lifting of that earlier darkness would also explain how the smoke from Babylon's destruction was visible at a distance (18:9–19). However, darkness will soon blanket the earth again, accentuating the flashing, brilliant glory of the returning Christ (Matt. 24:29).

As angels have frequently done in Revelation (7:2; 10:1–3; 14:15; 18:1–2), the angel **cried out with a loud voice.** He addresses **all the birds which fly in midheaven** (cf. 8:13; 14:6), inviting them to feed on the results of the carnage that will shortly ensue. The angel thus declares Christ's victory before the battle is ever fought. His invitation to the **birds** is reminiscent of Jesus' words in Matthew 24:27–28: "For just as the lightning comes from the east and flashes even to the west, so will the coming of the Son of Man be. Wherever the corpse is, there the vultures will gather" (cf. Luke 17:37).

The angel commands the **birds** to **come** and **assemble for the great supper of God.** This will not be the first time birds have feasted on human carrion in Scripture. Isaiah 18:6, describing the results of judgment on Cush (modern Ethiopia), reads, "They will be left together for mountain birds of prey, and for the beasts of the earth; and the birds of prey will spend the summer feeding on them." Jeremiah relates that, after the Babylonian destruction of Jerusalem, "the dead bodies of this people will be food for the birds of the sky and for the beasts of the earth; and no one will frighten them away" (Jer. 7:33). In a striking parallel to the present passage Ezekiel wrote,

> "As for you, son of man, thus says the Lord God, 'Speak to every kind of bird and to every beast of the field, "Assemble and come, gather from every side to My sacrifice which I am going to sacrifice for you, as a great sacrifice on the mountains of Israel, that you may eat flesh and drink blood. You shall eat the flesh of mighty men and drink the blood of the princes of the earth, as though they were rams, lambs, goats and bulls, all of them fatlings of Bashan. So you will eat fat until you are glutted, and drink blood until you are drunk, from My sacrifice which I have sacrificed for you. You will be glutted at My table with horses and charioteers, with mighty men and all the men of war," declares the Lord God.'" (Ezek. 39:17–20)

The brief but catastrophic Day of the Lord destruction will result in an unprecedented slaughter, with uncounted millions of dead bodies strewn throughout its entire two-hundred-mile length (14:20). Even after the **birds** have gorged themselves, it will still take seven months to bury the remaining corpses (Ezek. 39:12).

It is an important fact to consider that every year millions of birds of many species migrate south from Europe to Africa. They fly over the land of Israel on their journey. The numbers of these birds and their migrating patterns has been the special study of the Israeli government because of the threat they pose to aircraft. This can certainly answer the question as to where such vast numbers of birds will come from. The geographical setting of Israel, situated between the Mediterranean Sea on the west and the vast expanse of barren desert to the east, forms the natural corridor for these migrating birds.

At the great supper, the birds will **eat the flesh of kings and the flesh of commanders and the flesh of mighty men and the flesh of horses and of those who sit on them and the flesh of all men, both**

free men and slaves, and small and great. That all-inclusive statement reveals the worldwide extent of the slaughter. To have one's unburied body left as food for birds is the ultimate indignity, especially for proud **kings** and mighty military **commanders.** That same ignominious fate awaits all the proud, God-hating rebels everywhere in the world, **both free men and slaves, and small and great** (cf. 11:18; 13:16). Commentator Joseph Seiss writes about this awful scene,

> This tells already an awful story. It tells of the greatest of men made food for the vultures;—of kings and leaders, strong and confident, devoured on the field, with no one to bury them;—of those who thought to conquer Heaven's anointed King rendered helpless even against the timid birds;—of vaunting gods of nature turned into its cast off and most dishonoured dregs. And what is thus forintimated soon becomes reality. The Great Conqueror bows the heavens and comes down. He rides upon the cherub horse and flies upon the wings of the wind. Smoke goes up from his nostrils, and devouring fire out of his mouth. He moves amid storms and darkness, from which the lightnings hurl their bolts, and hailstones mingle with the fire. He roars out of Zion, and utters his voice from Jerusalem, till the heavens and the earth shake. He dashes forth in the fury of his incensed greatness amid clouds, and fire, and pillars of smoke. The sun frowns. The day is neither light nor dark. The mountains melt and cleave asunder at his presence. The hills bound from their seats and skip like lambs. The waters are dislodged from their channels. The sea rolls back with howling trepidation. The sky is rent and folds upon itself like a collapsed tent. It is the day for executing an armed world,—a world in covenant with Hell to overthrow the authority and throne of God,—and everything in terrified Nature joins to signalize the deserved vengeance. (*The Apocalypse* [reprint; Grand Rapids: Kregel, 1987], 441)

Zephaniah also prophesied of this terrifying scene:

> Near is the great day of the Lord,
> Near and coming very quickly;
> Listen, the day of the Lord!
> In it the warrior cries out bitterly.
> A day of wrath is that day,
> A day of trouble and distress,
> A day of destruction and desolation,
> A day of darkness and gloom,
> A day of clouds and thick darkness,
> A day of trumpet and battle cry
> Against the fortified cities
> And the high corner towers.
> I will bring distress on men

So that they will walk like the blind,
Because they have sinned against the Lord;
And their blood will be poured out like dust
And their flesh like dung.
Neither their silver nor their gold
Will be able to deliver them
On the day of the Lord's wrath;
And all the earth will be devoured
In the fire of His jealousy,
For He will make a complete end,
Indeed a terrifying one,
Of all the inhabitants of the earth.
(Zeph. 1:14–18)

As the next stage in his incredible vision unfolded, John **saw the beast and the kings of the earth and their armies assembled to make war against Him who sat on the horse and against His army.** The **beast** is Antichrist (11:7; 13:1–8), leader of the last and greatest empire in human history. The **kings of the earth** are the ten kings who rule the ten sectors into which Antichrist's worldwide empire is divided (17:12–14). **Their armies** have **assembled to make war against Him who sat on the horse** (v. 11) **and against His army** (v. 14; Zech. 14:5). The formidable and seemingly invincible armed might of the beast, with all its firepower, awaits the arrival of the Rider.

But before there is any battle, it is all over. In an instant, **the beast was seized, and with him the false prophet who performed the signs in his presence, by which he deceived those who had received the mark of the beast and those who worshiped his image** (13:11–17). These two demonically empowered political and religious leaders of the world are dealt a horrible blow; **these two were thrown alive into the lake of fire.** This is the first mention in Scripture of the **lake of fire,** the final hell, the ultimate destination of Satan, his angels, and the unredeemed (Matt. 25:41). Isaiah described it as the place where "their worm shall not die and their fire shall not be quenched" (Isa. 66:24), a description echoed by the Lord Jesus Christ in Mark 9:48. In Matthew 13:42 Jesus added that it will be a place where "there will be weeping and gnashing of teeth." Revelation 14:11 says of those who suffer there, "The smoke of their torment goes up forever and ever; they have no rest day and night." Apparently, these two don't die, but are transformed miraculously into eternal form to burn in hell. They are the first of millions of men (20:15) and angels (Matt. 25:41) to arrive in the **lake of fire.**

Hell has always existed, but this is its final form. Unlike Hades, the **lake of fire** is not a temporary holding place (cf. Luke 16:23) but a permanent place of incarceration and punishment. **Brimstone** is frequently associated with the fire of judgment (cf. 9:17; 14:10; 20:10; Luke 17:29). That the **beast** and the **false prophet** are still in the **lake of fire** a thousand years later when Satan is cast there (20:10) is a convincing refutation of the false doctrine of annihilationism. As the two most evil, vile, blasphemous people who have ever lived, it is only fitting that these two be the first to arrive in that awful place. The New Testament is clear on the eternality of punishment (cf. 14:10–11; Matt. 13:40–42; 25:41; Mark 9:43–48; Luke 3:17; 12:47–48).

And the rest were killed with the sword which came from the mouth of Him who sat on the horse, and all the birds were filled with their flesh. Bereft of their commanders, Antichrist's leaderless forces will then be destroyed, as the **rest** of those gathered to fight against Christ **were killed with the sword which came from the mouth of Him who sat on the horse.** As noted earlier in the discussion of verse 15, the rest of the unredeemed throughout the world will be judged at the sheep and goat judgment, which takes place at this time. Then, just as the angel foretold, **all the birds were filled with their flesh.** Describing the almost inconceivable carnage, John Phillips writes:

> Then suddenly it will all be over. In fact, there will be no war at all, in the sense that we think of war. There will be just a word spoken from Him who sits astride the great white horse. Once He spoke a word to a fig tree, and it withered away. Once He spoke a word to howling winds and heaving waves, and the storm clouds vanished and the waves fell still. Once He spoke to a legion of demons bursting at the seams of a poor man's soul, and instantly they fled. Now He speaks a word, and the war is over. The blasphemous, loud-mouthed Beast is stricken where he stands. The false prophet, the miracle-working windbag from the pit is punctured and still. The pair of them are bundled up and hurled headlong into the everlasting flames. Another word, and the panic-stricken armies reel and stagger and fall down dead. Field marshals and generals, admirals and air commanders, soldiers and sailors, rank and file, one and all—they fall. And the vultures descend and cover the scene. (*Exploring Revelation*, 236)

The prophet Zechariah filled in more of the details of this frightening scene:

> Behold, a day is coming for the Lord when the spoil taken from you will be divided among you. For I will gather all the nations against Jerusalem to battle, and the city will be captured, the houses plundered, the women ravished and half of the city exiled, but the rest of the people will not be cut off from the city. Then the Lord will go forth

and fight against those nations, as when He fights on a day of battle. In that day His feet will stand on the Mount of Olives, which is in front of Jerusalem on the east; and the Mount of Olives will be split in its middle from east to west by a very large valley, so that half of the mountain will move toward the north and the other half toward the south. You will flee by the valley of My mountains, for the valley of the mountains will reach to Azel; yes, you will flee just as you fled before the earthquake in the days of Uzziah king of Judah. Then the Lord, my God, will come, and all the holy ones with Him!

In that day there will be no light; the luminaries will dwindle. For it will be a unique day which is known to the Lord, neither day nor night, but it will come about that at evening time there will be light.

And it will come about in that day that living waters will flow out of Jerusalem, half of them toward the eastern sea and the other half toward the western sea; it will be in summer as well as in winter.

And the Lord will be king over all the earth; in that day the Lord will be the only one, and His name the only one.

All the land will be changed into a plain from Geba to Rimmon south of Jerusalem; but Jerusalem will rise and remain on its site from Benjamin's Gate as far as the place of the First Gate to the Corner Gate, and from the Tower of Hananel to the king's wine presses. People will live in it, and there will be no more curse, for Jerusalem will dwell in security.

Now this will be the plague with which the Lord will strike all the peoples who have gone to war against Jerusalem; their flesh will rot while they stand on their feet, and their eyes will rot in their sockets, and their tongue will rot in their mouth. It will come about in that day that a great panic from the Lord will fall on them; and they will seize one another's hand, and the hand of one will be lifted against the hand of another. (Zech. 14:1–13)

These sobering truths serve as a warning to unbelievers to repent (2 Pet. 3:9), and also to stimulate believers to godly living (2 Pet. 3:11). "The night is almost gone, and the day is near. Therefore let us lay aside the deeds of darkness and put on the armor of light. Let us behave properly as in the day, not in carousing and drunkenness, not in sexual promiscuity and sensuality, not in strife and jealousy. But put on the Lord Jesus Christ, and make no provision for the flesh in regard to its lusts" (Rom. 13:12–14).

The Coming Earthly Kingdom of the Lord Jesus Christ (Revelation 20:1–10)

16

Then I saw an angel coming down from heaven, holding the key of the abyss and a great chain in his hand. And he laid hold of the dragon, the serpent of old, who is the devil and Satan, and bound him for a thousand years; and he threw him into the abyss, and shut it and sealed it over him, so that he would not deceive the nations any longer, until the thousand years were completed; after these things he must be released for a short time.

Then I saw thrones, and they sat on them, and judgment was given to them. And I saw the souls of those who had been beheaded because of their testimony of Jesus and because of the word of God, and those who had not worshiped the beast or his image, and had not received the mark on their forehead and on their hand; and they came to life and reigned with Christ for a thousand years. The rest of the dead did not come to life until the thousand years were completed. This is the first resurrection. Blessed and holy is the one who has a part in the first resurrection; over these the second death has no power, but they will be priests of God and of Christ and will reign with Him for a thousand years.

When the thousand years are completed, Satan will be

released from his prison, and will come out to deceive the nations which are in the four corners of the earth, Gog and Magog, to gather them together for the war; the number of them is like the sand of the seashore. And they came up on the broad plain of the earth and surrounded the camp of the saints and the beloved city, and fire came down from heaven and devoured them. And the devil who deceived them was thrown into the lake of fire and brimstone, where the beast and the false prophet are also; and they will be tormented day and night forever and ever. (20:1–10)

Imagine a world dominated by righteousness and goodness, a world where there is no injustice, where no court ever renders an unjust verdict, and where everyone is treated fairly. Imagine a world where what is true, right, and noble marks every aspect of life, including interpersonal relations, commerce, education, and government. Imagine a world where there is complete, total, enforced, and permanent peace, where joy abounds and good health prevails, so much so that people live for hundreds of years. Imagine a world where the curse is removed, where the environment is restored to the pristine purity of the Garden of Eden, where peace reigns even in the animal kingdom, so that "the wolf will dwell with the lamb, and the leopard will lie down with the young goat, and the calf and the young lion and the fatling together; and a little boy will lead them" (Isa. 11:6). Imagine a world ruled by a perfect, glorious Ruler, who instantly and firmly deals with sin.

Humanly speaking, that description may seem far-fetched, a utopian fantasy that could never be reality. Yet it accurately describes conditions during the future earthly kingdom of the Lord Jesus Christ. The restored and radically reconstructed earth of the millennial kingdom will constitute paradise regained. The thousand-year reign of the Savior over the earth is the divinely planned and promised culmination of all of redemptive history and the realization of the hope of all the saints of all the ages.

The millennial kingdom is called by many names in Scripture. In Matthew 19:28 Jesus calls it "the regeneration." Acts 3:19 describes the kingdom as "times of refreshing," while verse 21 of that chapter calls it "the period of restoration of all things." The apostle Paul refers to it in Ephesians 1:10 as "an administration suitable to the fullness of the times."

The Bible's teaching on the kingdom is not confined to the New Testament. The kingdom is an important theme throughout Scripture; it is the goal toward which all of redemptive history progresses. In the words of John Bright, "The Bible is *one* book. Had we to give that book a title, we might with justice call it 'The Book of the Coming Kingdom of

God'" (*The Kingdom of God* [Nashville: Abingdon, 1953], 197; italics in original). Among the many Old Testament passages that speak of the earthly kingdom are Deuteronomy 30:1–5; 2 Samuel 7:12–16; Psalm 2:6–12; Isaiah 2:2–4; 11:1–10; 12:1–6; 24:23; 32:15–20; 35:1–2; 60:10–18; 65:20–22; Jeremiah 3:14–18; 23:5–6; 30:3; 31:35–40; 33:14–18; Ezekiel 34:23–24; 36:16–38; 37:15–28; Daniel 2:44–45; Hosea 3:4–5; Joel 3:18–21; Amos 9:11–15; Micah 4:1–8; Zephaniah 3:14–20; and Zechariah 14:9–11.

God's kingdom may be broadly defined as the sphere in which He reigns. In its universal, eternal sense, God's kingdom encompasses everything that exists, because God is the sovereign ruler over all of His creation. David declared that truth in Psalm 103:19: "The Lord has established His throne in the heavens, and His sovereignty rules over all." Historically, God has mediated His rule on earth through His people, first through Adam and Eve, then Abel, Seth, Enoch, Noah, Abraham, Isaac, Jacob, Joseph, Moses, Joshua, the judges of Israel (including Samuel), and the kings of Israel and Judah. In the present era, God mediates His rule politically through human governments (Rom. 13:1–7) and spiritually through the church (Acts 20:25; Rom. 14:17; Col. 1:13). In the millennial kingdom, the political and religious elements of God's temporal, earthly rule will be reunited in the Person of the Lord Jesus Christ.

Taking the text of Revelation 20 (and the numerous other biblical passages that speak of the earthly kingdom) at face value leads to a premillennial view of eschatology. That is, Christ will return, and then establish a literal kingdom on earth, which will last for a thousand years. There are two other major views of the Millennium in addition to premillennialism: postmillennialism and amillennialism.

Postmillennialism is in some ways the opposite of premillennialism. Premillennialism teaches that Christ will return before the Millennium; postmillennialism teaches that He will return at the end of the Millennium. Premillennialism teaches that the period immediately before Christ's return will be the worst in human history; postmillennialism teaches that before His return will come the best period in history, so that Christ will return at the end of a long golden age of peace and harmony. (Most postmillennialists deny that the Millennium will last for one thousand actual years; they arbitrarily view that number as symbolic of a long period of time.) "The millennium to which the postmillennialist looks forward is thus a golden age of prosperity during this present dispensation, that is, during the Church Age" (Loraine Boettner, "Postmillennialism," in *The Meaning of the Millennium: Four Views* Robert G. Clouse, ed. [Downers Grove, Ill: InterVarsity, 1977], 117). That golden age, according to postmillennialism, will result from the spread of the gospel throughout the world and the conversion of a majority of the human race to Christianity. Thus "Christ will return to a truly Christianized world"

(Boettner, "Postmillennialism," 118). The millennial kingdom, according to postmillennialists, will be established by the church, not by the personal intervention of Jesus Christ. Nor will Christ reign personally on earth during the Millennium, but rather through His church.

In keeping with the generally optimistic views of those eras, postmillennialism flourished in the eighteenth and nineteenth centuries. The impact of the Enlightenment, the Industrial Revolution, the rapid pace of scientific discovery, and Darwin's theory of evolution convinced many that society was progressing inevitably toward a utopia. That optimistic view was in harmony with postmillennialism, which also teaches that the world is going to get better and better (though by different means). But the numbing horror of the First World War, the moral decadence of the Roaring Twenties, the hard times of the Great Depression, the madness of the Nazi's slaughter of the Jews, and the worldwide catastrophe of the Second World War brought an end to the naive optimism that had prevailed before World War I. Postmillennialism accordingly also declined in popularity. In recent years, however, there has been a resurgence of postmillennialism in such movements as Liberation Theology, Kingdom Theology, and Theonomy.

The name "amillennialism" is somewhat misleading, since it implies that amillennialists do not believe in a millennium. While it is true that they reject the concept of an earthly millennium, and especially one that is actually a Millennium (one thousand years in duration), amillennialists do believe in a kingdom. They believe the Old Testament prophecies of the Messiah's kingdom are being fulfilled now, either by the saints reigning with Christ in heaven, or (spiritually, not literally) by the church on earth. (Amillennialists would also apply some of those Old Testament prophecies to the eternal state.) Far from disbelieving in the Millennium, amillennialists believe we are in it now: "As far as the thousand years of Revelation 20 are concerned, we are in the millennium now" (Anthony A. Hoekema, "Amillennialism," in *The Meaning of the Millennium: Four Views*, ed. Clouse, 181).

There is absolutely no exegetical reason or source for this conclusion and no warrant for abandoning the historical, grammatical hermeneutic when interpreting prophecy. Such is purely an arbitrary act on the part of the interpreter, based on his presuppositions. Furthermore, there is no reason to deny a literal one thousand years as the duration of the kingdom of Christ on earth. Robert L. Thomas writes:

> If the writer wanted a very large symbolic number, why did he not use 144,000 (7:1ff.; 14:1ff.;), 200,000,000 (9:16), "ten thousand times ten thousand, and thousands of thousands" (5:11), or an incalculably large number (7:9)? The fact is that no number in Revelation is verifiably a symbolic number. On the other hand, nonsymbolic usage of numbers

> is the rule. It requires multiplication of a literal 12,000 by a literal twelve to come up with 144,000 in 7:4–8. The churches, seals, trumpets, and bowls are all literally seven in number. The three unclean spirits of 16:13 are actually three in number. The three angels connected with the three last woes (8:13) add up to a total of three. The seven last plagues amount to exactly seven. The equivalency of 1,260 days and three and a half years necessitate a nonsymbolic understanding of both numbers. The twelve apostles and the twelve tribes of Israel are literally twelve (21:12–14). The seven churches are in seven literal cities. Yet confirmation of a single number in Revelation as symbolic is impossible. (*Revelation 8–22: An Exegetical Commentary* [Chicago: Moody, 1995], 408–9)

It is highly doubtful that any symbolic number would be repeated six times in a text, as one thousand is here.

For the first century and a half after the close of the New Testament era, the church was largely premillennial. Among the church fathers of that period who believed in a literal thousand-year earthly Millennium were Papias (a disciple of the apostle John), Irenaeus, Justin Martyr, Tertullian, and the author of the Epistle of Barnabas. That premillennial consensus was challenged by the members of the Alexandrian school (most notably Origen), who advocated an allegorical approach to interpreting Scripture. The famous church historian Eusebius also rejected a literal, earthly Millennium, as did the noted Bible scholar Jerome. But it was the influence of Augustine, the greatest theologian of the early church, that ensured that amillennialism would dominate the church for centuries. Amillennialism was the view of the Reformers, and today most scholars in the Reformed tradition are amillennialists.

At the heart of the debate over millennial views is the issue of hermeneutics. All sides in the debate agree that interpreting Old Testament prophecy literally leads naturally to premillennialism. Amillennialist Floyd E. Hamilton candidly acknowledges that truth: "Now we must frankly admit that a literal interpretation of the Old Testament prophecies gives us just such a picture of an earthly reign of the Messiah as the premillennialist pictures" (*The Basis of Millennial Faith* [Grand Rapids: Eerdmans, 1942], 38). Postmillennialist Loraine Boettner agrees with Hamilton's assessment: "It is generally agreed that if the prophecies are taken literally, they do foretell a restoration of the nation of Israel in the land of Palestine with the Jews having a prominent place in that kingdom and ruling over the other nations" ("A Postmillennial Response [to Dispensational Premillennialism]," in *The Meaning of the Millennium: Four Views*, ed. Clouse, 95).

In light of the above admissions, the question that naturally arises is "Why not take the Old Testament prophecies of the Millennium literally?"

Those who reject a literal interpretation argue that the New Testament appears to interpret some Old Testament prophecies nonliterally. But in most cases, the New Testament is not interpreting those prophecies, but merely applying principles found in them. In fact, scores of Old Testament prophecies relating to Christ's first coming were literally fulfilled.

There are several compelling reasons for interpreting Old Testament prophecies literally.

First, if the literal sense of a passage is rejected, who is to determine what the nonliteral or spiritual sense is, since the normal rules of interpretation do not apply? Walter C. Kaiser, Jr., poses the dilemma:

> Who or what will arbitrate among the various [nonliteral] meanings suggested and decide which are to be accepted as authoritative and which are spurious? Short of saying that every person's fancy is his or her own rule, there does not appear to be any final court of appeal. . . . There simply are no justifiable criteria for setting boundaries once the interpreter departs from the normal usage of language. (*Back Toward the Future* [Grand Rapids: Baker, 1989], 129–30)

Second, adopting a nonliteral view of the Old Testament kingdom prophecies raises some disturbing questions: What did those prophecies mean to those to whom they were addressed? If prophecies seemingly addressed to Israel really apply to the church (which did not exist at that time), did God give revelation that failed to reveal? And if those prophecies were meant to apply symbolically to the church, why were they addressed to Israel? What meaning could such prophecies have in their historical settings? Ironically, many who spiritualize Old Testament prophecies reject the futurist interpretation of Revelation because it allegedly robs the book of its meaning for those to whom it was written. Yet they do the very same thing with the Old Testament kingdom prophecies.

Third, spiritualizing those prophecies leads to some glaring inconsistencies. It is inconsistent ~~to argue that the cursings they~~ pronounce apply literally to Israel, while the blessings they promise apply symbolically and spiritually to the church. An example of inconsistency in the spiritualizing method of interpreting prophecy comes from the angel Gabriel's words to Mary in Luke 1:31–33: "And behold, you will conceive in your womb and bear a son, and you shall name Him Jesus. He will be great and will be called the Son of the Most High; and the Lord God will give Him the throne of His father David; and He will reign over the house of Jacob forever, and His kingdom will have no end." If, as all conservative scholars agree, Jesus was literally conceived in Mary's womb, literally named "Jesus," literally became great, was literally "the Son of the Most High," will He not also literally reign on David's throne over Israel? Can the same passage be interpreted both literally and nonliterally? Further, both amillennialists and postmillennialists interpret some prophetic events literally, such as Christ's second coming, the Great White Throne judgment, and the new heavens and the new earth. Why not interpret the millennial kingdom literally? Finally, amillennialists and postmillennialists interpret the nonprophetic portions of Scripture according to the literal, historical, grammatical, and contextual method of hermeneutics; why adopt a different method for interpreting prophecy? Such an adoption is utterly arbitrary.

Though not an exhaustive description of the earthly kingdom, this text caps off all the biblical revelation about the Millennium by revealing four essential truths about it: the removal of Satan, the reign of the saints, the return of Satan, and the revolt of society.

The Removal of Satan

Then I saw an angel coming down from heaven, holding the key of the abyss and a great chain in his hand. And he laid hold of the dragon, the serpent of old, who is the devil and Satan, and bound him for a thousand years; and he threw him into the abyss, and shut it and sealed it over him, so that he would not deceive the nations any longer, until the thousand years were completed; after these things he must be released for a short time. (20:1–3)

The first matter for the King's attention as He sets up His kingdom is the confinement of the chief rebel. The removal of "the god of this world" (2 Cor. 4:4), "the prince of the power of the air . . . the spirit that is now working in the sons of disobedience" (Eph. 2:2), will dramatically change the world. By this time, God will have destroyed all human rebels. Those who survived the Tribulation judgments will have been executed at Armageddon (19:11–21) or the goat judgment (Matt. 25:41–46). The ringleaders of the worldwide rebellion, the beast (Antichrist) and the false prophet, will have been thrown into the lake of fire (19:20). The final step in preparation for the kingdom will be the removal of Satan and his demon hosts, so that Christ reigns without the opposition of supernatural enemies.

As it frequently does in Revelation (cf. vv. 4, 11; 6:1, 2, 5, 8, 12; 7:2; 8:2, 13; 9:1; 10:1; 13:1, 11; 14:1, 6, 14; 15:1; 16:13; 17:3; 19:11, 17, 19; 21:1), the phrase *kai eidon* (**Then I saw**) indicates chronological progression. The location of this passage in the chronological flow of Revelation is consistent with a premillennial view of the kingdom. After the Tribulation (chaps. 6–19) Christ will return (19:11–21) and set up His kingdom (20:1–10), which will be followed by the new heavens and the new earth (21:1). Thus the millennial kingdom comes after Christ's second coming but before the establishing of the new heavens and the new earth. Amillennialist Anthony Hoekema has to acknowledge that, taken at face value, the chronology of Revelation supports premillennialism. He writes:

> Let us assume, for example, that the book of Revelation is to be interpreted in an exclusively futuristic sense. . . . Let us further assume that what is presented in Revelation 20 must necessarily follow, in chronological order, what was described in chapter 19. We are then virtually compelled to believe that the thousand-year reign depicted in 20:4 must come after the return of Christ described in 19:11. ("Amillennialism," in *The Meaning of the Millennium: Four Views*, ed. Clouse, 156)

The passage clearly teaches that Christ's return precedes the millennial kingdom—a scenario incompatible with postmillennialism and amillennialism, but exactly what premillennialism teaches. To get around the difficulty the chronology of Revelation poses for their views, postmillennialists and amillennialists must deny that chapter 20 follows chapter 19 chronologically. But such a denial ignores the chronological significance of the phrase *kai eidon*, as noted above. It also ignores the continuity of the context: Having dealt with Antichrist and the false prophet in chapter 19, Christ deals with their evil master, Satan, in chapter 20. Why reject such an obvious chronology? It is apparently done for no other reason than to eliminate premillennialism, not because there is any justification in Scripture.

The identity of the **angel** whom John saw **coming down from heaven** to bind Satan is not disclosed, but he may be Michael the archangel, the great adversary of Satan (12:7; cf. Dan. 10:13, 21; 12:1; Jude 9). Whoever the angel is, he possesses great power. He is sent to earth with a specific agenda: to seize Satan for the thousand-year duration of the kingdom, bind him, cast him into the abyss and seal it, and then release him at the end of the thousand years.

Abussos (**abyss**) appears seven times in Revelation (cf. 9:1, 2, 11; 11:7; 17:8), always in reference to the temporary place of incarceration for certain demons. The abyss is not their final place of punishment; the lake of fire is (Matt. 25:41). Nevertheless it is a place of torment to which the demons fear to be sent (Luke 8:31). The prisoners in the abyss are among the most vile and evil of all demons and include the "spirits now in prison, who once were disobedient, when the patience of God kept waiting in the days of Noah" (1 Pet. 3:19–20). Those demons, who attempted to corrupt the human race by cohabiting with human women (Gen. 6:1–4), will never be released (Jude 6). They will be transferred directly from their temporary incarceration in the **abyss** to their permanent place of punishment, the lake of fire (cf. Isa. 24:21–22). Other demons sentenced to the **abyss** will be released at the fifth trumpet judgment to torment sinners (9:1–12). (For further information on the **abyss,** see *Revelation 1–11,* The MacArthur New Testament Commentary [Chicago: Moody, 1999], 257–58.)

The **key** given to the angel by God signifies his delegated authority (cf. 9:1); he has the power to open the **abyss,** and then to shut it after casting Satan inside. The metaphor of binding demons with a **chain** also appears in Jude 6. This **chain** is a **great** one, because of Satan's greatness and power as the highest created being (cf. Ezek. 28:14). The angel **laid hold of** Satan, who is unmistakably identified by the same four titles given him in 12:9. First, he is called **the dragon,** a title given him twelve times in Revelation (cf. 12:3, 4, 7, 9, 13, 16, 17; 13:1, 2, 4; 16:13). It emphasizes his bestial nature, ferociousness, and oppressive cruelty. The title **serpent of old** hearkens back to the Garden of Eden and Satan's temptation of Eve (Gen. 3:1–6; 2 Cor. 11:3). *Diabolos* (**devil**) means "slanderer," or "malicious gossip" (1 Tim. 3:11; 2 Tim. 3:3; Titus 2:3)—an appropriate title for the "accuser of our brethren" (12:10). Satan is a malignant liar; in fact, he is "the father of lies" (John 8:44). *Satanas* (**Satan**) and its Hebrew root *satan* are used fifty-three times in Scripture. Both words mean "adversary," since Satan opposes God, Christ, and all believers.

The length of the period for which Satan will be **bound** is defined as a **thousand years,** the first of six precise and important references to the duration of the Millennium (cf. vv. 3, 4, 5, 6, 7). Satan's binding poses a serious difficulty for both postmillennialists and amillennialists. Amillennialists argue that Satan is already **bound,** since, as noted above, they believe we are in the Millennium now (though they do not view it as one thousand literal years in length). Many postmillennialists also believe that Satan is presently **bound,** because otherwise it is difficult to see how the church could usher in the Millennium. Yet the biblical description of Satan's activity in this present age makes it impossible to believe he has already been **bound.** Satan plants lying hypocrites in the church (Acts 5:3), schemes against believers (2 Cor. 2:11; Eph. 6:11), disguises himself as an angel of light to deceive people (2 Cor. 11:14), attacks believers (2 Cor. 12:7; Eph. 4:27) and must be resisted (James 4:7), hinders those in the ministry (1 Thess. 2:18), and leads believers astray (1 Tim. 5:15). Amillennialists and postmillennialists generally argue that Satan was bound at the Cross, and that his binding simply means that he can no longer deceive the nations and keep them from learning God's truth (e.g., Anthony A. Hoekema, *The Bible and the Future* [Grand Rapids: Eerdmans, 1979], 228]. But Satan did not keep the Gentile nations from the knowledge of the truth before his alleged binding at the Cross. The Egyptians heard about the true God from Joseph, and from the Israelites during the four hundred years they lived in Egypt. The Assyrians of Nineveh not only heard the truth from Jonah, but also repented (Matt. 12:41). The Queen of Sheba heard about the true God from Solomon (1 Kings 10:1–9); the Babylonians from Daniel and his Jewish friends; and the Persians from Esther, Mordecai, and Nehemiah. Further, in what sense is Satan restrained from deceiving the nations in the present age, since he blinds the minds of unbelievers (2 Cor. 4:4), "is now working in the sons of disobedience" (Eph. 2:2), and holds unbelievers captive (2 Tim. 2:26) in his kingdom (Col. 1:13)?

The testimony of Scripture is that Satan is anything but bound in this present age, but will be during the coming earthly kingdom of the Lord Jesus Christ. It is only then that he will be incarcerated in **the abyss,** which will be **shut . . . and sealed . . . so that he** cannot **deceive the nations any longer.** His activity in the world will not be merely restricted or restrained, but totally curtailed; he will not be permitted to influence the world in any way. As will be explained later, that does not mean that the living people in the Millennium will be incapable of sinning. Amazingly, a vast part of the population, born of the believers who alone entered the kingdom, will in that perfect environment love their sin and reject the King. They will be judged with a rod of iron (2:27; 12:5; Ps. 2:9), and those who engage in open rebellion under Satan's leadership when **the thousand years** are **completed** and Satan **must be released for a short time** will be utterly destroyed (see the discussion of vv. 8–10 below).

The Reign of the Saints

Then I saw thrones, and they sat on them, and judgment was given to them. And I saw the souls of those who had been beheaded because of their testimony of Jesus and because of the word of God, and those who had not worshiped the beast or his image, and had not received the mark on their forehead and on their hand; and they came to life and reigned with Christ for a thousand years. The rest of the dead did not come to life until the thousand years were completed. This is the first resurrection. Blessed and holy is the one who has a part in the first resurrection; over these the second death has no power, but they will be priests of God and of Christ and will reign with Him for a thousand years. (20:4–6)

With Satan, his demon hosts, and all God-rejecting sinners out of the way, the millennial kingdom of peace and righteousness will be established. The supreme ruler in that kingdom will, of course, be the Lord Jesus Christ. He alone is "King of kings, and Lord of lords" (19:16), and "the Lord God will give Him [alone] the throne of His father David" (Luke 1:32). Yet He has graciously promised that His saints will reign with Him. They will rule subordinately over every aspect of life in the kingdom, and being glorified and perfected, they will perfectly carry out His will.

In this vision, John sees the panorama of God's people resurrected, rewarded, and reigning with Christ. He **saw thrones,** symbolizing both judicial and regal authority, **and** God's people **sat on them, and judgment was given to them.** The glorified saints will both enforce God's will and adjudicate disputes.

Several suggestions have been offered concerning the identity of the saints who **sat on** the **thrones,** but they can best be identified by determining who God promised would reign. Daniel 7:27 promises that the Old Testament saints will reign in the millennial kingdom: "Then the sovereignty, the dominion and the greatness of all the kingdoms under the whole heaven will be given to the people of the saints of the Highest One; His kingdom will be an everlasting kingdom, and all the dominions will serve and obey Him." Jesus promised the apostles that "you who have followed Me, in the regeneration when the Son of Man will sit on His glorious throne, you also shall sit upon twelve thrones, judging the twelve tribes of Israel" (Matt. 19:28). New Testament believers are also promised that they will reign with Christ. In 1 Corinthians 6:2 Paul wrote, "Do you not know that the saints will judge the world?" while 2 Timothy 2:12 declares, "If we endure, we will also reign with Him." In Revelation 2:26 Jesus promises, "He who overcomes, and he who keeps My deeds until the end, to him I will give authority over the nations," and in Revelation 3:21 He adds, "He who overcomes, I will grant to him to sit down with Me on My throne, as I also overcame and sat down with My Father on His throne." Revelation 5:10 makes it clear that the saints will reign on the earth, not in a spiritual sense or in the heavenly sphere: "You have made them to be a kingdom and priests to our God; and they will reign upon the earth."

The present passage introduces the last group of saints who will reign with Christ in His kingdom. As his vision continued, John **saw the souls of those who had been beheaded because of their testimony of Jesus and because of the word of God, and those who had not worshiped the beast or his image, and had not received the mark on their forehead and on their hand.** These are the martyred believers from the Tribulation (6:9; 7:9–17; 12:11). *Pelekizō* (**beheaded**) literally means, "to cut off with an axe," and is a figure of speech meaning "to put to death," or "to execute." The empire of Antichrist exterminated Tribulation saints **because of their testimony of Jesus** (cf. 1:9; 12:17; 19:10), **because** they faithfully proclaimed the **word of God** (cf. 1:2; 6:9), **and** because they **had not worshiped the beast or his image, and had not received the mark on their forehead and on their hand** (cf. 13:16–17; 14:9–11; 16:2; 19:20).

Because the Tribulation saints were faithful to the death, evidencing their true salvation (cf. Matt. 24:13; Col. 1:21–23; Heb. 3:14), **they** too **came to life and reigned with Christ for a thousand years.** *Ezēsan* (**they came to life**) cannot refer to a spiritual resurrection (regeneration or the new birth), since the Tribulation martyrs were already spiritually alive. When used in connection with physical death, the root form of *ezēsan (zaō)* is used throughout the New Testament to describe physical, bodily resurrection (cf. 1:18; 2:8; 13:14; 20:5; Matt. 9:18; 27:63; Mark 5:23; Luke 24:23; John 11:25; Acts 1:3; 9:41; Rom. 14:9; 2 Cor. 13:4).

Then John adds the parenthetical footnote that **the rest of the dead did not come to life until the thousand years were completed.** These are the unbelieving dead of all ages, whose resurrection to judgment and damnation is described in verses 11–15. John calls the resurrection of the saints from all ages **the first resurrection.** That resurrection is also called in Scripture the "resurrection of the righteous" (Luke 14:14; Acts 24:15), the "resurrection of life" (John 5:29), the resurrection of "those who are Christ's at His coming" (1 Cor. 15:23), and the "better resurrection" (Heb. 11:35). The use of *anastasis* (**resurrection**) offers further evidence that the resurrection described in verse 4 is a physical resurrection. The word is used forty-two times in the New Testament, always of a physical resurrection (except in Luke 2:34, where the context clearly demands another meaning).

The phrase **blessed and holy is the one who has a part in the first resurrection** introduces the fifth of seven beatitudes in Revelation (cf. 1:3; 14:13; 16:15; 19:9; 22:7, 14). Those who have **a part in the first resurrection** are blessed first of all because **the second death has no power** over them. The **second death,** defined in verse 14 as "the lake of fire," is eternal hell. The comforting truth is that no true child of God will ever face God's eternal wrath. "Having now been justified by His blood," Paul wrote, "we shall be saved from the wrath of God through Him" (Rom. 5:9). To the Thessalonians he added, "Jesus . . . rescues us from the wrath to come. . . . For God has not destined us for wrath, but for obtaining salvation through our Lord Jesus Christ" (1 Thess. 1:10; 5:9).

Those who participate in the **first resurrection** are also blessed because **they will be priests of God and of Christ** (cf. 1:6; 5:10). Believers are already "a royal priesthood," called to "proclaim the excellencies of Him who has called [them] out of darkness into His marvelous light" (1 Pet. 2:9). Believers now serve as priests by worshiping God and leading others to the knowledge of Him, and will also serve in that capacity during the millennial kingdom.

A final blessing for the participants in the **first resurrection** is that they **will reign with** the Lord Jesus Christ **for a thousand years,** along with believers who survived the Tribulation. Politically and socially, the rule of Christ and His saints will be universal (Ps. 2:6–8; Dan. 2:35), absolute (Ps. 2:9; Isa. 11:4), and righteous (Isa. 11:3–5). Spiritually, their rule will be a time when the believing remnant of Israel is converted (Jer. 30:5–8; Rom. 11:26) and the nation is restored to the land God promised to Abraham (Gen. 13:14–15; 15:18). It will be a time when the Gentile nations also will worship the King (Isa. 11:9; Mic. 4:2; Zech. 14:16). The millennial rule of Christ and the saints will also be marked by the presence of righteousness and peace (Isa. 32:17) and joy (Isa. 12:3–4; 61:3, 7). Physically, it will be a time when the curse is lifted (Isa. 11:7–9; 30:23–24; 35:1–2, 7), when food will be plentiful (Joel 2:21–27), and when there will be physical health and well-being (Isa. 33:24; 35:5–6), leading to long life (Isa. 65:20).

THE RETURN OF SATAN

When the thousand years are completed, Satan will be released from his prison, (20:7)

As previously noted, Satan and his demon hordes will be imprisoned in the abyss for the duration of the Millennium, in which the Lord Jesus Christ will rule with unopposed sovereignty. They will not be permitted to interfere in the affairs of the kingdom in any way. Satan's binding will end, however, **when the thousand years are completed** and he is **released from his prison** to lead a final rebellion of sinners.

To review briefly, Scripture teaches that no unsaved people will enter the kingdom. Only the redeemed from among the Jewish (12:6, 13–17; Isa. 60:21; Rom. 11:26) and Gentile (7:9–17) survivors of the Tribulation will go into the kingdom in their normal, physical bodies. The perfect environmental and social conditions of the Millennium, coupled with the lengthened life spans of those physically alive (Isa. 65:20), will cause their children to proliferate.

Though the initial inhabitants of the millennial kingdom will all be redeemed, they will still possess a sinful human nature. And as all parents have done since the Fall, they will pass that sin nature on to their offspring. Each successive generation throughout the thousand years will be made up of sinners in need of salvation. Many will come to saving faith in the Lord Jesus Christ. But amazingly, despite the personal rule of Christ on earth, despite the most moral society the world will ever know, many others will love their sin and reject Him (cf. Rom. 8:7). Even the utopian conditions of the Millennium will not change the sad reality of human depravity. As they did during His incarnational presence on earth, sinners will refuse the grace and reject the lordship of the King of all the earth. That is not surprising, since even the perfect conditions of the Garden of Eden were not sufficient to keep sinless Adam and Eve from rebelling against God. The issue regarding salvation is never lack of information (cf. Rom. 1:18–20); it is love of sin (John 3:19). Those who openly rebel will face swift judgment (2:27; 12:5; 19:15; Ps. 2:9), including the withholding of rain on their land (Zech. 14:16–19). But enough unrepentant sinners will be alive at the end of the Millennium for Satan to lead a worldwide rebellion.

When Satan is loosed, he will provide the cohesive supernatural leadership needed to bring to the surface all the latent sin and rebellion left in the universe. He will pull together all the rebels, revealing the true character and intent of those Christ-rejecting sinners and making it evident that God's judgment of them is just. Satan's desperate wickedness and violent hatred of God and Christ will not be altered by his thousand years of imprisonment in the abyss. When he is released, he will immediately set about fomenting his final act of rebellion.

The Revolt of Society

[Satan] will come out to deceive the nations which are in the four corners of the earth, Gog and Magog, to gather them together for the war; the number of them is like the sand of the seashore. And they came up on the broad plain of the earth and surrounded the camp of the saints and the beloved city, and fire came down from heaven and devoured them. And the devil who deceived them was thrown into the lake of fire and brimstone, where the beast and the false prophet are also; and they will be tormented day and night forever and ever. (20:8–10)

At the end of his thousand-year imprisonment, Satan **will come out to deceive the nations** (cf. vv. 3, 10; 12:9). As noted above, Satan's imprisonment cannot alter his God-hating nature. In fact, he will hate Christ more than ever. And as also noted above, Satan will find fertile soil in which to sow his seeds of rebellion. Many unsaved descendants of those who entered the millennial kingdom in their physical bodies (all of whom will be redeemed) will love their sin and reject Christ. They will be as unmoved by the peace, joy, and righteousness of the Millennium as sinners were by the devastating judgments of the Tribulation (cf. 9:20–21; 16:9, 11, 21).

The actual strategy and method of Satan's deception is not revealed, but it will succeed in duping the unregenerate people of the world into revolting against the Lord Jesus Christ. His deception, however, will fit within God's purpose, which, as noted above, is to manifest His justice when He destroys the rebels. Satan's actions are always under God's sovereign control (cf. Job 1:12; 2:6), and his gathering together of these wicked rebels will be no exception.

Satan will collect the deceived **nations** from **the four corners of the earth** (cf. 7:1; Isa. 11:12), an expression referring, not to a flat earth, but to the four main points of the compass: north, south, east, and west. In other words, the rebels will come from all over the globe.

John gives these enemies of the King of Kings the symbolic title **Gog and Magog,** naming them after the invasion force that will assault Israel during the Tribulation (Ezek. 38–39). Some believe that Ezekiel 38 and 39 describe this battle at the end of the Millennium. There are, however, significant differences that argue against equating the two events. Ezekiel 39:4 and 17 describe the invaders perishing on the mountains of Israel, but according to Revelation 20:9 the rebels at the end of the Millennium will be destroyed on a "broad plain." Also, the language of Ezekiel 39:17–20 seems to be describing the same event depicted in Revelation 19:17–18. Finally, the events of Ezekiel 38–39 fit chronologically before the description of the millennial temple given in chapters 40–48, while the battle depicted in Revelation 20:7–10 takes place after the Millennium.

The name **Gog** appears to be used in Scripture as a general title for an enemy of God's people (the Septuagint uses it to translate "Agag" in Num. 24:7). In Ezekiel 38–39, the name **Gog** describes the final Antichrist of the Tribulation. Most likely, then, **Gog** is used in verse 8 to describe the human leader of Satan's forces. Some believe the people known as **Magog** to be the descendents of Noah's grandson of that same name (Gen. 10:2). They later became known as the Scythians and inhabited the region north of the Black and Caspian Seas. Others identify them with a people who lived farther south in Asia Minor. Whoever the historical people known as **Magog** may have been, the term is used in this passage to describe the sinful rebels from all the nations who will **gather together for the** final **war** in human history.

Amazingly, John saw that **the number of** the rebels will be **like the sand of the seashore**—a figure of speech used in Scripture to describe a vast, uncountable multitude (Gen. 22:17; Josh. 11:4; Judg. 7:12; 1 Sam. 13:5; 1 Kings 4:20; Heb. 11:12). As previously noted, the ideal conditions of health, prosperity, safety, and peace that will prevail during the Millennium, coupled with the long life spans of its inhabitants, will lead to a massive population explosion. Incredibly, vast numbers of those people will join Satan in his final act of rebellion against God.

The earth's topography will have been drastically reshaped by the catastrophic events of the Tribulation (cf. 16:20; Zech. 14:4, 9–11). That will allow the rebel forces to come **up on the broad plain of the earth** and surround the **camp of the saints and the beloved city.** *Parembolē* (**camp**) is used six times in Acts to describe a Roman military barrack (Acts 21:34, 37; 22:24; 23:10, 16, 32). The saints will be encamped around **the beloved city** of Jerusalem (cf. Pss. 78:68; 87:2), which is the place of Messiah's throne and the center of the millennial world (cf. Isa. 24:23; Ezek. 38:12; 43:7; Mic. 4:7; Zech. 14:9–11), enjoying the glorious presence of the Lord Jesus Christ (Isa. 24:23; Jer. 3:17) when the attack comes.

Like Armageddon a thousand years earlier (19:11–21), the "battle" will in reality be an execution. As the rebel forces moved in for the attack, **fire came down from heaven and devoured them.** They will be swiftly, instantly, and totally exterminated. Sending **fire . . . down from heaven** is often the way God judges sinners (cf. Gen. 19:24; Lev. 10:2; 2 Kings 1:10, 12; Luke 9:54). Satan's forces will be physically killed, and their souls will go into the realm of punishment, awaiting their final sentencing to eternal hell, which will take place shortly (20:11–15). Nor will their evil leader escape his fate: **the devil who deceived them was thrown into the lake of fire and brimstone.** There he will join his cronies, **the beast and the false prophet,** who by that time will have been in that place of torment for a thousand years (19:20). That those two humans are still there after that time refutes the false doctrine of annihilationism.

Hell is a place of both mental (Dan. 12:2; Matt. 8:12; 13:42, 50; 22:13; 24:51; 25:30; Luke 13:28) and physical torment (14:10–11; Matt. 25:41; Mark 9:43–44; Luke 16:23–24). Those sentenced to that terrible place **will be tormented day and night.** There will not be a moment's relief **forever and ever.** Scripture explicitly teaches that hell is eternal. The same Greek phrase translated **forever and ever** is used in 1:18 to speak of Christ's eternity; in 4:9–10, 10:6, and 15:7 of God's eternity; and in 11:15 of the duration of Christ's reign. Unbelievers will "be tormented with fire and brimstone in the presence of the holy angels and in the presence of the Lamb. And the smoke of their torment goes up forever and ever; they have no rest day and night" (14:10–11). Jesus taught that the punishment of the wicked is as eternal as the eternal life of the righteous (Matt. 25:46). He also taught that hell is a place of "unquenchable fire" (Mark 9:43), "where their worm does not die" (Mark 9:48). Second

Thessalonians 1:9 teaches that the destruction of the wicked in hell stretches throughout all eternity. (For a summary of the arguments that the punishment in hell is eternal, see Richard L. Mayhue, "Hell: Never, Forever, or Just for Awhile?" *The Master's Seminary Journal* 9 [Fall 1998]: 129–45. This entire issue of *The Master's Seminary Journal* is devoted to the topic of the eternality of hell.)

Believers are already citizens of God's kingdom (Phil. 3:20; Col. 1:13; 1 Thess. 2:12), blessed to be in fellowship with the King. But a glorious future inheritance awaits them, "imperishable and undefiled [which] will not fade away" (1 Pet. 1:4).

Man's Last Day in God's Court (Revelation 20:11–15)

17

Then I saw a great white throne and Him who sat upon it, from whose presence earth and heaven fled away, and no place was found for them. And I saw the dead, the great and the small, standing before the throne, and books were opened; and another book was opened, which is the book of life; and the dead were judged from the things which were written in the books, according to their deeds. And the sea gave up the dead which were in it, and death and Hades gave up the dead which were in them; and they were judged, every one of them according to their deeds. Then death and Hades were thrown into the lake of fire. This is the second death, the lake of fire. And if anyone's name was not found written in the book of life, he was thrown into the lake of fire. (20:11–15)

This passage describes the final sentencing of the lost and is the most serious, sobering, and tragic passage in the entire Bible. Commonly known as the Great White Throne judgment, it is the last courtroom scene that will ever take place. After this there will never again be a trial, and God will never again need to act as judge. The accused, all the unsaved who have ever lived, will be resurrected to experience a trial like no other that has ever been. There will be no debate over their guilt or innocence. There will be a prosecutor, but no defender; an accuser, but no advocate. There will be an indictment, but no defense mounted by the accused; the convicting evidence will be presented with no rebuttal or cross-examination. There will be an utterly unsympathetic Judge and no jury, and there will be no appeal of the sentence He pronounces. The guilty will be punished eternally with no possibility of parole in a prison from which there is no escape.

The language of this passage is plain, stark, and unembellished. Few details are given, and the description is utterly lacking in the vivid, eloquent modifiers that might be expected. But the scene is frightening enough in its own right that such language would be superfluous. The beloved apostle John, recording this vision in a cave or on a hillside on the island of Patmos, no doubt was shaken as he wrote of the eternal damnation of the wicked.

Ever since the Fall, Satan, the father of lies (John 8:44), has attempted to deceive people about the reality of the coming judgment. He has done his best to convince people that there will be no final tribunal. Satan has deceived sinners into believing that they can live as they please without fear of ultimate accountability or future punishment. Satan said to Eve, "You surely will not die!" (Gen. 3:4), thus voicing his denial of judgment on sin. The primary means the devil uses in his deception are atheism (particularly the godless theory of evolution) and false religion. Atheism's denial of God's existence means there is no moral Judge to whom people are accountable after they die. They wrongly believe that they are free to sin as they please and then simply pass out of existence. The gods of most false religions are not holy, requiring inward righteousness and heart obedience, and they are appeased by ritual and ceremony; thus these gods inspire no fear of accountability in their worshipers.

But despite the vain, foolish speculations of men, the true and living God is the Supreme Judge of the universe. His judgment of unbelievers will be just, because He is just. Deuteronomy 32:4 says of God, "His work is perfect, for all His ways are just; a God of faithfulness and without injustice, righteous and upright is He." Job 37:23–24 declares, "The Almighty—we cannot find Him; He is exalted in power and He will not do violence to justice and abundant righteousness. Therefore men fear Him." God cannot but be just, because the absolutely holy perfection of His nature will not allow Him to do anything but what is right. God's will is the supreme standard of justice and equity, and He wills nothing but what is just, right, and true. Nothing outside of Himself compels God to act justly; justice is His very nature. Thus, all of God's acts toward people are perfectly just; sinners have all wronged God's justice, but God's justice has not wronged them, nor could it ever.

No one at the Great White Throne judgment will have the slightest grounds for complaint about his or her sentence. Those who reject God's grace and mercy in this life will inevitably face His justice in the life to come. God said of wayward Israel, "My people did not listen to My voice, and Israel did not obey Me" (Ps. 81:11). To their equally stiff-necked descendants Jesus declared, "You are unwilling to come to Me so that you may have life" (John 5:40) and "You will die in your sins; for unless you believe that I am He, you will die in your sins" (John 8:24). Unrepentant sinners will experience God's justice at the Great White Throne judgment.

This simple, but powerful text describes the terrifying reality of the final verdict and sentence on sinners under four headings: the scene, the summons, the standard, and the sentence.

The Scene

Then I saw a great white throne and Him who sat upon it, from whose presence earth and heaven fled away, and no place was found for them. And I saw the dead, the great and the small, standing before the throne, (20:11–12*a*)

In one brief, straightforward, unembellished statement, John describes the appalling, terrifying scene before him. The apostle is shown the Judge seated on His throne of judgment, and all the accused standing before Him. The familiar phrase *kai eidon* once again introduces a new vision in Revelation (cf. vv. 1, 4; 6:1; 7:2; 8:2; 10:1; 13:1, 11; 14:1, 6, 14; 15:1; 17:3; 19:11; 21:1). This vision of the Great White Throne judgment follows those of the Millennium (20:1–10), and the Second Coming (19:11–21), and immediately precedes that of the new heaven and the new earth (21:1ff.).

The first thing John **saw** was **a great white throne.** Nearly fifty times in Revelation there is the mention of a throne. In this case it is the seat of God's sovereign rule (cf. 4:2–6, 9; 5:1–7, 13; 6:16; 7:10, 15; 19:4; 21:5). It is called **great** not only because of its size as greater than the thrones mentioned in 20:4, but also because of its significance, majesty, and authority. That it is **white** symbolizes its purity, holiness, and justice. The verdict handed down from this **throne** will be absolutely equitable, righteous, and just. "The Lord abides forever," wrote David, "He has established His throne for judgment, and He will judge the world in righteousness; He will execute judgment for the peoples with equity" (Ps. 9:7–8). Daniel described this scene in Daniel 7:9–10:

"I kept looking
Until thrones were set up,
And the Ancient of Days took His seat;
His vesture was like white snow
And the hair of His head like pure wool.
His throne was ablaze with flames,
Its wheels were a burning fire.
A river of fire was flowing
And coming out from before Him;
Thousands upon thousands were attending Him,
And myriads upon myriads were standing before Him;
The court sat,
And the books were opened."

Jesus described this scene as the "resurrection of judgment" (John 5:29). Of this judgment, the apostle Paul wrote, "Because of your stubbornness and unrepentant heart you are storing up wrath for yourself in the day of wrath and revelation of the righteous judgment of God" (Rom. 2:5).

Even more awe inspiring than the **throne** was the vision of **Him who sat upon it.** The judge on the throne is none other than the eternal, almighty God, described in the throne scene of 4:8–11:

> And the four living creatures, each one of them having six wings, are full of eyes around and within; and day and night they do not cease to say,
>
> "Holy, holy, holy is the Lord God, the Almighty, who was and who is and who is to come."
>
> And when the living creatures give glory and honor and thanks to Him who sits on the throne, to Him who lives forever and ever, the twenty-four elders will fall down before Him who sits on the throne, and will worship Him who lives forever and ever, and will cast their crowns before the throne, saying,
>
> "Worthy are You, our Lord and our God, to receive glory and honor and power; for You created all things, and because of Your will they existed, and were created."

Earlier in Revelation the Tribulation martyrs cried out, "Salvation to our God who sits on the throne, and to the Lamb" (7:10). In 19:4 "The twenty-four elders and the four living creatures fell down and worshiped God who sits on the throne saying, 'Amen. Hallelujah!'" (cf. 1:4; 4: 9–10; 5:6–7, 13; 6:16). Sharing the throne with the Father is the Lord Jesus Christ. In 3:21 Jesus promised, "He who overcomes, I will grant to him to sit down with Me on My throne, as I also overcame and sat down with My Father on His throne." In John's vision of the new heaven and the new earth, he saw "the throne of God and of the Lamb" (22:1,3).

Though the Father and the Son share the throne, it is the Son who is uniquely in view here, since Scripture teaches that He will judge sinners. In John 5:22 Jesus said, "Not even the Father judges anyone, but He has given all judgment to the Son," while in verses 26–27 He added, "Just as the Father has life in Himself, even so He gave to the Son also to have life in Himself; and He gave Him authority to execute judgment, because He is the Son of Man." In Acts 10:42 Peter declared that Jesus "is the One who has been appointed by God as Judge of the living and the dead." The apostle Paul warned the pagan philosophers of Athens that God "has fixed a day in which He will judge the world in righteousness through a Man whom He has appointed, having furnished proof to all men by raising Him from the dead" (Acts 17:31). In Romans he wrote of "the day when, according to my gospel, God will judge the secrets of men through Christ Jesus" (Rom. 2:16), while to Timothy he noted that "Christ Jesus . . . is to judge the living and the dead" (2 Tim. 4:1). It is God in the Person of the glorified Lord Jesus Christ who will sit in final judgment on unbelievers.

After describing the vision of the Judge on His throne, John noted the startling reality that **from** His **presence earth and heaven fled away.** That amazing, incredible statement describes the "uncreation" of the universe. The earth will have been reshaped by the devastating judgments of the Tribulation and restored during the millennial kingdom. Yet it will still be tainted with sin and subject to the effects of the Fall—decay and death; hence it must be destroyed, since nothing corrupted by sin will be permitted to exist in the eternal state (2 Pet. 3:13). God will in its place create "a new heaven and a new earth; for the first heaven and the first earth passed away" (21:1; cf. 21:5; Isa. 65:17; 66:22; 2 Pet. 3:13). The present **earth and heaven** will not merely be moved or reshaped, since John saw in his vision that **no place was found for them.** They will be uncreated and go totally out of existence. This is nothing less than the sudden, violent termination of the universe (cf. Ps. 102:25–26; Isa. 51:6; Matt. 5:18; 24:35; Luke 16:17; 21:33; Heb. 1:10–12; 12:26–27). Barnhouse wrote, "There is to be an end of the material heavens and earth which we know. It is not that they are to be purified and rehabilitated, but that the reverse of creation is to take place. They are to be uncreated. As they came from nothing at the word of God, they are to be sucked back into nothingness by this same word of God" (*Revelation: An Expository Commentary* [Grand Rapids: Zondervan, 1971], 391).

The details of God's uncreation of the universe are given by Peter in 2 Peter 3:10–13, which describes the final expression of the Day of the Lord:

> But the day of the Lord will come like a thief, in which the heavens will pass away with a roar and the elements will be destroyed with intense heat, and the earth and its works will be burned up.

> Since all these things are to be destroyed in this way, what sort of people ought you to be in holy conduct and godliness, looking for and hastening the coming of the day of God, because of which the heavens will be destroyed by burning, and the elements will melt with intense heat! But according to His promise we are looking for new heavens and a new earth, in which righteousness dwells.

The Day of the Lord will come suddenly, unexpectedly, and with disastrous consequences for the unprepared—just like the coming of a thief. When that Day comes, several things will happen. First, "the heavens will pass away with a roar." *Rhoizedon* ("roar") is an onomatopoetic word; that is, a word that sounds like what it means. It describes the loud whistling, crackling, rushing sound that will result when "the elements will be destroyed with intense heat, and the earth and its works will be burned up . . . [when] the heavens will be destroyed by burning, and the elements will melt with intense heat." *Stoicheion* ("elements") refers to the basic building blocks of matter, such as atomic and subatomic particles. "Destroyed" is from the verb *luō*, and could be translated "dissolved." The present universe will explode like a gigantic nuclear bomb, and the resulting "intense heat" will literally dissolve all the matter in it. The present laws of thermodynamics, which state that matter can neither be created nor destroyed, will no longer be in effect. As a result, the universe "will be burned up"; it will be totally consumed. The absolute reverse of creation will occur. It didn't take eons of evolution to create the universe, nor will it take eons to uncreate it. The uncreation of the universe, like its creation, will take place by the word of God.

Introducing the final element in this fearful scene, John writes that he **saw the dead, the great and the small, standing before the throne.** The setting is the indescribable void, the inconceivable nothingness between the end of the present universe and the creation of the new heaven and the new earth. The prisoners before the bar are all physically **dead,** since there are no longer any living people—none could possibly have survived the destruction of the present universe. The last living unbelievers will perish when God crushes the rebellion at the end of the Millennium (20:8–9). The last living believers will be translated and transformed into their eternal bodies, like Enoch (Gen. 5:24), Elijah (2 Kings 2:11), and the raptured church (1 Thess. 4:13–18).

The **dead** pictured here **standing before the throne** of divine judgment are not just from the millennial rebellion, but include all the unbelievers who ever lived. This is the "resurrection of judgment" (John 5:29), the resurrection "to disgrace and everlasting contempt" (Dan. 12:2), the "resurrection of . . . the wicked" (Acts 24:15). The Bible teaches that no believer will ever face God's judgment, because "there is now no condemnation for those who are in Christ Jesus" (Rom. 8:1). Everyone "who believes in Him is not judged" (John 3:18); they have "eternal life, and [do] not come into judgment, but [have] passed out of death into life" (John 5:24). Far from being judged, all the godly participants in the first resurrection (20:6) will have already received their rewards (cf. v. 4; 19:7–9; 1 Cor. 3:12–15; 2 Cor. 5:10).

To emphasize the all-encompassing scope of the judgment, John notes that the sweeping mass of unbelievers before God's throne includes both **the great and the small.** All will face judgment, the somebodies and the nobodies, "for there is no partiality with God" (Rom. 2:11; cf. Deut. 10:17; Job 34:19; Eph. 6:9; Col. 3:25; 1 Pet. 1:17). John Phillips provocatively wrote:

> There is a terrible fellowship there. . . . The dead, small and great, stand before God. Dead souls are united to dead bodies in a fellowship of horror and despair. Little men and paltry women whose lives were filled with pettiness, selfishness, and nasty little sins will be there. Those whose lives amounted to nothing will be there, whose very sins were drab and dowdy, mean, spiteful, peevish, groveling, vulgar, common, and cheap. The great will be there, men who sinned with a high hand, with dash, and courage and flair. Men like Alexander and Napoleon, Hitler and Stalin will be present, men who went in for wickedness on a grand scale with the world for their stage and who died unrepentant at last. Now one and all are arraigned and on their way to be damned: a horrible fellowship congregated together for the first and last time. (*Exploring Revelation,* rev. ed. [Chicago: Moody, 1987; reprint, Neptune, N.J.: Loizeaux, 1991], 242–43)

The Summons

And the sea gave up the dead which were in it, and death and Hades gave up the dead which were in them; (20:13*a*)

As the next scene in this ultimate courtroom drama unfolds, the prisoners are summoned from their cells to appear before the Judge. Since their deaths, their souls have been tormented in a place of punishment; now the time has come for them to be sentenced to the final, eternal hell. Before **the sea** was uncreated and went out of existence (cf. 21:1), it **gave up the dead which were in it.** The **sea** may be singled out because it is seemingly the most difficult place from which bodies could be resurrected. But God will summon from its depths new bodies for all who perished in the **sea** throughout human history, including those who drowned in the Flood, those who went down with the *Titanic,* the *Lusitania,* the *Arizona,* and the countless other ships that have sunk, as well as all the millions of other people who met their end at **sea. Death** symbolizes all the places on land from which God will resurrect new bodies for the unrighteous dead. The **sea** and **death** are pictured as voracious monsters that have swallowed those bodies and will be forced to disgorge them before their uncreation.

Hades is the Greek equivalent of the Hebrew word *sheol.* Both words describe the realm of the dead. *Sheol,* used sixty-seven times in the Old Testament, describes the realm of the dead in general. **Hades** is used ten times in the New Testament, always in reference to the place of punishment (cf. Luke 16:23) where the unrighteous dead are kept pending their sentencing to hell. In this incredible scene, **Hades** is emptied of its captive spirits, who are reunited with resurrection bodies before the bar of God's justice. Unbelievers, fitted with resurrection bodies suited for hell, will then be ready for their sentencing to the lake of fire where their punishment, unlike that in **Hades,** will last forever.

The Standard

and books were opened; and another book was opened, which is the book of life; and the dead were judged from the things which were written in the books, according to their deeds. . . . and they were judged, every one of them according to their deeds. (20:12*b*, 13*b*)

As the judgment commences, the Judge opens the **books.** The scene is reminiscent of the one described by Daniel:

> "I kept looking
> Until thrones were set up,
> And the Ancient of Days took His seat;
> His vesture was like white snow
> And the hair of His head like pure wool.
> His throne was ablaze with flames,
> Its wheels were a burning fire.
> A river of fire was flowing
> And coming out from before Him;
> Thousands upon thousands were attending Him,
> And myriads upon myriads were standing before Him;
> The court sat,
> And the books were opened."
>
> (Dan. 7:9–10)

The **books** contain the record of every thought, word, and deed of every unsaved person who ever lived. God has kept perfect, accurate, and comprehensive records of every person's life, **and the dead** will be **judged from the things which were written in the books, according to their deeds.** Sinners' **deeds** will be measured against God's perfect, holy standard, which Jesus defined in Matthew 5:48: "Therefore you are to be perfect, as your heavenly Father is perfect." In his first epistle Peter wrote, "Like the Holy One who called you, be holy yourselves also in all your behavior; because it is written, 'You shall be holy, for I am holy'" (1 Pet. 1:15–16). To the Galatians Paul wrote, "For as many as are of the works of the Law are under a curse; for it is written, 'Cursed is everyone who does not abide by all things written in the book of the law, to perform them'" (Gal. 3:10)—a truth also taught by James: "For whoever keeps the whole law and yet stumbles in one point, he has become guilty of all" (James 2:10). No prisoner before the bar of divine justice will be able to claim the perfect obedience to God's holy standards that He requires. They "all have sinned and fall short of the glory of God" (Rom. 3:23), and are "dead in [their] trespasses and sins" (Eph. 2:1).

God's justice demands payment for every person's sins. Christ paid that penalty for believers: "He was pierced through for our transgressions, He was crushed for our iniquities; the chastening for our well-being fell upon Him, and by His scourging we are healed. All of us like sheep have gone astray, each of us has turned to his own way; but the Lord has caused the iniquity of us all to fall on Him" (Isa. 53:5–6). "Christ redeemed us from the curse of the Law, having become a curse for us—for it is written, 'Cursed is everyone who hangs on a tree'" (Gal. 3:13). God "made Him who knew no sin to be sin on our behalf, so that we might become the righteousness of God in Him" (2 Cor. 5:21). "[Christ] Himself bore our sins in His body on the cross, so that we might die to sin and live to righteousness" (1 Pet. 2:24). But unbelievers, not having Christ's righteousness imputed to them (Phil. 3:9), will themselves pay the penalty for violating God's law—eternal destruction in hell (2 Thess. 1:9).

God's judgment of impenitent, unbelieving sinners' evil **deeds** will include their thoughts. "God . . . knows the secrets of the heart" (Ps. 44:21), and He "will judge the secrets of men through Christ Jesus" (Rom. 2:16), "For nothing is hidden that will not become evident, nor anything secret that will not be known and come to light" (Luke 8:17). Sinners will also be judged for their words. Jesus said in Matthew 12:37, "For by your words you will be justified, and by your words you will be condemned." Finally, unbelievers will be judged for their actions: "God will bring every act to judgment, everything which is hidden, whether it is good or evil" (Eccl. 12:14); "The Son of Man is going to come in the glory of His Father with His angels, and will then repay every man according to his deeds"

(Matt. 16:27). Nor will anyone be able to claim ignorance of God's standards, because both creation (Rom. 1:20) and the conscience (Rom. 2:14–15) reveal God's righteousness. Those without knowledge of God's law will be judged on the basis of the knowledge they did have (Rom. 2:12).

The absolute, unerring accuracy of God's judgment will ensure that unbelievers' punishment in hell fits their iniquity. Each person's life will be individually evaluated, and each person's punishment will be consistent with that evaluation. Thus, Scripture teaches that there will be varying degrees of punishment in hell. When He sent the twelve out on a preaching tour Jesus told them, "Whoever does not receive you, nor heed your words, as you go out of that house or that city, shake the dust off your feet. Truly I say to you, it will be more tolerable for the land of Sodom and Gomorrah in the day of judgment than for that city" (Matt. 10:14–15). Rebuking several cities for their unbelief, Jesus declared:

> "Woe to you, Chorazin! Woe to you, Bethsaida! For if the miracles had occurred in Tyre and Sidon which occurred in you, they would have repented long ago in sackcloth and ashes. Nevertheless I say to you, it will be more tolerable for Tyre and Sidon in the day of judgment than for you. And you, Capernaum, will not be exalted to heaven, will you? You will descend to Hades; for if the miracles had occurred in Sodom which occurred in you, it would have remained to this day. Nevertheless I say to you that it will be more tolerable for the land of Sodom in the day of judgment, than for you." (Matt. 11:21–24)

The hypocritical scribes "who like to walk around in long robes, and like respectful greetings in the market places, and chief seats in the synagogues and places of honor at banquets, who devour widows' houses, and for appearance's sake offer long prayers; these will receive greater condemnation" (Mark 12:38–40). Describing the final judgment in the parable of the faithful steward, Jesus taught that "[the] slave who knew his master's will and did not get ready or act in accord with his will, will receive many lashes, but the one who did not know it, and committed deeds worthy of a flogging, will receive but few" (Luke 12:47–48). The writer of Hebrews asks, "How much severer punishment do you think he will deserve who has trampled under foot the Son of God, and has regarded as unclean the blood of the covenant by which he was sanctified, and has insulted the Spirit of grace?" (Heb. 10:29).

It should be noted that while there are varying degrees of punishment in hell, everyone there will suffer intolerable, indescribable misery and torment. All sinners in hell will be utterly separated from God and all that comes from His goodness. Thus, they will be miserable, but not equally miserable.

After the **books** containing the prisoners' evil **deeds** were opened, **another book was opened, which is the book of life.** This book's imagery corresponds to the registry of citizens kept by ancient cities; it contains the names of all those whose "citizenship is in heaven" (Phil. 3:20). It is referred to several times in Revelation (v. 15; 3:5; 13:8; 17:8; 21:27). The **book of life** is the record of God's elect (cf. Dan. 12:1; Mal. 3:16; Luke 10:20; Phil. 4:3; Heb. 12:23), and all whose names are not recorded in it will be eternally damned.

Since their names were not in the **book of life,** the prisoners before the Great White Throne **were judged, every one of them according to their deeds.** Some, in shock and horror, will protest, "Lord, Lord, did we not prophesy in Your name, and in Your name cast out demons, and in Your name perform many miracles?" (Matt. 7:22). But they will hear in reply the most chilling, terrifying words that any human will ever hear: "I never knew you; depart from me, you who practice lawlessness" (Matt. 7:23). Those who refuse to plead guilty to their sins in this world, repent, and ask God for a pardon based on the substitutionary work of Christ will face trial after they die. And on that day, they will be pronounced guilty.

The Sentence

Then death and Hades were thrown into the lake of fire. This is the second death, the lake of fire. And if anyone's name was not found written in the book of life, he was thrown into the lake of fire. (20:14–15)

The evidence is irrefutable, the verdict rendered; judgment will be swiftly carried out. As the sentence is passed, **death and Hades** (the grave, and the temporary place of punishment for everyone whose **name was not found written in the book of life**) **were thrown into the lake of fire,** meaning that they will go out of existence, swallowed up by the final hell. Their inmates, currently suffering in their spirits only, will be united with specially designed resurrection bodies and cast into eternal hell (cf. Matt. 10:28). That final hell, described as **the lake of fire,** may already exist (cf. Matt. 25:41), but if so, it is currently unoccupied. Its first two occupants, the beast and the false prophet, will not arrive until the end of the Tribulation (19:20).

The clearest and most vivid of the New Testament terms used to describe the final hell, **the lake of fire,** is *geenna* (Gehenna). Gehenna is the New Testament word for the valley of Ben-Hinnom (also called Topheth; 2 Kings 23:10; Isa. 30:33; Jer. 7:31–32; 19:6), located southwest of

Jerusalem. In Old Testament times, idolatrous Israelites burned their children in the fire there as sacrifices to false gods (Jer. 19:2–6). In Jesus' day, it was the site of Jerusalem's garbage dump. The fires kept constantly burning there gave off foul-smelling smoke, and the dump was infested with maggots. Sometimes the bodies of criminals were dumped there. The valley of Ben-Hinnom was thus an apt picture of eternal hell, one used repeatedly by Jesus (Matt. 5:22, 29, 30; 10:28; 18:9; 23:15, 33; Mark 9:43, 45, 47; Luke 12:5). Hell will be God's eternal cosmic dump; its inmates will be burning as garbage forever.

The blessed and holy participants in the first resurrection will not experience the second death (20:6). But the rest of the dead, who did not participate in the first resurrection (20:5), will face **the second death,** which is defined here as **the lake of fire.** Those who die in their sins in this present world of time and space will die a **second death** in eternity—they will be sentenced to **the lake of fire** forever.

Scripture vividly portrays the various aspects of the final, fiery hell. **Fire** is used more than twenty times in the New Testament to depict the torment of hell (cf. vv. 10, 15; 14:10; 19:20; 21:8; Matt. 3:10–12; 5:22; 7:19; 13:40, 42, 50; 18:8–9; 25:41; Mark 9:44; Luke 3:9, 16–17; John 15:6; Heb. 10:27; Jude 7). Whether the **fire** of hell is literal, physical fire is unknown, since **the lake of fire** exists outside the created universe as we know it. If the fire here is symbolic, the reality it represents will be even more horrifying and painful. The Bible also depicts hell as a place of total darkness, which will isolate its inmates from each other (Matt. 8:12; 22:13; 25:30; 2 Pet. 2:17; Jude 13); as a place where the worm (possibly emblematic of an accusing conscience) devouring the wicked will never die (Isa. 66:24; Mark 9:48); as a place of banishment from God's kingdom (Matt. 8:12; 22:13); and as a place of unending sorrow, where there is "weeping and gnashing of teeth" (Matt. 8:12; 13:42, 50; 22:13; 24:51; 25:30; Luke 13:28).

There is only one way to avoid the terrifying reality of hell. Those who confess their sins and ask God to forgive them on the basis of Christ's substitutionary death on their behalf will be delivered from God's eternal wrath (Rom. 5:9; 1 Thess. 1:10; 5:9). For those who refuse to repent, the somber warning expressed by the writer of Hebrews will apply:

> For if we go on sinning willfully after receiving the knowledge of the truth, there no longer remains a sacrifice for sins, but a terrifying expectation of judgment and the fury of a fire which will consume the adversaries. Anyone who has set aside the Law of Moses dies without mercy on the testimony of two or three witnesses. How much severer punishment do you think he will deserve who has trampled under foot the Son of God, and has regarded as unclean the blood of the covenant by

which he was sanctified, and has insulted the Spirit of grace? For we know Him who said, "Vengeance is mine, I will repay." And again, "The Lord will judge His people." It is a terrifying thing to fall into the hands of the living God. (Heb. 10:26–31)

The New Heaven and the New Earth (Revelation 21:1–8)

18

Then I saw a new heaven and a new earth; for the first heaven and the first earth passed away, and there is no longer any sea. And I saw the holy city, new Jerusalem, coming down out of heaven from God, made ready as a bride adorned for her husband. And I heard a loud voice from the throne, saying, "Behold, the tabernacle of God is among men, and He will dwell among them, and they shall be His people, and God Himself will be among them, and He will wipe away every tear from their eyes; and there will no longer be any death; there will no longer be any mourning, or crying, or pain; the first things have passed away."

And He who sits on the throne said, "Behold, I am making all things new." And He said, "Write, for these words are faithful and true." Then He said to me, "It is done. I am the Alpha and the Omega, the beginning and the end. I will give to the one who thirsts from the spring of the water of life without cost. He who overcomes will inherit these things, and I will be his God and he will be My son. But for the cowardly and unbelieving and abominable and murderers and immoral persons and sorcerers and idolaters and all liars, their part will be in the lake that burns with fire and brimstone, which is the second death." (21:1–8)

Throughout the history of the church, God's people rightly have been preoccupied with heaven. They have longed for its joys because they have been only loosely tied to this earth. They have seen themselves as "strangers and exiles on the earth" who "desire a better country, that is, a heavenly one" (Heb. 11:13, 16). With the psalmist they have said to God, "Whom have I in heaven but You? And besides You, I desire nothing on earth. My flesh and my heart may fail, but God is the strength of my heart and my portion forever" (Ps. 73:25–26); and "As the deer pants for the water brooks, so my soul pants for You, O God. My soul thirsts for God, for the living God; when shall I come and appear before God?" (Ps. 42:1–2). Through the centuries, that desire to see God (Matt. 5:8) and to be in His presence and enjoy Him forever (Ps. 16:11), that intense longing that nothing on this earth can satisfy (Heb. 11:13–16), has marked believers.

Sadly, that is no longer true for many in today's church. Caught up in our society's mad rush for instant gratification, material comfort, and narcissistic indulgence, the church has become worldly. Nothing more graphically demonstrates that worldliness than the current lack of interest in heaven. The church doesn't sing or preach much about heaven, believers seldom discuss it, songs are no longer written about it, and books about heaven are few and far between. Believers who do not have heaven on their minds trivialize their lives, hinder the power of the church, and become absorbed with the fading things of this world.

The Bible makes it clear that believers are to focus on heaven. In Philippians 3:20 Paul notes that "our citizenship is in heaven." To the Colossians he wrote, "Therefore if you have been raised up with Christ, keep seeking the things above, where Christ is, seated at the right hand of God. Set your mind on the things above, not on the things that are on earth" (Col. 3:1–2). James rebukes worldliness in no uncertain terms: "You adulteresses, do you not know that friendship with the world is hostility toward God? Therefore whoever wishes to be a friend of the world makes himself an enemy of God" (James 4:4). The apostle John adds: "Do not love the world nor the things in the world. If anyone loves the world, the love of the Father is not in him. For all that is in the world, the lust of the flesh and the lust of the eyes and the boastful pride of life, is not from the Father, but is from the world. The world is passing away, and also its lusts; but the one who does the will of God lives forever" (1 John 2:15–17).

A heavenly perspective is vital, since everything connected to believers' spiritual life and destiny is there. Their Father is there, as are their Savior and their Comforter. The myriads of their fellow believers who have successfully run their earthly races are there (Heb. 12:23). Believers' names are recorded in heaven (3:5; 13:8; 17:8; 20:12, 15; 21:27; Phil. 4:3), they are citizens of heaven (Phil. 3:20), their inheritance is there (1 Pet. 1:4), and their reward (Matt. 5:12) and treasure (Matt. 19:21) are there. In short, everything of lasting importance to believers is in heaven; it is their home, and they are strangers, exiles, and pilgrims on earth (1 Chron. 29:15; Ps. 119:19; Heb. 11:13–16; 1 Pet. 2:11). Even death, the final enemy (1 Cor. 15:26), merely ushers believers into the presence of God. The words of the Preacher in Ecclesiastes 7:1, though cynical and pessimistic, are nevertheless true for the believer: "The day of one's death is better than the day of one's birth." His intense longing for heaven led Paul to write, "For to me, to live is Christ and to die is gain. . . . [I have] the desire to depart and be with Christ, for that is very much better" (Phil. 1:21, 23).

Desiring heaven exerts a powerful influence on believers' lives here on earth. In his first epistle the apostle John described one of the main reasons Christians desire heaven: "We know that when He appears, we will be like Him, because we will see Him just as He is" (1 John 3:2; cf. Phil. 3:21). Believers will receive glorified bodies, similar to Christ's resurrected body, in which they will "see Him just as He is" (cf. 1 Cor. 13:12). Then John gave the practical effect such knowledge should have on believers' lives: "Everyone who has this hope fixed on Him purifies himself, just as He is pure" (1 John 3:3; cf. 2 Pet. 3:14).

A genuine and strong longing for heaven has many important implications and benefits for the Christian. Such a longing is one of the surest indicators of genuine salvation, "for where your treasure is, there your heart will be also" (Luke 12:34).

A genuine and strong longing for heaven also produces the highest and noblest Christian character. Those who spend much time meditating on heavenly things cannot help but have their lives transformed.

A genuine and strong longing for heaven also brings joy and comfort in trials. Those who focus on heaven's glories can endure anything in this life and not lose their joy. When they suffer, they can say with Paul, "For momentary, light affliction is producing for us an eternal weight of glory far beyond all comparison" (2 Cor. 4:17).

A genuine and strong longing for heaven is also a preservative against sin. Those who set their minds on things above are less likely to become ensnared by earthly temptations. "For those who are according to the flesh set their minds on the things of the flesh, but those who are according to the Spirit, the things of the Spirit. For the mind set on the flesh is death, but the mind set on the Spirit is life and peace" (Rom. 8:5–6).

A genuine and strong longing for heaven will also maintain the vigor of believers' spiritual service. Those who are negligent in the Lord's work and make only a token, minimal effort to serve Him, demonstrate little regard for eternal things. They foolishly think that the reward for pursuing earthly things is greater than that for pursuing heavenly things.

Finally, a genuine and strong longing for heaven honors God

above everything else. Those who focus on heaven focus on the Supreme One in heaven. By setting their hearts on Him, they honor the One whose heart is set on them.

Scripture refers to heaven more than five hundred times. Revelation alone mentions heaven about fifty times. The Bible delineates three heavens (2 Cor. 12:2). The first heaven is the earth's atmosphere (Gen. 1:20; Job 12:7; Ezek. 38:20); the second heaven is interplanetary and interstellar space (Gen. 15:5; 22:17; Deut. 1:10; 4:19; Ps. 8:3; Isa. 13:10); the third heaven is the dwelling place of God (Deut. 4:39; 1 Kings 8:30; Job 22:12; Ps. 14:2; Dan. 2:28; Matt. 5:34; Acts 7:55; Heb. 9:24; 1 Pet. 3:22).

Heaven is an actual place, not a state of spiritual consciousness. That is evident because some have gone there in glorified bodies, such as Enoch (Gen. 5:24), Elijah (2 Kings 2:11), and the Lord Jesus Christ (Acts 1:9). That Christ is presently preparing a place for believers and will one day return to take them to heaven (John 14:2–3; 1 Thess. 4:16–17) offers further proof that heaven is a place. The Bible does not give a location for heaven, but views it from the perspective of the earth as up (4:1; 2 Cor. 12:2). Though heaven is far beyond the created world in another dimension, when believers die they will be there immediately (Luke 23:43; 2 Cor. 5:8). Those believers alive at the Rapture will also be transported to heaven immediately (1 Thess. 4:13–18; 1 Cor. 15:51–55).

This text unfolds six features of the final and eternal heaven, called the new heaven and the new earth: the appearance of the new heaven and the new earth, the capital of the new heaven and the new earth, the supreme reality of the new heaven and the new earth, the changes in the new heaven and the new earth, the residents of the new heaven and the new earth, and the outcasts from the new heaven and the new earth.

The Appearance of the New Heaven and the New Earth

Then I saw a new heaven and a new earth; for the first heaven and the first earth passed away, and there is no longer any sea. (21:1)

The phrase *kai eidon* (**then I saw**) is used throughout Revelation to indicate chronological progression (cf. 6:1, 2, 5, 8, 12; 7:2; 8:2, 13; 9:1; 10:1; 13:1, 11; 14:1, 6, 14; 15:1; 16:13; 17:3; 19:11, 17, 19; 20:1, 4, 11). It has introduced each of the climactic events beginning with the return of the Lord Jesus Christ in 19:11. As chapter 21 opens, all the sinners of all the ages, as well as Satan and his demons, have been sentenced to the lake of fire (20:10–15). With all ungodly men and angels banished forever and the present universe destroyed (20:11), God will create a new realm for the redeemed and the holy angels to dwell in forever.

The phrase **a new heaven and a new earth** derives from two passages in Isaiah. In Isaiah 65:17 God declared, "For behold, I create new heavens and a new earth; and the former things will not be remembered or come to mind." In Isaiah 66:22 He added, "'For just as the new heavens and the new earth which I make will endure before Me,' declares the Lord, 'so your offspring and your name will endure.'" What Isaiah predicted is now a reality in John's vision.

Kainos (**new**) does not mean new in a chronological sense, but new in a qualitative sense. The **new heaven** and the **new earth** will not merely succeed the present universe in chronological sequence; they will be something brand new, fresh, never before seen. God must create **a new heaven and a new earth** because **the first heaven and the first earth passed away.** God originally created the earth to be suitable as mankind's permanent home. The entrance of sin, however, corrupted the earth and the universe, and God will destroy them (cf. 20:11). What lies ahead for the earth is not a nuclear or an ecological holocaust, but a divine judgment.

The Old Testament describes the pollution and destruction of the present universe. Job 15:15 declares that "the heavens are not pure in His sight." Isaiah 24:5 adds, "The earth is also polluted by its inhabitants, for they transgressed laws, violated statutes, broke the everlasting covenant." The psalmist writes, "Of old You founded the earth, and the heavens are the work of Your hands. Even they will perish, but You endure; and all of them will wear out like a garment; like clothing You will change them and they will be changed" (Ps. 102:25–26). The Lord Jesus Christ confirmed that Old Testament teaching when He declared, "Heaven and earth will pass away" (Luke 21:33).

The first hint of what the **new heaven** and **new earth** will be like comes in John's observation that there will **no longer** be **any sea.** That will be a startling change from the present earth, nearly three-fourths of which is covered by water. The **sea** is emblematic of the present water-based environment. All life on earth is dependent on water for its survival, and the earth is the only known place in the universe where there is sufficient water to sustain life. But believers' glorified bodies will not require water, unlike present human bodies, whose blood is 90 percent water, and whose flesh is 65 percent water. Thus, the **new heaven** and the **new earth** will be based on a completely different life principle than the present universe. There will be a river in heaven, not of water, but of the "water of life" (22:1, 17). Without a sea, there can be no hydrological cycle, so that every feature of life and climate will be dramatically different.

From a metaphorical perspective, commentators have seen the absence of the sea as symbolic of the absence of evil. Robert L. Thomas summarizes:

> Most justifiably see this void as representing an archetypical connotation in the sea (cf. 13:1; 20:13), a principle of disorder, violence, or unrest that marks the old creation (cf. Isa. 57:20; Ps. 107:25–28; Ezek. 28:8).... It is not that the sea is evil in itself, but that its aspect is one of hostility to mankind. For instance, the sea was what stood guard over John in his prison on Patmos and separated him from the churches of Asia.... The sea is the first of seven evils that John says will no longer exist, the other six being death, mourning, weeping, pain (21:4), the curse (22:3), and night (21:25; 22:5). (*Revelation 8–22: An Exegetical Commentary* [Chicago: Moody, 1995], 440)

The Capital of the New Heaven and the New Earth

And I saw the holy city, new Jerusalem, coming down out of heaven from God, made ready as a bride adorned for her husband. (21:2)

As the next stage in his vision unfolds, the apostle John moves from a description of the new heaven and the new earth in general to a description of the capital city of the eternal state. Since the text plainly identifies it as such, there is no reason to doubt that **the holy city, new Jerusalem,** is an actual city. The **new Jerusalem** is not heaven, but heaven's capital. It is not synonymous with heaven, because its dimensions are given in 21:16. It will be the third city named Jerusalem in redemptive history. The first is the historic Jerusalem, the City of David, which currently exists in Palestine. Scripture repeatedly calls it **the holy city** (11:2; Neh. 11:1; Isa. 52:1; Dan. 9:24; Matt. 4:5; 27:53) because it was set apart for God's purposes. The second Jerusalem will be the restored Jerusalem where Christ will rule during the millennial kingdom.

But the **new Jerusalem** does not belong to the first creation, so it is neither the historic city, nor the millennial city; it is the altogether new eternal city (cf. v. 10; 3:12; Heb. 11:10; 12:22–24; 13:14). The old Jerusalem, in ruins for twenty-five years when John received this vision, is too stained with sin, too much a part of the old creation to survive into the eternal state. The **new Jerusalem** is called **the holy city** because everyone in it is holy, since "blessed and holy is the one who has a part in the first resurrection" (20:6). The concept of a city includes relationships, activity, responsibility, unity, socialization, communion, and cooperation.

Unlike the evil cities of the present earth, the perfectly holy people in the new Jerusalem will live and work together in perfect harmony.

In his vision, John saw the **new Jerusalem, coming down out of heaven from God,** its "architect and builder" (Heb. 11:10). The implication is that it already exists, a truth reinforced by Hebrews 12:22–23: "You have come to Mount Zion and to the city of the living God, the heavenly Jerusalem, and to myriads of angels, to the general assembly and church of the firstborn who are enrolled in heaven, and to God, the Judge of all, and to the spirits of the righteous made perfect." All of heaven is currently contained in the **new Jerusalem;** it is separate from the present universe, which is tainted by sin. Believers who die go to the "heavenly Jerusalem," where Jesus has gone before them to prepare a place for them (John 14:1–3). But when God creates the new heaven and the new earth, the **new Jerusalem** will descend into the midst of that holy new universe (21:10), and serve as the dwelling place of the redeemed for all eternity. Since the throne of God will be in the **new Jerusalem,** which will come down to the new earth, that city will be the bond between the new earth and the new heaven. (For a description of the **new Jerusalem,** see chapter 19 of this volume.)

Further describing heaven's capital city, John notes that it was **made ready as a bride adorned for her husband.** The city is pictured as a **bride** because it contains the bride and takes on her character. The imagery is drawn from a Jewish wedding, which typically had three parts. First was the betrothal, which was like a modern engagement, but more legally binding. The betrothal of the Lord's **bride** took place in eternity past when God pledged to His Son a redeemed people. The next stage was the presentation, a time of celebration and feasting leading up to the actual wedding ceremony. The presentation of the **bride** took place following the Rapture of the church, when believers are taken to heaven. The third stage was the ceremony, which for the Lord's **bride** began at the marriage supper of the Lamb (19:7–9) and stretched through the millennial kingdom. The final stage was the consummation, which corresponds to the eternal state. John saw the **bride adorned for her husband** because it was time for the consummation. **Adorned** is from the verb *kosmeō* ("to order," or "to arrange"); the related noun *kosmos* (translated "adornment" in 1 Pet. 3:3) is the root of the English word "cosmetics." The **bride** has become appropriately ordered in all her beauty. By this point in Revelation, the **bride** concept expands to include not only the church (as it has since Acts 2), but also all the rest of the redeemed from all the ages who live forever in that eternal city (see the discussion of 19:9 in chapter 14 of this volume). This is the moment described by Paul in 1 Corinthians 15:28: "When all things are subjected to Him, then the Son Himself also will be subjected to the One who subjected all things to Him, so that God may be all in all."

The Supreme Reality of the New Heaven and the New Earth

And I heard a loud voice from the throne, saying, "Behold, the tabernacle of God is among men, and He will dwell among them, and they shall be His people, and God Himself will be among them, (21:3)

The supreme glory and joy of heaven is the Person of God (cf. Ps. 73:25). Here, as twenty times previously in Revelation, a **loud voice** heralds an announcement of great importance. The source of the **voice** is not revealed. It is not God (who speaks in v. 5), but is probably an angel (cf. 5:2; 7:2; 14:9, 15, 18; 19:17). The portentous announcement he makes is **"Behold, the tabernacle of God is among men."** *Skenē* (**tabernacle**) can also mean "tent," or "dwelling place." God will pitch His tent among His people; no longer will He be far off, distant, transcendent. No more will His presence be veiled in the human form of Jesus Christ, even in His millennial majesty, or in the cloud and pillar of fire, or inside the Holy of Holies. The amazing reality that "the pure in heart . . . shall see God" (Matt. 5:8) will come to pass. Christ's prayer, recorded in John 17:24, will be answered: "Father, I desire that they also, whom You have given Me, be with Me where I am, so that they may see My glory which You have given Me" (cf. John 14:1–3; 1 Thess. 4:13–17). There will be "no temple in [heaven], for the Lord God the Almighty and the Lamb are its temple" (21:22). Their presence will permeate heaven and will not be confined to one place of manifestation.

So staggering is this truth that the heavenly voice repeats it several ways. To the mind-boggling reality that **the tabernacle of God is among men** he adds the statement that God **will dwell among them, and they shall be His people, and God Himself will be among them** (cf. 22:3–4). This will be a manifestation of God's glorious presence to **His people** like no other in redemptive history and the culmination of all divine promise and human hope (Lev. 26:11–12; Jer. 24:7; 30:22; 31:1, 33; 32:38; Ezek. 37:27; 48:35; Zech. 2:10; 8:8; 2 Cor. 6:16).

What will it be like to live in God's glorious presence in heaven? First, believers will enjoy fellowship with Him. The imperfect, sin-hindered fellowship that believers have with God in this life (1 John 1:3) will become full, complete, and unlimited. In his classic book on heaven entitled *The Saints' Everlasting Rest*, seventeenth-century Puritan Richard

Baxter describes the intimate communion with God that believers will enjoy in heaven:

> Doubtless as God advanceth our senses, and enlargeth our capacity, so will he advance the happiness of those senses and fill up with himself all that capacity. . . . We shall then have light without a candle, and perpetual day without the sun. . . . We shall then have enlightened understandings without Scripture, and be governed without a written law; for the Lord will perfect his law in our hearts, and we shall be all perfectly taught of God. We shall have joy, which we drew not from the promises, nor fetched home by faith or hope. We shall have communion without sacraments, without this fruit of the vine, when Christ shall drink it new with us in his Father's kingdom and refresh us with the comforting wine of immediate enjoyment. To have necessities, but no supply, is the case of them in hell. To have necessity supplied by means of the creatures, is the case of us on earth. To have necessity supplied immediately from God, is the case of the saints in heaven. To have no necessity at all, is the prerogative of God himself. (*The Practical Works of Richard Baxter* [reprint; Grand Rapids: Baker, 1981], 7, 16)

Second, believers will see God as He is. In 1 John 3:2 the apostle John writes, "Beloved, now we are children of God, and it has not appeared as yet what we will be. We know that when He appears, we will be like Him, because we will see Him just as He is." Such an unveiled view of God is impossible for mortal men. No living person has ever seen God in the fullness of His glory (John 1:18; 6:46; 1 John 4:12); He is invisible (Col. 1:15; 1 Tim. 1.17) and "dwells in unapproachable light" (1 Tim. 6:16; cf. Ps. 104:2), exposure to which would mean instant death for any living person (Ex. 33:20). But in heaven, "the pure in heart . . . shall see God" (Matt. 5:8), since they will be perfectly holy. They will be given an eternal and expanded vision of God manifest in His shining glory (21:11, 23; 22:5). Even the saints in heavenly glory will not be able to comprehend all the infinite majesty of God's wondrous being. But they will see all that glorified beings are able to comprehend. Is it any wonder that Paul, thinking of the glory of heaven, had "the desire to depart and be with Christ, for that is very much better" (Phil. 1:23)?

In her marvelous but seldom sung hymn, "My Savior First of All," Fanny Crosby echoed Paul's sentiments:

> When my life work is ended and I cross the swelling tide,
> When the bright and glorious morning I shall see,
> I shall know my Redeemer when I reach the other side,
> And His smile will be the first to welcome me.

Thru the gates to the city, in a robe of spotless white,
He will lead me where no tears will ever fall,
In the glad song of ages I shall mingle with delight—
But I long to meet my Savior first of all.

Third, believers will worship God. Every glimpse of heaven in Revelation reveals the redeemed and the angels in worship (4:10; 5:14; 7:11; 11:1, 16; 19:4). That is not surprising, since Jesus said in John 4:23 that "true worshipers will worship the Father in spirit and truth; for such people the Father seeks to be His worshipers." In heaven, the glorified, perfected saints will offer God perfect worship.

Fourth, believers will serve God (22:3). It is said of the saints in heaven pictured in 7:15 that "they serve [God] day and night in His temple." Believers' capacity for heavenly service will reflect their faithfulness in this life. All believers will be rewarded with capacities for heavenly service, but those capacities will differ (1 Cor. 3:12–15; 4:5).

Finally, and most astounding of all, the Lord will serve believers. Jesus told a parable reflecting that truth in Luke 12:35–40:

> Be dressed in readiness, and keep your lamps lit. Be like men who are waiting for their master when he returns from the wedding feast, so that they may immediately open the door to him when he comes and knocks. Blessed are those slaves whom the master will find on the alert when he comes; truly I say to you, that he will gird himself to serve, and have them recline at the table, and will come up and wait on them. Whether he comes in the second watch, or even in the third, and finds them so, blessed are those slaves.
>
> But be sure of this, that if the head of the house had known at what hour the thief was coming, he would not have allowed his house to be broken into. You too, be ready; for the Son of Man is coming at an hour that you do not expect.

Jesus pictures Himself as a wealthy nobleman, who returns to His estate after a long trip. Finding that his servants ministered faithfully in His absence, He rewards them by taking the role of a servant and preparing a feast for them. So will it be for believers in heaven, forever to be served a heavenly feast of joy by their Lord.

The Changes in the New Heaven and the New Earth

and He will wipe away every tear from their eyes; and there will no longer be any death; there will no longer be any mourning, or

crying, or pain; the first things have passed away." And He who sits on the throne said, "Behold, I am making all things new." And He said, "Write, for these words are faithful and true." Then He said to me, "It is done. I am the Alpha and the Omega, the beginning and the end." (21:4–6*a*)

Heaven will be so dramatically different from the present world that to describe it requires the use of negatives, as well as the previous positives. To describe what is totally beyond human understanding also requires pointing out how it differs from present human experience.

The first change from their earthly life believers in heaven will experience is that God **will wipe away every tear from their eyes** (cf. 7:17; Isa. 25:8). That does not mean that people who arrive in heaven will be crying and God will comfort them. They will not, as some imagine, be weeping as they face the record of their sins. There is no such record, because "there is now no condemnation for those who are in Christ Jesus" (Rom. 8:1), since Christ "bore our sins in His body on the cross, so that we might die to sin and live to righteousness; for by His wounds you were healed" (1 Pet. 2:24). What it declares is the absence of anything to be sorry about—no sadness, no disappointment, no pain. There will be no tears of misfortune, tears over lost love, tears of remorse, tears of regret, tears over the death of loved ones, or tears for any other reason.

Another dramatic difference from the present world will be that in heaven **there will no longer be any death** (cf. Isa. 25:8). The greatest curse of human existence will be no more. "Death," as Paul promised, "is swallowed up in victory" (1 Cor. 15:54). Both Satan, who had the power of death (Heb. 2:14) and death itself will have been cast into the lake of fire (20:10, 14).

Nor will there be any **mourning, or crying** in heaven. The grief, sorrow, and distress that produce **mourning** and its outward manifestation, **crying,** will not exist in heaven. This glorious reality will be the fulfillment of Isaiah 53:3–4: "He was despised and forsaken of men, a man of sorrows and acquainted with grief; and like one from whom men hide their face He was despised, and we did not esteem Him. Surely our griefs He Himself bore, and our sorrows He carried; yet we ourselves esteemed Him stricken, smitten of God, and afflicted." When Christ bore believers' sins on the cross, He also bore their sorrows, since sin is the cause of sorrow.

The perfect holiness and absence of sin that will characterize heaven will also mean that there will be no more **pain.** On the cross, Jesus was "pierced through for our transgressions, He was crushed for our iniquities; the chastening for our well-being fell upon Him, and by

His scourging we are healed" (Isa. 53:5). While the healing in view in that verse is primarily spiritual healing, it also includes physical healing. Commenting on Jesus' healing of Peter's mother-in-law, Matthew 8:17 says, "This was to fulfill what was spoken through Isaiah the prophet: 'He Himself took our infirmities and carried away our diseases.'" The healing ministry of Jesus was a preview of the well-being that will characterize the millennial kingdom and the eternal state. The glorified sin free bodies believers will possess in heaven will not be subject to **pain** of any kind.

All those changes that will mark the new heaven and the new earth indicate that **the first things have passed away.** Old human experience related to the original, fallen creation is gone forever, and with it all the mourning, suffering, sorrow, disease, pain, and death that has characterized it since the Fall. Summarizing those changes in a positive way, **He who sits on the throne said, "Behold, I am making all things new."** The One **who sits on the throne** is the same One "from whose presence earth and heaven fled away, and no place was found for them" (20:11). As noted in chapter 17 of this volume, the present universe will be uncreated. The new heaven and the new earth will be truly a new creation, and not merely a refurbishing of the present heaven and earth. In that forever new creation, there will be no entropy, no atrophy, no decay, no decline, and no waste.

Overwhelmed by all that he had seen, John seems to have lost his concentration. Thus, God Himself, the glorious, majestic One on the throne **said** to him **"Write, for these words are faithful and true"** (cf. 1:19). The **words** John was commanded by God to **write are** as **faithful and true** (cf. 22:6) as the One revealing them to him (3:14; 19:11). Though the present "heaven and earth will pass away," still God's "words will not pass away" (Luke 21:33). There will be an end to the universe, but not to the truth God reveals to His people. Whether or not men understand and believe that truth, it will come to pass.

Also by way of summary, the majestic voice of the One sitting on heaven's **throne said** to John, **"It is done."** Those words are reminiscent of Jesus' words on the cross, "It is finished!" (John 19:30). Jesus' words marked the completion of the work of redemption; these words mark the end of redemptive history. It is the time of which Paul wrote in 1 Corinthians 15:24–28:

> Then comes the end, when He hands over the kingdom to the God and Father, when He has abolished all rule and all authority and power. For He must reign until He has put all His enemies under His feet. The last enemy that will be abolished is death. For He has put all things in subjection under His feet. But when He says, "All things are put in subjection," it is evident that He is excepted who put all things in subjection to Him. When all things are subjected to Him, then the Son Himself also

> will be subjected to the One who subjected all things to Him, so that God may be all in all.

The One **who sits on the throne** is qualified to declare the end of redemptive history, because He is **the Alpha and the Omega** (the first and last letters of the Greek alphabet; cf. 1:8), **the beginning and the end** (cf. Isa. 44:6; 48:12). God started history, and He will end it, and all of it has unfolded according to His sovereign plan. That this same phrase is applied to the Lord Jesus Christ in 22:13 offers proof of His full deity and equality with the Father.

The Residents of the New Heaven and the New Earth

I will give to the one who thirsts from the spring of the water of life without cost. He who overcomes will inherit these things, and I will be his God and he will be My son. (21:6*b*–7)

Two descriptive phrases reveal who will live in the glorious new heaven and new earth. First, a citizen of heaven is described as **one who thirsts.** That phrase signifies those who, recognizing their desperate spiritual need, "hunger and thirst for righteousness" (Matt. 5:6). They are the ones to whom Isaiah cries out, "Ho! Every one who thirsts, come to the waters; and you who have no money come, buy and eat. Come, buy wine and milk without money and without cost" (Isa. 55:1). Those who will be redeemed and enter heaven are those who are dissatisfied with their hopeless, lost condition and crave God's righteousness with every part of their being. The psalmist expressed that strong desire in Psalm 42:1–2: "As the deer pants for the water brooks, so my soul pants for You, O God. My soul thirsts for God, for the living God; when shall I come and appear before God?" The promise to such earnest seekers is that their thirst will be satisfied. God **will give to the one who thirsts from the spring of the water of life without cost.** To the Samaritan woman at Jacob's well Jesus promised, "Everyone who drinks of this water will thirst again; but whoever drinks of the water that I will give him shall never thirst; but the water that I will give him will become in him a well of water springing up to eternal life" (John 4:13–14). It is the water of which He spoke in John 7:37–38: "Now on the last day, the great day of the feast, Jesus stood and cried out, saying, 'If anyone is thirsty, let him come to Me and drink. He who believes in Me, as the Scripture said, "From his innermost being will flow rivers of living water."'" This same promise is also repeated in 22:17 (cf. 7:17): "The Spirit and the bride say, 'Come.' And let the one who hears say,'Come.' And let the one who is thirsty come; let the one who wishes take the water of life without cost." The water in all those passages symbolizes eternal life. Those who thirst for and passionately seek salvation are the ones who will receive it and enjoy the eternal bliss of heaven.

Second, heaven belongs to **he who overcomes.** An overcomer, according to 1 John 5:4–5, is one who exercises saving faith in the Lord Jesus Christ. The overcomer is the person who in faith drinks the water of salvation freely offered by God. John uses this distinctive term for believers in the closing promise of each of the letters to the seven churches (see the discussion of 2:7, 11, 17, 26; 3:5, 12, 21 in *Revelation 1–11,* The MacArthur New Testament Commentary [Chicago: Moody, 1999], 53–141). The promise here to those who overcome is that they **will inherit these things.** They will "obtain an inheritance which is imperishable and undefiled and will not fade away, reserved in heaven for [them]" (1 Pet. 1:4). They will enjoy perfection of soul (Heb. 12:23) and body (20:6; John 5:28–29; Rom. 8:23; 1 Cor. 15:35–44; 2 Cor. 5:2; Phil. 3:21; 1 John 3:2) forever in the bliss of the new heaven and the new earth.

But the most wonderful promise to the one who overcomes, who thirsts for righteousness, is God's promise **I will be his God** (cf. Gen. 17:7–8; Ex. 6:7; 29:45; Lev. 26:12; Deut. 29:13; 2 Sam. 7:24; Jer. 7:23; 11:4; 24:7; 30:22; Ezek. 11:20; 34:24; 36:28; 37:23, 27; Zech. 8:8). Equally amazing is God's promise that the one who overcomes **will be My son.** Even in this life it is the believer's privilege to be the adopted son of the God of the universe (John 1:12; Rom. 8:14–17; 2 Cor. 6:18; Gal. 4:5; Eph. 1:5; Heb. 12:5–9; 1 John 3:1). But only in heaven, when believers come into their inheritance (1 Pet. 1:4), will that adoption be fully realized (Rom. 8:23).

The Outcasts from the New Heaven and the New Earth

"But for the cowardly and unbelieving and abominable and murderers and immoral persons and sorcerers and idolaters and all liars, their part will be in the lake that burns with fire and brimstone, which is the second death." (21:8)

John concludes his overview of the new heaven and the new earth with a serious and solemn warning. He delineates those who will be excluded from any participation in the blessings of heaven—all unforgiven and unredeemed sinners. There are similar lists of such sinners in 22:15; Romans 1:28–32; 1 Corinthians 6:9–10; Galatians 5:19–21; and 2 Timothy 3:2–5.

The first group excluded from heaven are the **cowardly.** These are the ones who lack endurance (cf. Matt. 24:13; Mark 8:35). They fell away when their faith was challenged or opposed, because their faith was not genuine. Jesus described such people in the parable of the soils: "The one on whom seed was sown on the rocky places, this is the man who hears the word and immediately receives it with joy; yet he has no firm root in himself, but is only temporary, and when affliction or persecution arises because of the word, immediately he falls away" (Matt. 13:20–21). These are the ones who "shrink back to destruction" (Heb. 10:39). In John 8:31 Jesus defined those whose faith is genuine as those who continue in His Word. (For further discussion of this issue, see my books *The Gospel According to Jesus* [rev. ed., Grand Rapids: Zondervan, 1994], and *The Gospel According to the Apostles* [Nashville: Word, 2000].)

Because they lack saving faith and are **unbelieving,** their disloyalty excludes them from heaven. They are also **abominable** (vile, polluted, detestable, wholly caught up in wickedness and evil), **murderers, immoral persons, sorcerers** (from the Greek word *pharmakos,* from which the English words "pharmacy" and "pharmaceuticals" derive; that indicates the inclusion of those who use mind-altering drugs in occult religion), **idolaters,** and **liars.** Those whose lives are characterized by such things give evidence that they are not saved and will never enter the heavenly city. On the contrary, **their part will be in the lake that burns with fire and brimstone, which is the second death.** In contrast to the eternal bliss of the righteous in heaven, the wicked will suffer eternal torment in hell. (For a further discussion of the **lake that burns with fire and brimstone, which is the second death,** see chapter 17 of this volume.)

The new heaven and the new earth await believers and the final hell awaits resurrected unbelievers. For believers, it will be a universe of eternal happiness as they dwell forever in the glorious presence of God. For unbelievers, it will be a terrifying place of unbearable torment and unrelieved misery away from God's presence (2 Thess. 1:9). The choices men and women make in this life determine in which of those realms they will live forever.

The Capital City of Heaven (Revelation 21:9–22:5)

19

Then one of the seven angels who had the seven bowls full of the seven last plagues came and spoke with me, saying, "Come here, I will show you the bride, the wife of the Lamb." And he carried me away in the Spirit to a great and high mountain, and showed me the holy city, Jerusalem, coming down out of heaven from God, having the glory of God. Her brilliance was like a very costly stone, as a stone of crystal-clear jasper. It had a great and high wall, with twelve gates, and at the gates twelve angels; and names were written on them, which are the names of the twelve tribes of the sons of Israel. There were three gates on the east and three gates on the north and three gates on the south and three gates on the west. And the wall of the city had twelve foundation stones, and on them were the twelve names of the twelve apostles of the Lamb.

The one who spoke with me had a gold measuring rod to measure the city, and its gates and its wall. The city is laid out as a square, and its length is as great as the width; and he measured the city with the rod, fifteen hundred miles; its length and width and height are equal. And he measured its wall, seventy-two yards, according to human measurements, which are also angelic

measurements. The material of the wall was jasper; and the city was pure gold, like clear glass. The foundation stones of the city wall were adorned with every kind of precious stone. The first foundation stone was jasper; the second, sapphire; the third, chalcedony; the fourth, emerald; the fifth, sardonyx; the sixth, sardius; the seventh, chrysolite; the eighth, beryl; the ninth, topaz; the tenth, chrysoprase; the eleventh, jacinth; the twelfth, amethyst. And the twelve gates were twelve pearls; each one of the gates was a single pearl. And the street of the city was pure gold, like transparent glass.

I saw no temple in it, for the Lord God the Almighty and the Lamb are its temple. And the city has no need of the sun or of the moon to shine on it, for the glory of God has illumined it, and its lamp is the Lamb. The nations will walk by its light, and the kings of the earth will bring their glory into it. In the daytime (for there will be no night there) its gates will never be closed; and they will bring the glory and the honor of the nations into it; and nothing unclean, and no one who practices abomination and lying, shall ever come into it, but only those whose names are written in the Lamb's book of life.

Then he showed me a river of the water of life, clear as crystal, coming from the throne of God and of the Lamb, in the middle of its street. On either side of the river was the tree of life, bearing twelve kinds of fruit, yielding its fruit every month; and the leaves of the tree were for the healing of the nations. There will no longer be any curse; and the throne of God and of the Lamb will be in it, and His bond-servants will serve Him; they will see His face, and His name will be on their foreheads. And there will no longer be any night; and they will not have need of the light of a lamp nor the light of the sun, because the Lord God will illumine them; and they will reign forever and ever. (21:9–22:5)

On the night before His death, the Lord Jesus Christ made a wonderful promise to all who believe in Him. He said, "Do not let your heart be troubled; believe in God, believe also in Me. In My Father's house are many dwelling places; if it were not so, I would have told you; for I go to prepare a place for you. If I go and prepare a place for you, I will come again and receive you to Myself, that where I am, there you may be also" (John 14:1–3). The "Father's house" Jesus referred to is the New Jerusalem, where God will live with His people forever. It is the present heaven where God dwells with the holy angels, and where the redeemed go when they die. As noted in the previous chapter of this volume, the place that the Lord has prepared for them will descend in the eternal state, where it will be the capital city of the new heaven and the new earth.

Just as a person preparing to travel to a foreign country desires information about that country, so believers long for a glimpse of that glorious place where they will live eternally. Knowing their eager sense of anticipation, God has provided believers with a description of heaven. Though only a select few details are given, they are staggering, mind-boggling, and overwhelming.

As the vision of the New Jerusalem unfolds, history has ended, and time is no more. John and his readers are transported to the eternal state. Having described the fearful eternal destination of the damned, the lake of fire (v. 8; 20:14–15), the vision takes the beloved, exiled apostle to the blissful eternal resting place of the redeemed. Because it is the capital city of heaven and the link between the new heaven and the new earth, the New Jerusalem is central to the vision and is described in far more detail than the rest of the eternal state.

The book of Hebrews also mentions the glorious capital city of heaven. Describing Abraham's faith, the writer of Hebrews stated that

> by faith Abraham, when he was called, obeyed by going out to a place which he was to receive for an inheritance; and he went out, not knowing where he was going. By faith he lived as an alien in the land of promise, as in a foreign land, dwelling in tents with Isaac and Jacob, fellow heirs of the same promise; for he was looking for the city which has foundations, whose architect and builder is God. (Heb. 11:8–10)

In the next chapter, the writer penned the following description of the New Jerusalem:

> But you have come to Mount Zion and to the city of the living God, the heavenly Jerusalem, and to myriads of angels, to the general assembly and church of the firstborn who are enrolled in heaven, and to God, the Judge of all, and to the spirits of the righteous made perfect, and to Jesus, the mediator of a new covenant, and to the sprinkled blood, which speaks better than the blood of Abel. (Heb. 12:22–24)

As he closed out that epistle, he reminded his readers that "here we do not have a lasting city, but we are seeking the city which is to come" (Heb. 13:14).

What Abraham, the writer of Hebrews, and the rest of the redeemed have anticipated by faith was revealed to and described by John. His view of heaven's capital includes several features: its general appearance, exterior design, internal character, and the privileges of its inhabitants.

Its General Appearance

Then one of the seven angels who had the seven bowls full of the seven last plagues came and spoke with me, saying, "Come here, I will show you the bride, the wife of the Lamb." And he carried me away in the Spirit to a great and high mountain, and showed me the holy city, Jerusalem, coming down out of heaven from God, having the glory of God. Her brilliance was like a very costly stone, as a stone of crystal-clear jasper. (21:9–11)

As the vision opened, an angel appeared to call John's attention to the city. The last appearance of an angel was one thousand years earlier at the beginning of the Millennium (20:1). Angels play a significant role in Revelation, and this particular angel was involved in the Tribulation judgments. Those judgments unfolded in three telescoping series: the seal, trumpet, and, climactically, the bowl judgments. This angel was **one of the seven angels who had the seven bowls full of the seven last plagues** (cf. 15:1). Either he or another of those **seven angels** also introduced the impending judgment of the harlot city of Babylon (17:1), making the contrast between the two cities apparent.

Inaugurating John's personal tour of heaven's capital city, the angel **came and spoke with** the apostle, **saying, "Come here, I will show you the bride, the wife of the Lamb."** As noted in the discussion of 21:2 in chapter 18 of this volume, the New Jerusalem is described as a **bride** because it draws its character from its occupants. Those occupants consist of the **bride** of the **Lamb,** a title originally given to the church (19:7), but now enlarged to encompass all the redeemed of all the ages, who live there forever. The New Jerusalem is likened to a **bride** because the redeemed are forever united to God and the Lamb. It is further defined as **the wife of the Lamb** because the marriage has taken place (19:7).

John's incredible vision began when the angel **carried** him **away in the Spirit.** When he received the visions that comprise the book of Revelation, the aged apostle was a prisoner of the Romans on the island of Patmos (1:9). But he was transported from there in an amazing spiritual journey to see what unaided human eyes could never see. John's visions were not dreams, but spiritual realities, like those Paul saw when he was also caught up to the third heaven (2 Cor. 12:2–4).

The first stop was **a great and high mountain.** From that vantage point, the angel **showed** John **the holy city, Jerusalem.** The apostle repeats his observation from verse 2 that the New Jerusalem came **down out of heaven from God.** That emphasizes its divine origin; it is the city "whose architect and builder is God" (Heb. 11:10). It should be noted that what is described here is not the creation of heaven; it is merely the descent of what already existed from eternity past, and is now situated in the center of the new heaven and the new earth.

The most distinguishing characteristic of the capital city of eternity is that it is the throne of the eternal, almighty One, and therefore had **the glory of God** in it. That **glory** will reach its fullest expression there (John 17:24); it will be unlimited and unconfined, flashing from that city throughout the re-created universe. The **glory of God** is the sum total of His attributes (cf. Ex. 33:18–19) and is manifested as blazing light (Ex. 13:21; 19:18; 24:17; 34:29–30, 35; 40:34; 1 Kings 8:10–11; Ps. 104:2; Isa. 4:5; Ezek. 10:4; Hab. 3:3–4; Luke 2:9) and in His Son (Matt. 17:2; 24:27, 30; 1 Tim. 6:16). Sadly, though God revealed His glory, disobedient, rebellious people rejected Him. Even the Lord Jesus Christ, the embodiment of God's glory in human form (John 1:14), "was despised and forsaken of men" (Isa. 53:3). Radiating from the New Jerusalem will be the brilliance of the full manifestation of God's glory, so much so that "the city has no need of the sun or of the moon to shine on it, for the glory of God has illumined it, and its lamp is the Lamb" (v. 23). Isaiah foresaw that same reality: "No longer will you have the sun for light by day, nor for brightness will the moon give you light; but you will have the Lord for an everlasting light, and your God for your glory" (Isa. 60:19).

Describing the effect of God's glory radiating from the new Jerusalem, John notes that **her brilliance was like a very costly stone, as a stone of crystal-clear jasper.** *Phōstēr* (**brilliance**) refers to something from which light radiates. The Septuagint, the Greek translation of the Old Testament, uses it in Genesis 1:14 and 16 to describe heavenly light-bearing objects. To John, the heavenly city appeared like a giant lightbulb, with the brilliant light of God's glory streaming out of it. But that light did not shine through the thin glass of a lightbulb, but through what looked to John **like a very costly stone, as a stone of crystal-clear jasper.** The city appeared to the apostle like one gigantic precious stone. **Jasper** does not refer to the modern stone of the same name, which is opaque; it is a transliteration of the Greek word *iaspis,* which describes a translucent stone. The word **jasper** in this passage is best understood as referring to a diamond, **a very costly** one because it is **crystal-clear** and unblemished. Heaven's capital city is thus pictured as a huge, flawless diamond, refracting the brilliant, blazing glory of God throughout the new heaven and the new earth.

Its Exterior Design

It had a great and high wall, with twelve gates, and at the gates twelve angels; and names were written on them, which are the

names of the twelve tribes of the sons of Israel. There were three gates on the east and three gates on the north and three gates on the south and three gates on the west. And the wall of the city had twelve foundation stones, and on them were the twelve names of the twelve apostles of the Lamb.

The one who spoke with me had a gold measuring rod to measure the city, and its gates and its wall. The city is laid out as a square, and its length is as great as the width; and he measured the city with the rod, fifteen hundred miles; its length and width and height are equal. And he measured its wall, seventy-two yards, according to human measurements, which are also angelic measurements. The material of the wall was jasper; and the city was pure gold, like clear glass. The foundation stones of the city wall were adorned with every kind of precious stone. The first foundation stone was jasper; the second, sapphire; the third, chalcedony; the fourth, emerald; the fifth, sardonyx; the sixth, sardius; the seventh, chrysolite; the eighth, beryl; the ninth, topaz; the tenth, chrysoprase; the eleventh, jacinth; the twelfth, amethyst. And the twelve gates were twelve pearls; each one of the gates was a single pearl. (21:12–21*a*)

Human language is inadequate to fully describe the unimaginable magnificence of the believers' indescribable eternal home. Unwilling to take the language of Scripture at face value, many seek for some hidden meaning behind John's description. But if the words do not mean what they say, who has the authority to say what they do mean? Abandoning the literal meaning of the text leads only to baseless, groundless, futile speculation. The truth about the heavenly city is more than is described, but not less and not different from what is described. It is a material creation, yet so unique as to be unimaginable to us. The words of John provide all the detail we have been given by God to excite our hope.

That the city **had a great and high wall** indicates that it is not an amorphous, nebulous, floating place. It has specific dimensions; it has limits; it can be entered and left through its **twelve gates. At** those **gates twelve angels** were stationed, to attend to God's glory and to serve His people (cf. Heb. 1:14). The **gates** had **names . . . written on them, which are the names of the twelve tribes of the sons of Israel,** celebrating for all eternity God's covenant relationship with Israel, the people of the promises, the covenants, the Scriptures, and the Messiah. They were arranged symmetrically; **there were three gates on the east and three gates on the north and three gates on the south and three gates on the west.** That arrangement is reminiscent of the way the twelve tribes camped around the tabernacle (Num. 2), and of the allotment of the tribal lands around the millennial temple (Ezek. 48).

The massive **wall of the city** was anchored by **twelve foundation stones, and on them were the twelve names of the twelve apostles of the Lamb.** Those **stones** commemorate God's covenant relationship with the church, of which the apostles are the foundation (Eph. 2:20). At the top of each gate was the name of one of the tribes of Israel; at the bottom of each gate was the name of one of the apostles. Thus, the layout of the city's gates pictures God's favor on all His redeemed people, both those under the old covenant, and those under the new covenant.

Then a curious thing occurred. The angel **who spoke with** John **had a gold measuring rod to measure the city, and its gates and its wall.** This interesting event is reminiscent of the measuring of the millennial temple (Ezek. 40:3ff.) and the measuring of the Tribulation temple (11:1). The significance of all three measurements is that they mark out what belongs to God.

The results of the angel's measuring revealed that **the city is laid out as a square, and its length is as great as the width; and he measured the city with the rod, fifteen hundred miles** (lit. "12,000 *stadia*"; a *stadion* was about 607 feet. Thus, the city walls are about 1,380 miles in each direction); **its length and width and height are equal.** Some commentators have suggested that the city is in the shape of a pyramid. It is best seen as a cube, however, as Henry M. Morris points out:

> Such an interpretation is quite forced, however, the language of the passage being much more naturally understood to mean a cube, with the length and breadth and height all the same. . . .
>
> The pyramidal shape . . . (whether as in Egypt, Mexico, or the stepped-towers of practically all ancient nations), seems always to have been associated with paganism, with the pyramid's apex being dedicated to the worship of the sun, or of the host of heaven. The first such structure was the Tower of Babel, and the Bible always later condemns worship carried in high places (Leviticus 26:30) whether these were simply natural high hills or artificially constructed hills in the form of a pyramid or ziggurat.
>
> The cube . . . was the shape specified by God for the holy place . . . in Solomon's temple (1 Kings 6:20), where God was to "dwell" between the cherubim. Both the language and the symbology thus favor the cubical, rather than the pyramidal, shape. (*The Revelation Record* [Wheaton, Ill.: Tyndale, 1983], 450)

Morris also points out that a cube-shaped city is well suited for the existence of glorified beings:

> It should also be remembered that the new bodies of the resurrected saints will be like those of angels, no longer limited by gravitational or electromagnetic forces as at present. Thus it will be as easy for the inhabitants to travel vertically as horizontally, in the new Jerusalem. Consequently, the "streets" of the city (verse 21) may well include vertical passageways as well as horizontal avenues, and the "blocks" could be real cubical blocks, instead of square areas between streets as in a present-day earthly city. (*The Revelation Record,* 451)

Based on certain assumptions about the design of the city and the number of the redeemed who will live in it, Morris calculates that each person's "cube" would be approximately seventy-five acres on each side (*The Revelation Record,* 451). Were that city to be superimposed on the present-day United States, it would extend from Canada to the Gulf of Mexico, and from Colorado to the Atlantic Ocean (*The Revelation Record,* 450). Obviously, God will design the new Jerusalem with plenty of room for all the redeemed (cf. John 14:2–3).

The angel next **measured** the city's wall at **seventy-two yards** (most likely its thickness). Then, as if to emphasize that the city's dimensions are literal and not mystical, John adds the parenthetical footnote that those dimensions were given **according to human measurements, which are also angelic measurements.** A yard is a yard, a foot is a foot, and a mile is a mile, whether for humans or angels.

The **material** that the massive city **wall** was made out of **was jasper**—the same diamond-like stone mentioned in verse 11. Not only was the wall translucent, but also **the city** itself **was pure gold, like clear glass.** The new Jerusalem's walls and buildings must be clear for the city to radiate the glory of God. Some may be concerned that the city's translucence will preclude any privacy. There will be nothing in heaven, however, that calls for privacy.

John next turns his attention in the vision to **the foundation stones of the city wall,** which he describes in amazing detail. They **were adorned with every kind of precious stone,** twelve of which the apostle names. The names of some of the stones have changed through the centuries, making their identification uncertain. Eight of these stones were mounted on the high priest's breastpiece (Ex. 28:17–20; 39:10–13). **The first foundation stone was jasper** which, as previously noted, is best identified as a diamond; **the second** was **sapphire,** a brilliant blue stone; **the third** was **chalcedony,** an agate stone from the Chalcedon region of what is now modern Turkey, sky blue in color with colored stripes; **the fourth** was **emerald,** a bright green stone; **the fifth** was **sardonyx,** a red and white striped stone; **the sixth** was **sardius,** a common quartz stone found in various shades of red; **the seventh** was **chrysolite,** a transparent gold or yellow-hued stone;

the eighth was **beryl,** a stone found in various colors, including shades of green, yellow, and blue; **the ninth** was **topaz,** a yellow-green stone; **the tenth** was **chrysoprase,** a gold-tinted green stone; **the eleventh** was **jacinth,** a blue or violet-colored stone in John's day, though the modern equivalent is a red or reddish-brown zircon; **the twelfth** was **amethyst,** a purple stone. These brightly-colored stones refract the shining brilliance of God's glory into a panoply of beautiful colors. The scene was one of breathtaking beauty, a spectrum of dazzling colors flashing from the New Jerusalem throughout the re-created universe.

The next facet of the heavenly city that caught John's eye was **the twelve gates,** which **were twelve pearls.** Pearls were highly prized and of great value in John's day. But these **pearls** were like no pearl ever produced by an oyster, because **each one of the gates was a single** gigantic **pearl** nearly 1,400 miles high. There is a spiritual truth illustrated by the fact that the **gates** were made of **pearls,** as John Phillips explains:

> How appropriate! All other precious gems are metals or stones, but a pearl is a gem formed within the oyster—the only one formed by living flesh. The humble oyster receives an irritation or a wound, and around the offending article that has penetrated and hurt it, the oyster builds a pearl. The pearl, we might say, is the answer of the oyster to that which injured it. The glory land is God's answer, in Christ, to wicked men who crucified heaven's beloved and put Him to open shame. How like God it is to make the gates of the new Jerusalem of pearl. The saints as they come and go will be forever reminded, as they pass the gates of glory, that access to God's home is only because of Calvary. Think of the size of those gates! Think of the supernatural pearls from which they are made! What gigantic suffering is symbolized by those gates of pearl! Throughout the endless ages we shall be reminded by those pearly gates of the immensity of the sufferings of Christ. Those pearls, hung eternally at the access routes to glory, will remind us forever of One who hung upon a tree and whose answer to those who injured Him was to invite them to share His home. (*Exploring Revelation,* rev. ed. [Chicago: Moody, 1987; reprint, Neptune, N. J.: Loizeaux, 1991], 254)

Its Internal Character

And the street of the city was pure gold, like transparent glass.

I saw no temple in it, for the Lord God the Almighty and the Lamb are its temple. And the city has no need of the sun or of the moon to shine on it, for the glory of God has illumined it, and its lamp is the Lamb. The nations will walk by its light, and the kings of the earth will bring their glory into it. In the daytime (for

there will be no night there) its gates will never be closed; and they will bring the glory and the honor of the nations into it; and nothing unclean, and no one who practices abomination and lying, shall ever come into it, but only those whose names are written in the Lamb's book of life.

Then he showed me a river of the water of life, clear as crystal, coming from the throne of God and of the Lamb, in the middle of its street. On either side of the river was the tree of life, bearing twelve kinds of fruit, yielding its fruit every month; and the leaves of the tree were for the healing of the nations. (21:21*b*–22:2)

As if just seeing the magnificent capital city of heaven from a distance was not privilege enough, John's angelic guide took him inside. As he entered the city, the apostle noted that **the street of the city was pure gold, like transparent glass.** The streets in the New Jerusalem were made of the highest quality **pure gold** which, like everything else in the heavenly city, was **transparent** like **glass.** Translucent gold is not a material familiar to us on this earth. But everything there is transparent to let the light of God's glory blaze unrestricted.

Once inside the city, the first thing John noted was that there was **no temple in it.** Up to this point, there has been a temple in heaven (cf. 7:15; 11:19; 14:15, 17; 15:5–8; 16:1, 17). But there will be no need for a temple in the new Jerusalem, **for the Lord God the Almighty and the Lamb are its temple.** Their blazing glory will fill the new heaven and the new earth, and there will be no need for anyone to go anywhere to worship God. Life will be worship and worship will be life. Believers will be constantly in His presence (cf. 21:3); there will never be a moment when they are not in perfect, holy communion with **the Lord God the Almighty and the Lamb.** Thus, there will be no need to go to a **temple,** cathedral, church, chapel, or any other house of worship. Believers will be the true worshipers God has always sought (John 4:23).

Returning to the theme of God's brilliant, shining glory, John notes that **the city has no need of the sun or of the moon to shine on it, for the glory of God has illumined it, and its lamp is the Lamb.** The new heaven and the new earth will be radically different from the present earth, which is totally dependent on the sun and moon. They provide the cycles of light and darkness, and the moon causes the ocean tides. But in the new heaven and the new earth, they will be unnecessary. There will be no seas (21:1) and hence no tides. Nor will the **sun** and **moon** be needed to provide light, **for the glory of God** will **illumine** the New Jerusalem **and its lamp** will be **the Lamb.** Once again in Revelation, **God** the Father and the **Lamb,** the Lord Jesus Christ, share authority (cf. 3:21).

Commenting on the brilliant light emanating from the New Jerusalem, J. A. Seiss writes:

> That shining is not from any material combustion,—not from any consumption of fuel that needs to be replaced as one supply burns out; for it is the uncreated light of Him who is light, dispensed by and through the Lamb as the everlasting Lamp, to the home, and hearts, and understandings of his glorified saints. When Paul and Silas lay wounded and bound in the inner dungeon of the prison of Philippi, they still had sacred light which enabled them to beguile the night-watches with happy songs. When Paul was on his way to Damascus, a light brighter than the sun at noon shone round about him, irradiating his whole being with new sights and understanding, and making his soul and body ever afterwards light in the Lord. When Moses came down from the mount of his communion with God, his face was so luminous that his brethren could not endure to look upon it. He was in such close fellowship with light that he became informed with light, and came to the camp as a very lamp of God, glowing with the glory of God. On the Mount of Transfiguration that same light streamed forth from all the body and raiment of the blessed Jesus. And with reference to the very time when this city comes into being and place, Isaiah says, "the moon shall be ashamed and the sun confounded,"—ashamed because of the out-beaming glory which then shall appear in the new Jerusalem, leaving no more need for them to shine in it, since the glory of God lights it, and the Lamb is the light thereof. (*The Apocalypse* [reprint, Grand Rapids: Kregel, 1987], 499)

The reference to the **nations . . . and the kings of the earth** has led some to view this passage as a recapitulation of the millennial kingdom. But such an interpretation fails to do justice to the chronology of Revelation, particularly the repeated use of *kai eidon* to indicate chronological progression (see the discussion of 21:1 in chapter 18 of this volume). There will be living human beings in the Millennium (Isa. 65:20–23), but no physically alive people could possibly exist in an environment without sea (v. 1), sun, or moon (v. 23). **Nations** translates *ethnos,* which can also mean "people," and is most frequently translated "Gentiles." The idea is not that national identities will be preserved in the eternal state, but rather the opposite. People from every tongue, tribe, and nation—both Jews and Gentiles—will be united as God's people. Every believer will be fully equal in the eternal capital city.

It may be that the truth that **the kings of the earth will bring their glory into it** offers further proof of the absolute equality in heaven. That phrase may indicate that there will be no social or class structure, that those who enter the city will surrender their earthly **glory.** Thus, everyone would be at the same level. Another possible interpretation is that this phrase refers to the believers living at the end of the Millennium. According to that view, the statement that **the kings of the earth will bring their glory into** the New Jerusalem refers to the translation of those believers before the uncreation of the present universe (see the discussion of 20:11 in chap. 17 of this volume).

Then John adds another detail to his description of the New Jerusalem. Throughout the never-ending **daytime** of the eternal state (**for there will be no night there**) **its gates will never be closed.** In an ancient walled city, the gates were closed at nightfall to keep invaders, marauders, criminals, and other potentially dangerous individuals from entering the city under cover of darkness. That **there will be no night** in eternity, and the **gates** of the New Jerusalem **will never** need to **be closed,** depicts the city's complete security. It will be a place of rest, safety, and refreshment, where God's people will "rest from their labors" (14:13).

The kings will not be the only ones to surrender their earthly prestige and glory when they enter heaven. The **glory and the honor of the nations** will also dissolve, as it were, into the eternal worship of God the Father and the Lord Jesus Christ. Like the twenty-four elders, all who enter heaven "will cast their crowns before the throne" of God (4:10).

All in heaven will be perfectly holy. Thus, **nothing unclean, and no one who practices abomination and lying, shall ever come into** the New Jerusalem (see the discussions of 21:7–8 in chap. 18 of this volume and 22:15 in chap. 21). The **only** ones there will be **those whose names are written in the Lamb's book of life.** (For a discussion of the book of life, see 3:5; 13:8; and the comments on 20:12 in chap. 17 of this volume.)

John's angelic tour guide next **showed** him **a river of the water of life.** With no sea in the eternal state (21:1), there could be no hydrologic cycle, and hence no rain to fill a river. Thus, the **water of life** is not water as we know it; it is a symbol of eternal life (cf. Isa. 12:3; John 4:13–14; 7:38). Like everything else in the New Jerusalem, the **river** was **clear as crystal** so it could reflect the glory of God. It cascaded down **from the throne of God and of the Lamb** in a dazzling, sparkling, never-ending stream. Its pure, unpolluted, unobstructed flow symbolizes the constant flow of everlasting life from God's throne to God's people.

The phrase **in the middle of its street** is best translated "in the middle of its path" and connected with the following phrase **on either side of the river was the tree of life.** The **tree of life** is the celestial counterpart to the tree of life in Eden (Gen. 2:9; 3:22–24), and this tree provides for those who are immortal. The **tree of life** was a familiar Jewish concept that expressed blessing (cf. 2:7; Prov. 3:18; 11:30; 13:12; 15:4), and the celestial tree symbolizes the blessing of eternal life. That the **tree** bears **twelve kinds of fruit, yielding its fruit every month** emphasizes the infinite variety that will fill heaven. The use of the term **month** does not refer to time, since this is the eternal state and time is no more. It is an anthropomorphic expression of the joyous provision of eternity couched in the familiar terms of time.

Then John makes the intriguing observation that **the leaves of the tree were for the healing of the nations.** At first glance, that seems confusing, since obviously there will be no illness or injury in heaven that would require **healing.** *Therapeia* (**healing**), however, does not imply illness. Perhaps a better way to translate it would be "life-giving," "health-giving," or "therapeutic." The **leaves of the tree** can be likened to supernatural vitamins, since vitamins are taken not to treat illness, but to promote general health. Life in heaven will be fully energized, rich, and exciting.

The text does not say whether the saints will actually eat the **leaves of the tree,** though that is possible. Angels ate food with Abraham and Sarah (Gen. 18:1–8), as did the Lord Jesus Christ with His disciples after His resurrection (Luke 24:42–43; Acts 10:41). It is conceivable that the saints in heaven will eat, not out of necessity, but for enjoyment.

The Privileges of Its Inhabitants

There will no longer be any curse; and the throne of God and of the Lamb will be in it, and His bond-servants will serve Him; they will see His face, and His name will be on their foreheads. And there will no longer be any night; and they will not have need of the light of a lamp nor the light of the sun, because the Lord God will illumine them; and they will reign forever and ever. (22:3–5)

As John toured the New Jerusalem, he couldn't help but notice that life was very different for its inhabitants. The most dramatic change from the present earth is that **there will no longer be any curse.** As noted in the discussion of 21:4 in chapter 18 of this volume, the removal of the curse will mean the end forever of sorrow, pain, and especially death—the most terrible aspect of the curse (Gen. 2:17).

Though, as previously noted, there will be no temple in the New Jerusalem, **the throne of God and of the Lamb will be in it** (cf. the detailed description of the throne scene in 4:2–11). **God** the Father and the **Lamb,** the Lord Jesus Christ, will reign throughout eternity. Since God will continue forever as heaven's sovereign ruler, **His bond-servants**

will serve Him forever (cf. 7:15). They will spend all eternity carrying out the infinite variety of tasks that the limitless mind of God can conceive. Incredibly, as the parable in Luke 12:35–40 indicates, the Lord will also serve them.

The saints in the New Jerusalem **will** also **see** God's **face** (cf. Matt. 5:8). Being perfectly holy and righteous, they will be able to endure the heavenly level of the blazing, glorious light from God's presence without being consumed—something impossible for mortal men (Ex. 33:20; John 1:18; 6:46; 1 Tim. 6:16; 1 John 4:12).

The redeemed will also be God's personal possession; **His name will be on their foreheads** (cf. 3:12; 14:1). That identification will leave no doubt as to who they belong to forever. John repeats the earlier description of heaven's magnificence: **And there will no longer be any night; and they will not have need of the light of a lamp nor the light of the sun, because the Lord God will illumine them** (cf. 21:22–26). Then he adds a final crescendo describing the saints' heavenly experience: it will never end, because **they will reign forever and ever.** That will be the fulfillment of Christ's promise in 3:21: "He who overcomes, I will grant to him to sit down with Me on My throne, as I also overcame and sat down with My Father on His throne." "If we endure," Paul wrote to Timothy, "we will also reign with Him" (2 Tim. 2:12).

The eternal capital city of heaven, the New Jerusalem, will be a place of indescribable, unimaginable beauty. From the center of it the brilliant glory of God will shine forth through the gold and precious stones to illuminate the new heaven and the new earth. But the most glorious reality of all will be that sinful rebels will be made righteous, enjoy intimate fellowship with God and the Lamb, serve Them, and reign with Them forever in sheer joy and incessant praise.

The Believer's Immediate Response to Christ's Imminent Return (Revelation 22:6–12) 20

And he said to me, "These words are faithful and true"; and the Lord, the God of the spirits of the prophets, sent His angel to show to His bond-servants the things which must soon take place.

"And behold, I am coming quickly. Blessed is he who heeds the words of the prophecy of this book."

I, John, am the one who heard and saw these things. And when I heard and saw, I fell down to worship at the feet of the angel who showed me these things. But he said to me, "Do not do that. I am a fellow servant of yours and of your brethren the prophets and of those who heed the words of this book. Worship God."

And he said to me, "Do not seal up the words of the prophecy of this book, for the time is near. Let the one who does wrong, still do wrong; and the one who is filthy, still be filthy; and let the one who is righteous, still practice righteousness; and the one who is holy, still keep himself holy."

"Behold, I am coming quickly, and My reward is with Me, to render to every man according to what he has done. (22:6–12)

Verses 6–21 of this chapter form the epilogue to the book of Revelation. Having taken the reader through the amazing sweep of future history all the way into the eternal state, all that is left for John to record is this divine postscript. By this point in the Apocalypse, all the glorious and gracious purposes that God ordained before the foundation of the world will have been attained. The devastating judgments of the Tribulation will have been carried out, and their memory will remain only in the torment of the damned. The Lord Jesus Christ will have returned in blazing glory, executed His enemies, and reigned on earth for a thousand years. All rebels, both angels and humans, will have been sentenced to their final, eternal punishment in the lake of fire. The present universe will have been "uncreated," and the eternal new heaven and the new earth created, in which the King of Kings will be reigning with His Father. The holy angels and the redeemed of all the ages will be dwelling in eternal bliss with Him in the new creation, particularly in heaven's capital city, the New Jerusalem. From His throne in the center of that majestic city, the brilliant, blazing glory of God will radiate throughout the re-created universe. Absolute and unchanging holiness will characterize all who dwell in the universal and eternal kingdom of God. They will constantly praise, worship, and serve Him throughout eternity in an environment of perfect peace, joy, and fulfillment.

Bracketing the book of Revelation along with the epilogue is the prologue, recorded in 1:1–3:

> The Revelation of Jesus Christ, which God gave Him to show to His bond-servants, the things which must soon take place; and He sent and communicated it by His angel to His bond-servant John, who testified to the word of God and to the testimony of Jesus Christ, even to all that he saw. Blessed is he who reads and those who hear the words of the prophecy, and heed the things which are written in it; for the time is near.

The prologue introduces the theme of Revelation, the second coming of Jesus Christ. The epilogue provides a fitting conclusion to the Apocalypse by pointing out what is to be the believer's response to the Second Coming (vv. 6–12). This postscript also, one final time in Scripture, invites nonbelievers to come to saving faith in Christ before it is forever too late (vv. 13–21).

In a series of rapid-fire, staccato statements that move breathlessly from theme to theme, verses 6–12 delineate the responses every believer should have to the imminent coming of the Lord Jesus Christ. These verses convey a furious rush of energy, a wild flurry of excited effort to call forth immediate reaction to the vital truth they communicate. The text is pregnant with urgency, pressuring every reader to take action based on the truths it presents.

Nothing more clearly communicates that sense of urgency than the repetition of the phrase "Behold, I am coming quickly" (vv. 7, 12; cf. v. 20). That declaration is the refrain of this passage. The phrase appears three other places in Revelation; in 3:11 it is a promise of blessing, as it is in its three uses in chapter 22. In 2:5 and 2:16, on the other hand, the phrase warns of Jesus' coming in judgment. In 3:3 and 16:15, Jesus likens His coming to the unexpected coming of a thief. (Unlike a thief, of course, Jesus will come not to steal, but to take back what is rightfully His.) Since Jesus could rapture His church at any moment, triggering all the end-time events culminating in His return, believers (and unbelievers) need to be ready.

A natural reading of the New Testament yields the truth that to the early church Jesus' coming was imminent; that is, that it could happen at any time. They believed that He could come back for them in their lifetime. For the early church, imminence contained elements both of certainty and uncertainty. They were certain that Jesus would one day return, but (unlike numerous modern date setters) were uncertain when. Not knowing when He might return, they wisely lived prepared for and hoping for Jesus to return at any moment.

There are a number of New Testament texts that reflect the early church's belief in imminence. Paul commended the Corinthians because they were "awaiting eagerly the revelation of our Lord Jesus Christ" (1 Cor. 1:7). He further exhorted them, "Therefore do not go on passing judgment before the time, but wait until the Lord comes who will both bring to light the things hidden in the darkness and disclose the motives of men's hearts; and then each man's praise will come to him from God" (1 Cor. 4:5). The apostle included the untranslated Aramaic word *maranatha* ("O Lord, come") in a letter to the Greek-speaking Corinthians (1 Cor. 16:22). That word had evidently become a familiar byword, expressing believers' longing for Christ's imminent return. To the Philippians Paul wrote, "For our citizenship is in heaven, from which also we eagerly wait for a Savior, the Lord Jesus Christ" (Phil. 3:20). He commended the Thessalonians because they "turned to God from idols to serve a living and true God, and to wait for His Son from heaven" (1 Thess. 1:9–10). Later in that same epistle, Paul expressed his own hope that he might be alive at the Lord's return: "For this we say to you by the word of the Lord, that we who are alive and remain until the coming of the Lord, will not precede those who have fallen asleep" (1 Thess. 4:15). The apostle rebuked those believers at Thessalonica who were so preoccupied with the Second Coming that they were not working:

> For even when we were with you, we used to give you this order: if anyone is not willing to work, then he is not to eat, either. For we hear that

> some among you are leading an undisciplined life, doing no work at all, but acting like busybodies. Now such persons we command and exhort in the Lord Jesus Christ to work in quiet fashion and eat their own bread. (2 Thess. 3:10–12)

Though they drew improper conclusions from it, they nonetheless believed in Christ's imminent return. Paul reminded Titus that Christians are to be "looking for the blessed hope and the appearing of the glory of our great God and Savior, Christ Jesus" (Titus 2:13). James encouraged his readers to "be patient, brethren, until the coming of the Lord" (James 5:7). In his first epistle the apostle John exhorted his readers, "Now, little children, abide in Him, so that when He appears, we may have confidence and not shrink away from Him in shame at His coming. . . . Beloved, now we are children of God, and it has not appeared as yet what we will be. We know that when He appears, we will be like Him, because we will see Him just as He is" (1 John 2:28; 3:2). These passages demonstrate the early believers' anticipation of their Savior's coming again.

The threefold repetition of the phrase "I am coming quickly" in this passage (vv. 7, 12, 20) reinforces the reality of the imminent return. The adverb *tachu* ("quickly") does not refer to the speed at which Christ will travel from heaven to earth when He returns; instead, it has the connotation of "soon," or "before long." The point is that "the Judge is standing right at the door" (James 5:9), poised to return at any moment.

As the epilogue opens, John records that **he** (the angel who had shown him the New Jerusalem; 21:9; 22:1) **said to me, "These words are faithful and true."** The angel's **words** provide heavenly attestation to the validity of all that John had heard and seen throughout the Apocalypse. The angel repeats the same affirmation given earlier to John by God Himself: "He who sits on the throne said . . . 'Write, for these words are faithful and true'" (21:5). The phrase **faithful and true** also appears twice in Revelation as a title for the Lord Jesus Christ (3:14; 19:11). The words of the Apocalypse are as faithful and true as the One who revealed them to John.

The angel's words reinforce an important truth: Everything John has seen in Revelation will come to pass. What the inspired apostle has written is not mystical; the Apocalypse is not a record of his bizarre dreams or the result of an overactive imagination. It is not an allegory from which readers can extract hidden meanings of their own concoction. It is an accurate description of events and persons yet to come. Verses 18 and 19 of this chapter give a sobering warning against tampering with Revelation: "I testify to everyone who hears the words of the prophecy of this book: if anyone adds to them, God will add to him the plagues which are written in this book; and if anyone takes away from the words of the book of this prophecy, God will take away his part from the tree of life and from the holy city, which are written in this book."

John affirmed the angel's emphatic testimony to the truthfulness of what he had seen and heard, writing that **the Lord, the God of the spirits of the prophets, sent His angel to show to His bond-servants the things which must soon take place.** The **God** who moved **the spirits of** His spokesmen **the prophets** to inspire both the Old and New Testaments is the same God who **sent His angel to show to His bond-servants** (believers; cf. v. 3; 1:1; 2:20; 7:3; 11:18; 15:3; 19:2, 5; Luke 2:29; Acts 4:29; 16:17; Rom. 1:1; Gal. 1:10; Phil. 1:1; Col. 1:7; 4:7; James 1:1; 2 Pet. 1:1; Jude 1) **the things which must soon take place** (cf. Luke 1:70; 2 Pet. 3:2). That is nothing short of a claim by John for the full and complete inspiration of Revelation. The prophecies recorded by those earlier biblical **prophets** were literally fulfilled, and those in Revelation will be also (see the discussion in chapter 16 of this volume).

The exactness, detail, and precision with which earlier prophecies already fulfilled came to pass form the pattern for those yet to be fulfilled. God's prophetic record is perfect. He predicted Israel would go into captivity, and the nation did (Lev. 26:33–39). He predicted the destruction of Babylon (Isa. 13:1–14:27; Jer. 50–51) and Tyre (Isa. 23:1ff.), and those cities were destroyed. He predicted that Messiah would be born in Bethlehem (Mic. 5:2), to a virgin (Isa. 7:14), and be killed by sinners (Isa. 53:7–10) and He was. Thus, when God predicts future events, such as the rapture of the church, the rise of Antichrist, the seal, trumpet, and bowl judgments, the Battle of Armageddon, the return of Jesus Christ, and His thousand-year earthly kingdom, those events will just as certainly come to pass. God will do exactly what He says He will do, as He Himself declares in Isaiah 46:9–11:

> Remember the former things long past,
> For I am God, and there is no other;
> I am God, and there is no one like Me,
> Declaring the end from the beginning,
> And from ancient times things which have not been done,
> Saying, "My purpose will be established,
> And I will accomplish all My good pleasure"; . . .
> Truly I have spoken; truly I will bring it to pass.
> I have planned it, surely I will do it.

The reality of our Lord's imminent return calls for four responses on the part of every believer: immediate obedience, immediate worship, immediate proclamation, and immediate service.

Immediate Obedience

"And behold, I am coming quickly. Blessed is he who heeds the words of the prophecy of this book." (22:7)

Kai (**and**) marks a change in speakers (cf. vv. 8, 9). The speaker is no longer the angel who spoke in verse 6, but the Lord Jesus Christ, the One who is **coming quickly.** He pronounces the sixth of seven beatitudes in Revelation (cf. v. 14; 1:3; 14:13; 16:15; 19:9; 20:6): **"Blessed is he who heeds the words of the prophecy of this book."** Three other times **the words of . . . this book** (Revelation) are called **prophecy** (vv. 10, 18, 19). Though **prophecy** by definition can refer to any message about the past, present, or future, the Apocalypse is a book largely consisting of future predictions and promises. **Heeds** translates a participial form of the verb *tēreō*, which means "to keep," "to hold fast," or "to guard." The same term is used in 14:12 to describe "the perseverance of the saints who keep the commandments of God and their faith in Jesus."

Believers are called to guard or protect the book of Revelation. It must be defended against detractors who deny its relevance, against critics who deny its veracity and authority, as well as against confused interpreters who obscure its meaning. In fact, all of Scripture is to be so guarded. Paul commanded Timothy, "Guard what has been entrusted to you. . . . Retain the standard of sound words which you have heard from me, in the faith and love which are in Christ Jesus. Guard, through the Holy Spirit who dwells in us, the treasure which has been entrusted to you" (1 Tim. 6:20; 2 Tim. 1:13–14).

But believers are called not only to guard Scripture, but also to obey it. Jesus said, "If you love Me, you will keep My commandments. . . . If you keep My commandments, you will abide in My love; just as I have kept My Father's commandments and abide in His love" (John 14:15; 15:10; cf. John 14:21, 23). The need to obey the commands of Scripture was a foundational theme in John's first epistle: "By this we know that we have come to know Him, if we keep His commandments. The one who says, 'I have come to know Him,' and does not keep His commandments, is a liar, and the truth is not in him" (1 John 2:3–4); "By this we know that we love the children of God, when we love God and observe His commandments. For this is the love of God, that we keep His commandments; and His commandments are not burdensome" (1 John 5:2–3). Those who live as if Jesus could come at any moment will live in obedience to Scripture.

The question arises as to what **words** in Revelation believers are called to heed. Before this command, there are no specific commands addressed to Christians in the portion of the Apocalypse covering future events (chaps. 4–22), though there are some addressed to the seven churches (chaps. 2–3). What does it mean, then, to heed the book of Revelation? It is a general command to long for Christ's return and our eternal fellowship with Him. It calls on believers to desire heaven, to desire holiness, to desire to see Christ vindicated and triumphant over His enemies, to desire the end of the curse, and to desire the glories of Christ's earthly kingdom and the new heaven and the new earth. After reading Revelation, Christians should love Christ more, long to see Him vindicated in His glory, live in light of the reality that they will one day see Him, disconnect themselves from the perishing world system, pursue heavenly realities, seek to be made like Christ, hope for their resurrection bodies, and anticipate their eternal rewards. They should also understand the fearful judgment that awaits non-Christians, and call those sinners to repentance and saving faith in the Lord Jesus.

God does not command believers to read Revelation merely to satisfy their curiosity about the future. He did not inspire it to provide material for detailed chronological charts of end-time events. There is a seemingly endless stream of books on prophecy being churned out, with speculative prophetic schemes proliferating *ad infinitum, ad nauseam.* But it was not God's purpose to give Christians a detailed analysis of the prophetic significance (if any) of contemporary cultural, political, military, and social events or trends. God inspired Revelation for one purpose: to reveal the glory of His Son and call believers to live godly, obedient lives in light of His soon return. The purpose of Revelation is not to provide entertainment, but to provide motivation for godly living.

The apostle Peter also taught that believers' knowledge of end-time events should cause them to live holy lives. In a passage describing the future Day of the Lord, the destruction of the present universe, and the coming of the new heaven and the new earth, Peter wrote, "Since all these things are to be destroyed in this way, what sort of people ought you to be in holy conduct and godliness, looking for and hastening the coming of the day of God. . . . Therefore, beloved, since you look for these things, be diligent to be found by Him in peace, spotless and blameless" (2 Pet. 3:11–12, 14). The glorious future realities described in Revelation compel a commitment on the part of believers to lead holy lives. Christ's imminent return demands immediate obedience.

Immediate Worship

I, John, am the one who heard and saw these things. And when I heard and saw, I fell down to worship at the feet of the angel who showed me these things. But he said to me, "Do not do that. I am a

fellow servant of yours and of your brethren the prophets and of those who heed the words of this book. Worship God." (22:8–9)

Though not expressed in the *New American Standard Bible* Updated Edition, a form of *kai* (*kagō;* from *kai*, "and," and *egō*, "I") begins verse 8. As it did in verse 7, it marks a change of speakers; the speaker is no longer Christ, but John, who names himself for the first time since 1:9. The inspired apostle adds his testimony of the truthfulness of Revelation to that of the angel (v. 6), declaring **I, John, am the one who heard and saw these things.** Then, overcome by what he **heard and saw,** John **fell down to worship at the feet of the angel who showed** him **these things.** He had the proper response, worship, but being overwhelmed with amazement, John inadvertently directed it to the wrong object. The apostle knew that angels were not to be worshiped; in fact, he had earlier been rebuked for attempting to do so (19:10). But like Ezekiel (Ezek. 1:28), Daniel (Dan. 8:17; 10:9), and Peter, James, and he himself at the Transfiguration (Matt. 17:6), John simply collapsed in wonder and worship.

Because God alone is to be worshiped (Ex. 34:14; Matt. 4:10), the angel **said to** John, **"Do not do that."** He hastily reminded the apostle that he, too, was a created being, declaring **I am a fellow servant of yours and of your brethren the prophets and of those who heed the words of this book.** Far from being a legitimate object of worship for John, the angel was actually his created **fellow servant,** and not only his, but also of John's **brethren the prophets,** and of all believers, defined here as **those who heed the words of this book.** Throughout Scripture, angels are seen serving God's people. They were involved in giving the Law to Israel (Acts 7:53; Gal. 3:19; Heb. 2:2) and are frequently seen protecting believers (cf. Ex. 23:20; 2 Chron. 32:21; Ps. 91:11; Dan. 3:28; 6:22; Acts 5:19; 12:7–11). Summing up the ministry of angels to believers, the author of Hebrews asks rhetorically, "Are they not all ministering spirits, sent out to render service for the sake of those who will inherit salvation?" (Heb. 1:14).

Calling the bewildered apostle back to the one and only object of worship, the angel commanded John to **worship God.** A proper understanding of Revelation should elicit worship; thus, worship is a major theme in the Apocalypse (cf. 4:8–11; 5:8–14; 7:9–12; 15:2–4; 19:1–6). As noted above, **God** alone is the only acceptable Person to worship. The Bible forbids the worship of anyone else, including angels, saints, the Virgin Mary, or any other created being (cf. Col. 2:18).

Immediate Proclamation

And he said to me, "Do not seal up the words of the prophecy of this book, for the time is near. Let the one who does wrong, still do wrong; and the one who is filthy, still be filthy; and let the one who is righteous, still practice righteousness; and the one who is holy, still keep himself holy." (22:10–11)

Continuing his message to John, the angel commanded him, **"Do not seal up the words of the prophecy of this book."** The message of the Apocalypse is not to be hidden (cf. 10:11); it is a message to be spread and proclaimed to produce obedience and worship. Thus, unlike Daniel (Dan. 8:26; 12:4–10), John was instructed **not** to **seal up the words of** Revelation. Immediate proclamation of **this book** is called for because the coming of Christ has been imminent for every generation from John's day until the present.

That the specific **words** of Revelation are not to be sealed up stresses again that there is no hidden, secret meaning apart from the normal sense of the text. If the truth is not clear in those **words** then this command is nonsense. If the plain, normal understanding of the **words** of Revelation does not convey the meaning God intended its readers to grasp, then those **words** *are* sealed.

At the beginning of Revelation, John was commanded, "Write in a book what you see, and send it to the seven churches" (1:11). The message of the Apocalypse, that Jesus will return bringing blessing for His own and horrifying judgment on the ungodly, is too critical not to spread. Thus, to fail to preach Revelation is not only foolish (cf. 1:3), but sinful. Any Christian who fails to learn its truths is forfeiting blessing; any preacher who fails to proclaim its truths is sinfully unfaithful to his mandate. Not to preach the book of Revelation is to fail to exalt the Lord Jesus Christ with the glory that is due Him. More than just a failure to teach the whole counsel of God (Acts 20:27), it is outright disobedience to the command not to **seal up the words** of the Apocalypse. It robs believers of the end of the divine story of history in all its wonder and fullness. No one should preach who doesn't rightly divide and proclaim this book.

The angel's next statement seems strangely out of place in this context: **"Let the one who does wrong, still do wrong; and the one who is filthy, still be filthy; and let the one who is righteous, still practice righteousness; and the one who is holy, still keep himself holy."** Some may think its connection with the command that preceded it is not immediately apparent. But the truth it dramatically conveys is that people's response to the proclamation of the truth will fix their eternal destinies. Those who hear the truth but continue to **do wrong** and **be filthy** will by that hardened response fix their eternal destiny in hell. On the other hand, the one who continues to practice **righteousness** and **keep himself holy** gives evidence of genuine saving faith. The adverb *eti* (**still**) may have the sense of "yet more." In that case, the meaning is that those who do **wrong** and are **filthy** in this life will be even more so in eternal hell, where there will be absolutely no good influences to mitigate their evil. In contrast, those who are **righteous** and **holy** in this life will be perfectly holy in their glorified bodies in heaven.

It is sobering to realize that people's response to God's gospel truth in this life will determine their eternal destiny. When they die, or when the Lord returns, their character will be forever fixed. Those who respond to the warnings in Revelation will live forever in heaven. But those who fail to heed those warnings and repent will remain forever in their sinful state. It is also true that God's Spirit will not always call sinners to repentance, and Scripture warns sinners not to harden their hearts to the point where God judicially abandons them (Ps. 95:7–8; Heb. 3:15; 4:7). Yet, tragically, those warnings often go unheeded, and the opportunity to repent and believe the gospel is wasted (cf. Matt. 25:1–13; Luke 13:24–25). Speaking of the wayward sinners of the northern kingdom (Israel), God declared, "Ephraim is joined to idols; let him alone" (Hos. 4:17). Jesus said of the equally hardened Pharisees, "Let them alone; they are blind guides of the blind" (Matt. 15:14; cf. Matt. 23:16, 24; Luke 6:39). Both of those passages express God's wrath of abandonment (Rom. 1:18–32), when He turns hardened, unrepentant sinners over to the consequences of their own choices.

Preaching Revelation draws the line. Its truths will melt the hearts of the repentant and harden the hearts of the unrepentant. Those same truths thus become either an instrument of salvation, or an instrument of damnation (cf. 1 Cor. 1:18; 2 Cor. 2:15–16). They must be proclaimed so men and women can hear them while there is still time.

Immediate Service

"Behold, I am coming quickly, and My reward is with Me, to render to every man according to what he has done. (22:12)

The speaker is no longer the angel, but the Lord Jesus Christ, who repeats His declaration of verse 7, "**Behold, I am coming quickly.**" As noted in the introduction to this chapter, Jesus' statement means that His coming is imminent. It teaches the same truth that He expressed in Mark 13:33–37:

> Take heed, keep on the alert; for you do not know when the appointed time will come. It is like a man away on a journey, who upon leaving his house and putting his slaves in charge, assigning to each one his task, also commanded the doorkeeper to stay on the alert. Therefore, be on the alert—for you do not know when the master of the house is coming, whether in the evening, at midnight, or when the rooster crows, or in the morning—in case he should come suddenly and find you asleep. What I say to you I say to all, "Be on the alert!"

When He comes, Jesus will bring His **reward . . . with** Him, **to render to every man according to what he has done.** Believers' eternal rewards will be based on their faithfulness in serving Christ in this life. Their works will be tested, and only those with eternal value will survive (1 Cor. 3:9–15; 2 Cor. 5:9–10). The rewards believers enjoy in heaven will be capacities for serving God; the greater their faithfulness in this life, the greater will be their opportunity to serve in heaven (cf. Matt. 25:14–30). Knowing that, John exhorted believers, "Watch yourselves, that you do not lose what we have accomplished, but that you may receive a full reward" (2 John 8).

The knowledge that Jesus could return at any moment should not lead Christians to a life of idle waiting for His coming (cf. 2 Thess. 3:10–12). Rather, it should produce diligent, obedient, worshipful service to God, and urgent proclamation of the gospel to unbelievers.

God's Last Invitation (Revelation 22:13–21)

"I am the Alpha and the Omega, the first and the last, the beginning and the end."

Blessed are those who wash their robes, so that they may have the right to the tree of life, and may enter by the gates into the city. Outside are the dogs and the sorcerers and the immoral persons and the murderers and the idolaters, and everyone who loves and practices lying.

"I, Jesus, have sent My angel to testify to you these things for the churches. I am the root and the descendant of David, the bright morning star."

The Spirit and the bride say, "Come." And let the one who hears say, "Come." And let the one who is thirsty come; let the one who wishes take the water of life without cost.

I testify to everyone who hears the words of the prophecy of this book: if anyone adds to them, God will add to him the plagues which are written in this book; and if anyone takes away from the words of the book of this prophecy, God will take away his part from the tree of life and from the holy city, which are written in this book.

He who testifies to these things says, "Yes, I am coming quickly." Amen. Come, Lord Jesus.
The grace of the Lord Jesus be with all. Amen. (22:13–21)

In these its concluding verses, the Bible comes full circle. It opened with the promise of a coming Savior, who would redeem His people from their sins. That promise, which came immediately after the Fall, is recorded in Genesis 3:15: "I will put enmity between you and the woman, and between your seed and her seed; he shall bruise you on the head, and you shall bruise him on the heel." Just as the Bible opens with the promise of Christ's first coming, so it ends with the promise of His second coming. The faithful Southern Baptist expositor W. A. Criswell writes:

> First, the Saviour is to come that He might be crushed, bruised, crucified and made an offering for sin. He is to come to die as the Redeemer for the souls of men. After God made that promise in Eden, hundreds of years passed, millenniums passed, and the Lord did not come. When finally He did arrive He came unto His own and His own received Him not. He was in the world and the world was made by Him and the world knew Him not. The thousands of humanity had forgotten the promise or else they scoffed at its fulfillment. When finally announcement came that he had arrived, the learned scribes pointed out the place where He was to be born, but never took the time to journey the five miles from Jerusalem to Bethlehem to welcome this promised Saviour of the world. But however long he delayed and however men forgot and scoffed and however few of a faithful band waited for the consolation of Israel, as old Simeon, yet He came. In keeping with the holy, faithful promise of God, the Lord Jesus came. It is thus in the text that God speaks in closing His Bible, "Surely, I come quickly." Here a second time, however infidels may scoff and however others may reject and however the centuries may grow into the millenniums, this is the immutable Word and promise of the Lord God, "Surely, I come." (*Expository Sermons on Revelation* [Grand Rapids: Zondervan, 1969], 5:176–77)

The second coming of the Lord Jesus Christ is a compelling theme in both the Old and New Testaments (e.g., Zech. 14:4; Mal. 3:2; 4:5; Matt. 16:28; 24:27; 1 Cor. 1:7; 15:23; 1 Thess. 2:19; 3:13; 4:15; 5:23; 2 Thess. 2:1; James 5:8; Jude 14). But nowhere is it given greater emphasis than in the Apocalypse, the "Revelation of Jesus Christ" (1:1). It is only fitting that this book, whose focus is on the Second Coming, ends with a final invitation in light of that glorious reality. Verses 6–12 of this chapter are addressed to believers, demanding their proper response to Christ's imminent return (see the discussion in chap. 20 of this volume). Verses 13–21 call unbelievers to repentance. The inspired canon of Scripture closes with an urgent invitation, pleading with sinners to come to Jesus Christ and receive the free gift of eternal life before it is forever too late.

God's final invitation to sinners comes in verse 17. But surrounding that invitation are several incentives designed to motivate people to respond to it.

THE INVITATION

The Spirit and the bride say, "Come." And let the one who hears say, "Come." And let the one who is thirsty come; let the one who wishes take the water of life without cost. (22:17)

There are two distinct invitations in this verse, delineated by the two exclamations, **"Come."** The first part of the verse is a prayer addressed to Christ; the second part is an invitation addressed to sinners. The first part calls for Christ to come; the second part is the last call for sinners to come to faith in Christ.

To Jesus' promise of His imminent return (vv. 7, 12, 20), the Holy **Spirit,** the third Member of the Trinity responds, **"Come."** The text does not specify why the **Spirit** especially desires Jesus to return, but the rest of Scripture suggests both a negative and a positive reason.

Negatively, men and women throughout history have continually rejected, ignored, and denied Christ. They have mocked and blasphemed the work of the **Spirit** (Matt. 12:31), whose ministry is to point them to Christ (John 15:26; 16:8). Speaking of the wicked sinners before the Flood, God said, "My Spirit shall not strive with man forever, because he also is flesh; nevertheless his days shall be one hundred and twenty years" (Gen. 6:3). The stubborn, stiff-necked, hard-hearted Israelites provoked the **Spirit** repeatedly during their forty years of wilderness wandering (Heb. 3:7–8)—something they would continue to do throughout their history (cf. Neh. 9:30; Isa. 63:10; Acts 7:51). The sinful world's blasphemous rejection of Jesus Christ will reach its apex during the Tribulation. That seven-year period will see Satan promote to power the two most vile and evil blasphemers who will ever live: the beast (Antichrist) and the false prophet. To those two wretched, demon-possessed sinners will go the dubious honor of being the first people cast into the final hell, the lake of fire (19:20).

Throughout the long, dark centuries of mankind's sin and rebellion, the **Spirit** has worked to bring about conviction and repentance (cf. John 16:8–11). So when the Lord Jesus Christ says He is coming, the long-suffering, grieved, blasphemed Holy **Spirit** echoes, **"Come."** He pleads with Christ to return, subdue His enemies, judge sinners, and end the Spirit's long battle to produce conviction in stubborn, hard-hearted sinners.

On the positive side, it is the desire and ministry of the **Spirit** to glorify the Lord Jesus Christ (John 16:14). But the last view the world had of Jesus was of Him on a cross between two criminals, rejected, despised, and mocked. The **Spirit** longs to see His fellow Member of the Trinity exalted in beauty, splendor, power, and majesty. That will happen when Christ returns in triumph at His second coming.

The Holy **Spirit** is not the only one who longs for Christ's return. Echoing His plea for Christ to **come** is the **bride** (the church; see the discussion of 19:7 in chap. 14 of this volume). Throughout the centuries, God's people have waited for, prayed for, hoped for, and watched for Christ's return. They are weary of the battle against sin and long to see Jesus Christ exalted, glorified, and honored. They long for Him to return and take them to heaven to live with Him forever (John 14:3; 1 Thess. 4:17). They long for the day when their perishable, mortal bodies will be transformed into their imperishable, immortal resurrection bodies (1 Cor. 15:53–54). They know that in that glorious day there will be no more sorrow, no more tears, no more crying, no more pain, and no more death. Rebellion will be swiftly dealt with; God and the Lamb will be glorified and will reign forever over the new heaven and the new earth.

Believers are, in the words of Paul, those "who have loved His appearing" (2 Tim. 4:8). It is incongruous for someone to claim to love Jesus Christ and not long for His return. Believers are destined for eternal fellowship with Him, and the anticipation of that fellowship should be their chief joy. The church will never be satisfied until it is presented to God "in all her glory, having no spot or wrinkle or any such thing; but that she would be holy and blameless" (Eph. 5:27).

The second use of the exclamation **"Come"** signals a change in perspective. The invitation is no longer for Christ to return, but for sinners to come to saving faith in Him. The phrase **let the one who hears say, "Come"** invites those who hear the **Spirit** and the **bride** to join with them in calling for Christ's return. Obviously, they cannot do so until they come to faith in Him; only the redeemed can truly long for Him to appear. The implicit warning is not to be like those who "having ears, do . . . not hear" (Mark 8:18; cf. Deut. 29:4; Jer. 5:21; 6:10; Ezek. 12:2). The **one who hears** with faith and believes is the one who will be saved, because "faith comes from hearing, and hearing by the word of Christ" (Rom. 10:17). Hearing is often associated with obedience in Scripture (e.g., Matt. 7:24; Luke 6:47; 8:21; 11:28; John 5:24; 18:37). Those who hear and obey the gospel will join with the **Spirit** and the **bride** in calling for the return of Jesus Christ, because they desire His glory—and their own deliverance from sin's presence—in the realm of perfect holiness.

The **one who hears** is further defined as **the one who is thirsty.** Thirst is a familiar biblical metaphor picturing the strong sense of spiritual need that is a prerequisite for repentance. In Isaiah God calls "every one who thirsts [to] come to the waters" of salvation (Isa. 55:1). Jesus pronounced those "blessed . . . who hunger and thirst for righteousness, for they shall be satisfied" (Matt. 5:6). In John 7:37 He gave the invitation, "If anyone is thirsty, let him come to Me and drink," while earlier in Revelation He promised, "I will give to the one who thirsts from the spring of the water of life without cost" (21:6; cf. Ps. 107:9; John 4:14; 6:35).

Adding another dimension to the invitation, John writes **let the one who wishes take the water of life without cost.** That unlimited invitation is typical of the broad, sweeping, gracious offers of salvation made in Scripture (cf. Isa. 45:22; 55:1; Matt. 11:28; John 3:15–16). It also illustrates the biblical truth that salvation involves both God's sovereign choice (cf. John 6:44) and human volition. God saves sinners, but only those who recognize their need and repent. The **water of life** (or the washing of regeneration, Titus 3:5) is offered **without cost** (cf. Isa. 55:1) to the sinner because Jesus paid the price for it through His sacrificial death on the cross (Rom. 3:24). God freely offers the **water of life** to those whose hearts are thirsty for forgiveness, whose minds are thirsty for truth, and whose souls are thirsty for Him.

The Incentives

"I am the Alpha and the Omega, the first and the last, the beginning and the end."

Blessed are those who wash their robes, so that they may have the right to the tree of life, and may enter by the gates into the city. Outside are the dogs and the sorcerers and the immoral persons and the murderers and the idolaters, and everyone who loves and practices lying.

"I, Jesus, have sent My angel to testify to you these things for the churches. I am the root and the descendant of David, the bright morning star." . . .

I testify to everyone who hears the words of the prophecy of this book: if anyone adds to them, God will add to him the plagues which are written in this book; and if anyone takes away from the words of the book of this prophecy, God will take away his part from the tree of life and from the holy city, which are written in this book.

He who testifies to these things says, "Yes, I am coming quickly." Amen. Come, Lord Jesus.

The grace of the Lord Jesus be with all. Amen. (22:13–16, 18–21)

Surrounding the invitation in verse 17 are four incentives for sinners to accept it: because of the Lord's Person, because of the exclusivity of heaven, because of the truthfulness of Scripture, and because of the certainty of the Savior's return.

BECAUSE OF CHRIST'S PERSON

"I am the Alpha and the Omega, the first and the last, the beginning and the end."...

"I, Jesus, have sent My angel to testify to you these things for the churches. I am the root and the descendant of David, the bright morning star." (22:13, 16)

The first reason for sinners to accept God's final invitation is because it comes personally from the exalted, majestic, glorious Lord Jesus Christ. The Lord's threefold identification of Himself repeats the same truth for emphasis. Since the original readers of Revelation spoke Greek, Jesus identifies Himself first as **the Alpha and the Omega** (cf. 1:8; 21:6). **Alpha** and **Omega** are, respectively, the first and last letters of the Greek alphabet. Together with the parallel phrases **the first and the last** (cf. 1:17) and **the beginning** (the source of all things) **and the end** (the goal of all things), it expresses Christ's infinity, eternity, and boundless life transcending all limitations. This threefold description describes the completeness, timelessness, and sovereign authority of the Lord Jesus Christ.

This description of Jesus Christ is also a statement of His deity. Obviously, there can be only one **Alpha** and **Omega, first** and l**ast,** and **beginning** and **end**—God. In 1:8 God says, "I am the Alpha and the Omega," while 21:6 describes Him as "the beginning and the end." In Isaiah 44:6 God declares, "I am the first and I am the last" (cf. Isa. 41:4; 48:12). That all three titles, which can apply only to God, are used here of Jesus Christ offers convincing testimony to His deity. He is not a created being; He is not merely a great prophet or a great moral teacher; He is not a misguided martyr. He is God the Son, the second Person of the eternal Trinity.

Salvation in Jesus Christ is the theme of Scripture. In the Old Testament the ark in which Noah and his family were saved, the Passover lamb, and the kinsman redeemer are all pictures of Christ. In addition, Christ fulfilled more than 300 Old Testament prophecies at His first coming. He is the focus of the New Testament as well. The gospels record His life and ministry, and the rest of the New Testament expounds their doctrinal and practical implications. To be saved is to be saved by Christ; to be a Christian is to be in Christ; to have forgiveness is to be forgiven by Christ; to have hope is to have hope in Christ; in short, for the Christian "to live is Christ" (Phil. 1:21).

Christ further identifies Himself in His own words in verse 16. But before doing so He tells John, **"I, Jesus, have sent My angel to testify to you."** Though angels communicated the Apocalypse to John (v. 6; 1:1; 17:1, 7; 21:9), its source was Jesus. The expression **"I, Jesus"** appears only here in the Bible. It establishes that this final invitation in Scripture is not a human invitation, but a divine call issued personally to sinners by the Lord Jesus Christ. The Apocalypse is addressed to **the churches** (1:11), but though it is written to believers (1:1), they are to proclaim it to the entire world (cf. 22:10).

Then, in an astounding, seemingly paradoxical statement, Jesus declares Himself to be both **the root** (ancestor) **and the descendant of David.** That phrase sums up the biblical teaching on Christ's two natures; only the God-man can be both David's ancestor and his descendant. In His deity, Christ is David's **root** (cf. Mark 12:35–37); in His humanity, He is David's **descendant** (2 Sam. 7:12–16; Ps. 132:11–12; Matt. 1:1; Rom. 1:3; 2 Tim. 2:8).

Finally, Jesus describes Himself as **"the bright morning star."** To call someone a star was in biblical times (as it is today) to exalt him (cf. Dan. 12:3). In extrabiblical Jewish writings, the coming Messiah was called a **star** (Robert H. Mounce, *The Book of Revelation*, The New International Commentary on the New Testament [Grand Rapids: Eerdmans, 1977], 395). Though Balaam was a greedy prophet for hire, God nevertheless used him to make an accurate prediction of the coming Messiah: "A star shall come forth from Jacob, a scepter shall rise from Israel" (Num. 24:17). Peter wrote of the time when "the day dawns and the morning star arises in your hearts" (2 Pet. 1:19). Jesus promised to give the overcomers at Thyatira the "morning star" (2:28)—that is, Himself. As the morning star heralds the arrival of the day, so Jesus' coming will herald the end of the darkness of man's night, and the glorious dawn of His kingdom. Christ is the "Light of the world" (John 8:12) who calls sinners to drink of the water of life. And to those who heed that call He promises, "Come to Me, all who are weary and heavy-laden, and I will give you rest" (Matt. 11:28); and "The one who comes to Me I will certainly not cast out" (John 6:37).

BECAUSE OF THE EXCLUSIVITY OF HEAVEN

Blessed are those who wash their robes, so that they may have the right to the tree of life, and may enter by the gates into the

city. Outside are the dogs and the sorcerers and the immoral persons and the murderers and the idolaters, and everyone who loves and practices lying. (22:14–15)

This section begins with the last of the seven beatitudes in Revelation (v. 7; 1:3; 14:13; 16:15; 19:9; 20:6), each introduced by the pronouncement **blessed.** This blessing is pronounced (most likely by the Lord Jesus Christ) on **those who wash their robes.** That phrase graphically portrays the believer's participation in the death of Christ. In 7:14 one of the twenty-four elders said to John, "These [the Tribulation martyrs; 7:9] are the ones who come out of the great tribulation, and they have washed their robes and made them white in the blood of the Lamb." Soiled clothes represent sinfulness in Isaiah 64:6 and Zechariah 3:3, whereas Psalm 51:7; Isaiah 1:18; and Titus 3:5 speak of the cleansing of sin that accompanies salvation. The agency through which that cleansing comes is the blood of Christ (1:5; 5:9; 7:14; Matt. 26:28; Acts 20:28; Rom. 3:24–25; 5:9; Eph. 1:7; 2:13; Col. 1:20; Heb. 9:12, 14; 10:19; 13:12; 1 Pet. 1:2, 18–19; 1 John 1:7).

Those who have experienced the washing from sin that marks salvation will forever **have the right to the tree of life.** As noted in the discussion of 22:2 in chapter 19 of this volume, the **tree of life** is located in the capital city of heaven, the New Jerusalem. This will be the fulfillment of Jesus' promise, "To him who overcomes, I will grant to eat of the tree of life which is in the Paradise of God" (2:7). Those granted access to the **tree of life** will be allowed to **enter by the gates into the city** (cf. the discussion of 21:21 in chap. 19 of this volume).

Heaven is exclusively for those who have been cleansed from their sins by faith in the blood of Christ and whose names have been "written from the foundation of the world in the book of life of the Lamb who has been slain" (13:8). In contrast, everyone else will remain forever **outside** the New Jerusalem in the lake of fire (20:15; 21:8), because "nothing unclean, and no one who practices abomination and lying, shall ever come into it, but only those whose names are written in the Lamb's book of life" (21:27). As in 21:8, a representative (though not exhaustive) list of the type of sins that exclude people from heaven is given to John.

The inclusion of **dogs** on the list seems puzzling at first glance. But in ancient times **dogs** were not the domesticated household pets they are today. They were despised scavengers that milled about cities' garbage dumps (cf. Ex. 22:31; 1 Kings 14:11; 16:4; 21:19, 23–24; 22:38). Thus, to call a person a dog was to describe that person as someone of low character (cf. 1 Sam. 17:43; 24:14; 2 Sam. 3:8; 9:8; 16:9; 2 Kings 8:13; Phil. 3:2); in fact, the first time blatantly impure sinners are called dogs is in Deuteronomy 23:18, where male homosexual prostitutes are in view. **Sorcerers** (from *pharmakos*, the root of the English word "pharmacy") refers to those engaged in occult practices and the drug abuse that often accompanies those practices (cf. 9:21; 21:8; Gal. 5:20). **Immoral persons** (from *pornos*, the root of the English word "pornography") are those who engage in illicit sexual activities. **Murderers** are also excluded from heaven in the list given in 21:8 (cf. 9:21; Rom. 1:29). **Idolaters** are those who worship false gods, or who worship the true God in an unacceptable manner (cf. 21:8). The final group excluded from heaven also includes **everyone who loves and practices lying.** It is not all who have ever committed any of these sins who are excluded from heaven (cf. 1 Cor. 6:11). Rather, it is those who love and habitually practice any such sin, stubbornly cling to it, and refuse Christ's invitation to salvation who will be cast into the lake of fire.

BECAUSE OF THE TRUTHFULNESS OF SCRIPTURE

I testify to everyone who hears the words of the prophecy of this book: if anyone adds to them, God will add to him the plagues which are written in this book; and if anyone takes away from the words of the book of this prophecy, God will take away his part from the tree of life and from the holy city, which are written in this book. (22:18–19)

It is of great significance that the Bible closes with an affirmation of its truthfulness. Because the words of Scripture are "faithful and true" (22:6), they must not be sealed up, but proclaimed (22:10). Sinners are to be called to respond to the warnings in the Word of the living God or suffer the consequences. All the prophecies of Revelation regarding the doom of sinners will come true. That terrifying certainty should drive people to Jesus Christ to escape the wrath to come (1 Thess. 1:10).

The speaker who testifies to the authority and finality of **the words of the prophecy of this book** is none other than the Lord Jesus Christ (cf. v. 20). His solemn warning against tampering with Scripture applies first of all to the **prophecy** of the **book** of Revelation (cf. 1:3). Its stern rebukes of Jezebel and her followers (2:20–23), those who had embraced the "deep things of Satan" (2:24), and those of the "synagogue of Satan" (3:9) would have prompted them to assault it. Down through the centuries there have been others who have both attacked Revelation and seriously misinterpreted it. But in light of the repeated warnings against altering God's Word, Christ's warning must be broadened to include all of Scripture. In Deuteronomy 4:2 Moses cautioned, "You shall not add to the word which I am commanding you, nor take away from it, that you may keep the commandments of the Lord your God which I command you." In Deuteronomy 12:32 he added, "Whatever I command you, you shall be careful to do; you shall not add to nor take away from it." Proverbs 30:5–6 warns, "Every word of God is tested; He is a shield to those who take refuge in Him. Do not add to His words or He will reprove you, and you will be proved a liar." Thus, the prohibition against altering the Apocalypse by implication extends to all of Scripture. Because Revelation describes the entire sweep of history from the close of the apostolic age to the eternal state, any alteration of it would be an alteration of Scripture, as Robert L. Thomas notes:

> The predictive portions project from John's lifetime all the way into the eternal state. Any type of prophetic utterance would intrude into the domain of this coverage and constitute either an addition to or subtraction from Revelation's content. So the final book of the Bible is also the concluding product of NT prophecy. It also marks the close of the NT canon since the prophetic gift was the divinely chosen means for communicating the inspired books of the canon. (*Revelation 8–22: An Exegetical Commentary* [Chicago: Moody, 1995], 517)

The canon of Scripture was closed at the end of the first century when Revelation was finished. Thus, any false prophet, fraud, or charlatan who **adds** alleged new revelations to it (as the Montanists did in the early church and Joseph Smith, Mary Baker Eddy, and other false prophets have done in recent times) will face divine vengeance. **God will add to** such people **the plagues which are written** in the **book** of Revelation. God's judgment will be equally severe on **anyone** who **takes away from the words** of Scripture (as the heretic Marcion did in the early church and liberal higher critics have done in modern times)—**God will take away** their **part from the tree of life and from the holy city.** Both warnings contain a play on words. Those who add to Scripture will have plagues added to them; those who take away from Scripture will have the blessings of heaven taken away from them.

No true believer would ever deliberately tamper with Scripture. Those who know and love God will treat His Word with the utmost respect. They will say with the psalmist, "O how I love Your law!" (Ps. 119:97; cf. Pss. 119:113, 163, 167; John 14:23); and, "I delight in Your law" (Ps. 119:70; cf. Pss. 1:2; 119:77, 92, 174). That does not, of course, mean that believers will never make errors in judgment or mistakenly interpret Scripture incorrectly or inadequately. The Lord's warning here is addressed to those who engage in deliberate falsification or misinterpretation of Scripture, those whom Paul denounces as peddlers of the Word of God (2 Cor. 2:17).

At the conclusion of his commentary on Revelation, J. A. Seiss expressed the humble reverence for Scripture that marks true believers:

> O, my friends, it is a fearful thing to suppress or stultify the word of God, and above all "the words of the prophecy of this Book." To put forth for truth what is not the truth,—denounce as error, condemn, repudiate, or emasculate what God himself hath set his seal to as his mind and purpose, is one of those high crimes, not only against God, but against the souls of men, which cannot go unpunished. With an honest and ever-prayerful heart, and with these solemn and awful warnings ever before my eyes, I have endeavoured to ascertain and indicate in these Lectures what our gracious Lord and Master has been so particular to make known and defend. If I have read into this Book anything which he has not put there, or read out of it anything which he has put there, with the profoundest sorrow would I recant, and willingly burn up the books in which such mischievous wickedness is contained. If I have in anything gone beyond the limits of due subjection to what is written, or curtailed in any way the depth and measure of what Jesus by his angel has signified for the learning of the Churches, I need not the condemnation of men to heap upon me the burden of censure which I deserve. If feebleness, or rashness, or overweening confidence in my own understanding has distorted anything, I can only deplore the fault, and pray God to send a man more competent to unfold to us the mighty truths which here stand written. According to the grace and light given me, have I spoken. . . . If I err, God forgive me! If I am right, God bless my feeble testimony! In either case, God speed his everlasting truth! (*The Apocalypse* [reprint, Grand Rapids: Kregel, 1987], 527)

Revelation and the rest of Scripture are true, and the redeemed will believe the Bible, guard the Bible, love the Bible, and obey the Bible. That Scripture speaks truly when it describes the joys of heaven and the terrors of hell should motivate sinners to heed God's gracious call to salvation.

BECAUSE OF THE CERTAINTY OF CHRIST'S RETURN

He who testifies to these things says, "Yes, I am coming quickly." Amen. Come, Lord Jesus. The grace of the Lord Jesus be with all. Amen. (22:20–21)

The book of Revelation and the Bible close with one final reminder and a benediction. In His last recorded words in Scripture the Lord Jesus Christ, **He who testifies to these things,** affirms **"Yes, I am coming quickly."** His **coming** is imminent, just as Revelation (and the rest of the New Testament) teaches. John speaks for all true believers when he responds, **Amen. Come, Lord Jesus,** since Christians are those "who have loved His appearing" (2 Tim. 4:8). Scoffers may mockingly ask, "Where is the promise of His coming? For ever since the fathers fell asleep, all continues just as it was from the beginning of creation" (2 Pet. 3:4). But things will not continue forever as they are. Jesus will return, just as Revelation predicts. If the certainty of Christ's return to judge sinners does not motivate people to repent, then nothing will.

For the glorious, comforting truth is that those who humble themselves and accept God's offer of salvation will find Him gracious. Fittingly, the last words of the Bible, **the grace of the Lord Jesus be with all. Amen,** are an expression of God's **grace** toward fallen humanity. The Lord of glory, as He promised in Scripture, offers heaven exclusively to those who, in light of His certain return, accept His gracious invitation and return to Him.

Bibliography

Allen, James. *What the Bible Teaches: Revelation*. Kilmarnock, Scotland: John Ritchie, 1997.

Barclay, William. *The Revelation of John*. Vol. Two. Philadelphia: Westminster, 1976.

Beasley-Murray, G. R. *The Book of Revelation*. The New Century Bible. London: Oliphants, 1974.

Beckwith, Isbon T. *The Apocalypse of John*. New York: Macmillan, 1919.

Criswell, W. A. *Expository Sermons on Revelation*. Grand Rapids: Zondervan, 1969.

Erdman, Charles R. *The Revelation of John*. Reprint. Philadelphia: Westminster, 1977.

Johnson, Alan F. *Revelation*. The Expositor's Bible Commentary. Grand Rapids: Zondervan, 1996.

Lenski, R. C. H. *The Interpretation of St. John's Revelation*. Minneapolis: Augsburg, 1943.

MacArthur, John F. *Revelation 1–11*. The MacArthur New Testament Commentary. Chicago: Moody, 1999.

Morris, Henry M. *The Revelation Record*. Wheaton, Ill.: Tyndale, 1983.

Morris, Leon. *The Revelation of St. John*. The Tyndale New Testament Commentaries. Grand Rapids: Eerdmans, 1969.

Mounce, Robert H. *The Book of Revelation*. The New International Commentary on the New Testament. Grand Rapids: Eerdmans, 1977.

Phillips, John. *Exploring Revelation*. Rev. ed. Chicago: Moody, 1987; reprint; Neptune, N.J.: Loizeaux, 1991.

Ryrie, Charles C. *Revelation*. Everyman's Bible Commentary. Chicago: Moody, 1996.

Seiss, Joseph A. *The Apocalypse*. Reprint, Grand Rapids: Kregel, 1987.

Swete, Henry Barclay. *Commentary on Revelation*. Reprint, Grand Rapids: Kregel, 1977.

Tenney, Merrill C. *Interpreting Revelation*. Grand Rapids: Eerdmans, 1957.

Thomas, Robert L. *Revelation 1–7: An Exegetical Commentary*. Chicago: Moody, 1992.

________. *Revelation 8–22: An Exegetical Commentary*. Chicago: Moody, 1995.

Trench, Richard C. *Synonyms of the Greek New Testament*. Reprint, Grand Rapids: Eerdmans, 1983.

Vincent, Marvin R. *Word Studies in the Greek New Testament*. Reprint, Grand Rapids: Eerdmans, 1946.

Walvoord, John F. *The Revelation of Jesus Christ*. Chicago: Moody, 1966.

Indexes

Index of Greek Words

Index of Hebrew Words

Index of Scripture

Index of Subjects

Titles in the MacArthur New Testament Commentary Series

Matthew 1-7
Matthew 8-15
Matthew 16-23
Matthew 24-28
Luke 1-5
Luke 6-10
John 1-11
John 12-21
Acts 1-12
Acts 13-28
Romans 1-8
Romans 9-16
First Corinthians
Second Corinthians
Galatians
Ephesians
Philippians
Colossians and Philemon
First and Second Thessalonians
First Timothy
Second Timothy
Titus
Hebrews
James
First Peter
Second Peter & Jude
First-Third John
Revelation 1-11
Revelation 12-22

MOODY
PUBLISHERS
THE NAME YOU CAN TRUST.
1-800-678-6928 www.MoodyPublishers.org